McCLOSKEY

ART AND ILLUSTRATIONS OF ROBERT McCLOSKEY

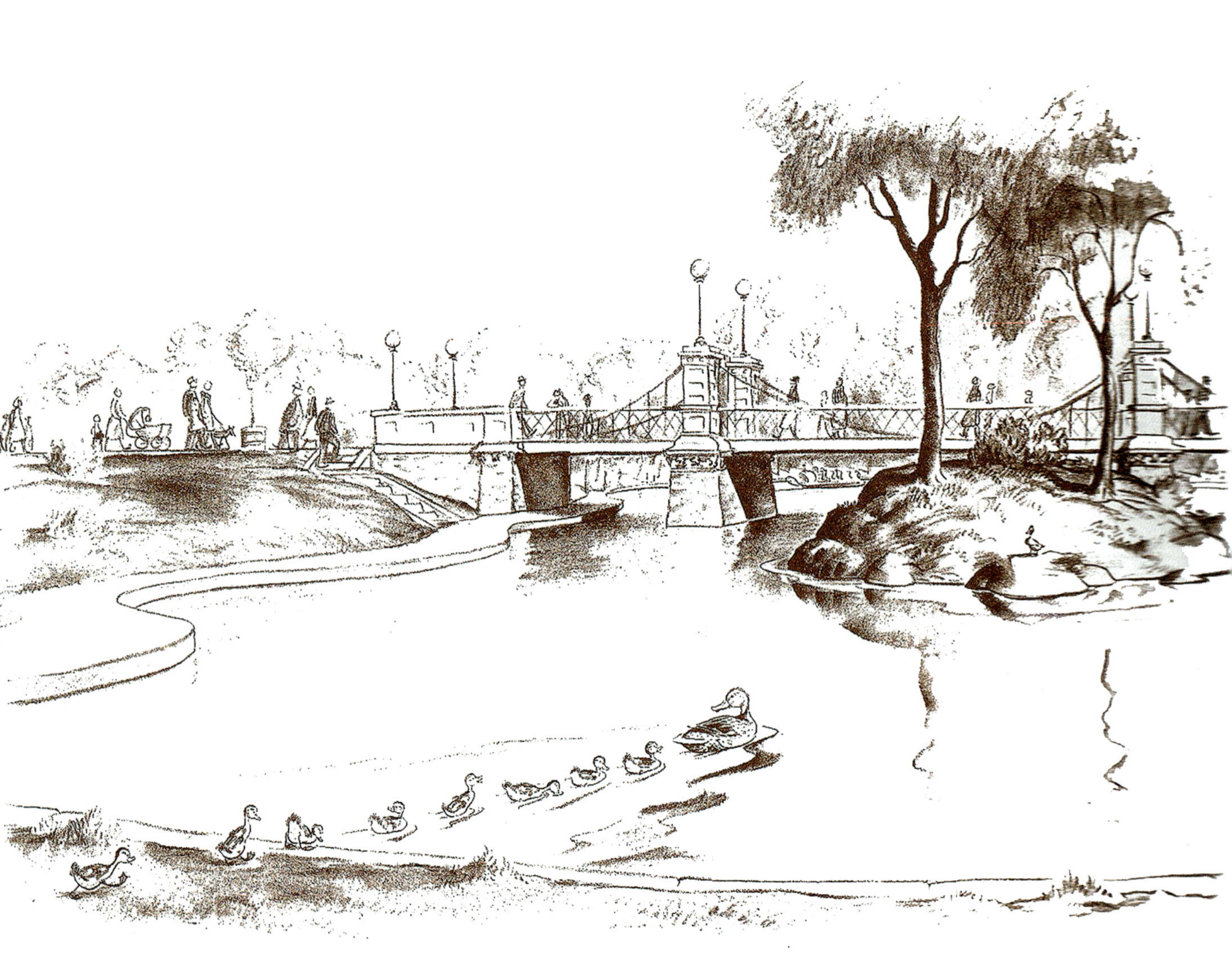

McCLOSKEY

ART AND ILLUSTRATIONS OF ROBERT McCLOSKEY

JANE McCLOSKEY

Down East Books

Down East Books
An imprint of Globe Pequot

Distributed by NATIONAL BOOK NETWORK

First Down East Books paperback edition, 2018

British Library Cataloguing in Publication Information available

The Library of Congress has previously catalogued an earlier edition of this book under the LCCN: 2015954329

ISBN 978-1-60893-958-9 (paperback)
ISBN 978-1-60893-493-5 (hardback)
ISBN 978-1-60893-494-2 (e-book)

∞™ The paper used in this publication meets the minimum requirements of American National Standard for Information Sciences—Permanence of Paper for Printed Library Materials, ANSI/NISO Z39.48-1992.

Printed in the United States of America

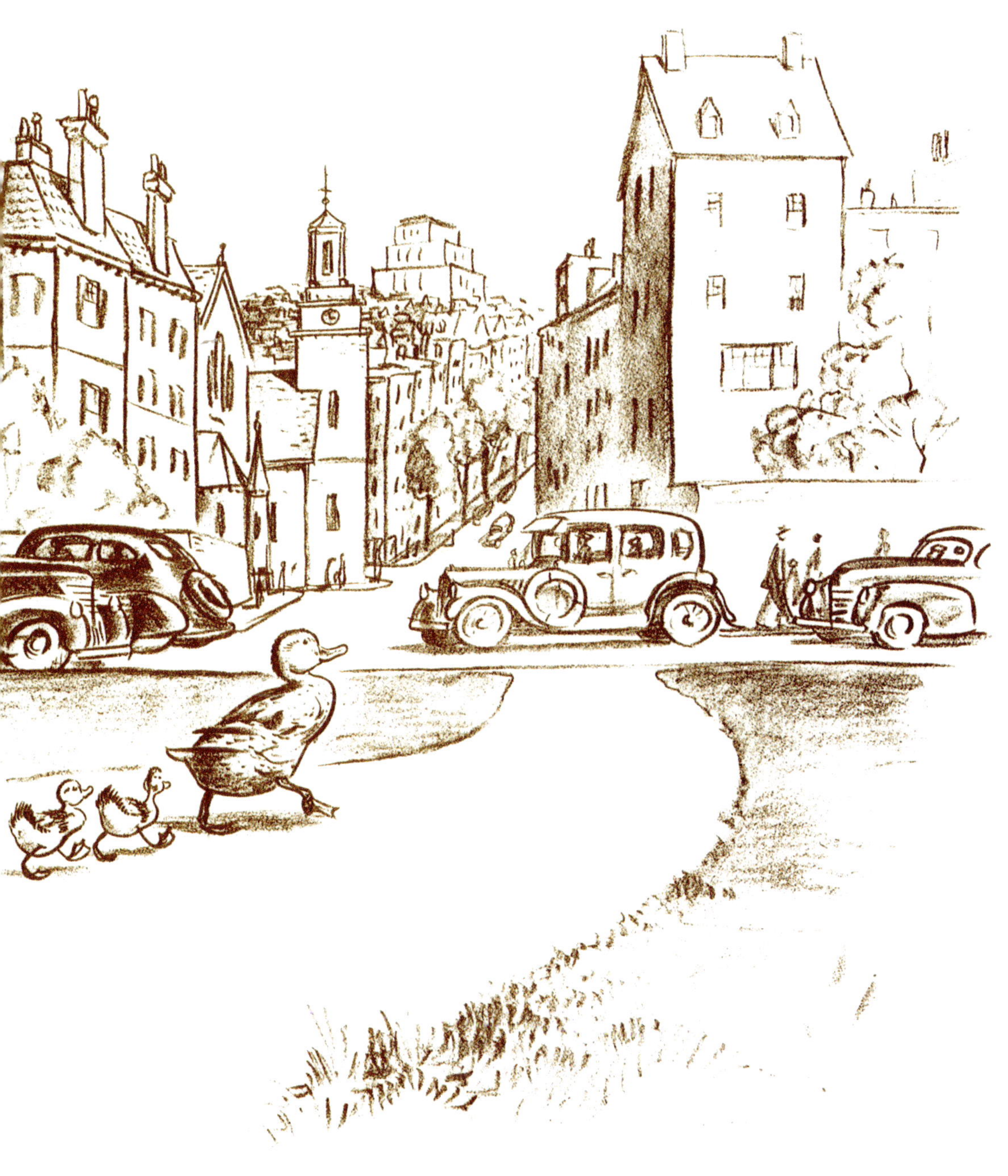

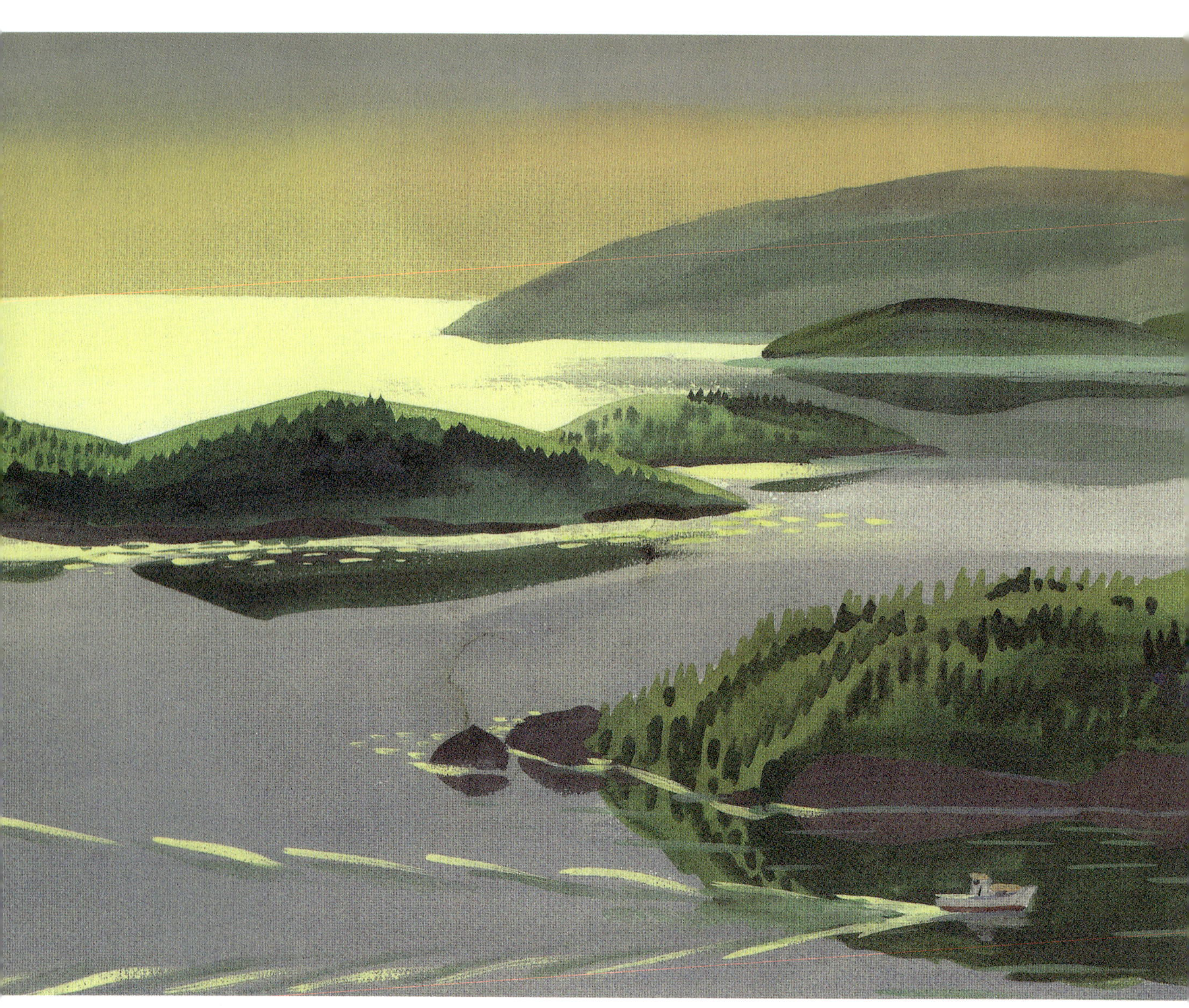

CONTENTS

Introduction

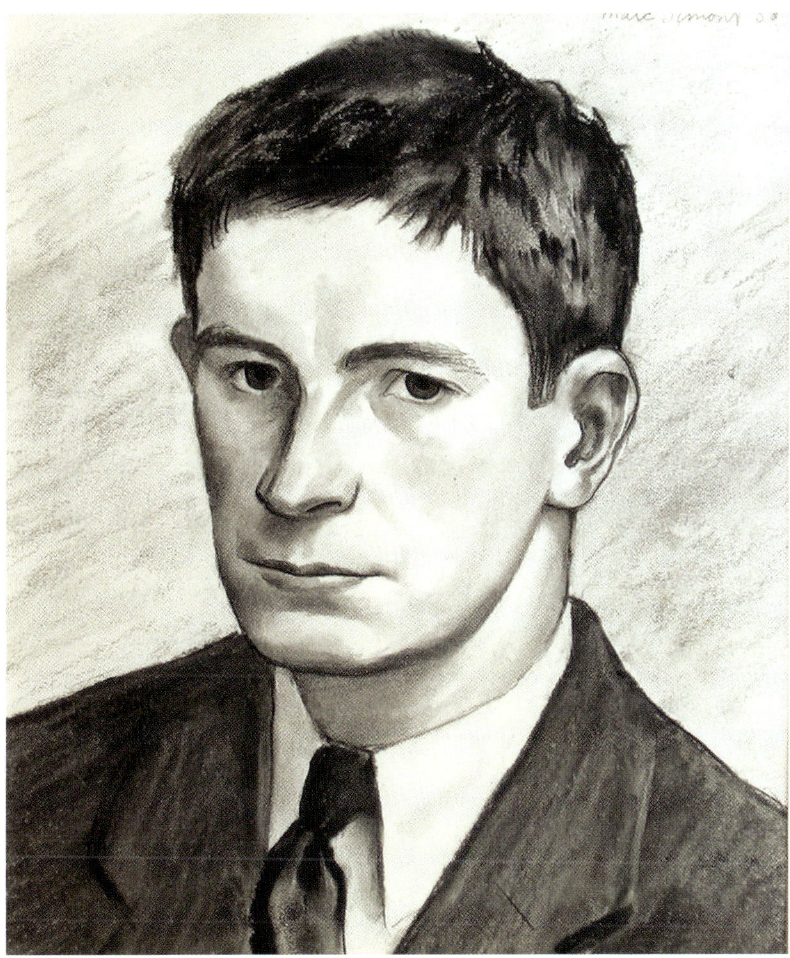

"Robert McCloskey," pencil drawing by Marc Simont, 1938. *From Make Way for McCloskey,* Viking Press, 2004.

My father, Robert McCloskey, was one of the best known and loved children's authors and illustrators of the 20th century. My sister Sal and I always called him Bob, even when we were kids, so I will call him that here.

His best known book is probably *Make Way for Ducklings,* about a family of ducks who move to the Boston Public Garden. It won the Caldecott Medal in 1941 for the most distinguished illustrated picture book of the year.

In 1985, the sculptor Nancy Schön made bronze statues of the ducks, which were placed in the Public Garden. In 1991, the United States and Soviet Union made peace after the long cold war. When Raisa Gorbachev, wife of the Soviet Premiere, was visiting the United States, Barbara Bush took herto see the ducks in the Boston Public Garden. After talking it over, Mrs. Bush decided to give a replica set of ducks from the children of the U.S. to the children of the U.S.S.R. Bob and Nancy Schön went to Moscow with the Bushes for the signing of the START treaty and the installation of the new ducks in Moscow.

Another well loved book of my father's is *Blueberries for Sal*, a make-believe story about my sister and mother, who go blueberry picking and get mixed up with a little bear and her mother.

A favorite book in the state of Maine is *One Morning in Maine*, about Sal, who loses her tooth when she goes clam digging with my father. Later, Sal, my father, and I make a trip to Bucks Harbor for groceries, and come home to Mom, who has made Clam Chowder For Lunch!

My favorite of Bob's books is *Time of Wonder.* It is the story of a summer Sal and I spent on our family's island in Maine. I like to think that this book was written for me, since I am the dreamer and wonderer in our family. *Time of Wonder* won the Caldecott Medal in 1957 for the most distinguished children's book of the year. My father was the first person ever to win the Caldecott twice. He won two Caldecott medals and three Caldecott Honors.

Bob wrote about his life with his children in Maine, and also about his own boyhood in Ohio. *Lentil* was his first book, about a boy who cannot whistle or sing, so he learns to play the harmonica. What with one thing and another, Lentil's harmonica playing saves the day when the local town dignitary returns home.

Homer Price and *Centerburg Tales* are about a boy in a small town who has various adventures, including one with a run-amok doughnut machine.

Where I live in Maine, many local people say that *Burt Dow, Deep-Water Man* is their favorite. Burt Dow was a real person who lived here and sailed on one of the last working barkentines to go around Cape Horn. When Burt died, his friends, Stace, Vic, my father, and others got together and inscribed his grave stone.

BURT DOW
DEEP WATER MAN

Bob also illustrated a number of books, including *Henry Reed, Inc.* and its sequels; and *The Man Who Lost His Head, Journey Cake Ho!* and *Yankee Doodle's Cousins.*

My father was a very private and shy man. He didn't talk a lot, and when he did, he was often cryptic. Sometimes people approached him with an idea for a children's book, the way they approach lawyers about legal problems and carpenters about woodworking problems. His standard response to people who told him their idea was: Don't talk about it. Do it. He took his own advice.

As a result, much of my understanding of my father's art came from detective work—watching him, thinking about him and what he said and didn't say, reading his books, and looking at his pictures.

Jane McCloskey
Deer Isle, Maine

NOTE: This introduction is very similar to the introduction I wrote for my memoir about growing up with my father: *Robert McCloskey: A Private Life in Words and Pictures.*

Ohio 1

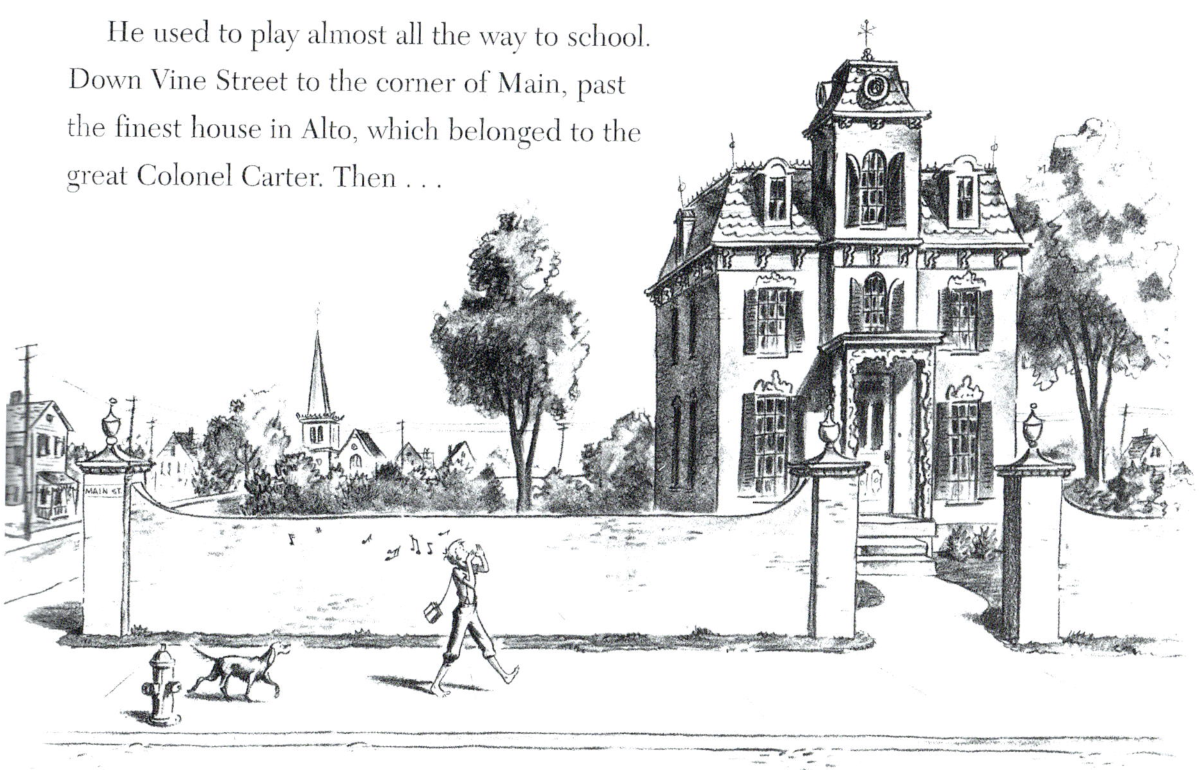

Lentil. "Lentil With his Dog and Harmonica, Going to School," Viking Press, 1939.

Bob was born in Hamilton, Ohio, in 1914, where he spent his boyhood until he graduated from high school. His father was Howard McCloskey, who managed the American Can Company, while his mother, Mabel Wismeyer McCloskey, was a housewife. He had two sisters, Dorothy and Mabel. He was musical, and played both the piano and the harmonica, his first love. In Bob's first book, *Lentil,* Lentil plays the harmonica as he walks to school.

Sixty years later, the sculptor Nancy Schön made Bob's illustration of Lentil and his dog into a sculpture in Hamilton. It is located next to Heritage Hall, which houses the Robert McCloskey Museum. Lentil's dog was named

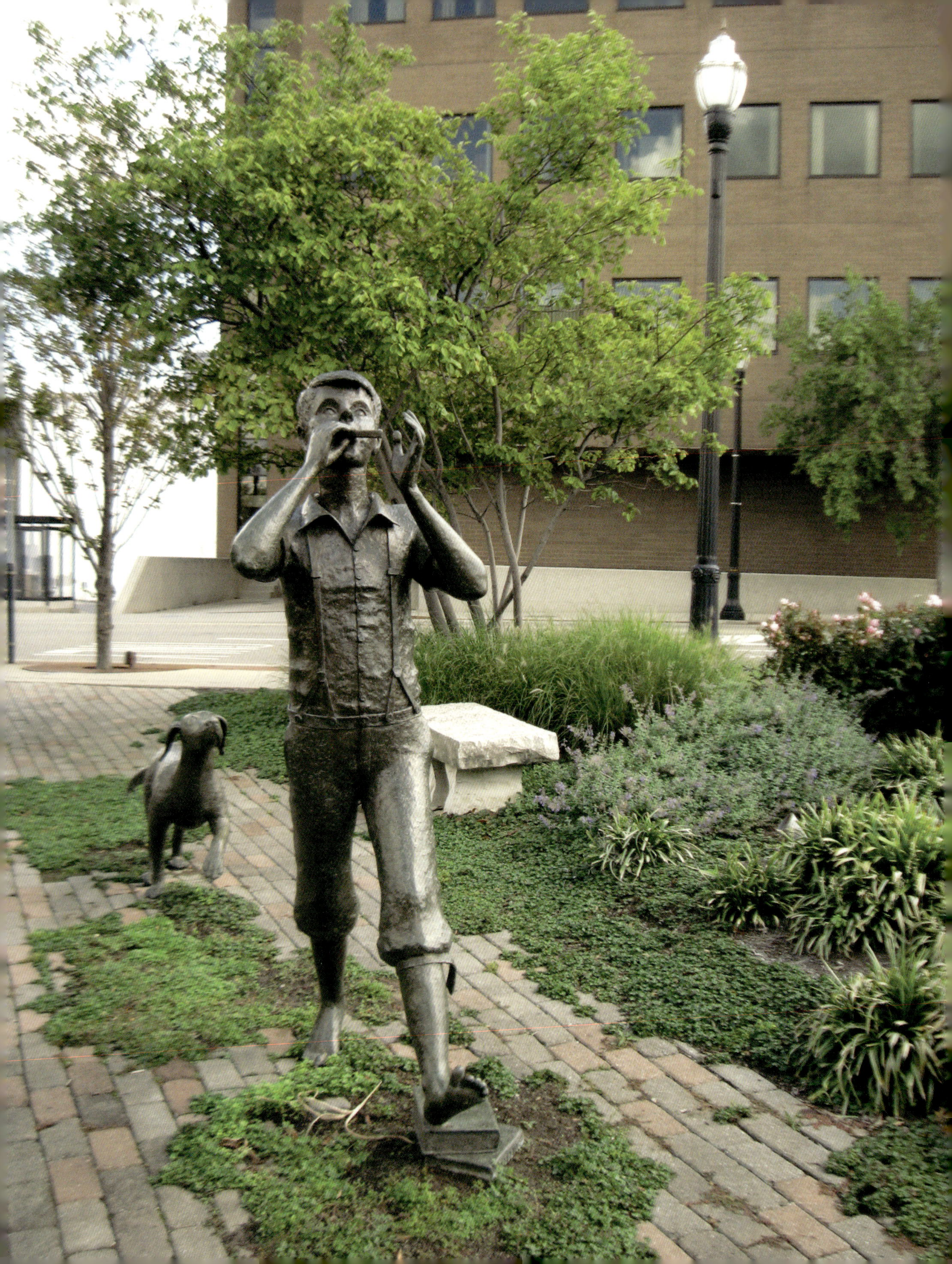

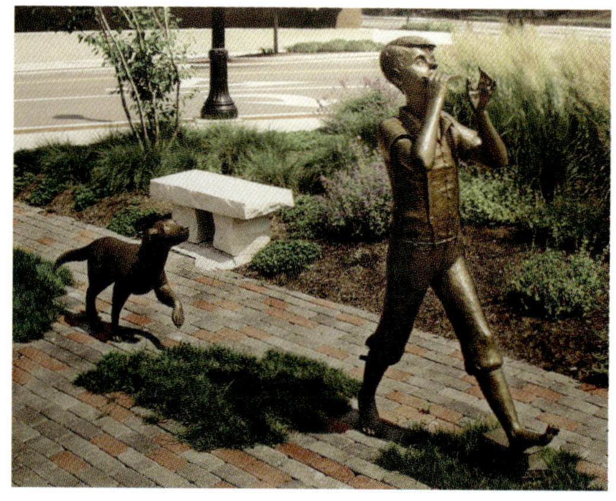

"Lentil and his dog at Heritage Hall," Hamilton. Statue by Nancy Schön, photo by Pat Brown, Brown Studios, Hamilton.

Harmony by the children of Hamilton.

When Bob was in high school, he worked in the summertime at the YMCA Camp Campbell Gard near Hamilton. Bob was dining hall steward and also in charge of musical activities and arts and crafts. Many years later, fellow camper Charles Klippel wrote a memoir about the camp, with a long section about Bob.

Klippel wrote that one night, the archery instructor, Russel, and Bob put on a show at the lodge. Russel was supposed to shoot an apple off the top of Bob's head. Klippel wrote, "Russ made a great show of reluctance, then of losing his nerve, while Bob stood apparently terrified . . . Suddenly Russ drew the bow and aimed." With a great BOOM, the lights went out. "A minute later, when the lights came on, Bob was standing on his head with the apple, pierced by the arrow, balanced on his feet." With his harmonica on a wire frame around his neck, Bob tore into the *William Tell Overture.*

Klippel writes,

> Bob was a harmonica virtuoso, and had an act that involved playing something on his "Super Chromonica, a two or three octave, high volume concert instrument with a provision for chromatic scales . . . In the midst of the performance, he'd blow a sour note or two, and take the instrument away from his mouth, pretending that there was something wrong with it. But the music would continue as he worked on it. He'd learned to conceal a small but high quality oneoctave harmonica in his mouth and could shift it to the front and play the simpler tunes "no hands."

In the wintertime, Bob was active in the YMCA, and was so creative, he was given a room of his own. Klippel writes, "He used it to teach harmonica playing, airplane model building, drawing, linoleum block print making, and soap carving. The [soap carving] proved so popular and so messy that it had to be moved to the boys' shower room where the clean up could be done by turning on the taps."

While at camp, my father carved a totem pole. James E. Schwartz, Ph.D. (henceforward called Jim), who wrote the time line at the end of this book, says that a Native American named Isaac Grayearth gave Bob guidance on the symbolism in the totem pole.

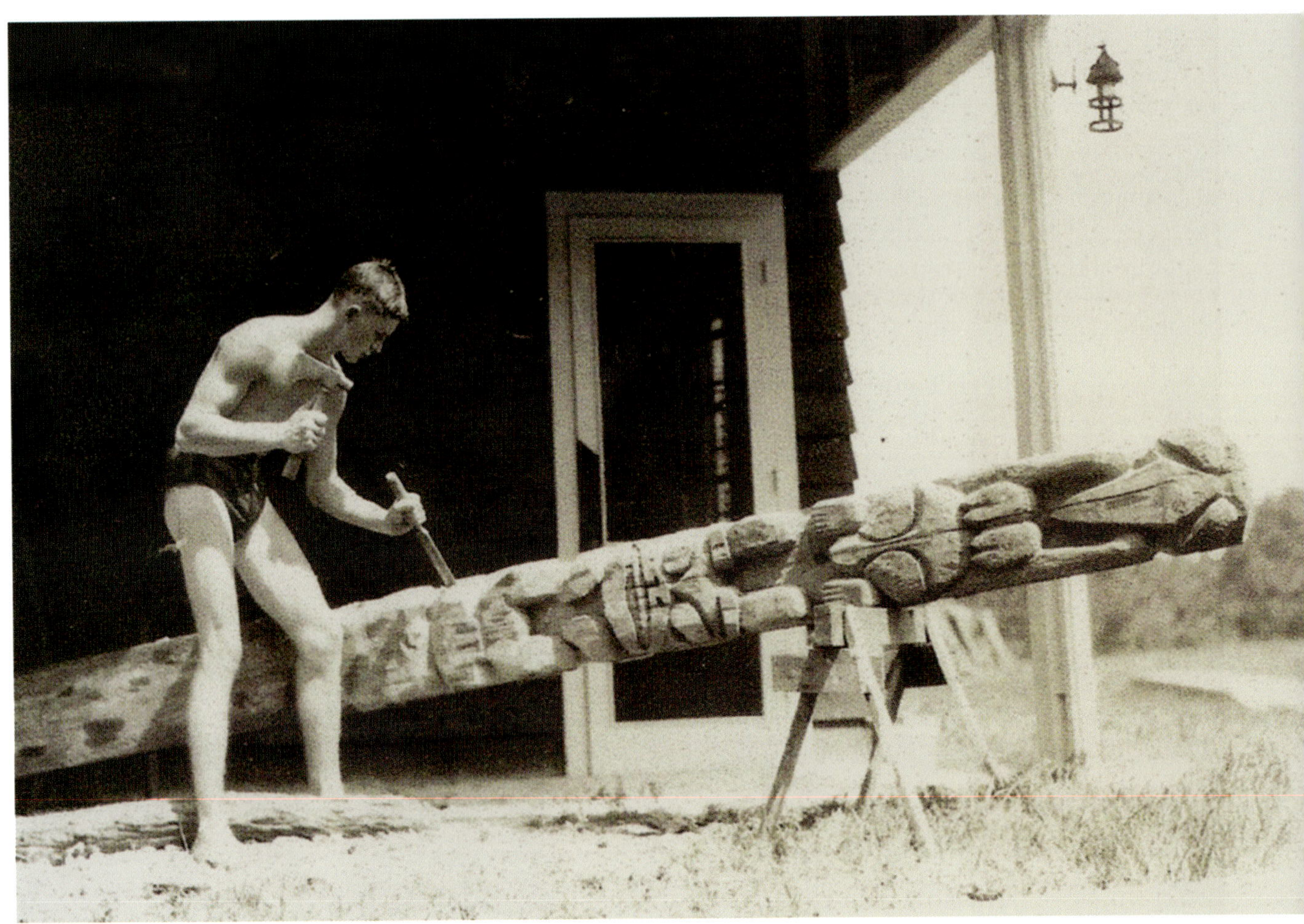

Bob Carving his totem pole, ca 1931. Courtesy of Jim Schwartz Photoshopped to remove glare.

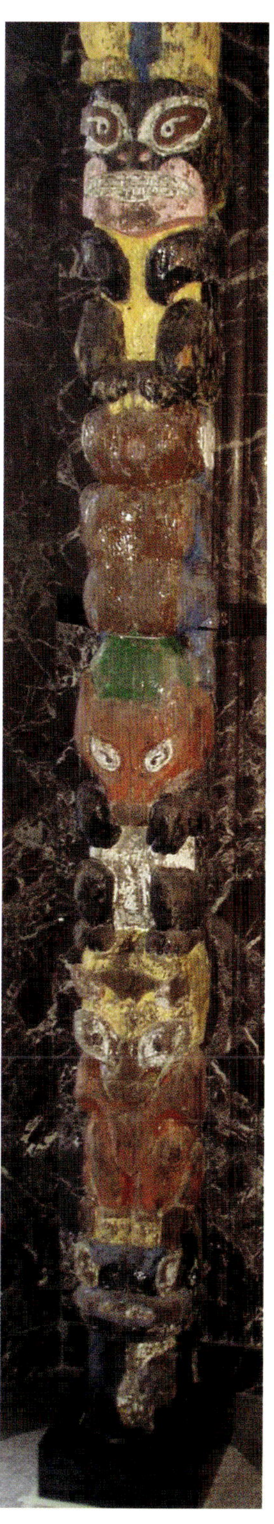

The totem pole was erected in the center of camp, where it stood for fifty years, but when it became rotten and dangerous, it was taken down. Neil Sohngen orchestrated its renovation and transport to its present site at Heritage Hall. The Wiebold Art Conservation Company did the work.

Totem pole, about 1' x 10', ca 1930, Heritage Hall, Hamilton. Photo by Janet Sohngen.

Bob's totem pole led to a commission from the City of Hamilton the following year, when he was 18, to carve the architectural details on the new Hamilton Municipal Building. Bob also created a leaded window for the building.

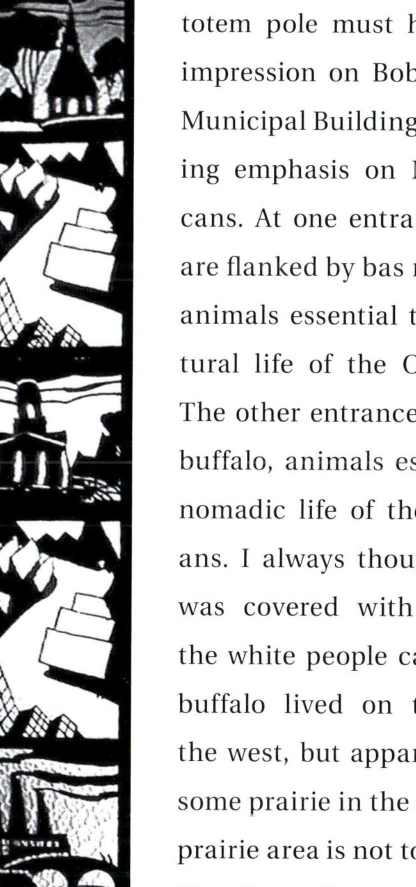

Leaded window, about 1' x 5', Heritage Hall, Hamilton, 1933. Photo by Janet Sohngen,

Greyearth's guidance on the totem pole must have made an impression on Bob, because the Municipal Building has a surprising emphasis on Native Americans. At one entrance, the steps are flanked by bas reliefs of oxen, animals essential to the agricultural life of the Ohio pioneers. The other entrance is flanked by buffalo, animals essential to the nomadic life of the Plains Indians. I always thought that Ohio was covered with trees before the white people came, and that buffalo lived on the plains to the west, but apparently there is some prairie in the state, and one prairie area is not too far north of Hamilton. Also, wood bison can

"Bas relief of Buffalo," entrance of the Hamilton Municipal Building, sandstone, about 4' x 6', 1933.

live in sparse forest, so there could have been bison around Hamilton before white people came.

The oxen look like oxen, but the buffalo have the faces of men—Greyearth must have told Bob that, for Native Americans, animals were people, like humans.

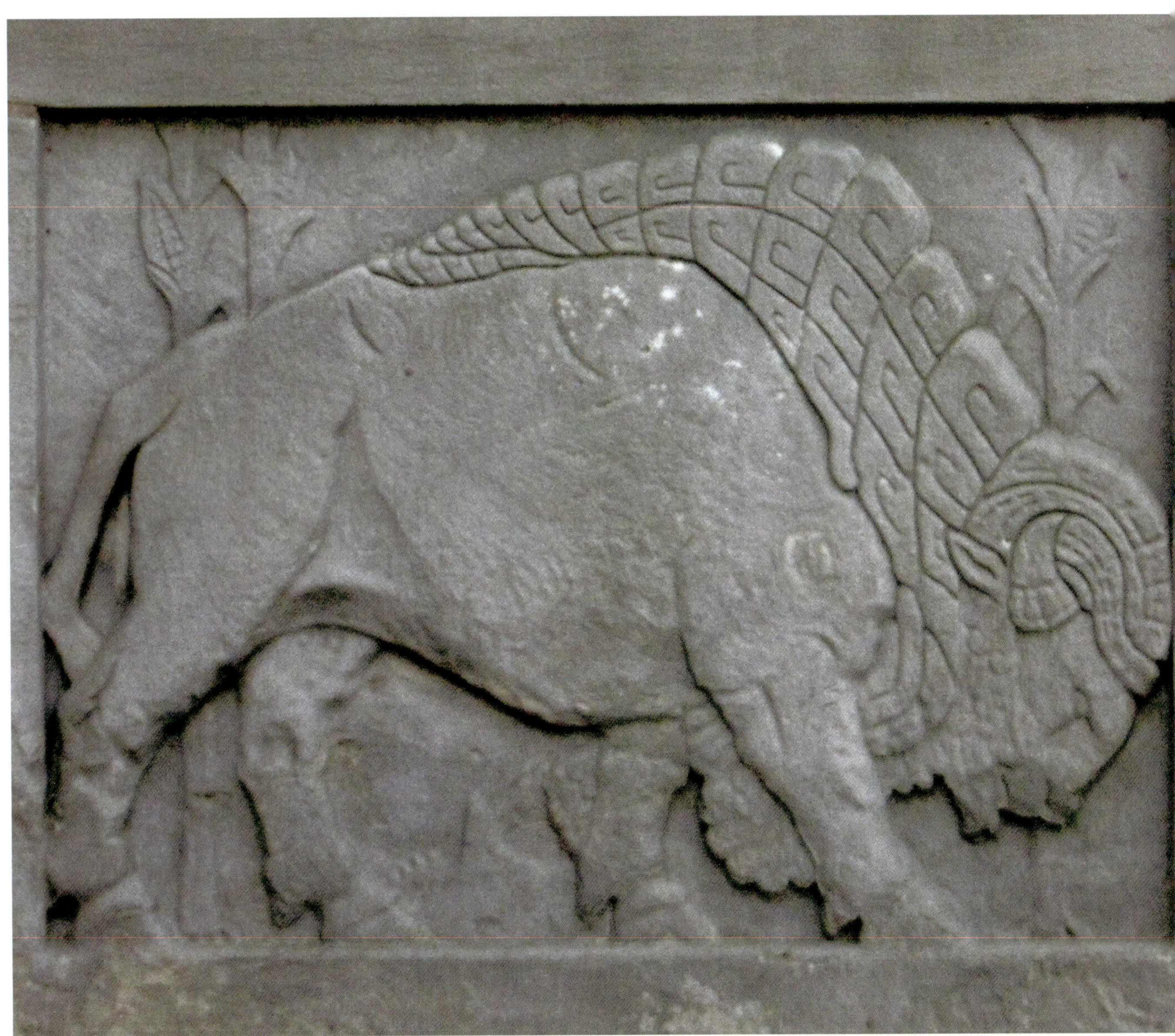

A series of scenes over the buffalo entrance show the subjugation of the area around Hamilton by white men with rifles, axes, and plows. The final scene shows the white man brought to his knees by the struggle; but victorious and still strong, he is gesturing, "bring it on." In front of him, an Indian lying on the ground hangs his head in defeat.

At the oxen entrance, a series of circles show the many trades that white settlers adopted in their new home. One circle shows an artist with brush and palette in hand. But the background to all the circles is corn, corn, corn, the great gift of the Native Americans to the white settlers. The settlers transmuted corn cultivation into a much more agricultural way of life, felling the forests and plowing the prairies. Corn was the gift of the Native Americans to the white people, but became the instrument of destroying the Native way of life.

Jim Schwartz says that the Hamilton town fathers were not happy with Bob's edgy view of Hamilton's history.

In 1932, at the age of 18, Bob won a scholarship to the Vesper George School of Art and left Hamilton for Boston. In 1934, he showed his classically inspired drawings to May Massee, children's book editor for Viking Press in New York City. She told him to go back to Hamilton and draw what he knew. The following pictures are from the time when he returned to Hamilton.

"Sketch of Melba McCloskey," pencil on paper, 1930s.

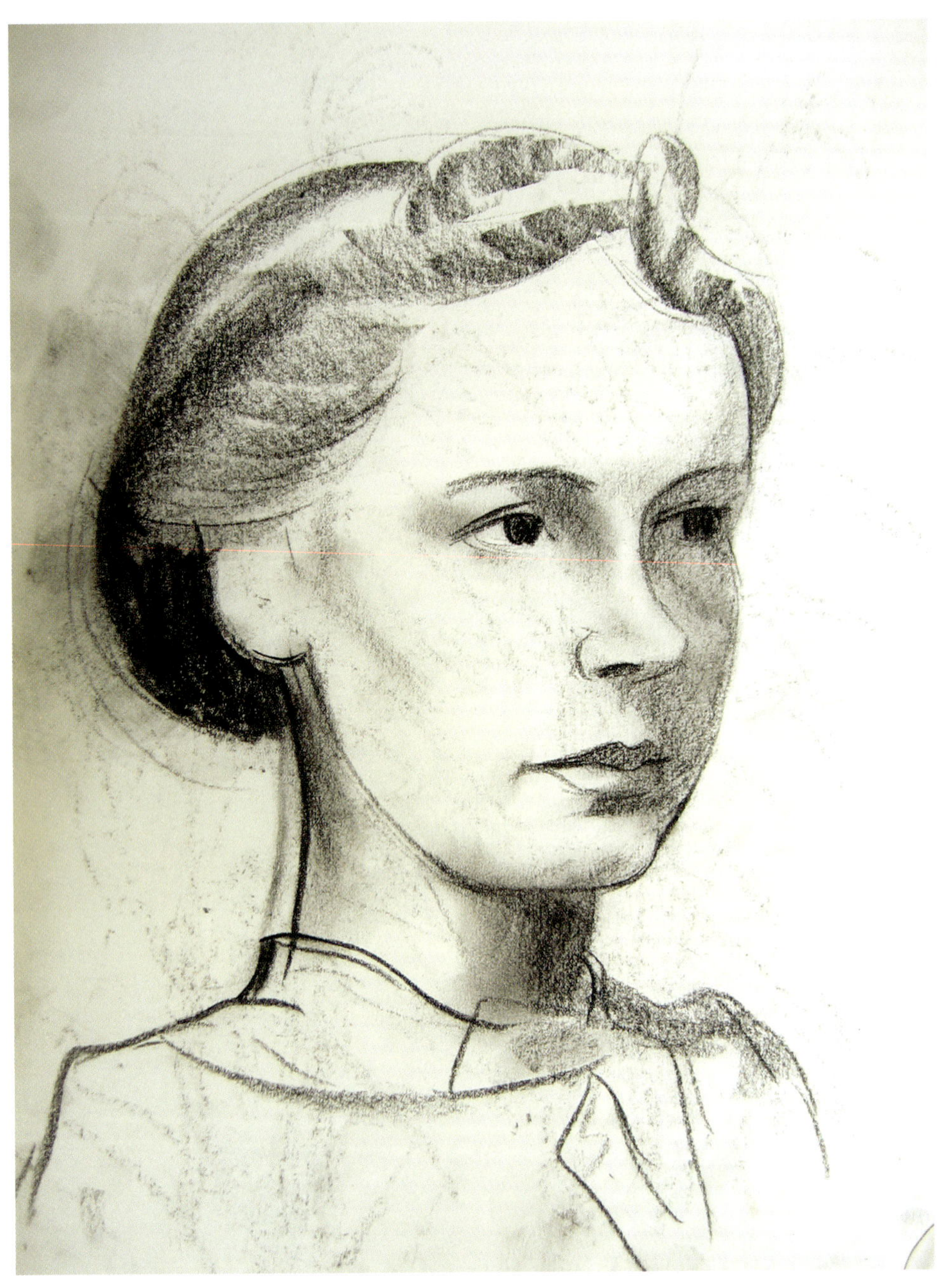

My father's sister, Melba, has the McCloskey nose. My cousin Kathy says that the nose is actually from Bob's mother's family, whose name was Wismeyer. Out of habit, however, I continue to call it the McCloskey nose.

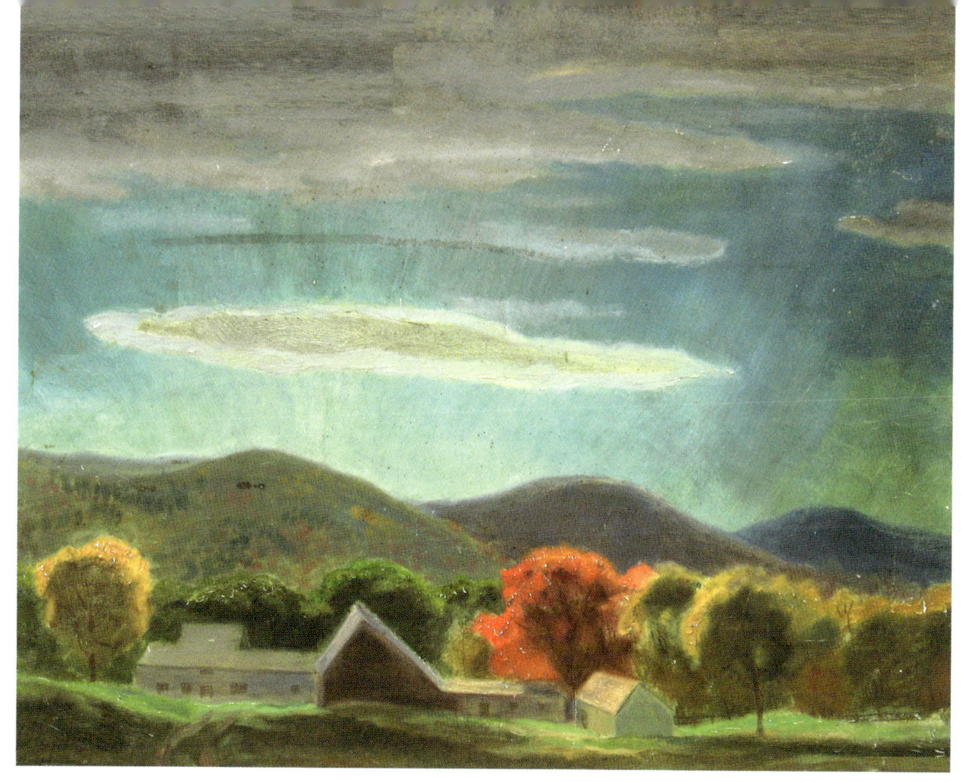

"Trees and Barn," oil on canvas board, slightly Photoshopped, 1930s.

"Men Working on Steel," charcoal on paper, 1930s.

This image (right) is one of a number of pictures Bob did of men working in industrial settings. Jim Schwartz wrote in an email,

> ***"Your father would have known the Armco as the American Rolling Mill Company. It was headquartered in Middletown, Ohio, and owned coke ovens and blast furnaces in New Miami (a village a few miles north of Hamilton) that was often referred to as Coke Otto. Coke Otto refers to the coke made there and the first name of the German native . . . an immigrant who introduced this process. Your father certainly was familiar with Coke Otto's operations as trains daily took molten iron in special rail cars from Coke Otto to the mill in Middletown."***

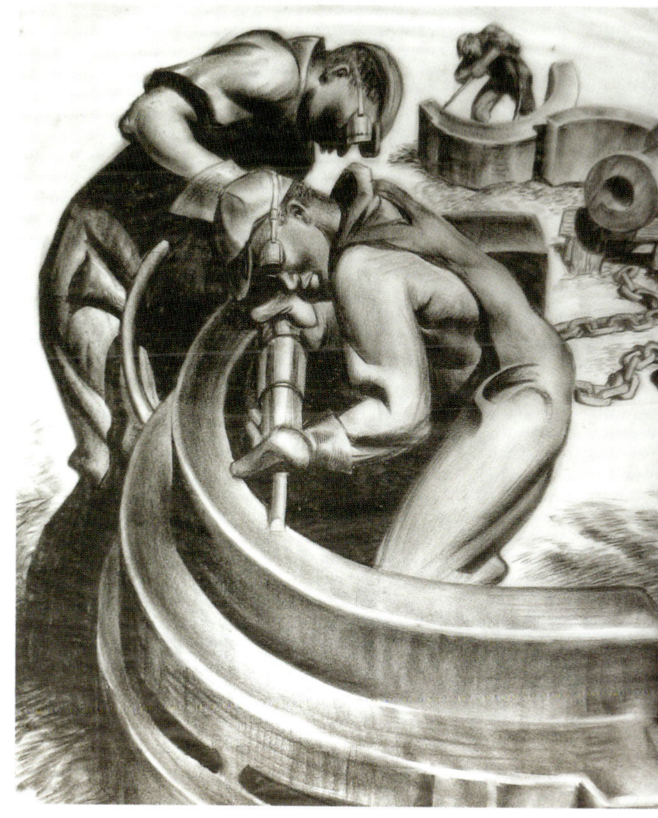

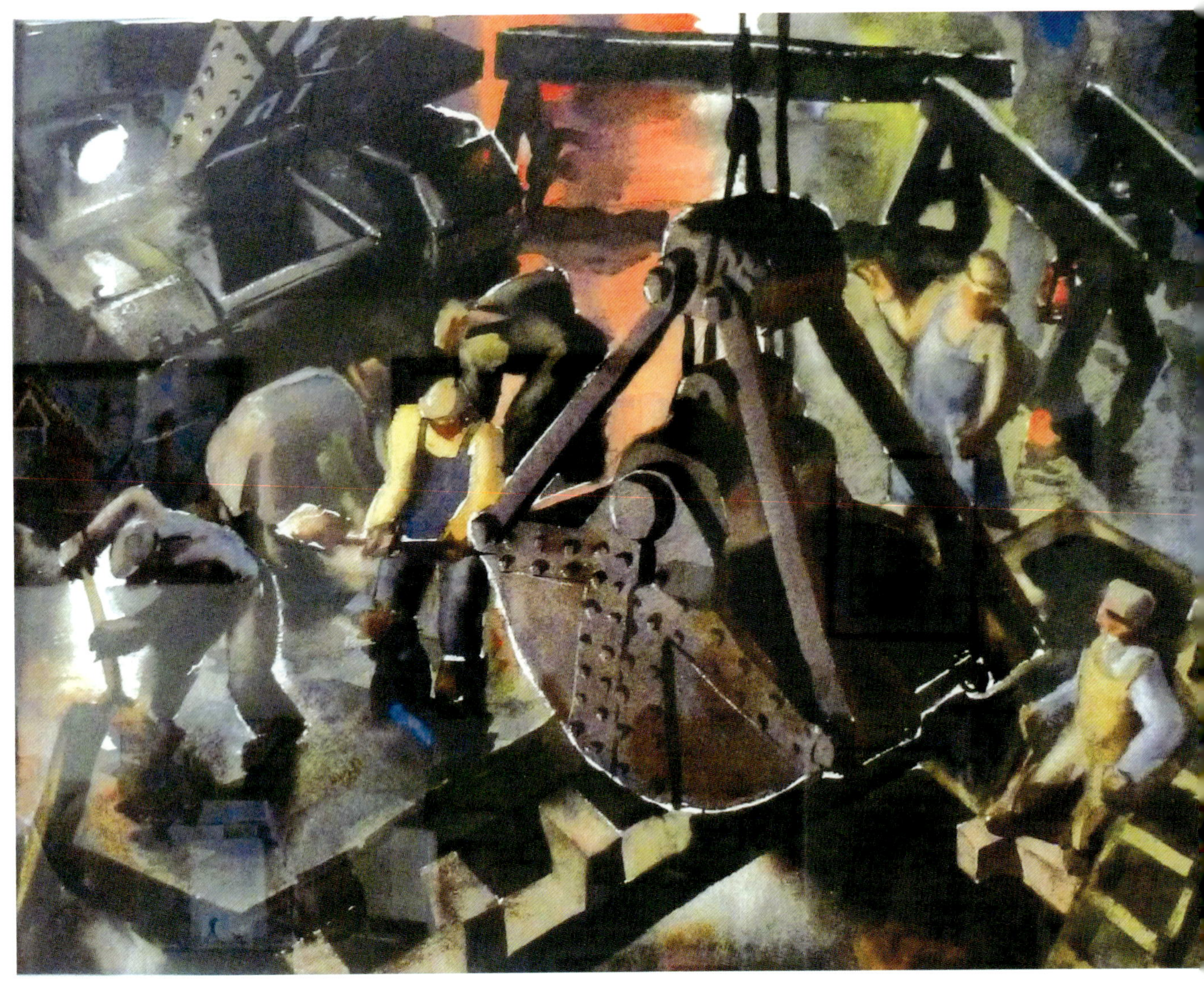

"Men in Coke Ovens," watercolor on paper, 1930s, photo by Janet Sohngen, courtesy of the Robert McCloskey Museum, Heritage Hall, Hamilton, Ohio.

The pictures have the feel of Soviet-era propaganda, with its hammer-and-sickle glorification of industrial workers. Maybe that was also an American art style in the 1930s.

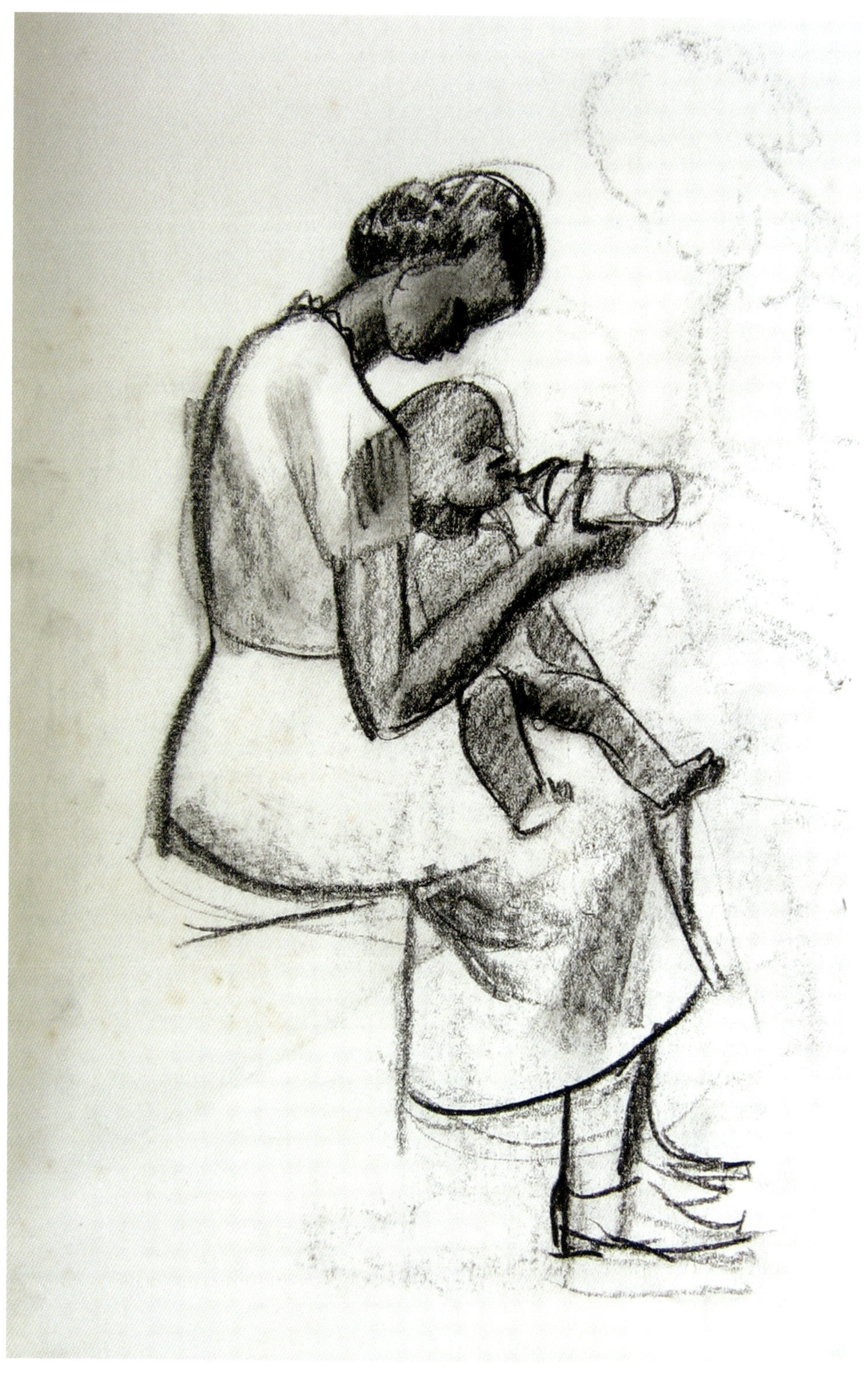

"Sketch of Woman Nursing her Baby," pencil on paper, 1930s.

"Sketch of Couple Dancing," pencil on paper, 1930s.

"Sketch of Man Playing Bass," pencil on paper, 1930s.

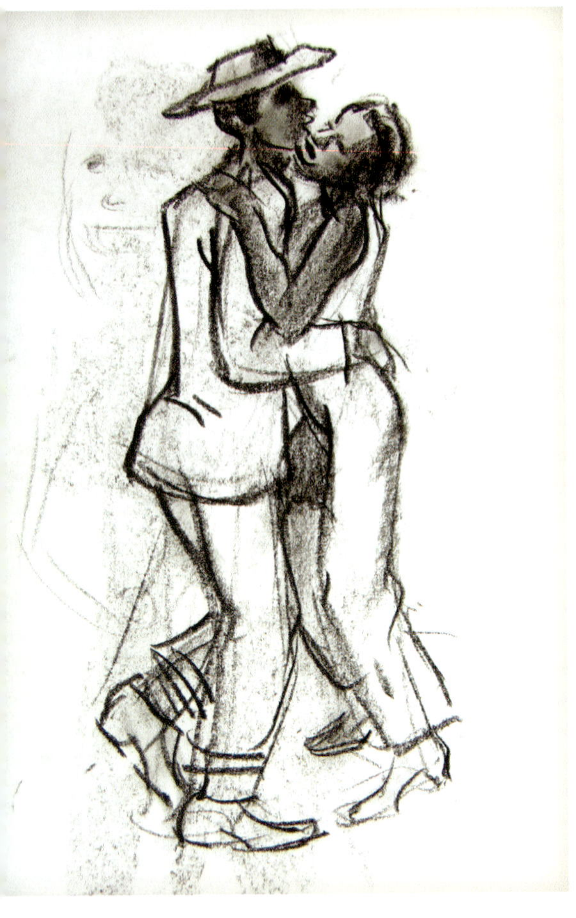

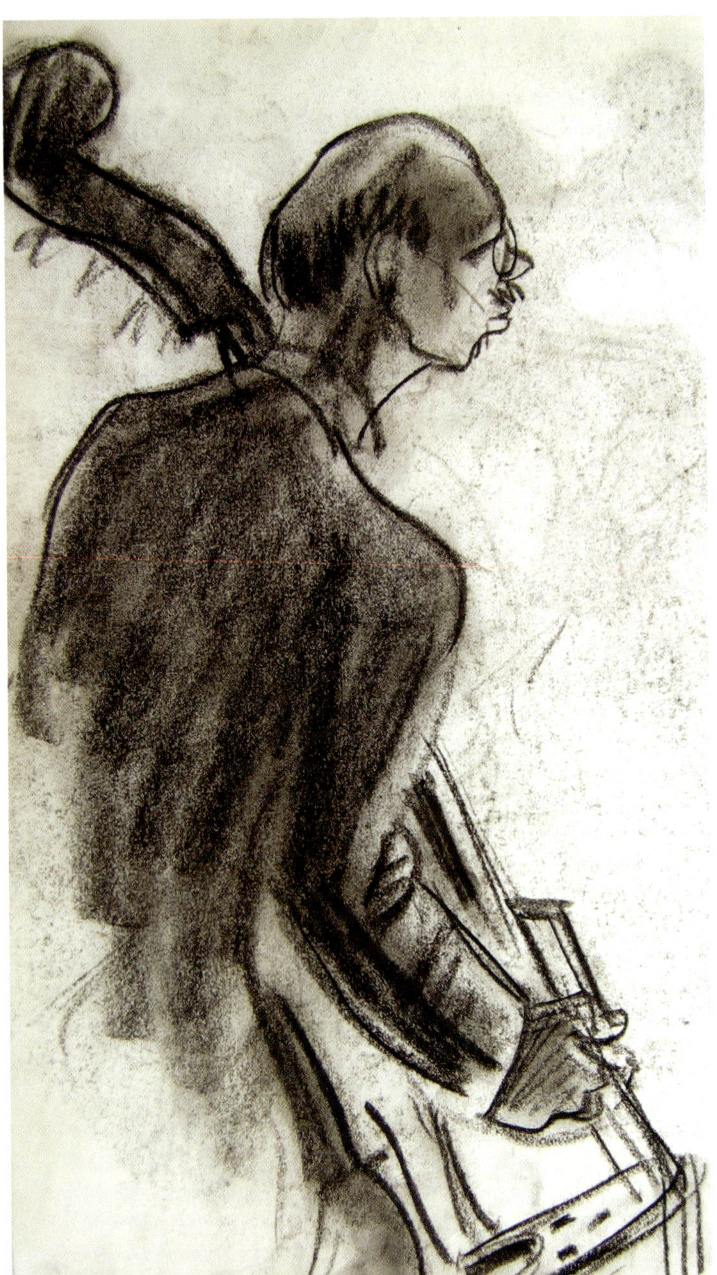

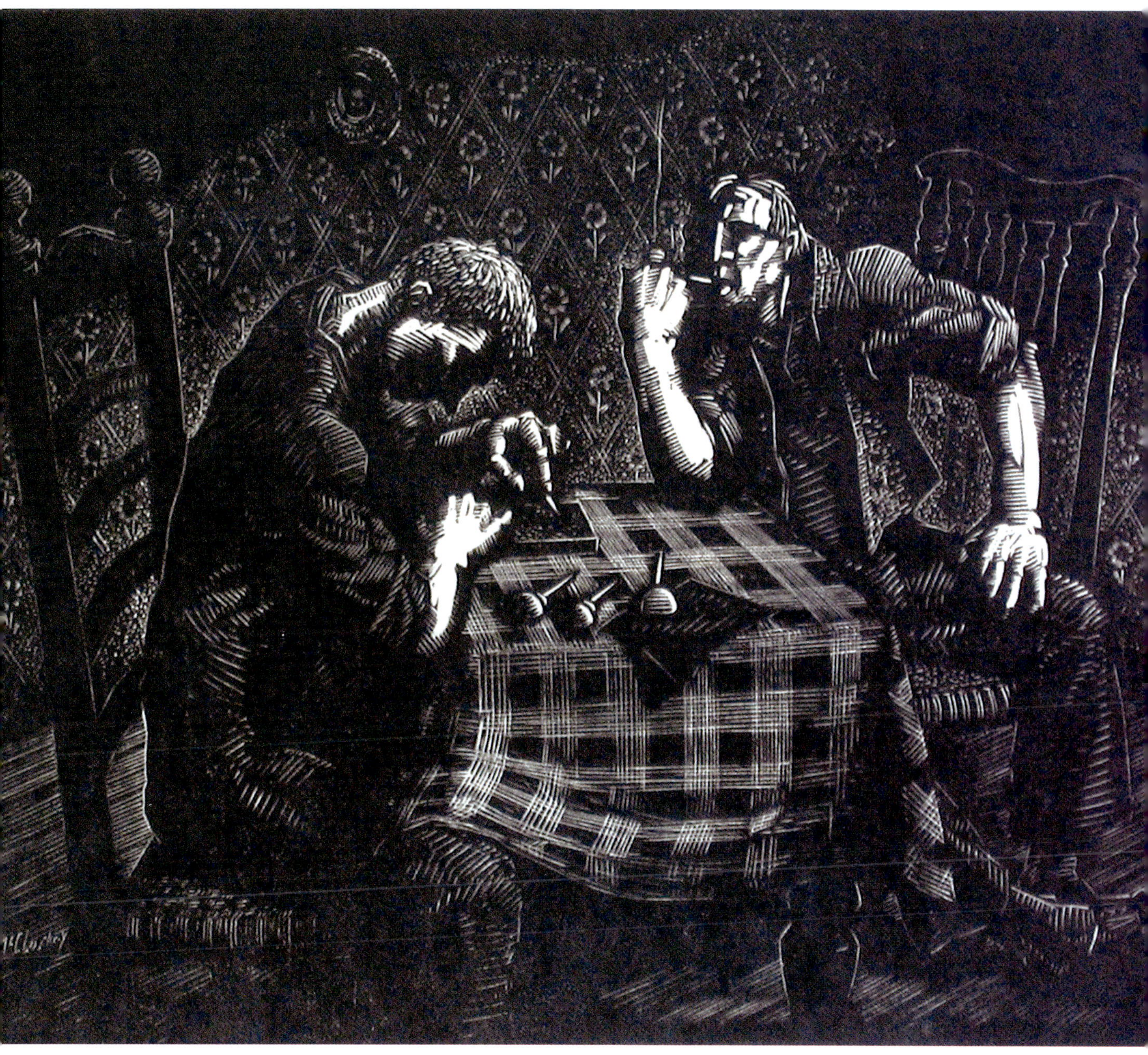

Here is a woodcut Bob made of himself making a woodcut. He liked pattern: wall paper, the checks on tablecloths, seat caning (and look at his nose!) Jim wondered if his friend wasn't Grayearth, Bob's Native American mentor.

"Robert McCloskey Carving a Woodcut, with a Friend," woodcut, 1930s.

Bob filled several sketchbooks with drawings of horses in the countryside around Hamilton.

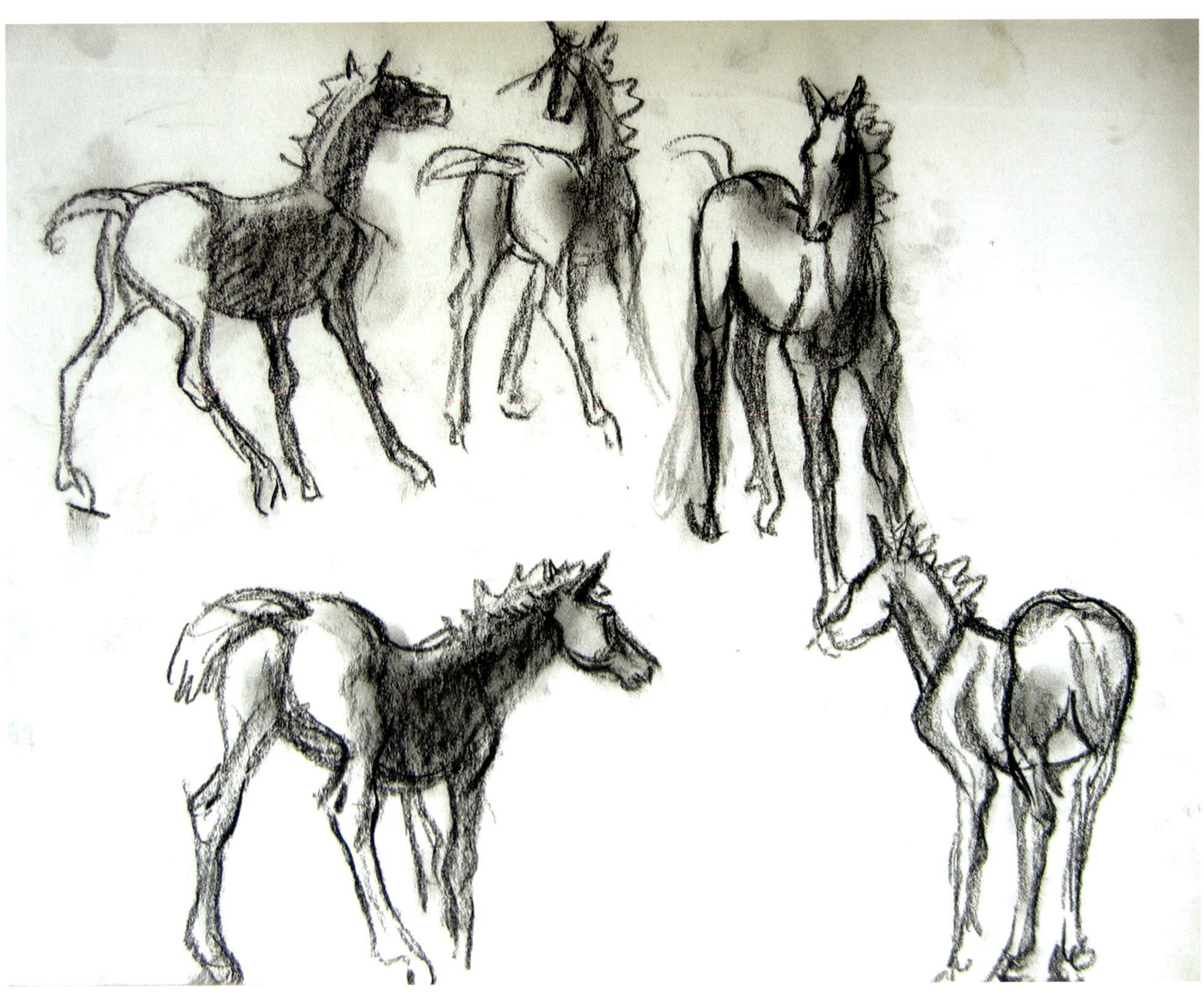

"Sketch of Colts Playing," pencil on paper, 1930s.

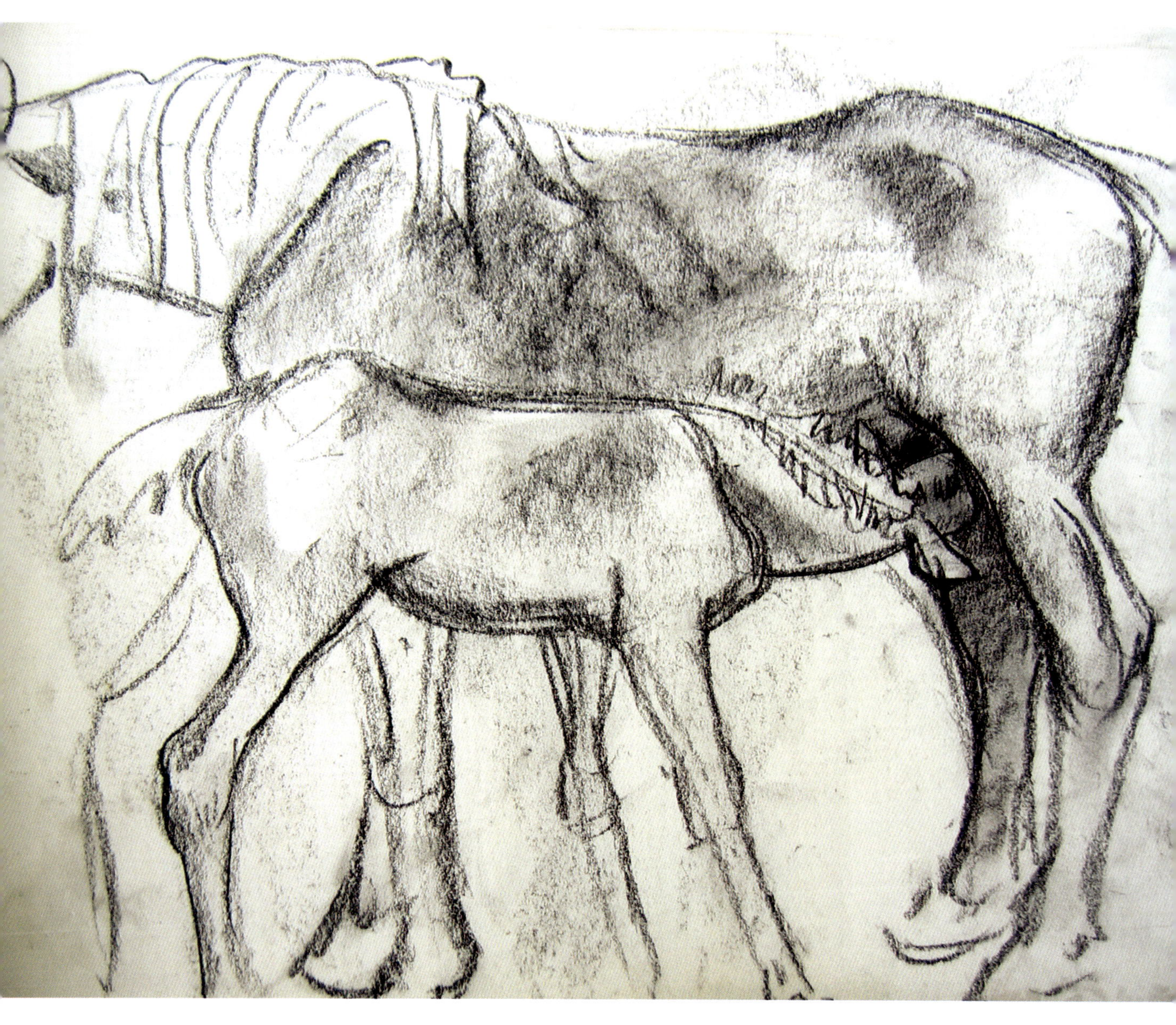

"Sketch of Mother and Colt Nursing," pencil on paper, 1930s.

Three of Bob's books were inspired by his childhood and youth in Hamilton: *Lentil* was about a boy who couldn't whistle or sing, so he learned to play the harmonica. *Homer Price* was about a resourceful boy who pulls the adults in his life out of trouble. Its sequel, *Centerburg Tales,* has more stories about Homer. Centerburg is probably named for Middletown, Ohio, which is about fifteen miles from Hamilton.

Bob did a number of prototype sketches for *Lentil.* You can see in these pictures that Bob returned to his old haunts to see if he could make a story from them. He went into the woods to dream and whistle melodies, and stare into a brook . . . and go fishing.

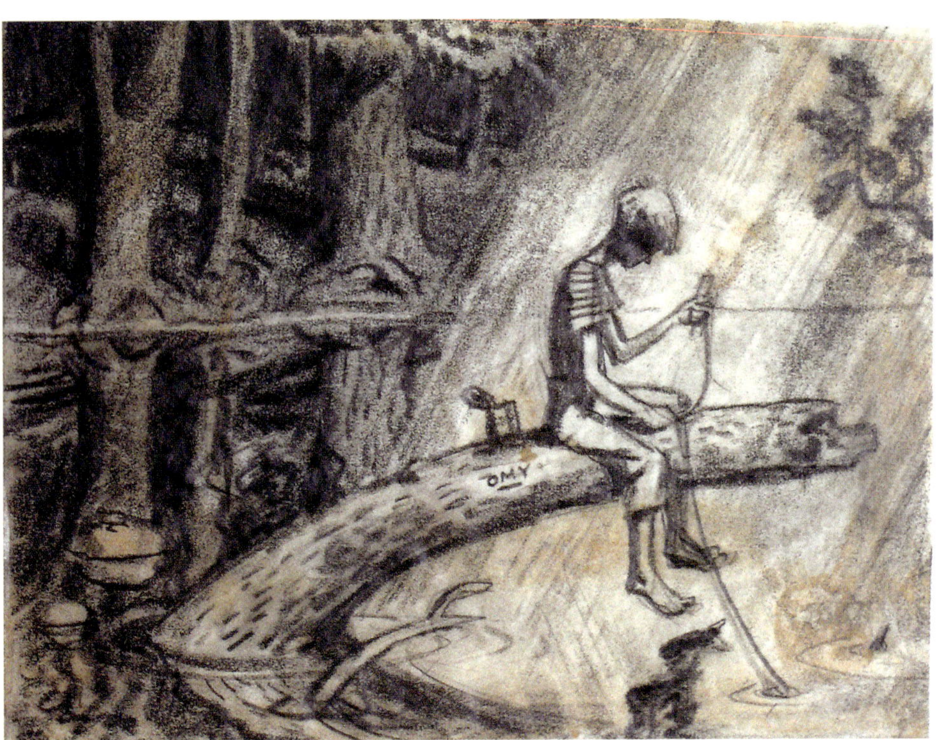

"Sketch of Lentil Fishing," pencil on paper, 1939.

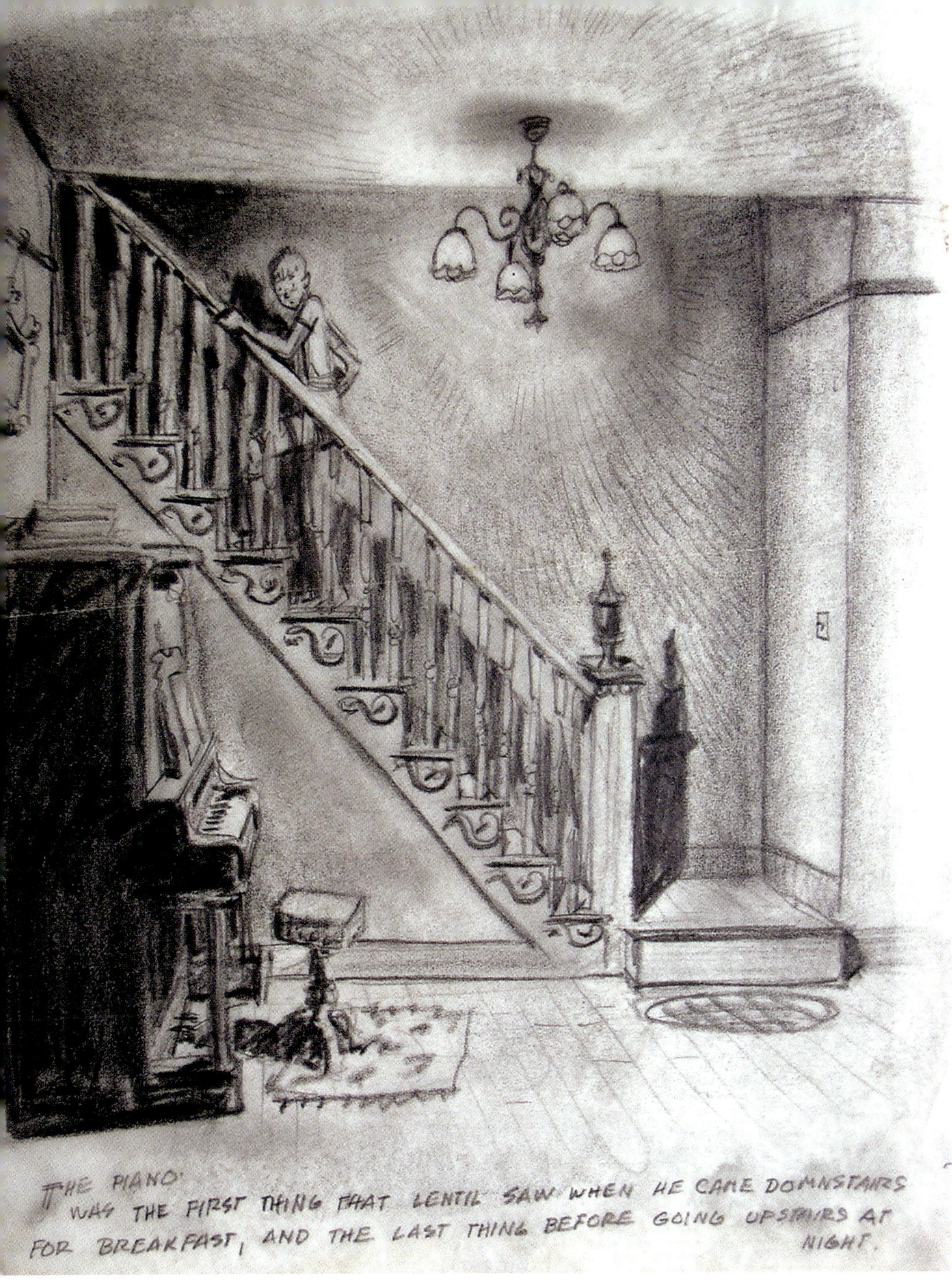

"Sketch of Lentil Looking at Piano," pencil on paper, ca 1939.

He remembered forced piano lessons and the pain when his uncle rapped him on the fingers if he made a mistake.

The text reads, "The piano was the first thing that Lentil saw when he came downstairs for breakfast, and the last thing before going upstairs at night."

"Sketch of Lentil's Mother Nagging him to Practice," pencil on paper, ca 1939.

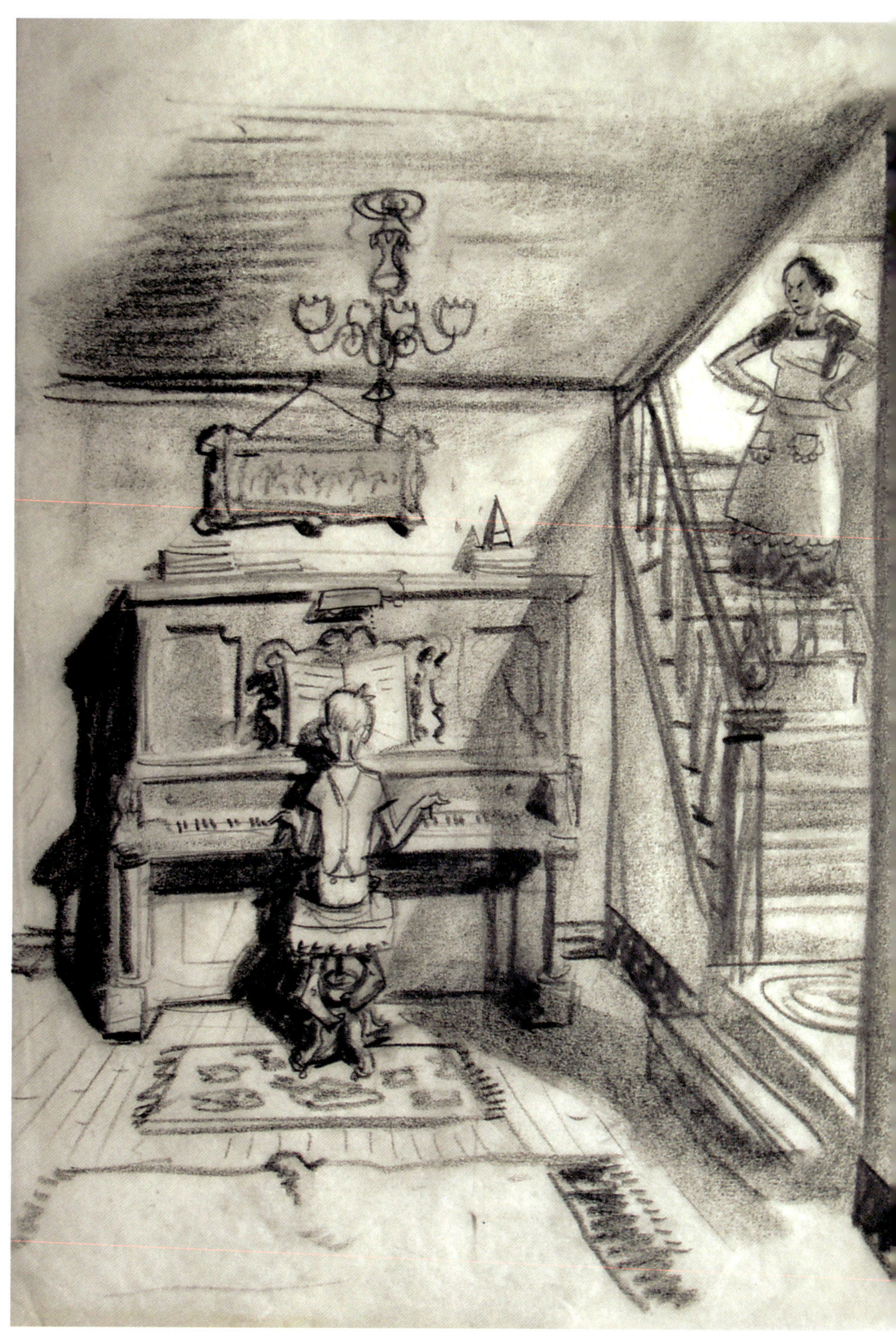

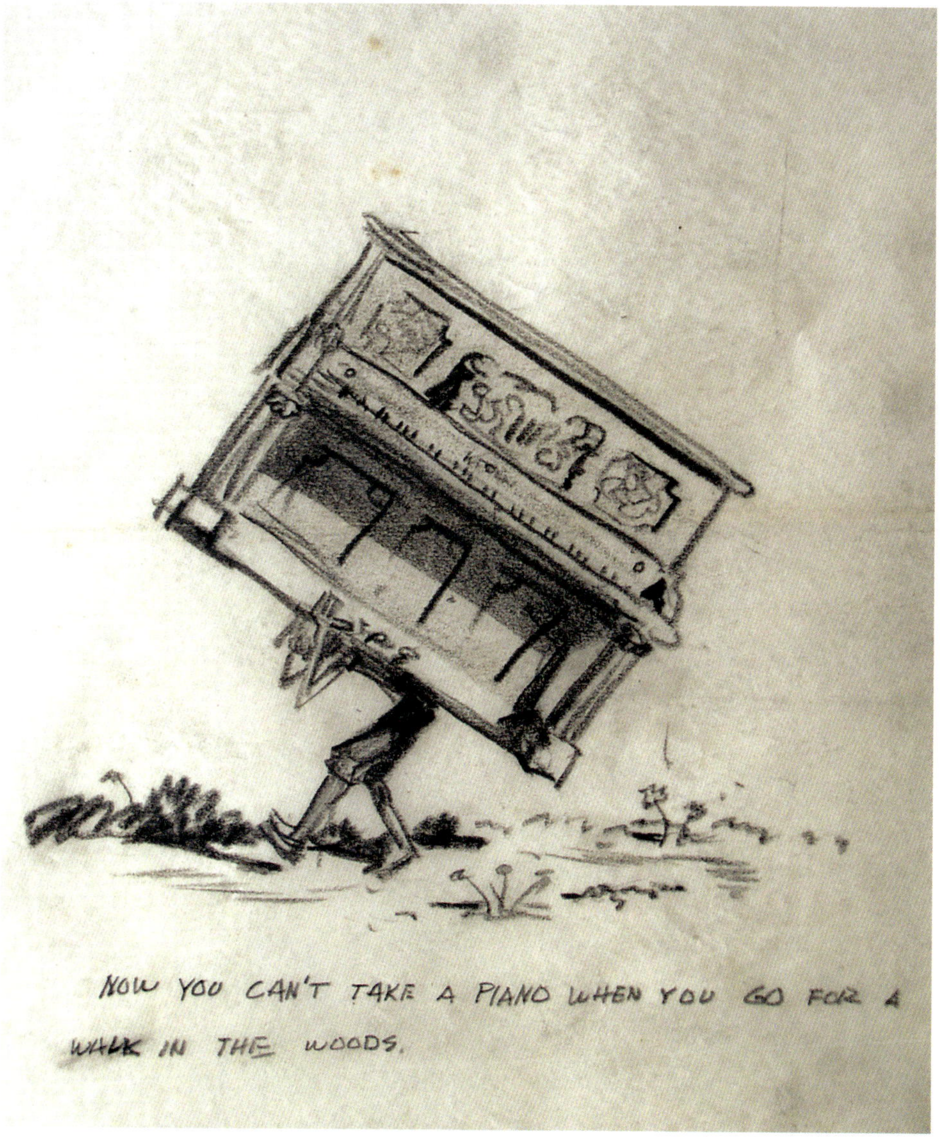

"Sketch of Lentil Carrying a Piano," pencil on paper, ca 1939.

And his mother nagged him to practice.

Bob wrote, "Now you can't take a piano when you go for a walk in the woods."

But then Lentil learned how to play the harmonica. You can take the harmonica into the woods. And he got good enough that he could entertain his friends, and a bird and an old dead tree, too.

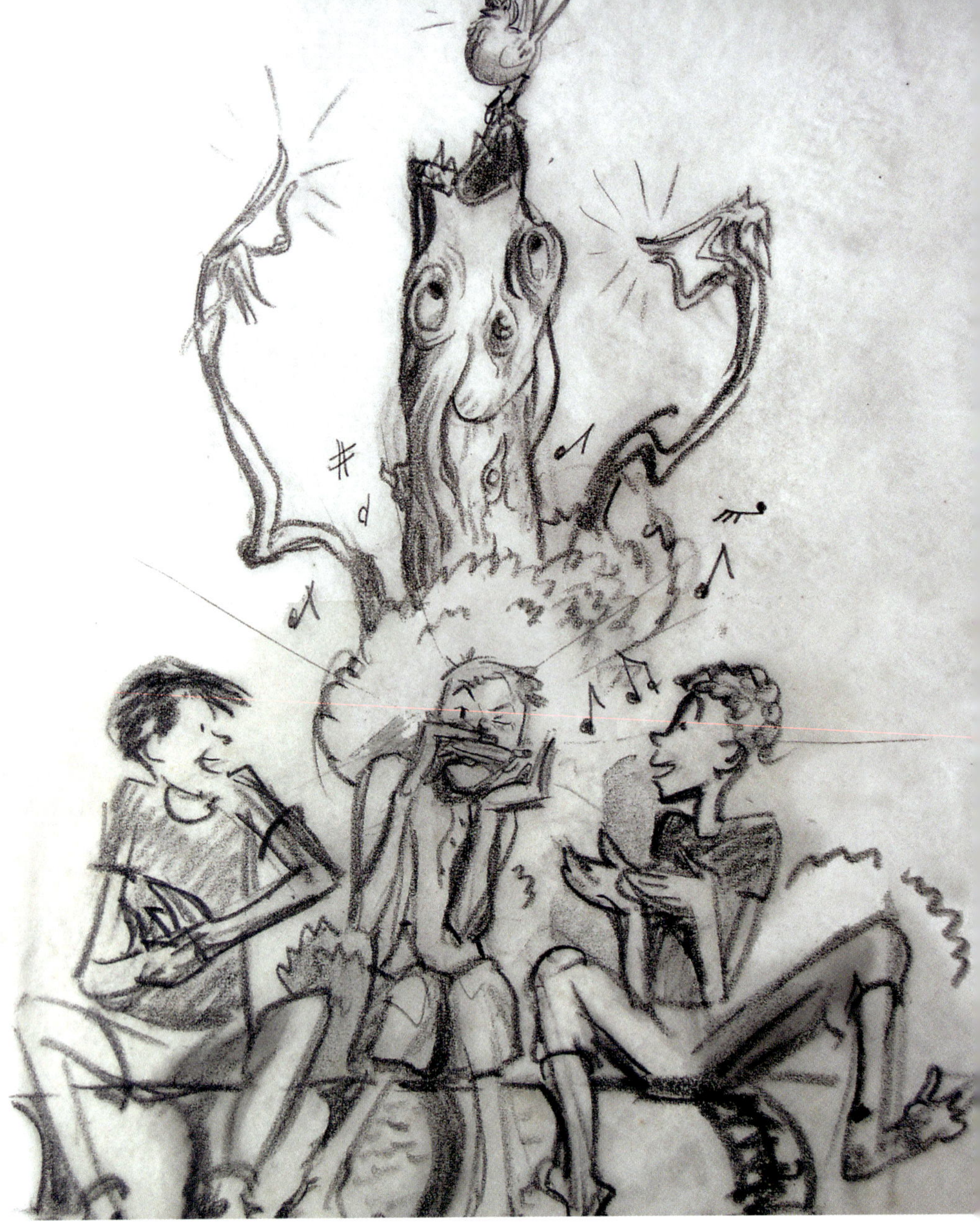

"Sketch of Lentil Playing Harmonica for His Friends and a Tree," pencil on paper, ca 1939.

These first ideas are a far cry from the finished book. In the book, Lentil learned to play the harmonica because he couldn't sing, and he couldn't even whistle because he couldn't pucker his lips. One day, the whole town of Alto turned out at the train station to welcome Colonel Carter home. But at the last minute, they were distracted by a guy sitting on a rooftop sucking on a lemon.

Everybody's lips puckered at the sight and sound of Old Sneep and his lemon. "The mayor gave the signal to play, but the cornetist couldn't play

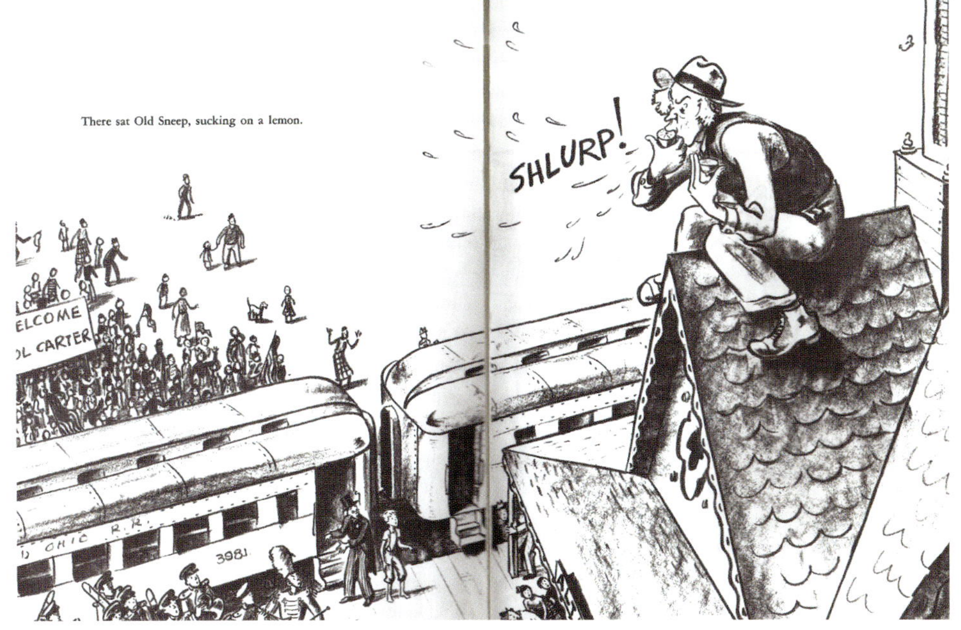

Lentil, "Old Sneep Sucking on a Lemon," Viking Press, 1940.

his cornet, the piccolo player couldn't play his piccolo, the trombone player couldn't play his trombone, and the tuba player couldn't play his tuba, because their lips were all puckered up." But the reason Lentil couldn't whistle is that he couldn't pucker his lips, so he could still play his harmonica. He saved the day, and Colonel Carter had a fine welcome home.

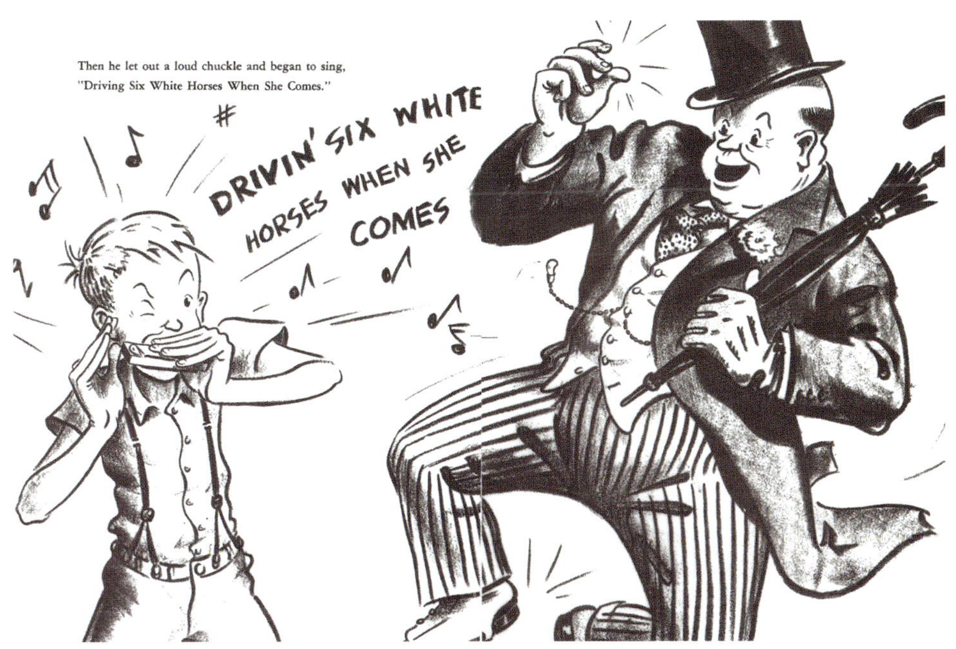

Lentil, "Playing the Harmonica," Viking Press, 1940.

If Lentil expressed my father's musical side, Homer Price expressed his mechanical side. Bob loved to tinker with gadgets, and gadgets abound in *Homer Price* and *Centerburg Tales.* My favorite is a steam calliope musical mouse trap.

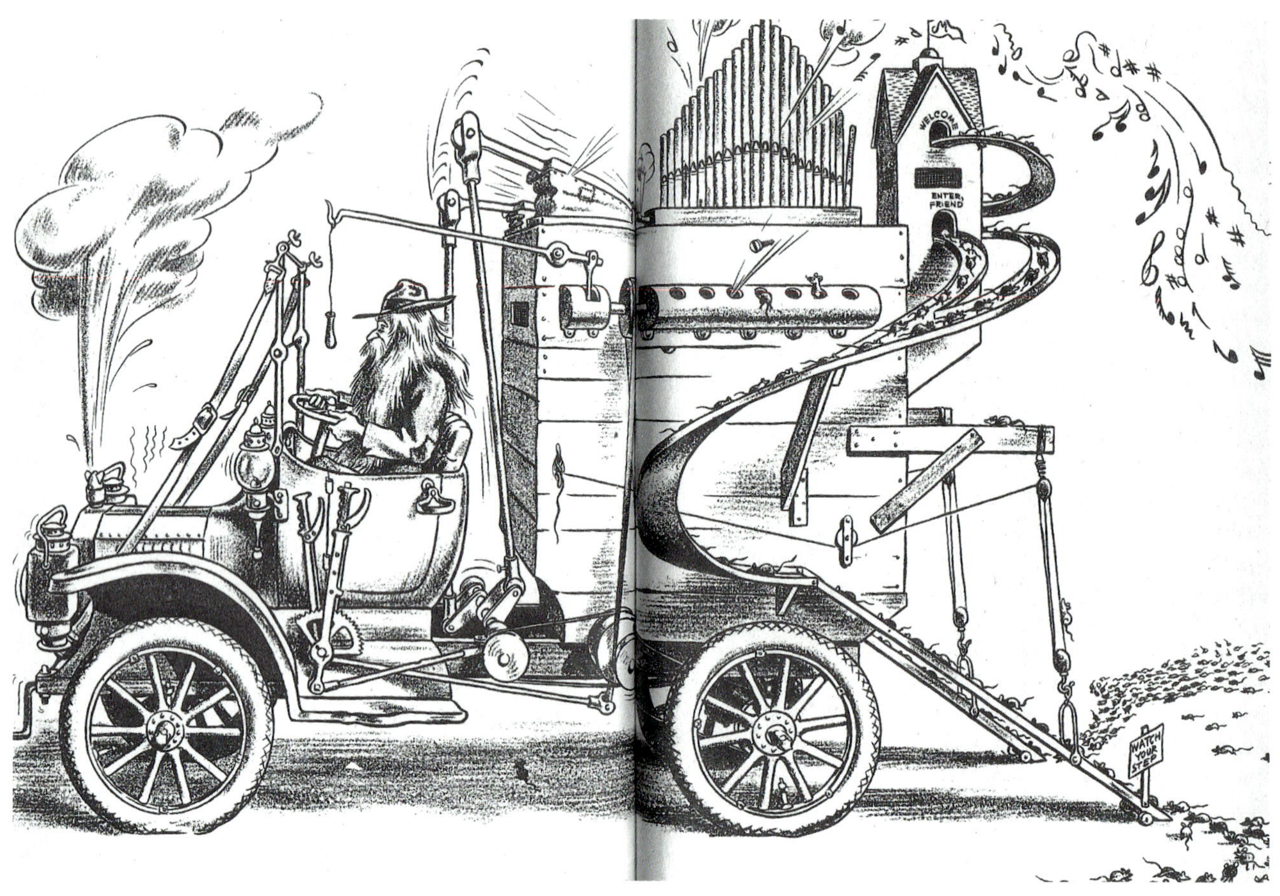

Homer Price, "The Musical Mousetrap," Viking Press, 1943.

But Robert McCloskey's best known gadget is the fabulous doughnut machine. In the episode of the Doughnuts, the Homer's Uncle Ulysses tinkers with the doughnut machine and without knowing it, disables the off button. When a lady stops by and makes a large batch of batter, the doughnuts cranked out by the machine take over the restaurant. Homer and his friends use good old American advertizing to sell the doughnuts and save the day.

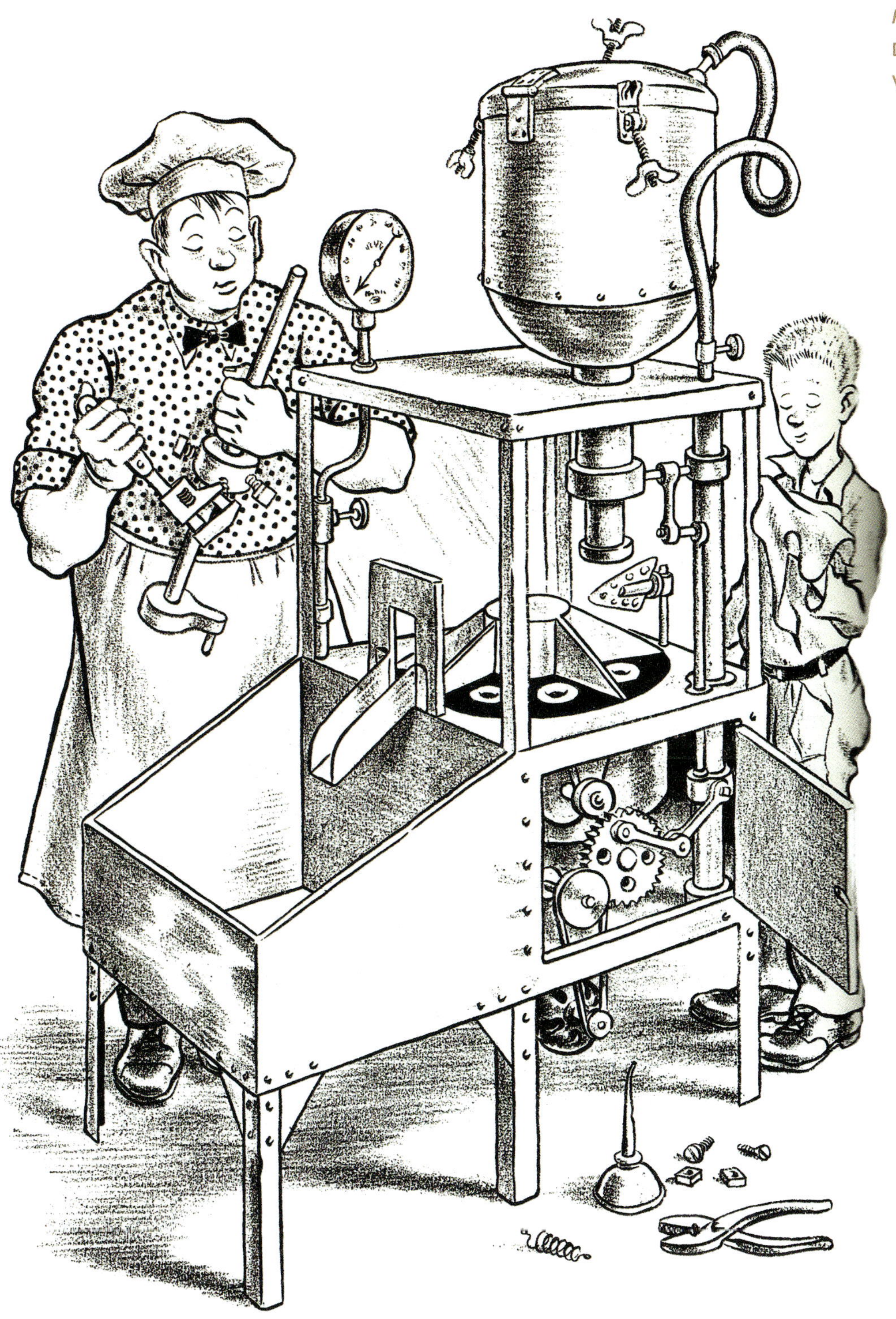

Homer Price, "The Doughnut Machine," Viking Press, 1943.

"Sketch of the Doughnut Machine for *Homer Price*," pencil on paper, ca 1942.

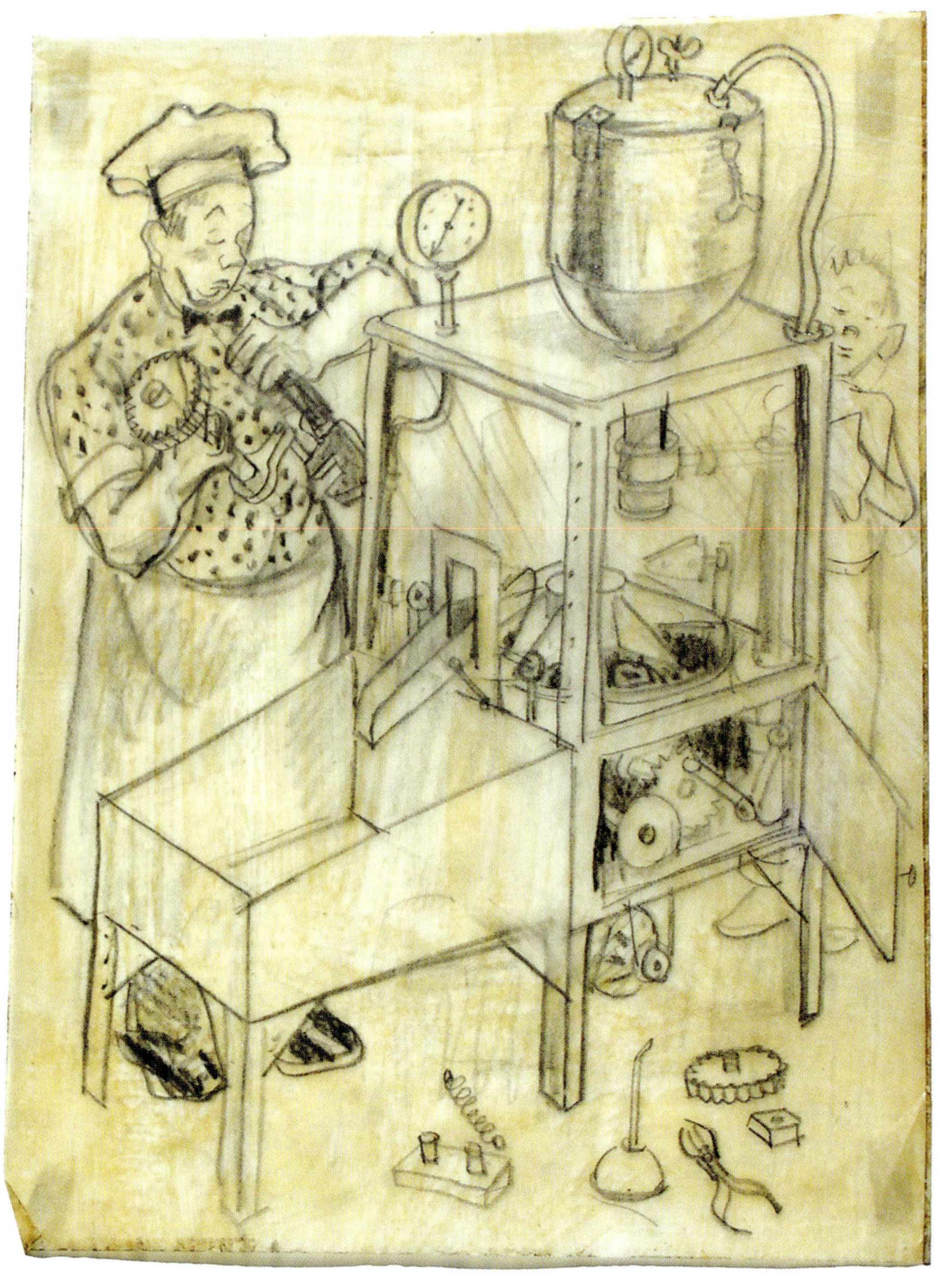

There is a doughnut machine at the McCloskey Museum in Hamilton.

"Oh, gracious! I've lost my diamond bracelet, and I know I left it here on the counter," she said, pointing to a place where the doughnuts were piled in stacks of two dozen.

"Yes, Ma'm, I guess you forgot it when you helped make the batter," said Homer.

Then they moved all the doughnuts around and looked for the diamond bracelet, but they couldn't find it anywhere. Meanwhile the doughnuts kept rolling down the little chute, just as regular as a clock can tick.

After they had looked all around the sheriff cast a suspicious eye on Mr. Gabby, but Homer said, "He's all right, sheriff, he didn't take it. He's a friend of mine."

Then the lady said, "I'll offer a reward of one hundred dollars for that bracelet! It really *must* be found! . . . it *really* must!"

"Now don't you worry, lady," said the sheriff. "I'll get your bracelet back!"

"Zeus! This is terrible!" said Uncle Ulysses. "First all of these doughnuts and then on top of all that, a lost diamond bracelet . . ."

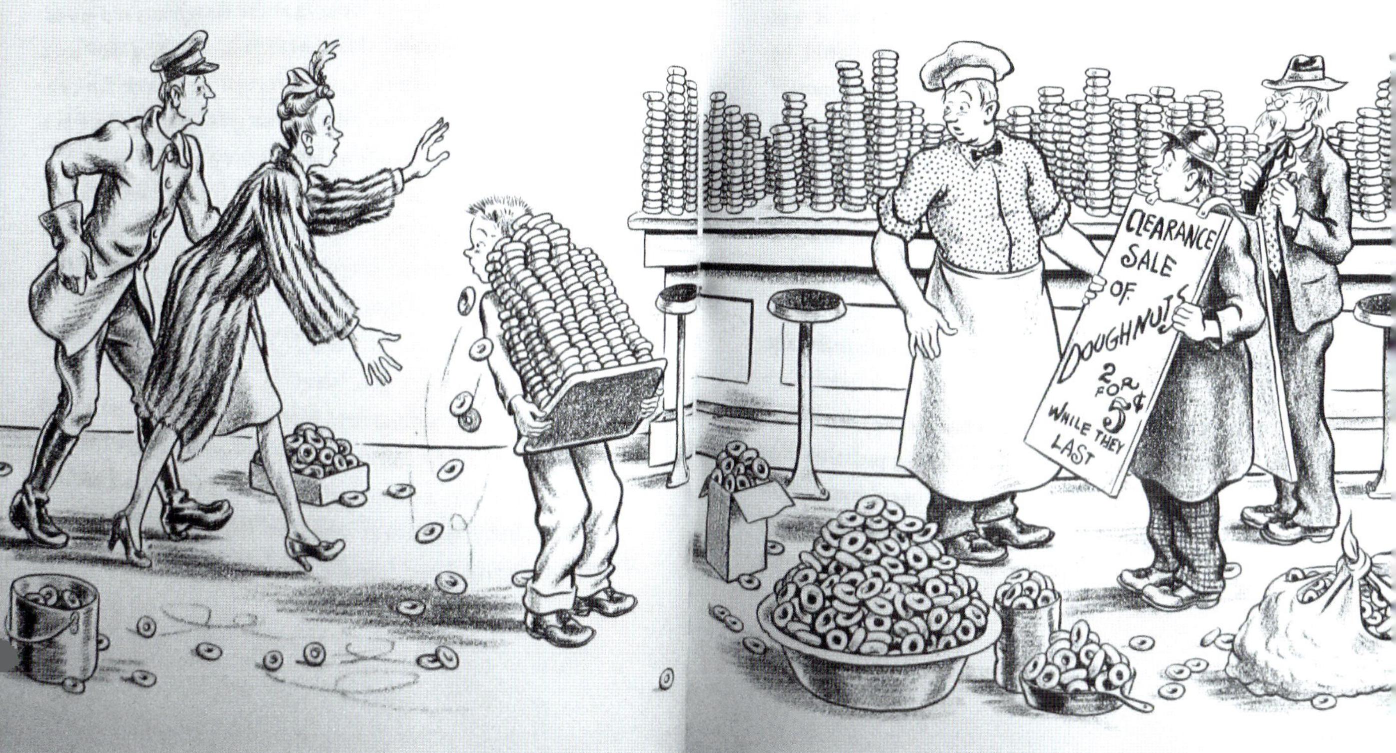

My father always liked libraries and librarians (he married one) but that didn't mean he couldn't poke fun at them. In *Centerburg Tales,* a library is turned upside down when a catchy song gets a little too catchy. Everybody sings and dances, including the librarian.

Homer Price, "What To Do with the Doughnuts," Viking Press, 1943.

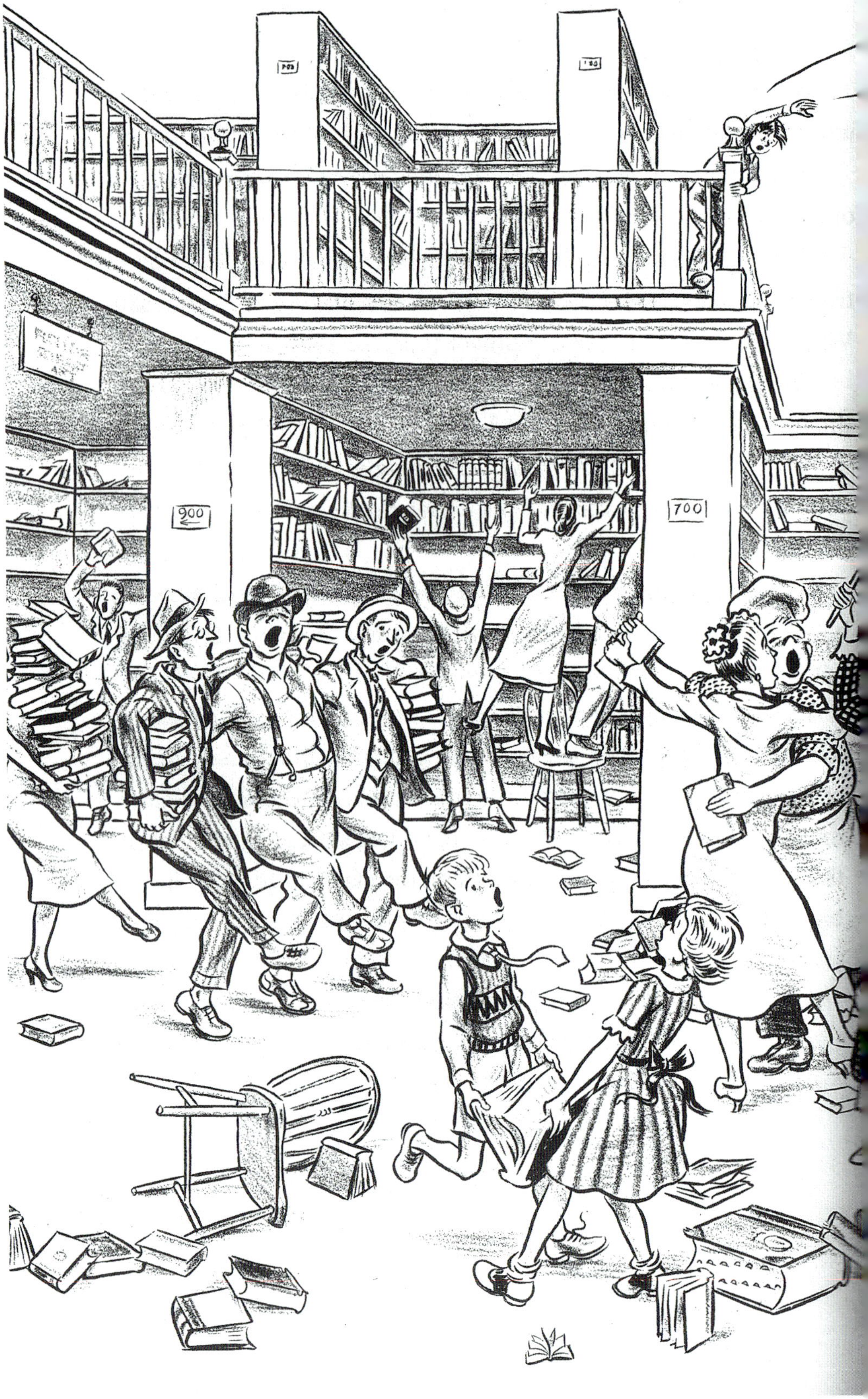

Centerburg Tales,
"Singing at the Library,"
Viking Press, 1951.

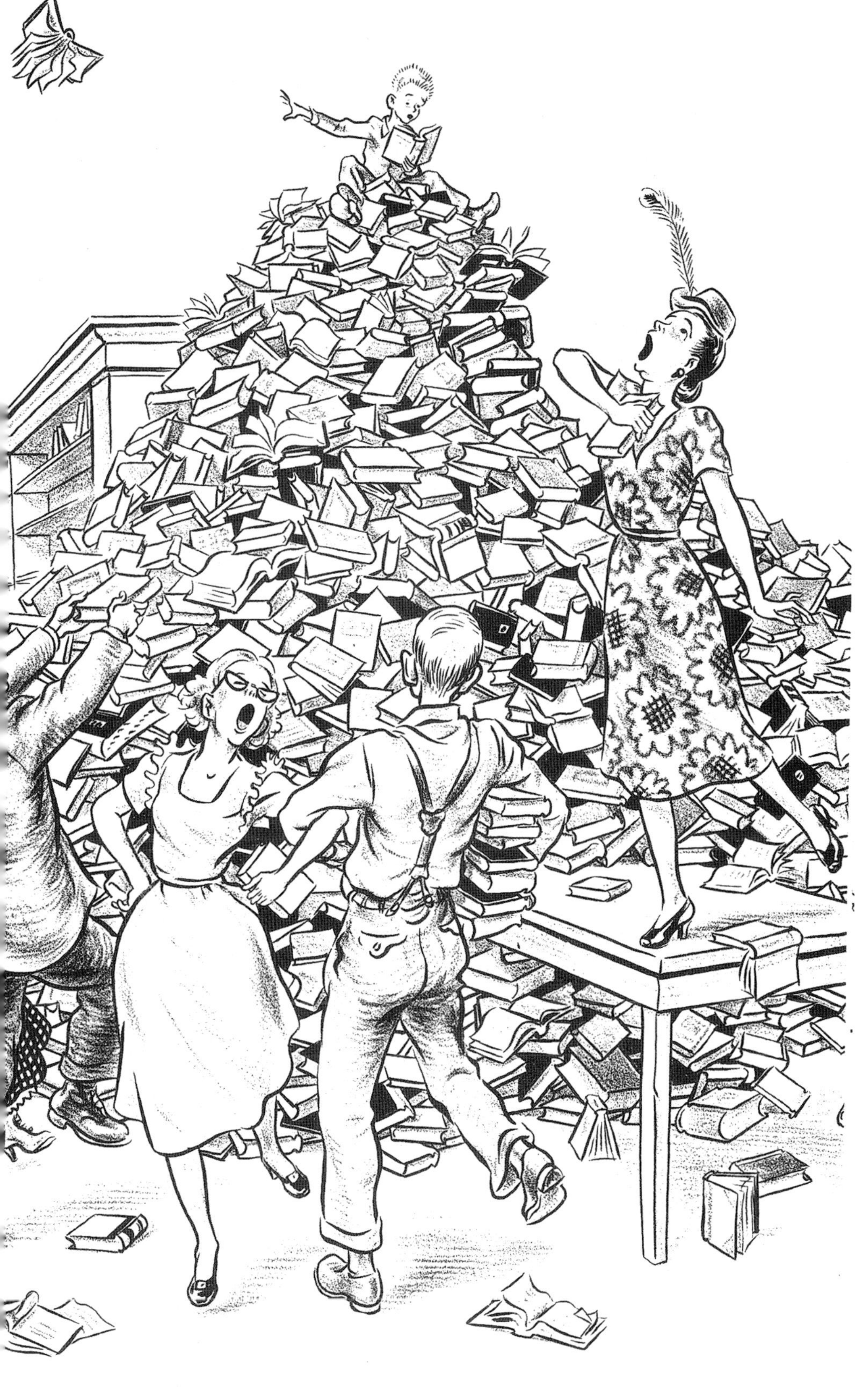

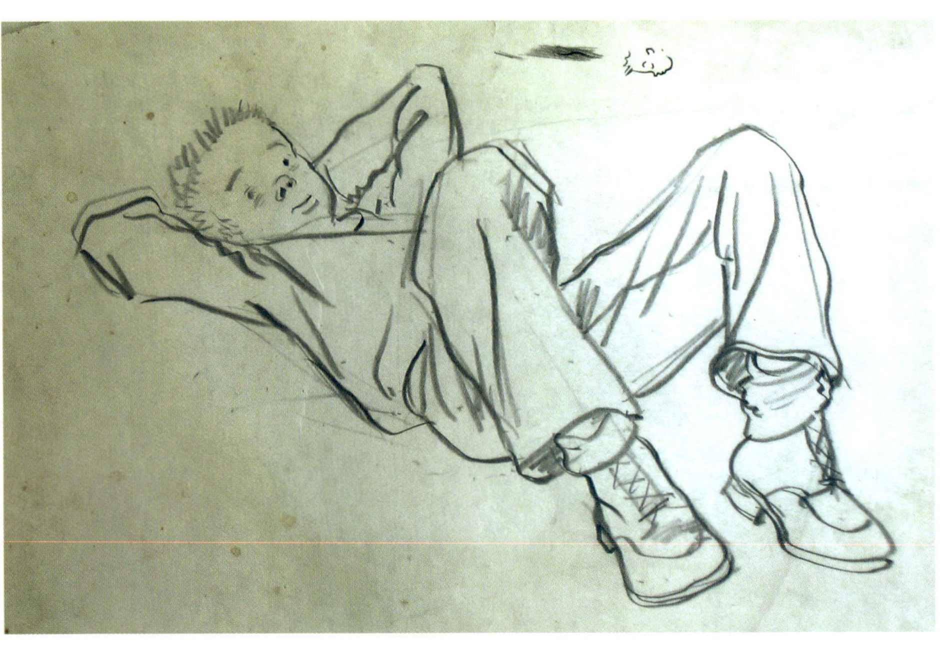

"Sketch of Homer," pencil on paper, ca 1951.

Here is a sketch of Homer in a moment of repose. If this sketch was done for *Homer Price,* then it was done during World War II, but if it was done for *Centerburg Tales,* it was done about 1950. The reason this matters is that the Cliffords, who were caretakers of our island, say that they believe that Earl Clifford posed for my father in sketches for Homer. But my family did not buy the island until 1946, after *Homer Price* was published, so Earl could not have posed for *Homer Price,* but he could have posed for *Centerburg Tales.*

Boston 2

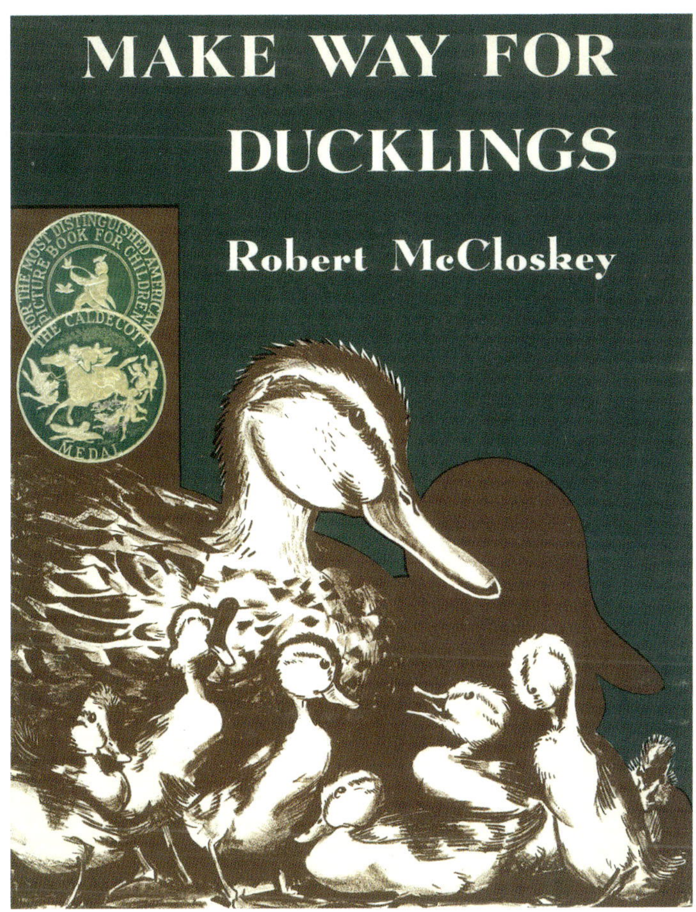

Make Way for Ducklings cover, Viking Press, 1941.

In 1932, my father won a scholarship to the Vesper George School of Art in Boston.

Then he went to the American Academy of Design in New York. After graduation, he returned to Boston, working for a syndicated newspaper cartoonist, and also for Francis Scott Bradford on a mural. He spent summers in Provincetown on Cape Cod and he hoped to become a painter, but he said later that he only sold two pictures in two years.

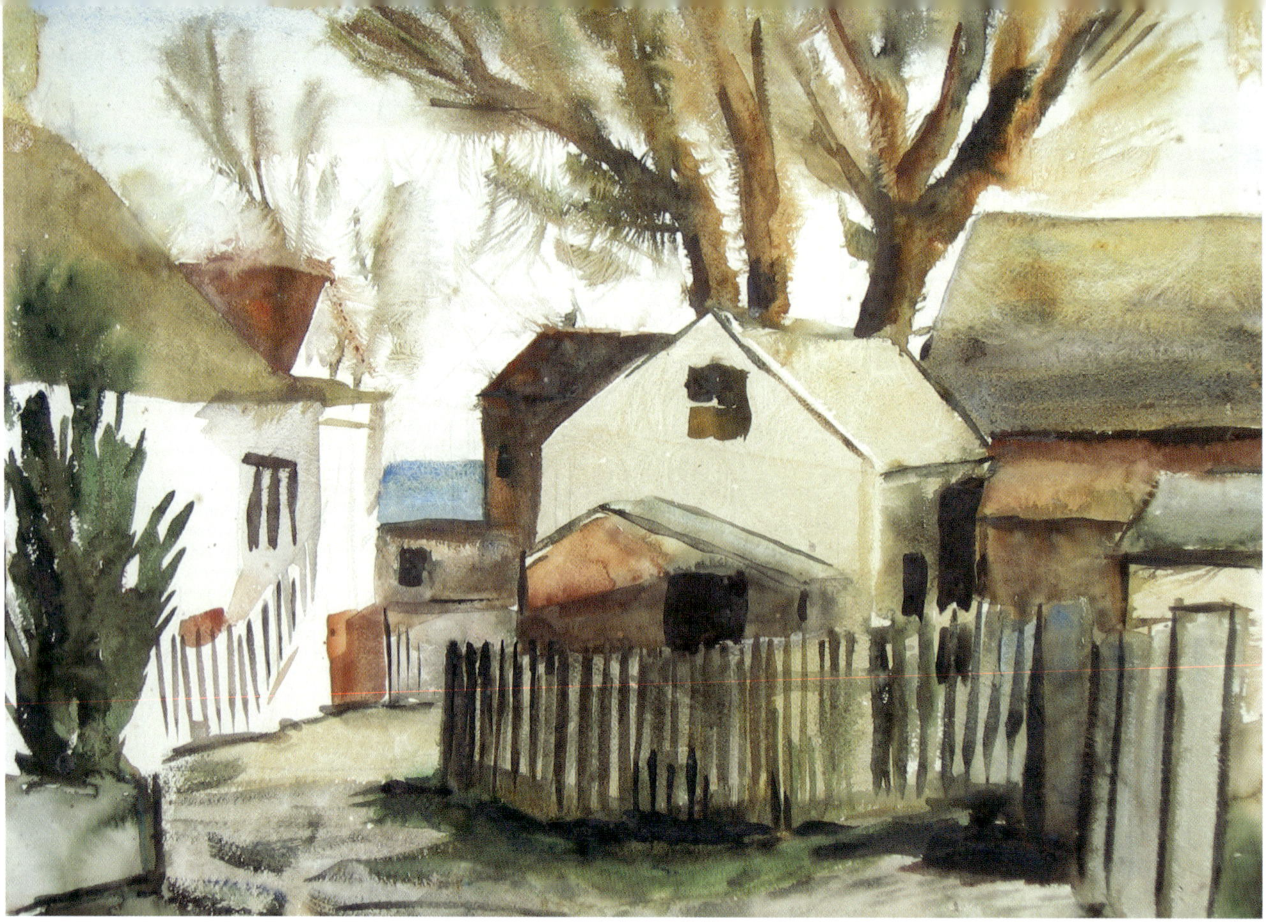

"Provincetown," watercolor on paper, 1930s.

His time in Boston was the inspiration for his best known book, *Make Way for Ducklings,* about a family of ducks who, with the help of Michael the police officer, stop traffic when they move from the Charles River to the Boston Public Garden.

Here are some of the other pictures he made during his time in Massachusetts.

In 1939, Francis Scott Bradford, a well known muralist, was

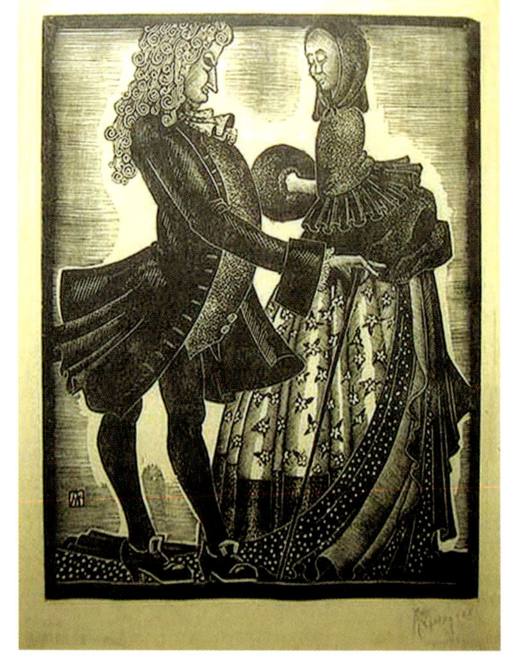

"Lord and Lady," woodcut, ca 1932. Courtesy of James Noble.

commissioned to do a series of six murals for the Lever Brothers of Cambridge. Brad, as my father called him, hired my father and his friend, Marc Simont, to help him paint the murals.

The murals are now at the Sloan School of Management at MIT. By coincidence, my mother's brother, David Durand, taught statistics at the Sloan School for most of his career.

The following images are some of my father's sketches for the murals.

"Study for Bradford Mural," charcoal on paper, 30" x 21", 1939.

"Study for Bradford Mural, Woman with Hat," charcoal on paper, 30" x 21" 1939.

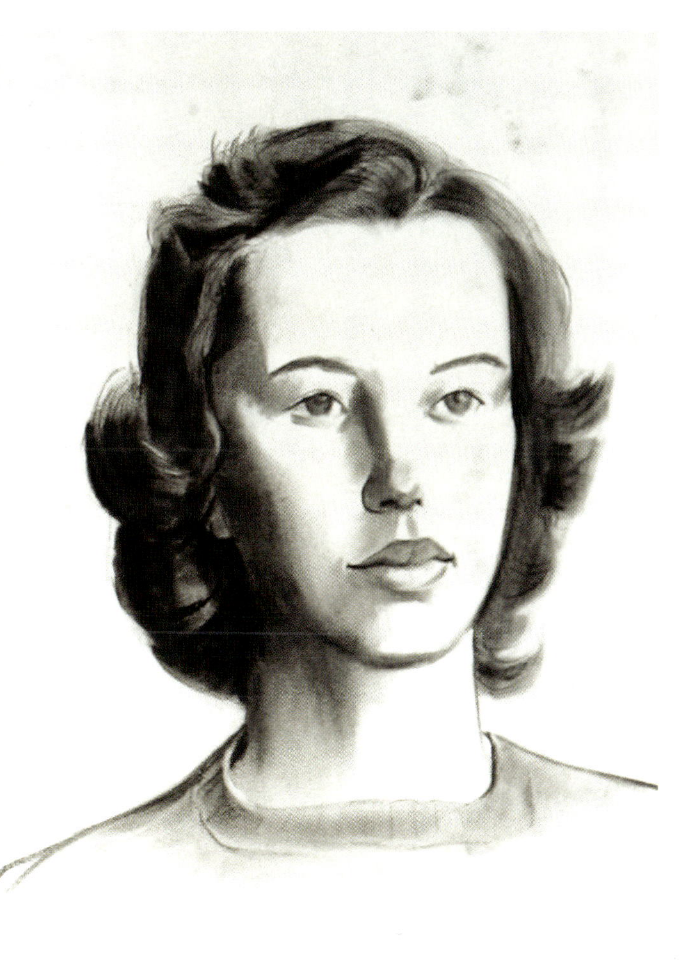

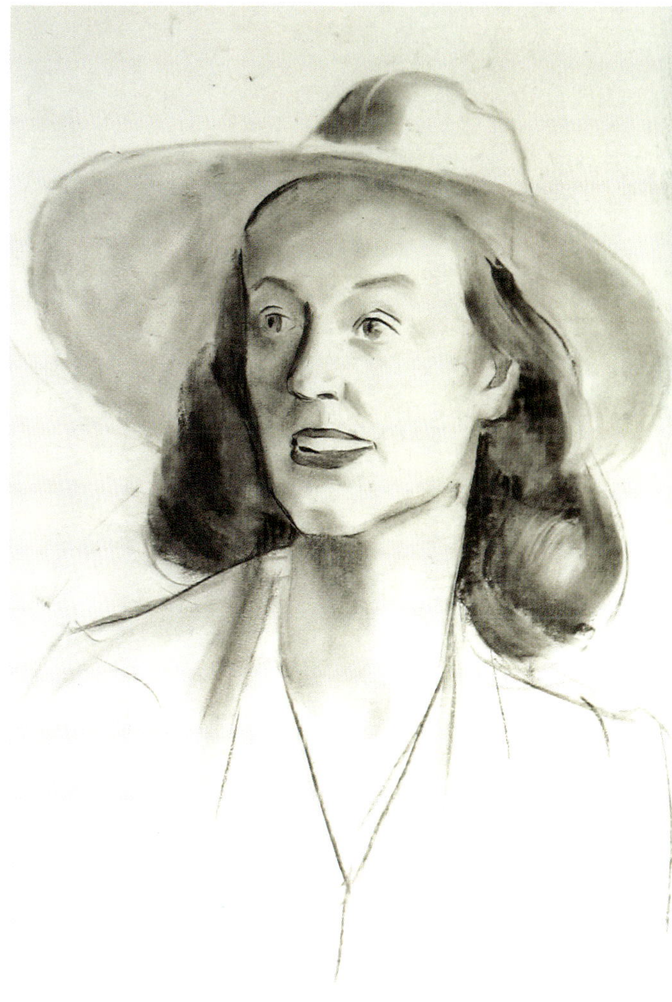

"Study for MIT Mural, Bust of Man," charcoal on paper, 30" x 21", 1939.

"Study for Bradford Mural, Young Woman Curtsying," charcoal on paper, 30" x 21", 1939.

"Study for Bradford Mural, Man in Uniform," charcoal on paper, 30" x 21", 1939.

"Study for Bradford Mural, Skates," charcoal on paper, 30" x 21", 1939.

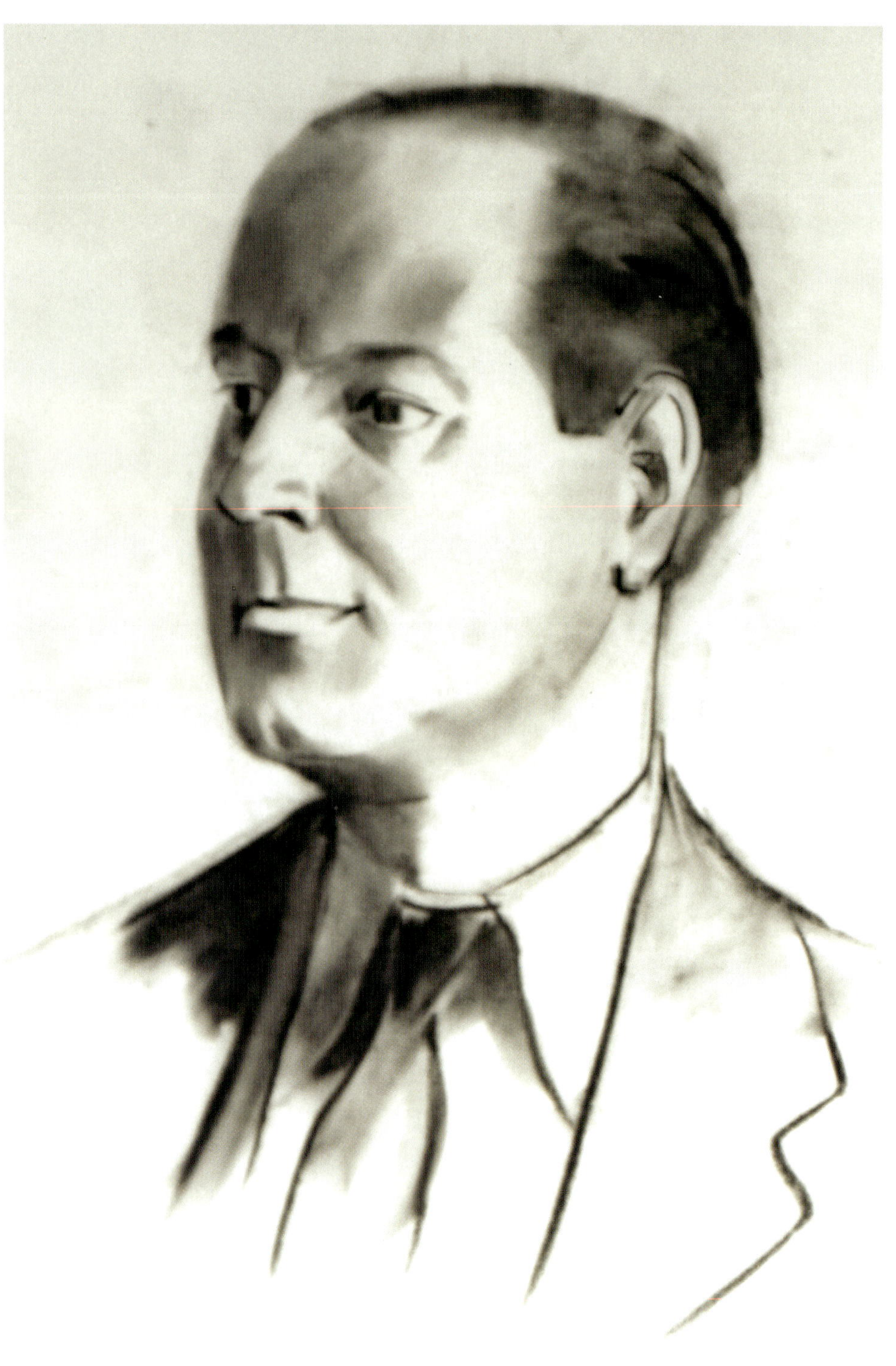

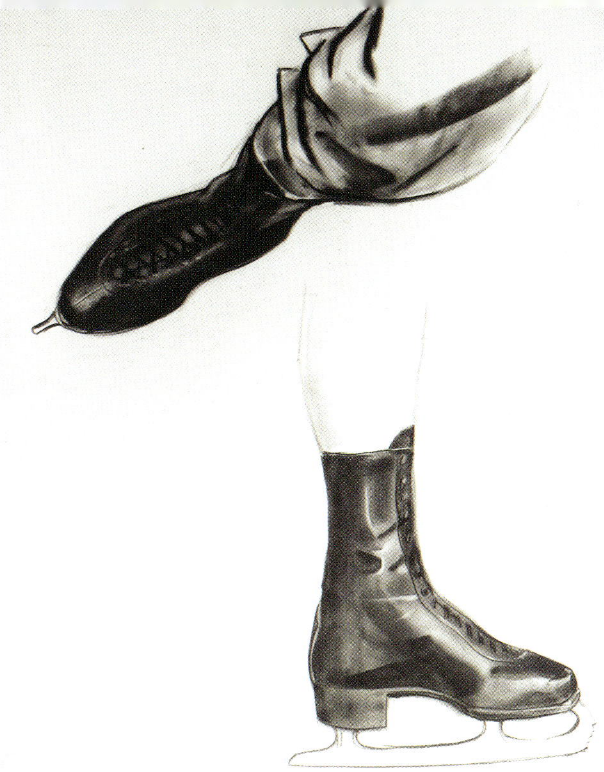

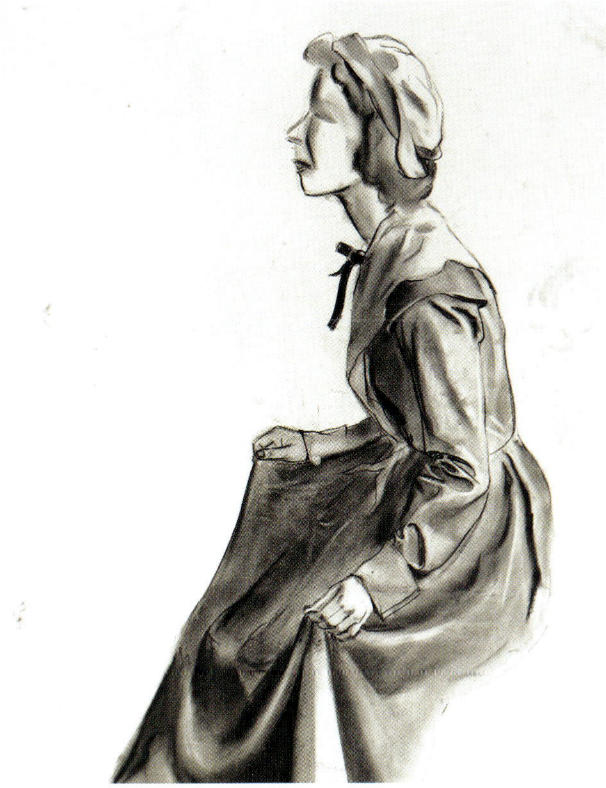

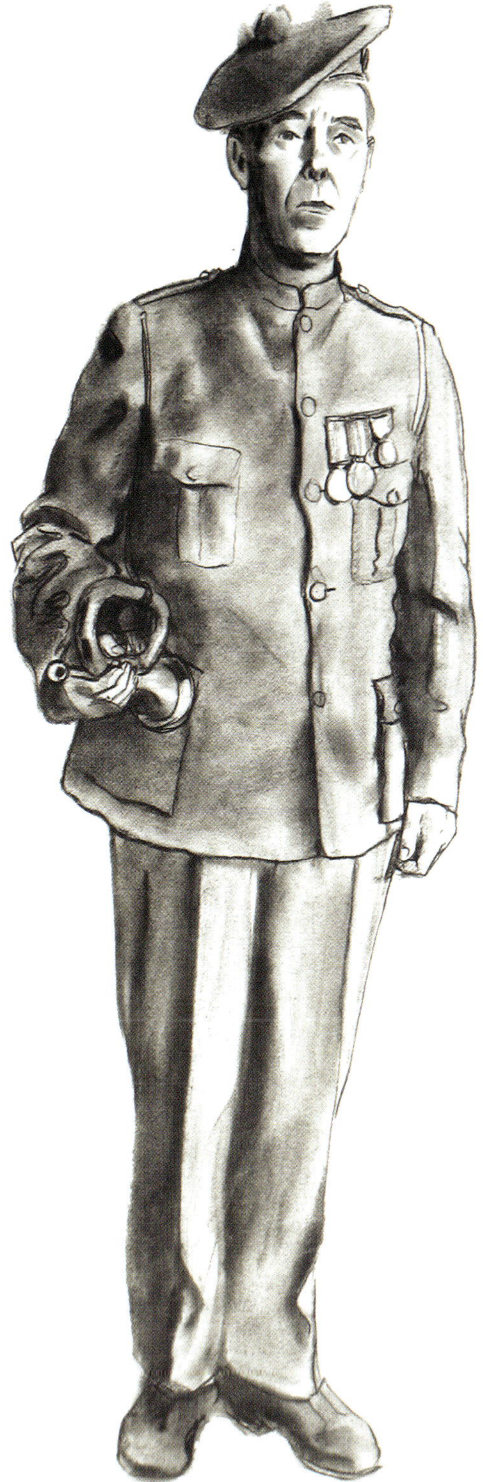

Here are some of the preliminary sketches for *Make Way for Ducklings.*

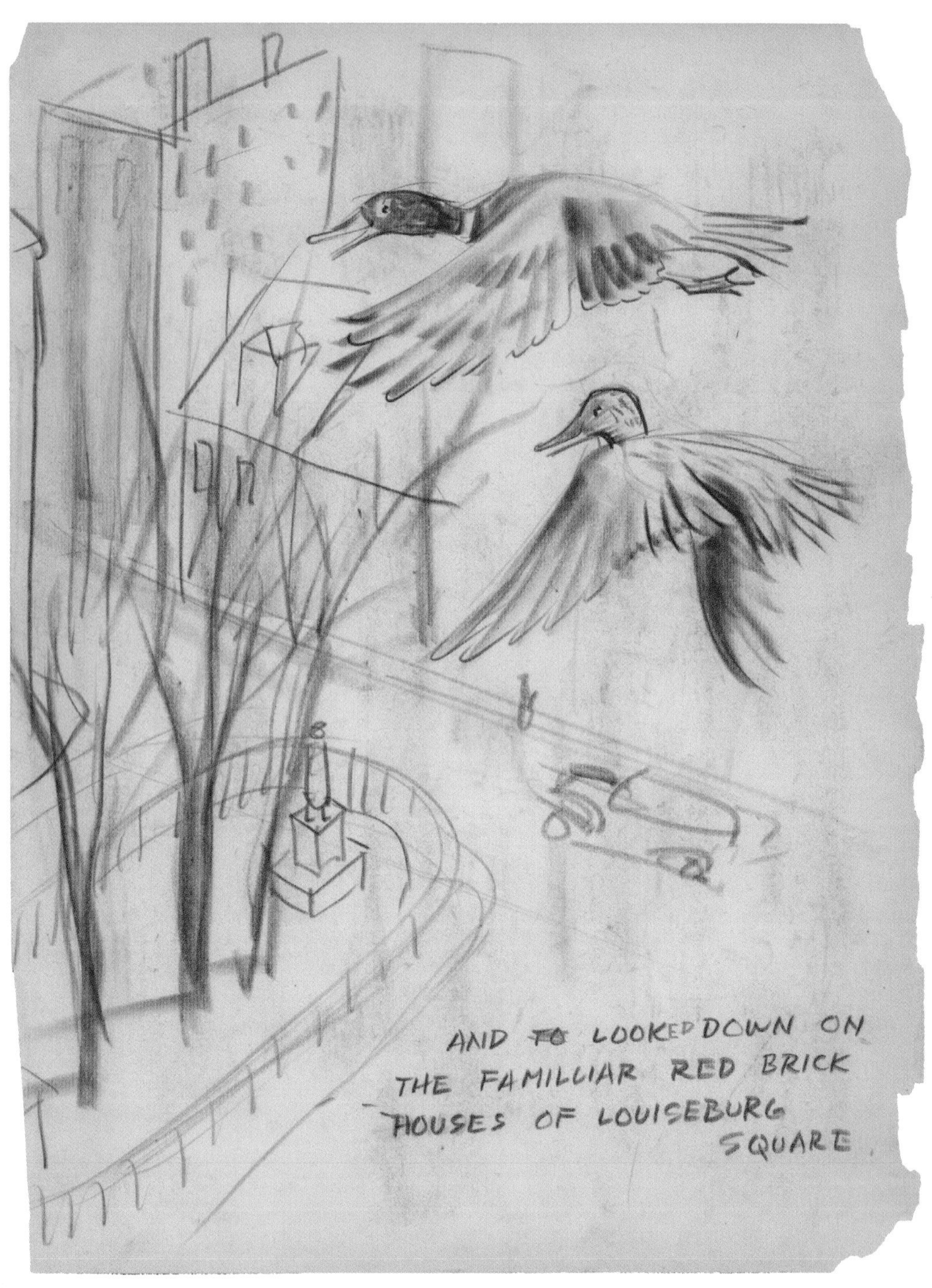

"Sketch Mr. and Mrs. Mallard over Louisburg Square," pencil on paper, ca 1940.

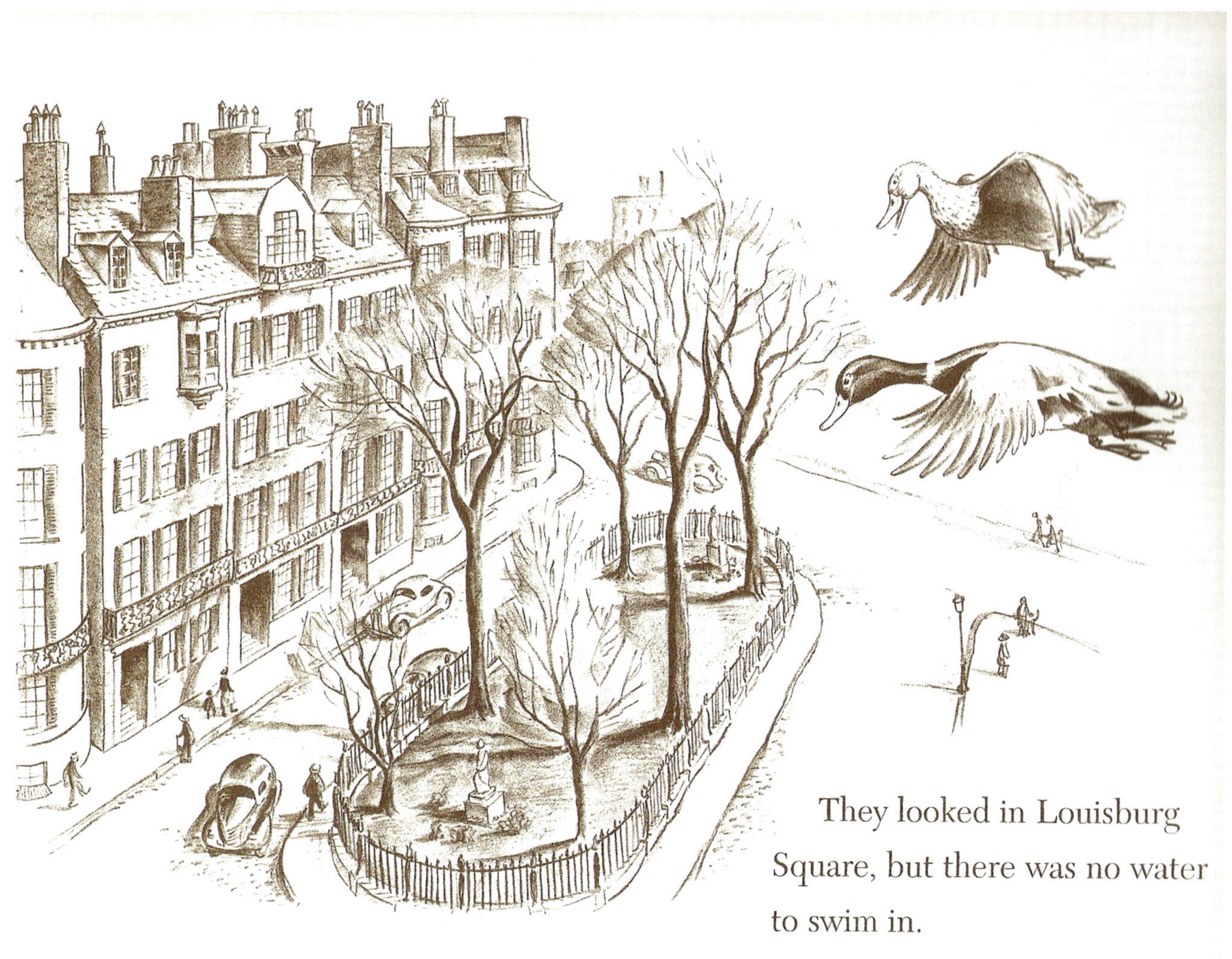

Make Way for Ducklings, "Mr. and Mrs. Mallard over Louisburg Square," Viking Press, 1941.

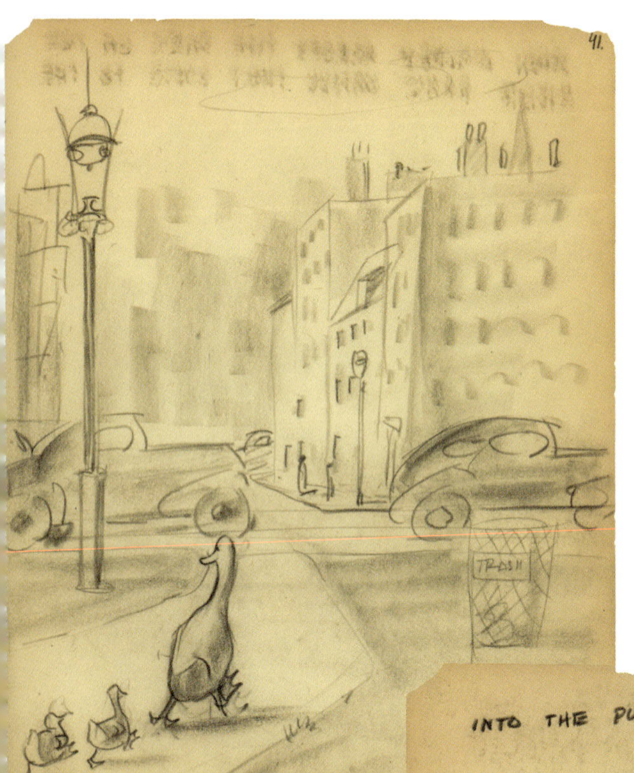

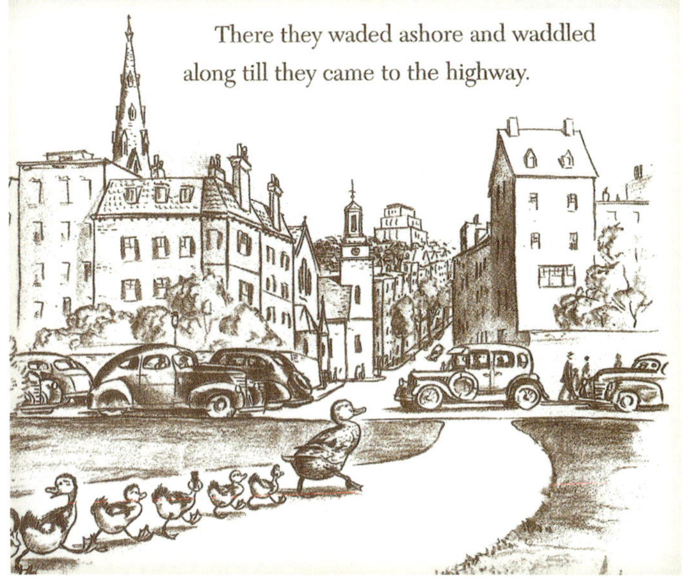

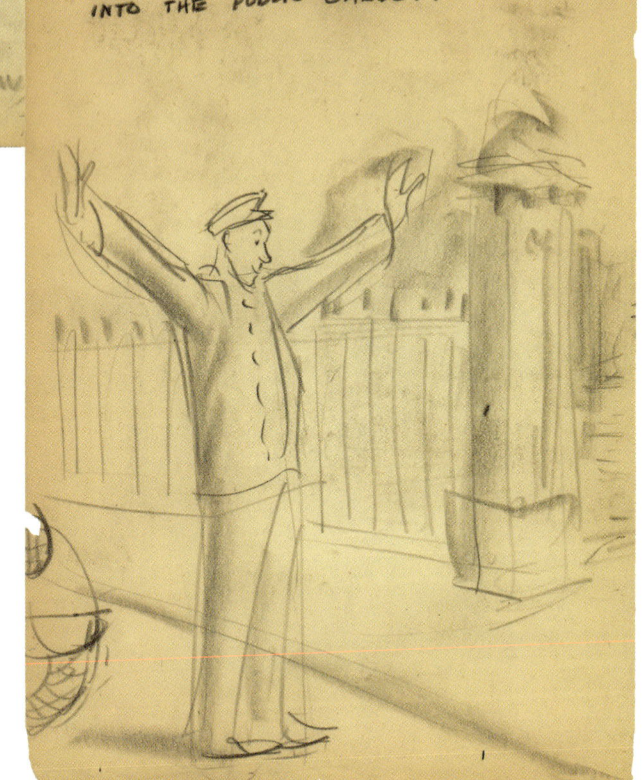

"Sketch of 'Mother Duck leading the Way'," pencil on paper, ca 1940.

Make Way for Ducklings, Viking Press, 1941.

"Sketch of 'Into the Public Garden'," pencil on paper, ca 1940.

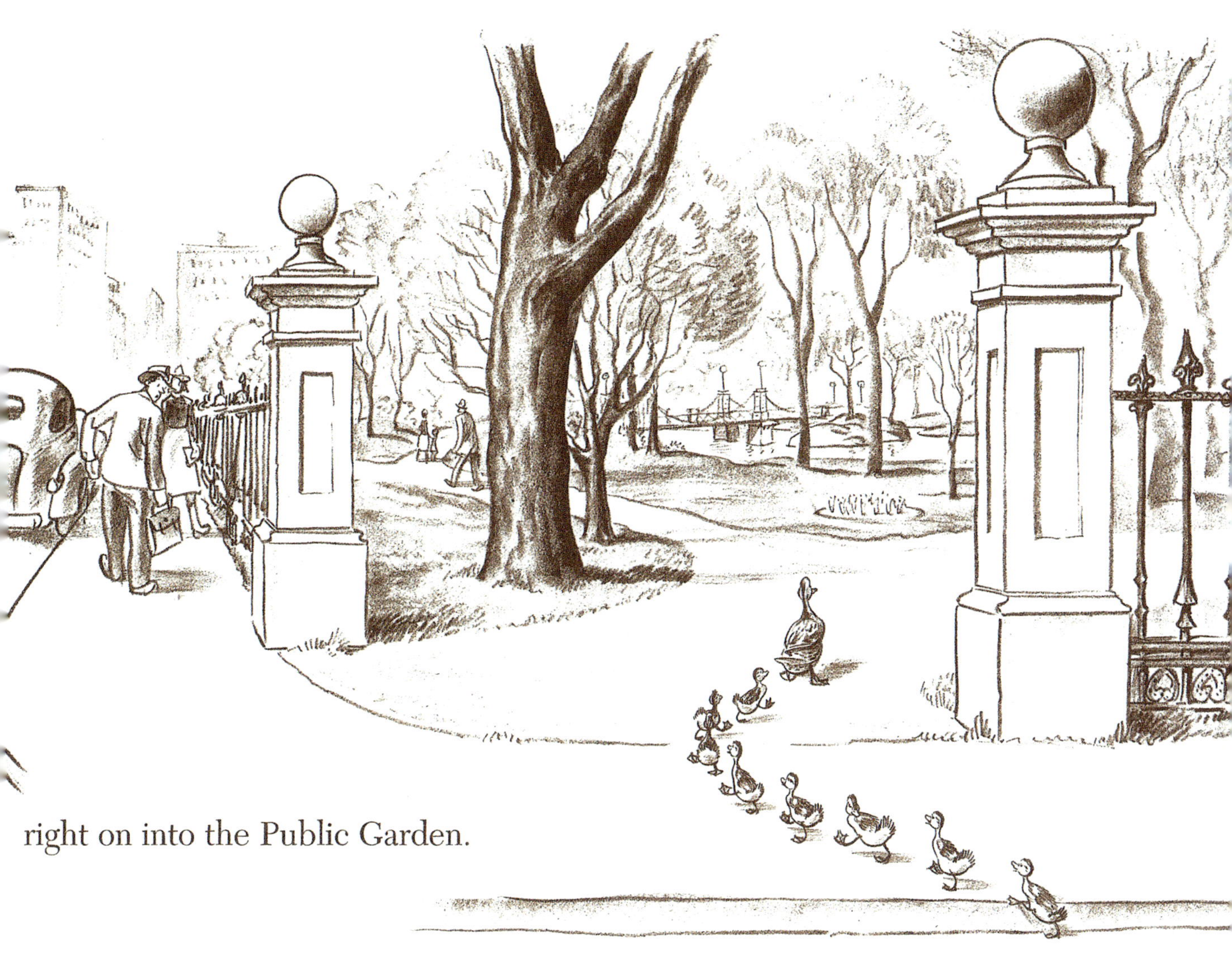

right on into the Public Garden.

Make Way for Ducklings, "Into the Public Garden," Viking Press, 1941.

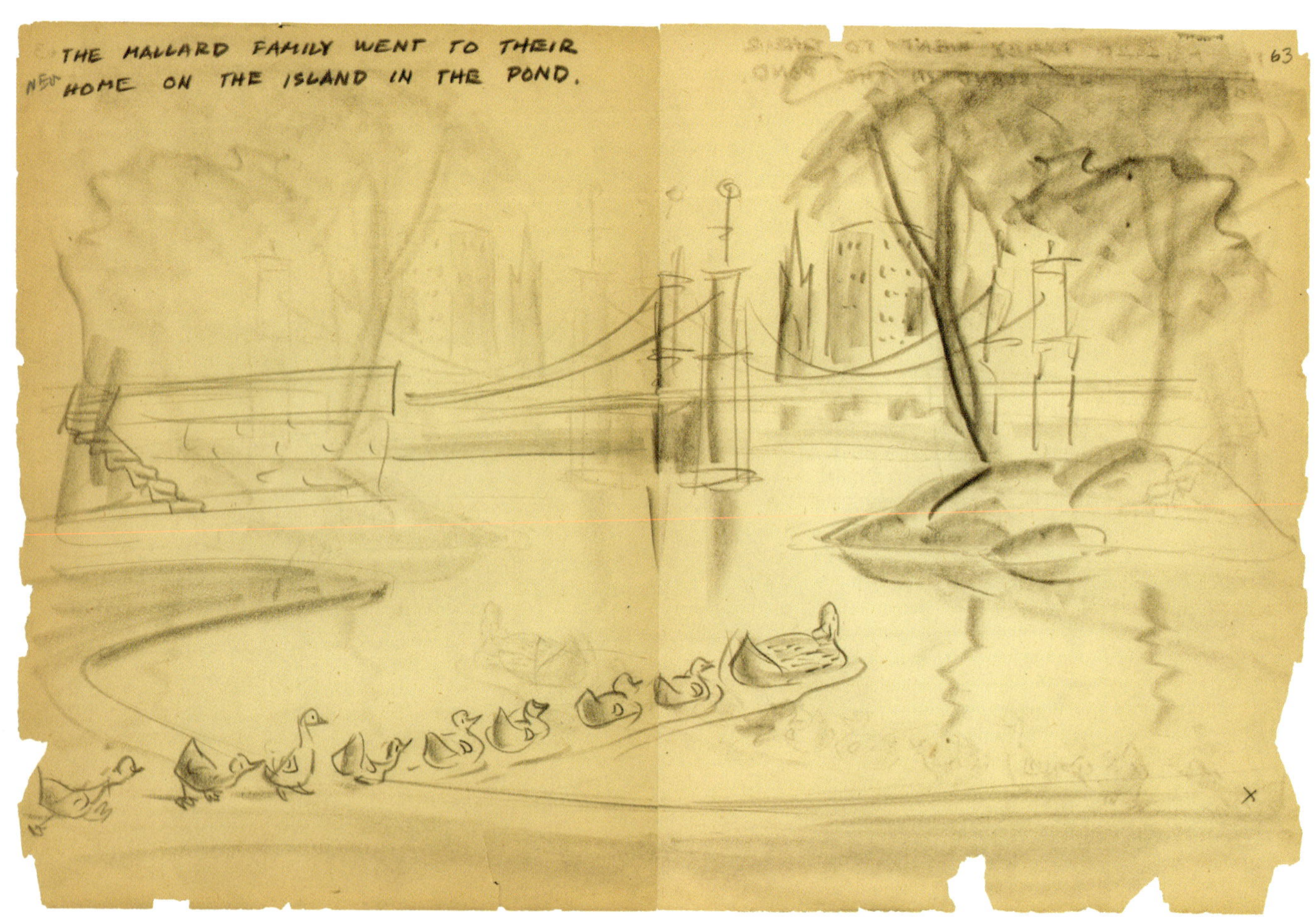

"Sketches of 'Ducklings Coming Home to their Island'," pencil on paper, 1940.

28 • Make Way for McCloskey

When they reached the pond and swam across to the little island, there was Mr. Mallard waiting for them, just as he had promised.

The ducklings liked the new island so much that they decided to live there. All day long they follow the swan boats and eat peanuts.

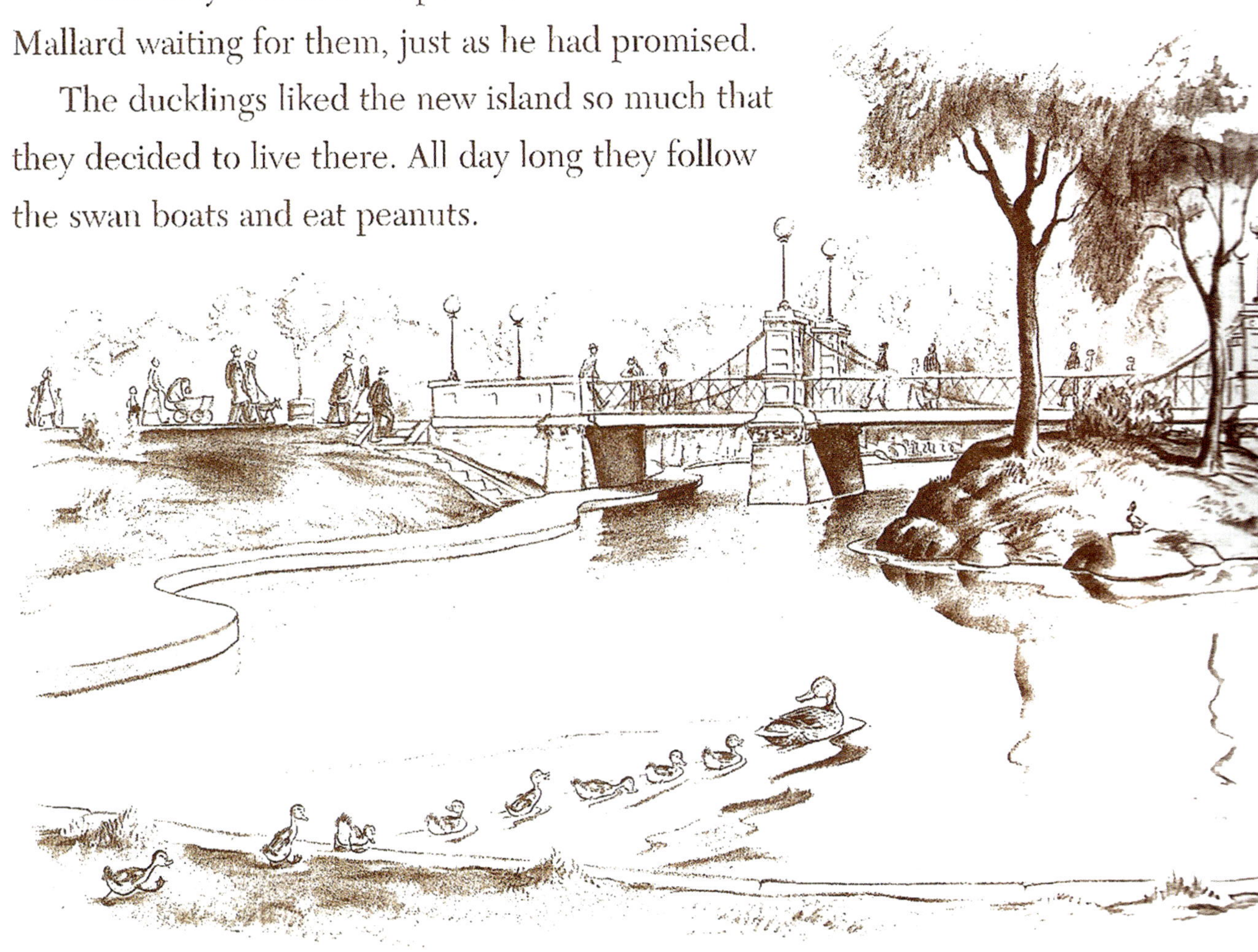

Make Way for Ducklings, "Ducklings Coming Home to their Island," Viking Press, 1941.

Maine 3

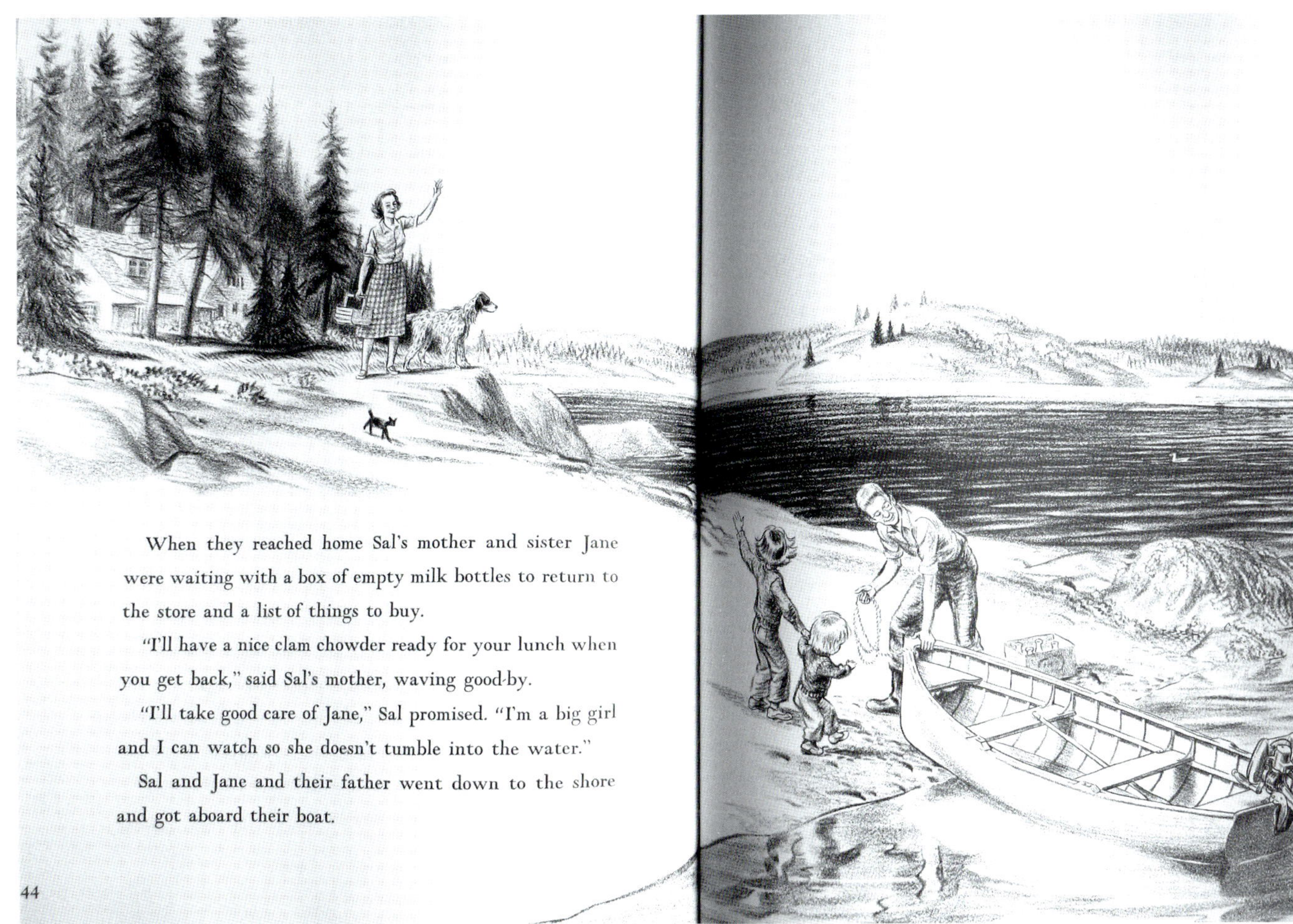

When they reached home Sal's mother and sister Jane were waiting with a box of empty milk bottles to return to the store and a list of things to buy.

"I'll have a nice clam chowder ready for your lunch when you get back," said Sal's mother, waving good-by.

"I'll take good care of Jane," Sal promised. "I'm a big girl and I can watch so she doesn't tumble into the water."

Sal and Jane and their father went down to the shore and got aboard their boat.

44

One Morning in Maine, "Waving Goodbye," Viking Press, 1952.

In 1946, after World War II ended, my parents came to visit my mother's parents at their home in Hancock, Maine. Bob fell in love with the beautiful coast (Mom already loved it) and my parents bought an island in Penobscot Bay in 1946. This island became the summer home of our family for the rest on their lives. To my knowledge, this is the only picture that father drew of our house on the island.

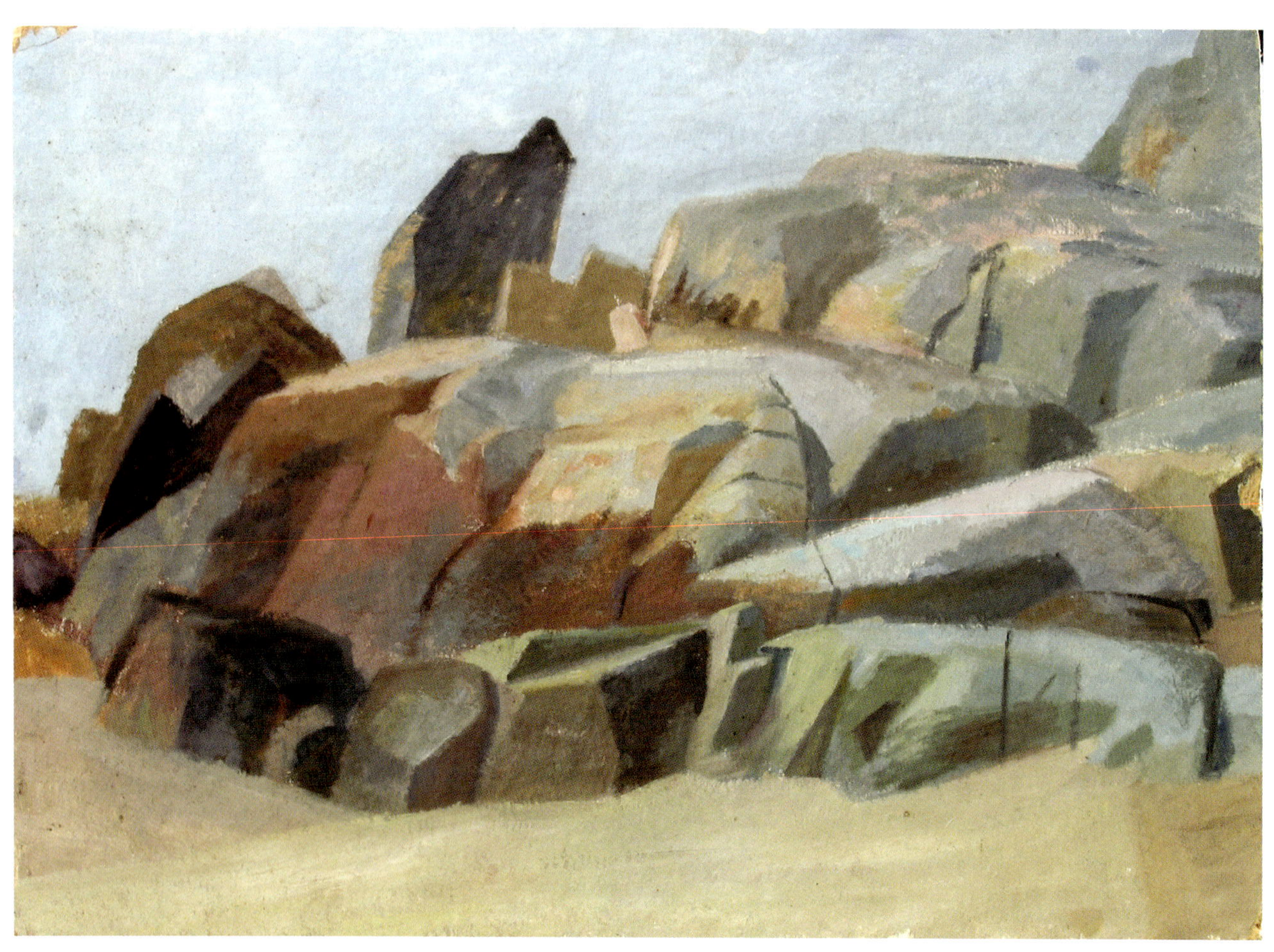

"Rocks on the South Beach," oil on wallboard, 17" x 25", ca 1960s.

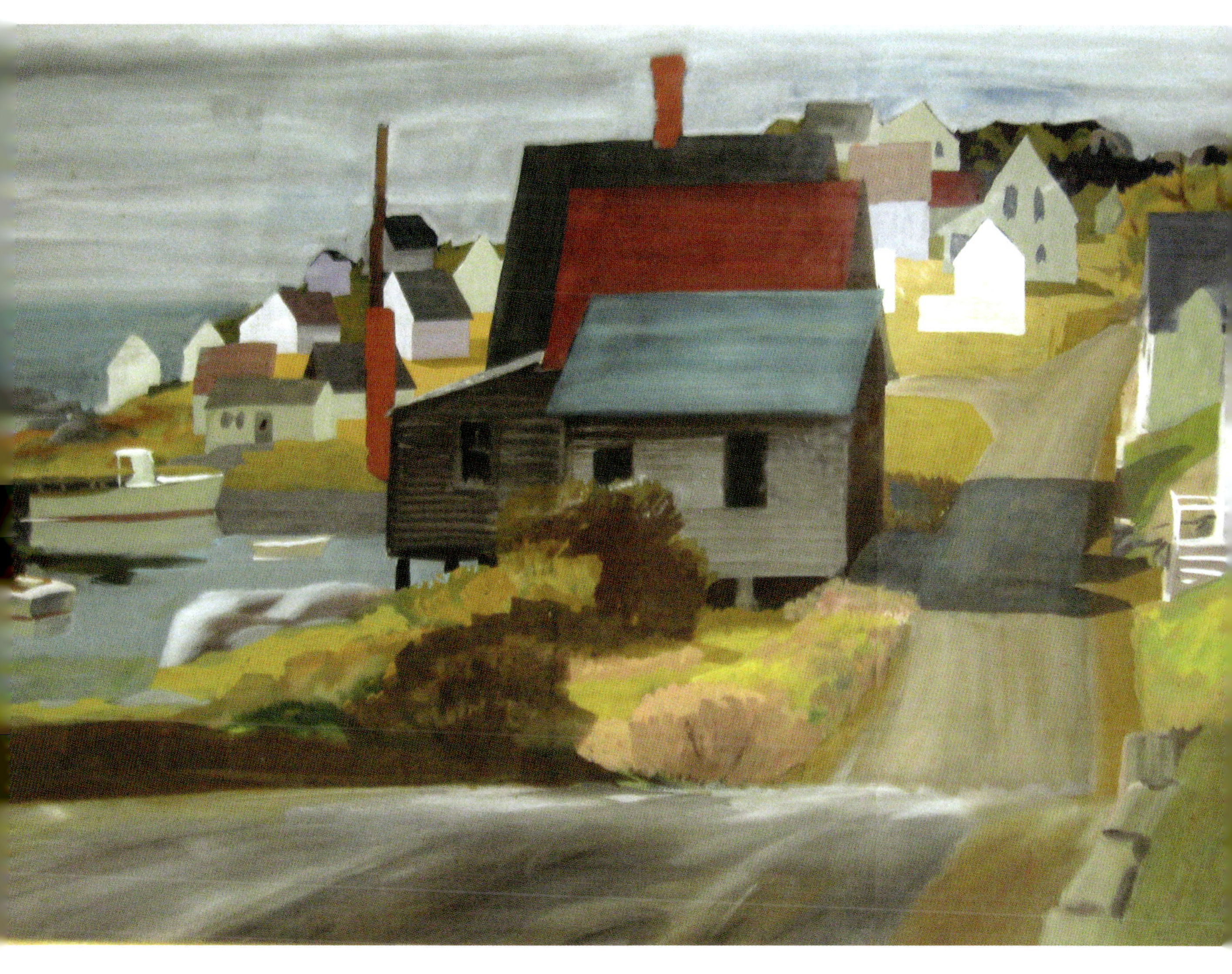

"Stonington," (probably Clam City), oil on Masonite, 1940s. Courtesy of Kathryn Lee.

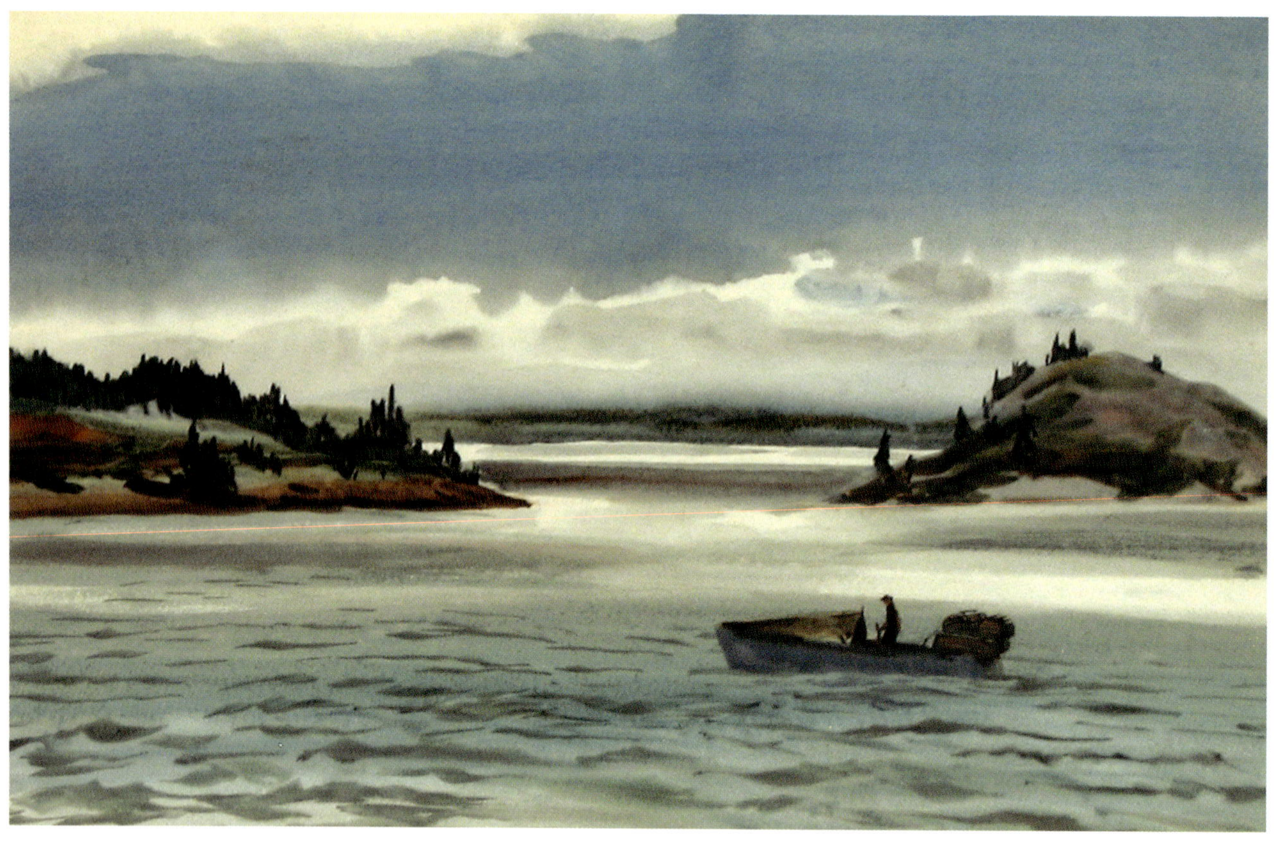

"Lobster Boat Off Little Deer Isle," casein 21" by 29", 1940s.

Before wooden cabins on lobster boats came into fashion, the old lobster boats had canvas awnings stretched over the forward part of the boat. We had a boat like this for a year, until we got one of the new lobster boats with a real cabin. The island on the right, behind the boat, is Sheep Island. The one on the left is Little Deer Isle. Sheep Island shows up in several of Bob's paintings and in the picture "Waving Goodbye" from *One Morning in Maine*.

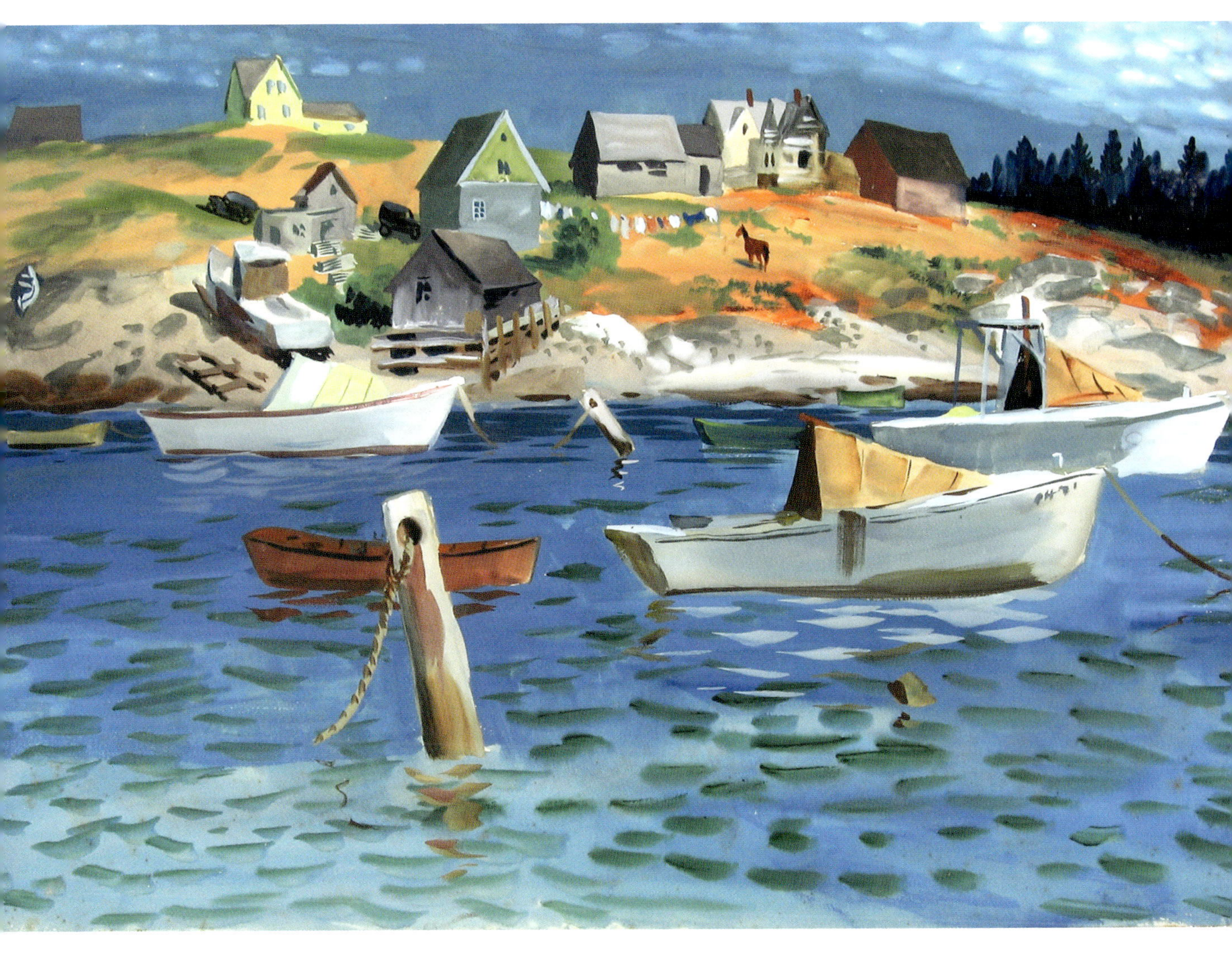

"Lobster Boats, Houses, and Horse," casein on cardboard, 20" x 30", 1940s.

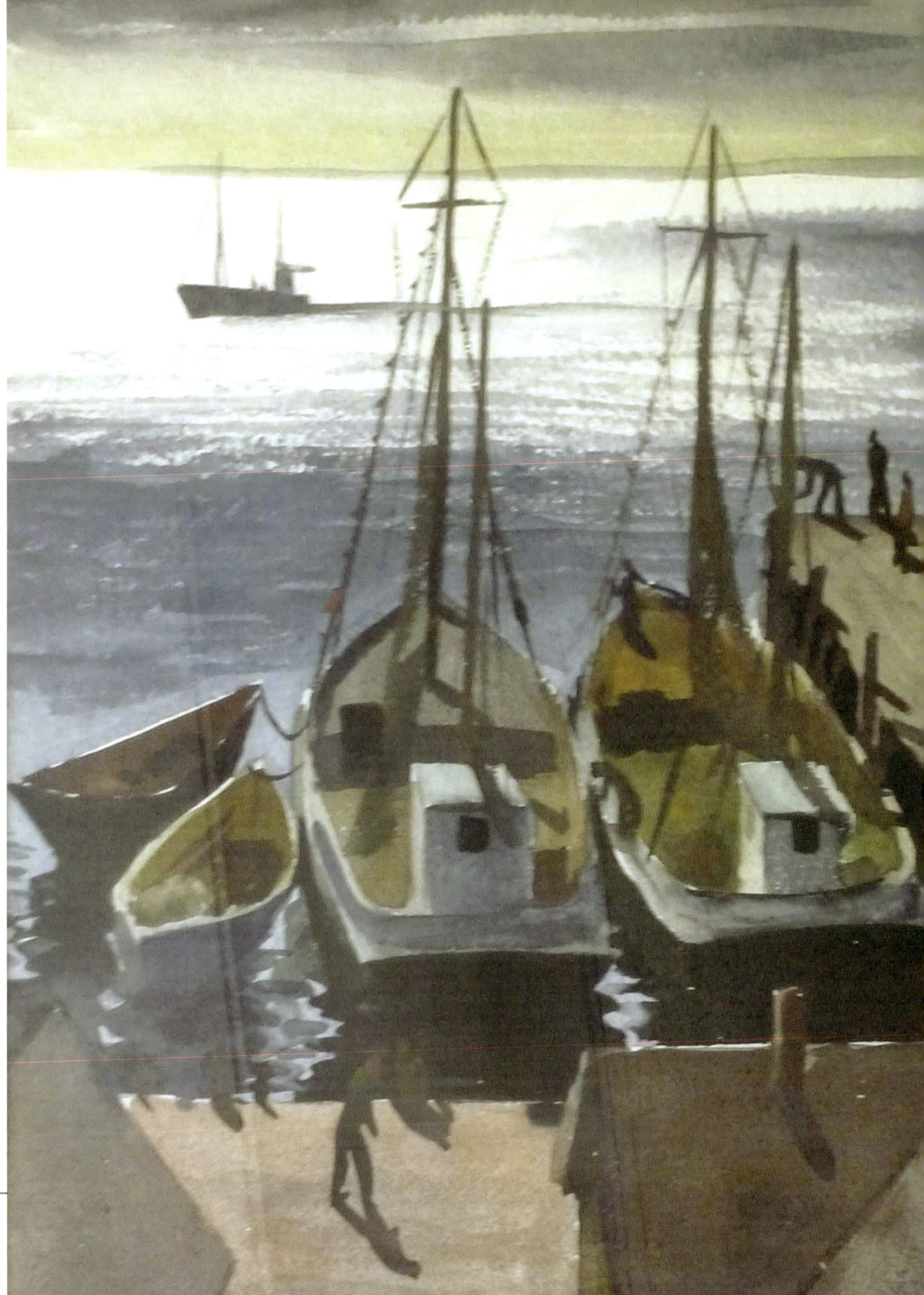

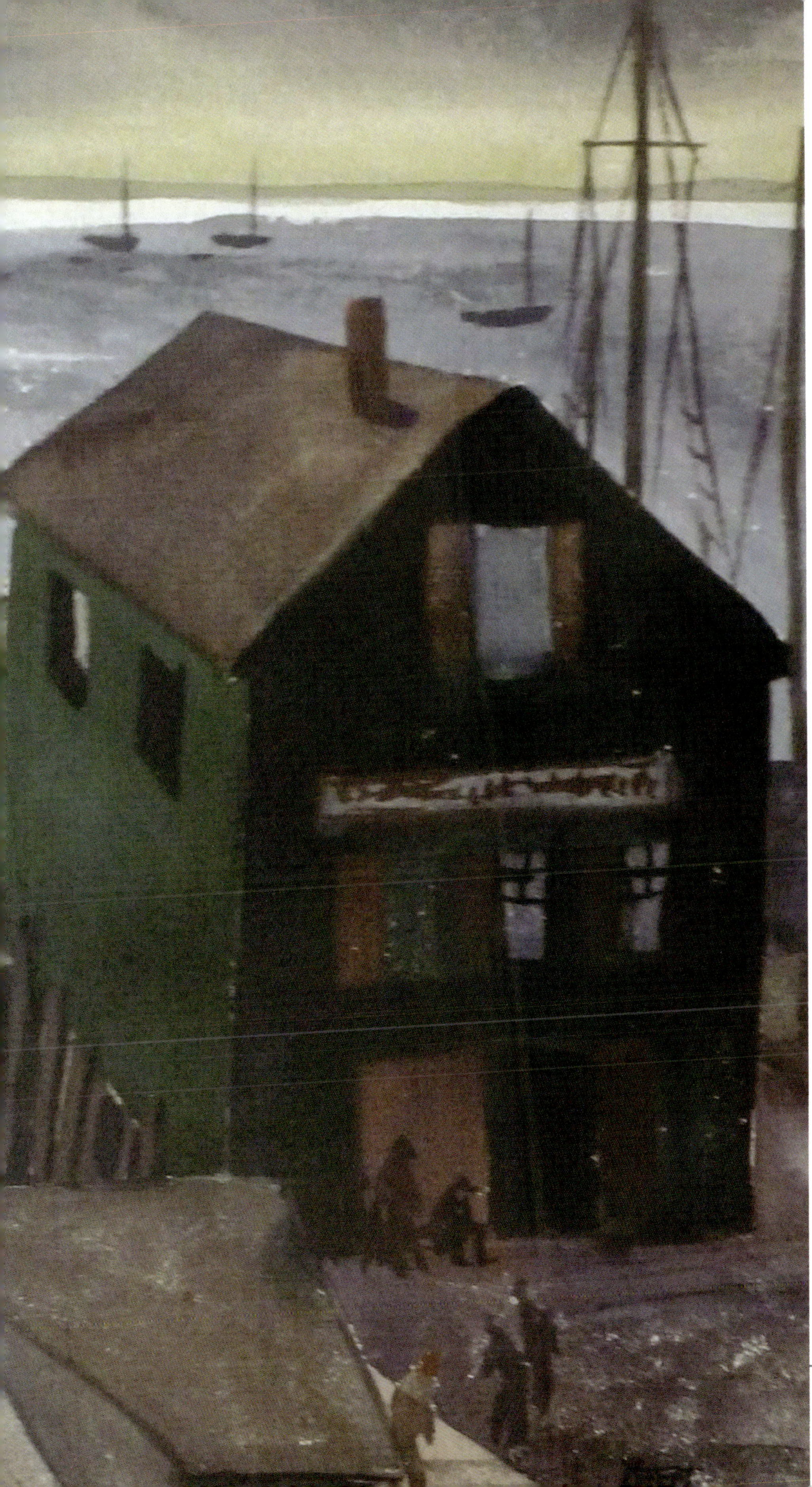

"Boats in Stonington, Maine," watercolor on paper, 19.5" x 25.5", 1940s. Courtesy of Robert McCloskey Museum.

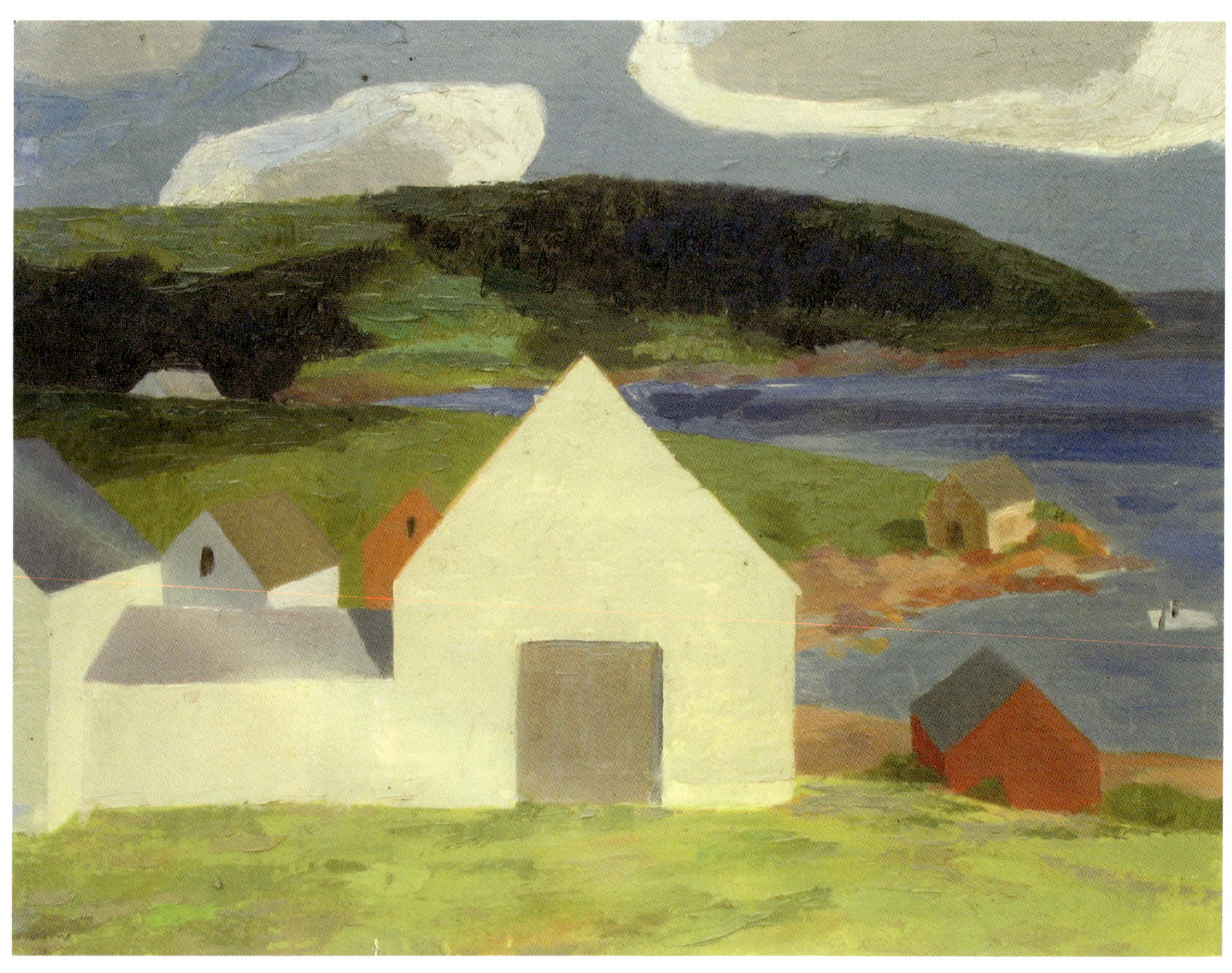

"Houses on Shore," oil on Masonite, 12" x 16", 1950s.

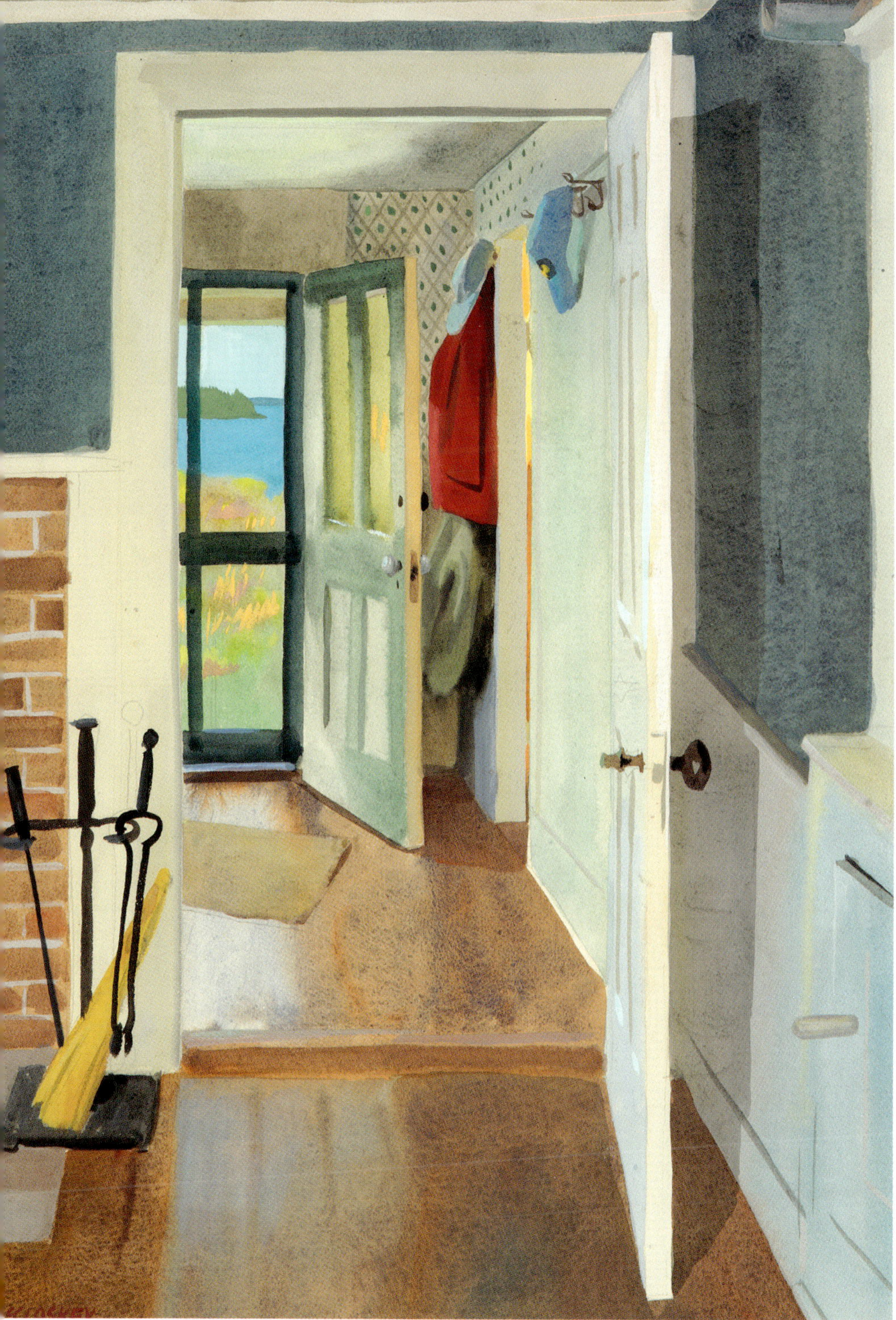

"Cove Acres," acrylic on canvas board, 21" x 14.5", ca 1960, Courtesy of Edee Howland.

Cove Acres was the summer home of the Howlands, who were friends of our family. The island visible through the screen door is our island.

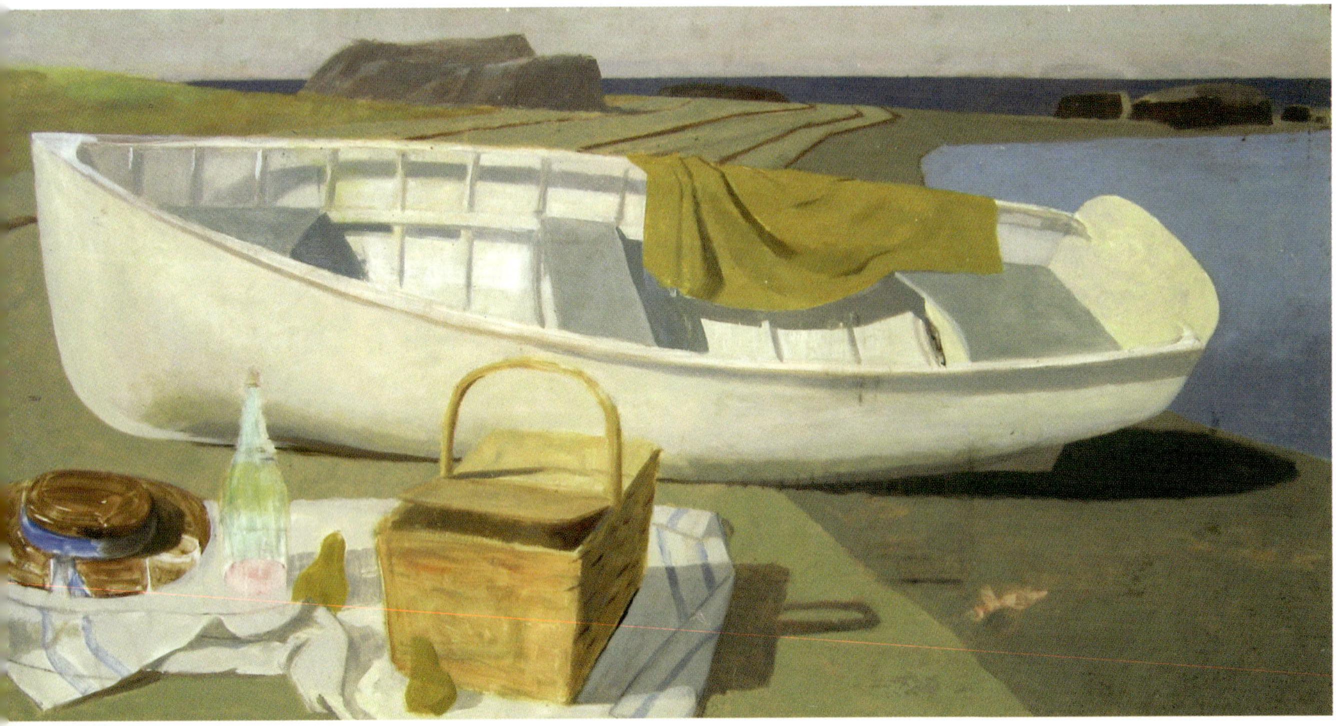

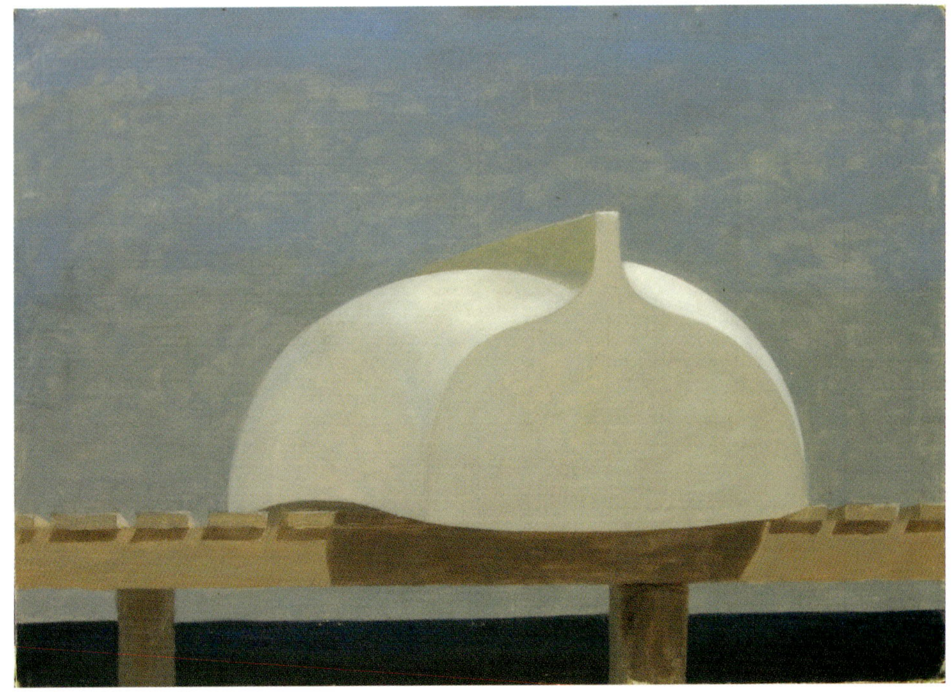

"Rowboat and Picnic Still Life, Little Island," oil on Masonite, 20" x 32", 1960s.

"Dinghy on a Dock," oil on canvas board, 20" x 27", 1960s.

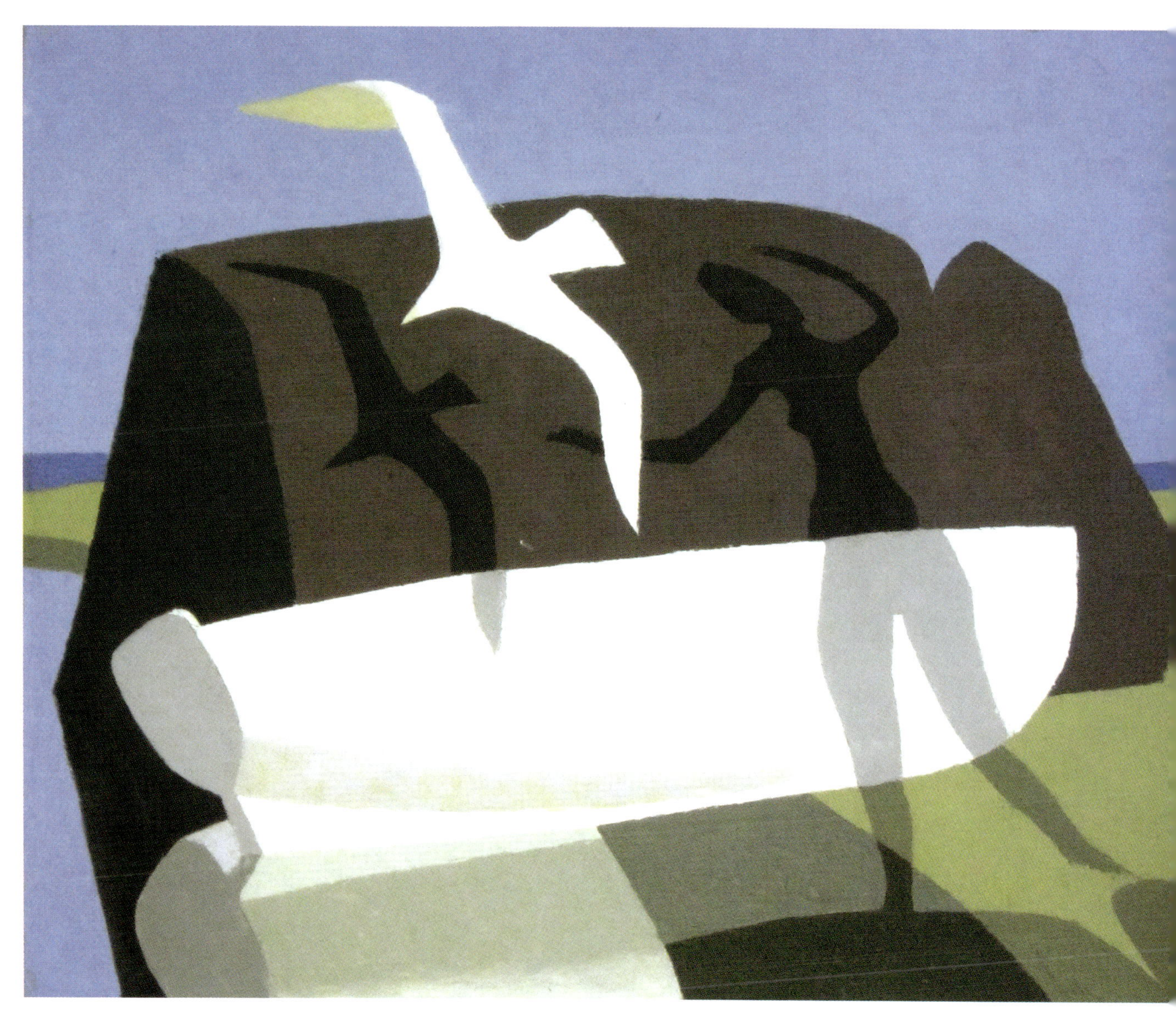

"Woman, Dinghy, Seagull, and Rock," oil on hardboard, 24" x 31", 1960s.

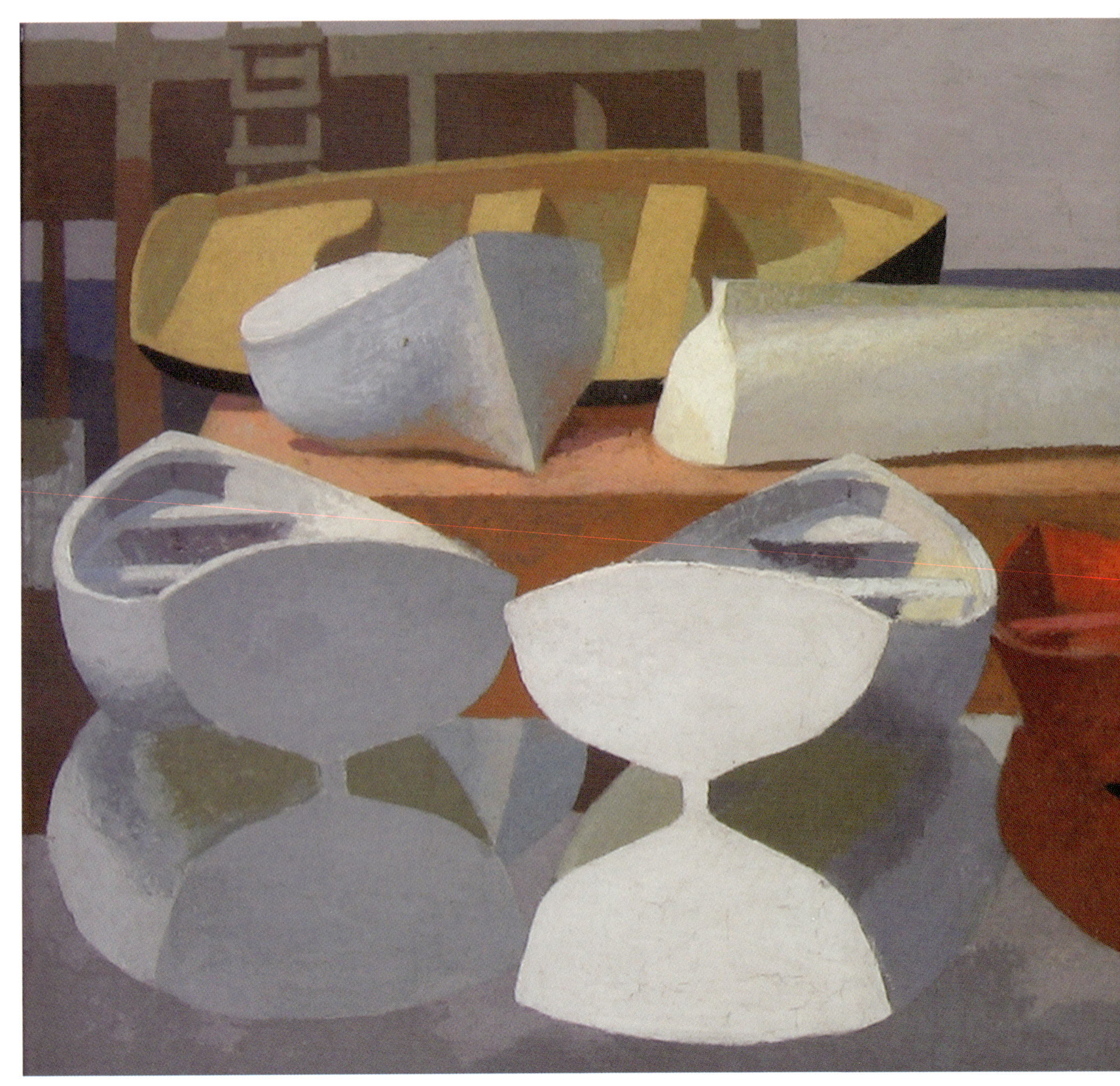

Bob liked to paint rowboats. I think that this was my father's favorite painting. It sat on the mantel of our house in Maine for fifty years, and he often just sat and looked at it.

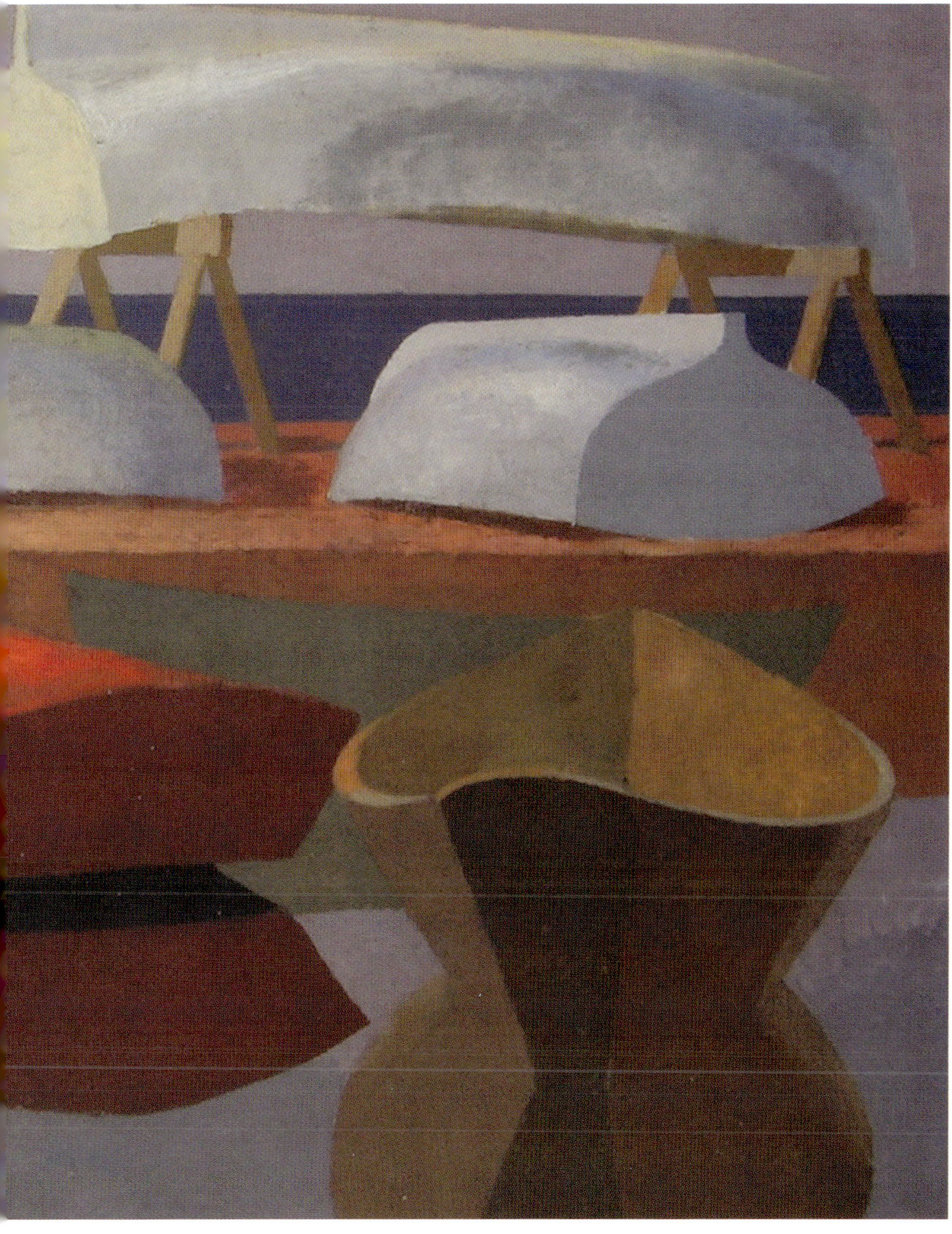

"Rowboats on a Dock,"
oil on Masonite,
56" x 30", 1950s.

"Seagulls on Rowboat on Dock," oil on Masonite, 32" x 24", 1960s.

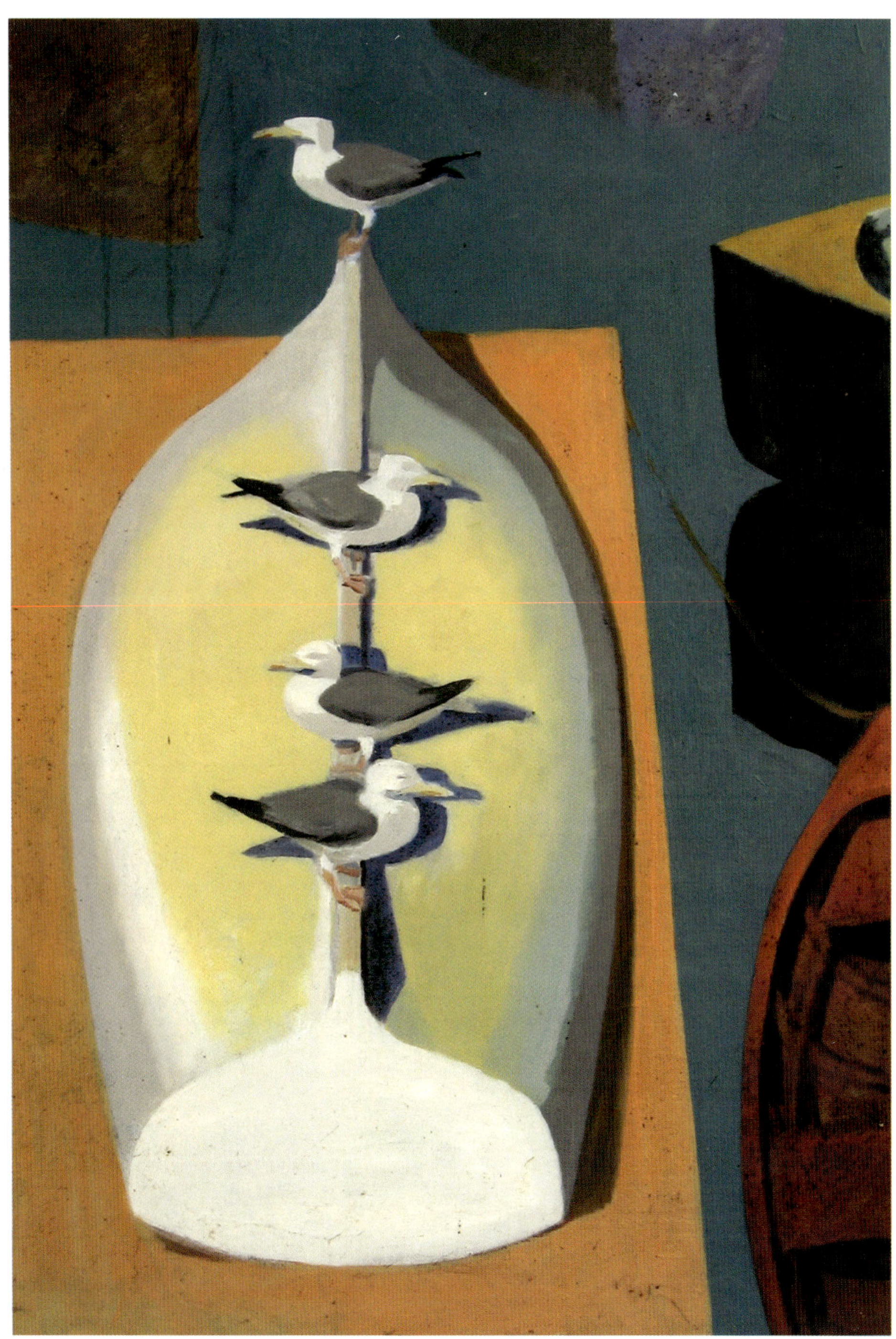

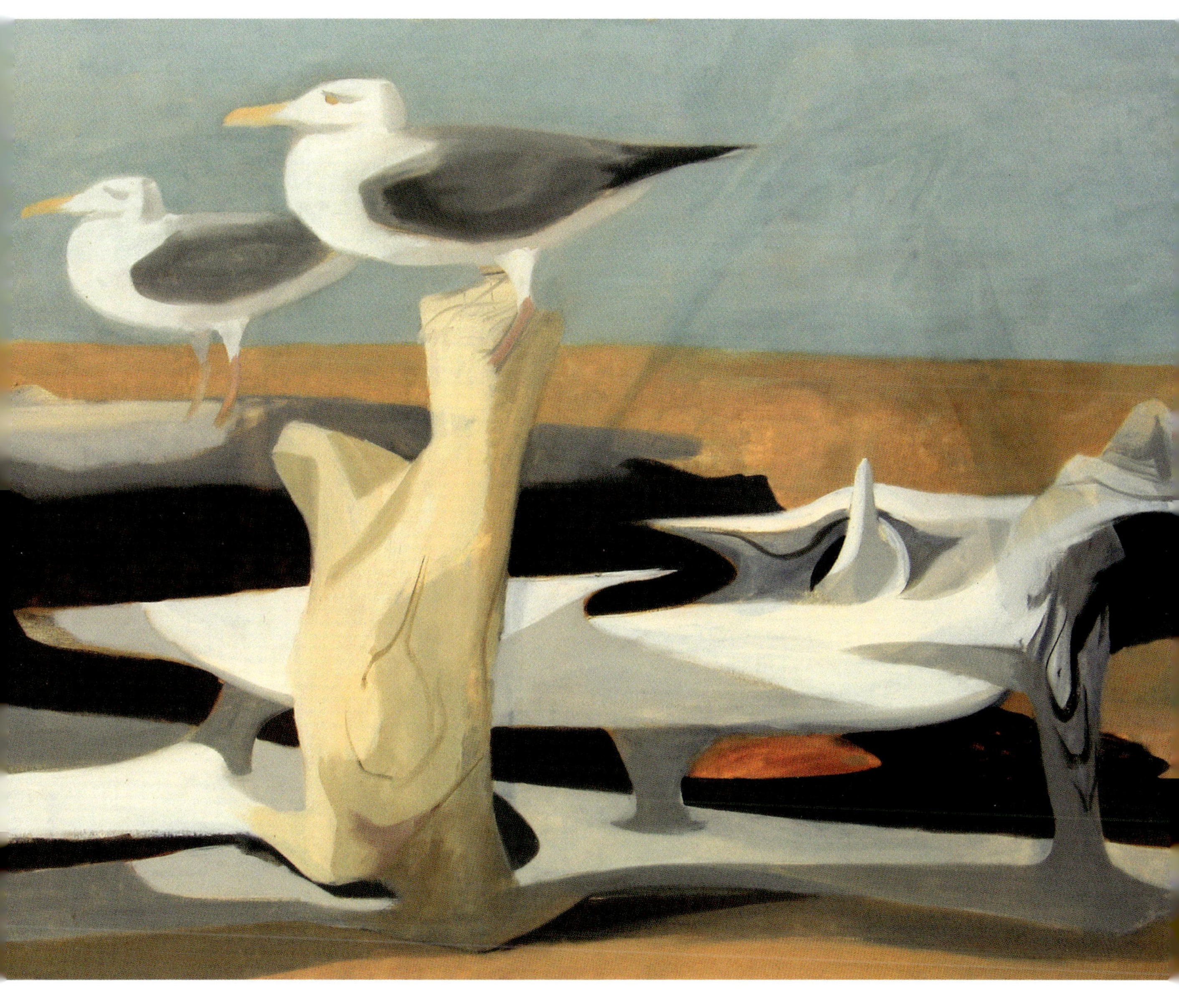

"Seagulls with Driftwood," oil on Masonite, 30" x 40", 1970s.

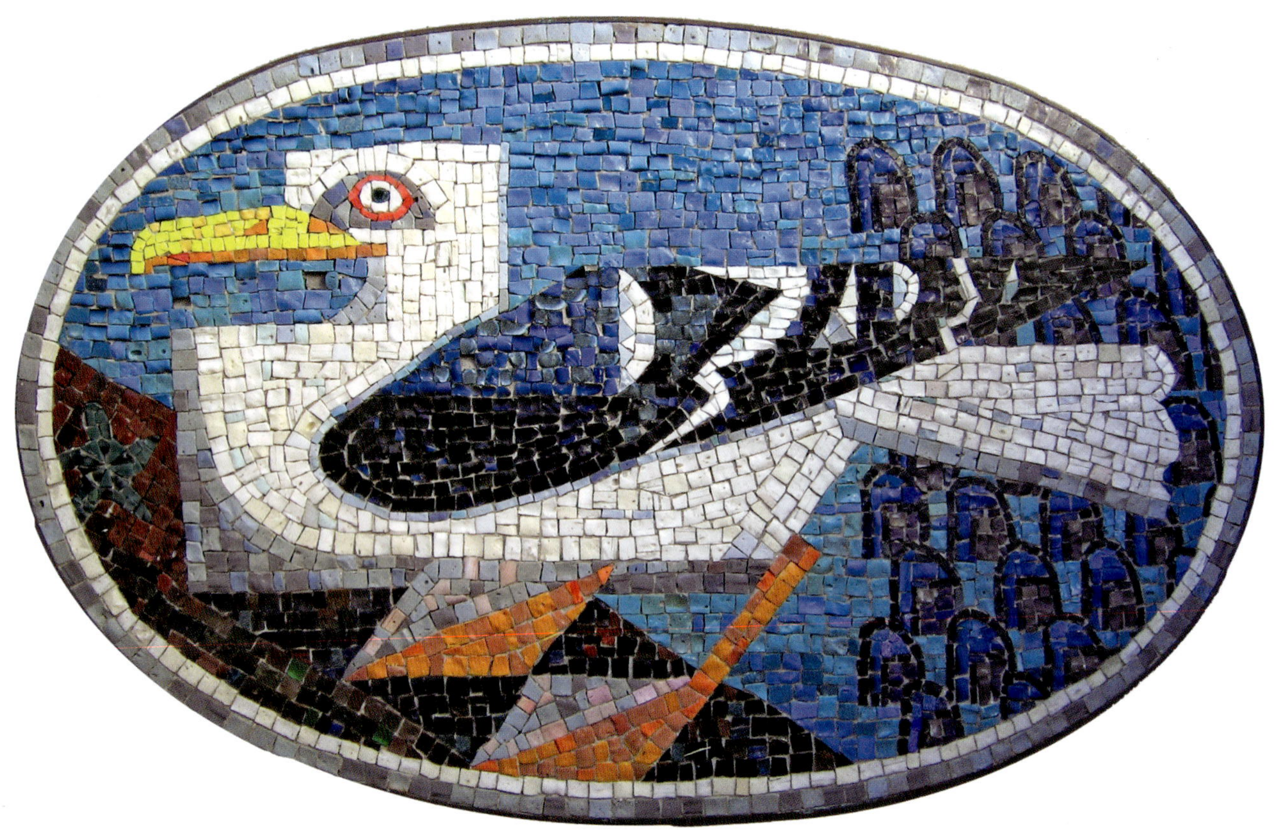

"Seagull," mosaic, 18" x 29", ca 1949.

This was one of three mosaics that my father did in Rome. He also frequently used seagulls as subjects in his paintings.

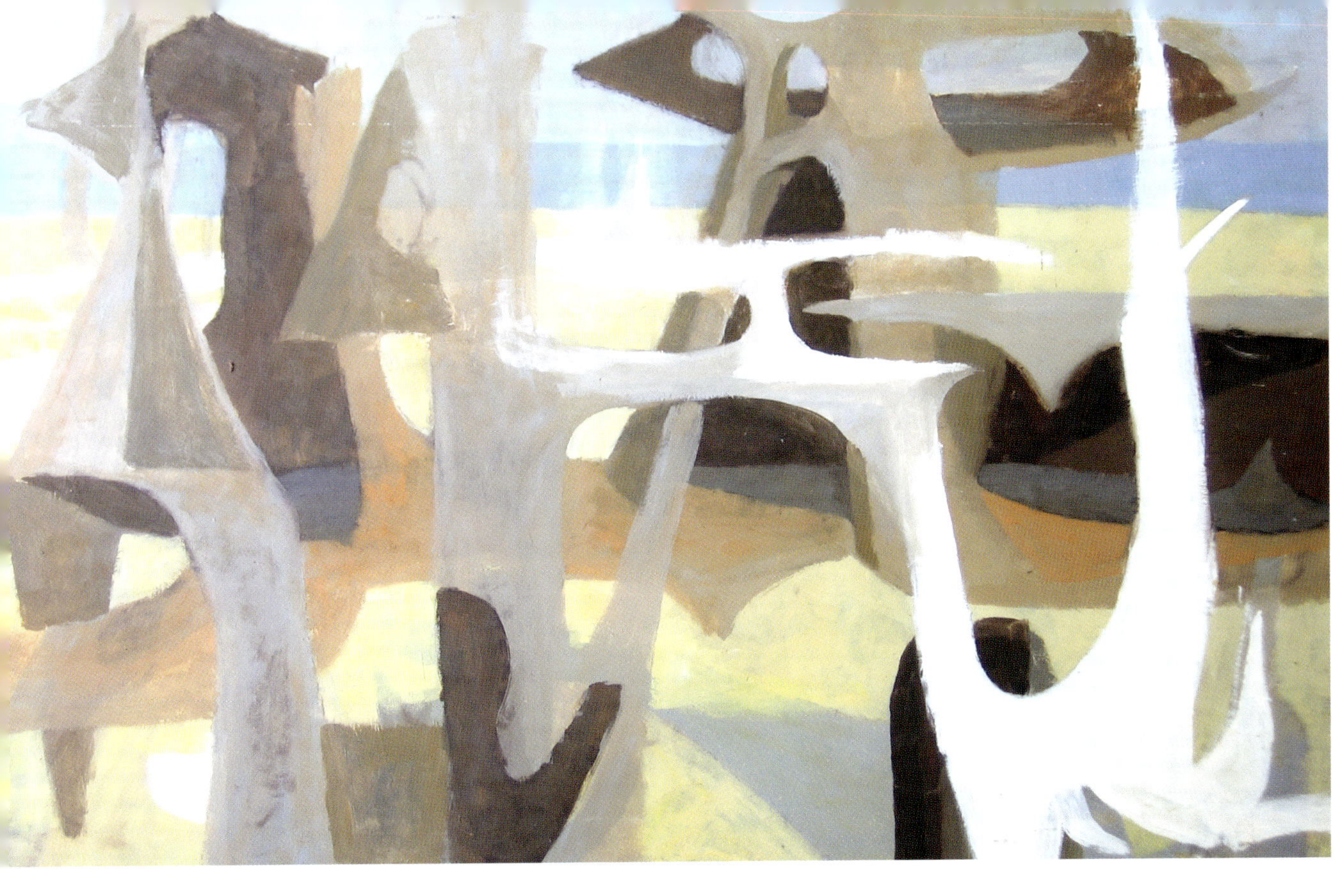

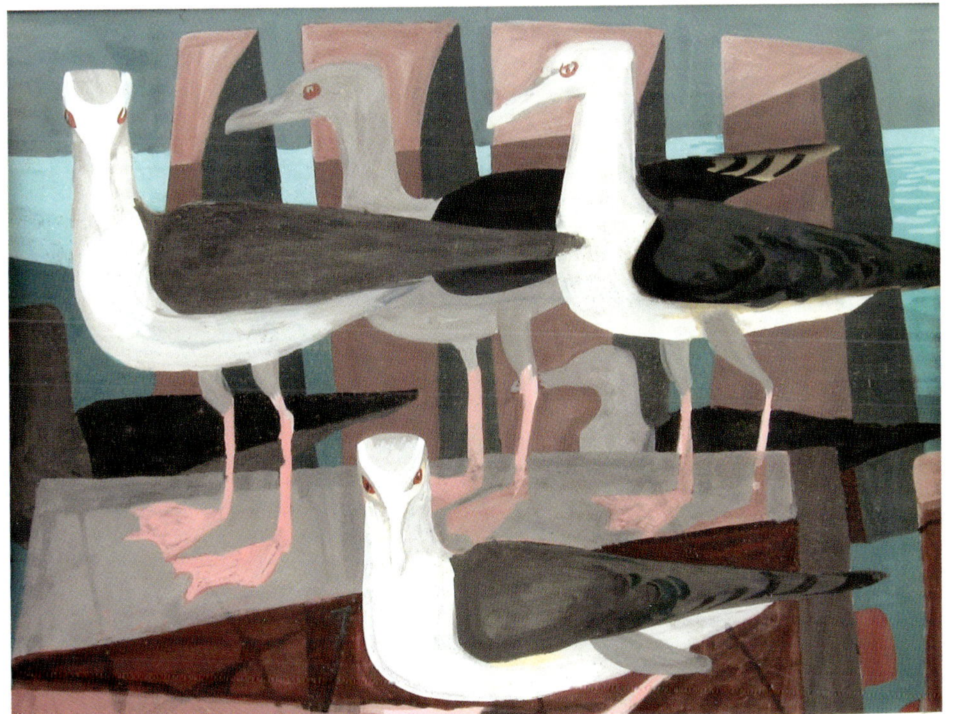

"Driftwood Fantasy," oil on Masonite, 24" x 32", 1970s.

"Seagulls on Rocks," oil on canvas board, 21" x 28", 1980s.

"Sketeches of Sal for *Blueberries for Sal,*" pencil on paper, ca 1947. Courtesy of May Massee Collection, Emporia State University.

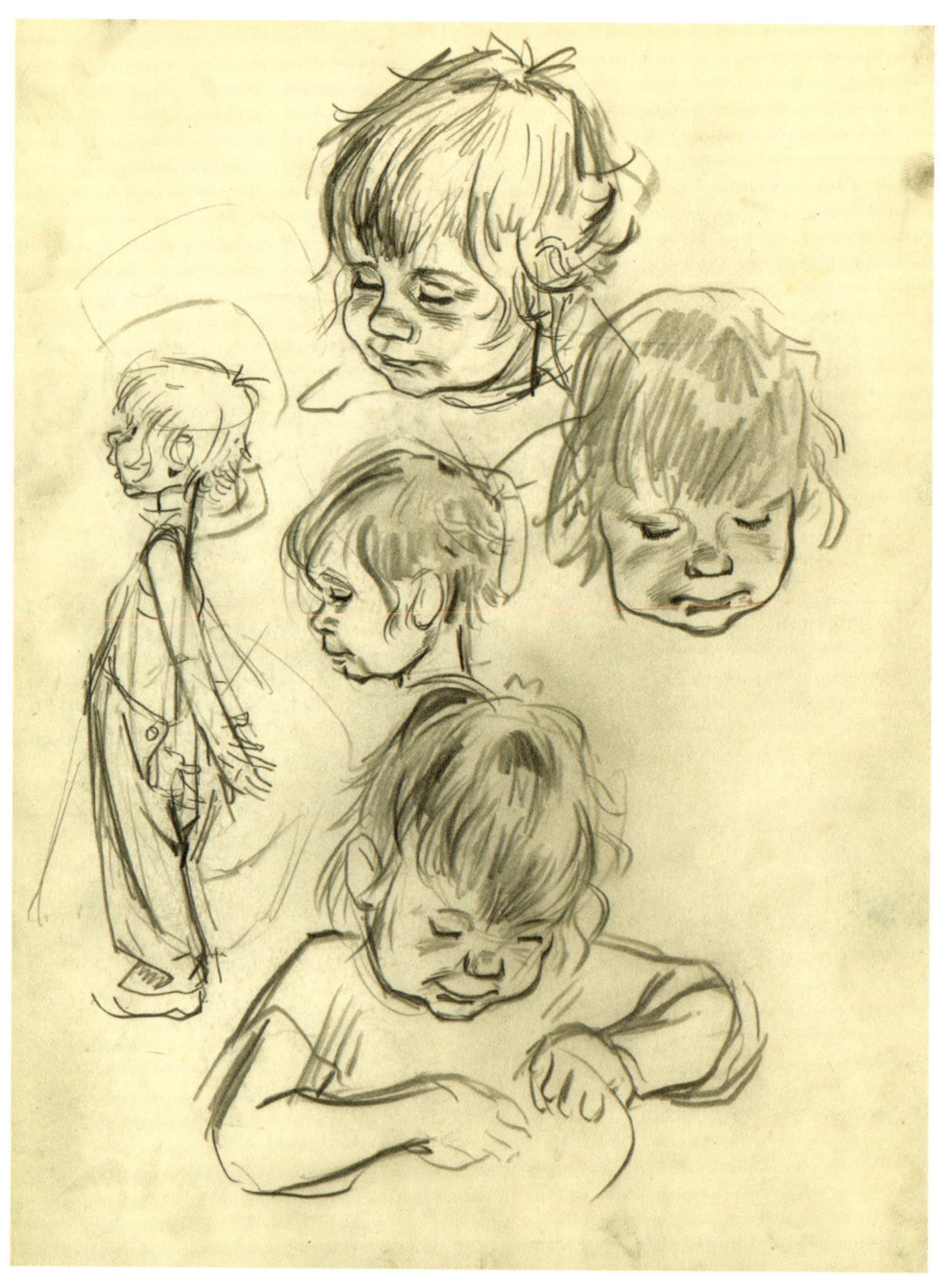

Four of my father's books were about Maine: *Blueberries for Sal, One Morning in Maine, Time of Wonder,* and *Burt Dow, Deep-Water Man*. These are some sketches for *Blueberries for Sal.*

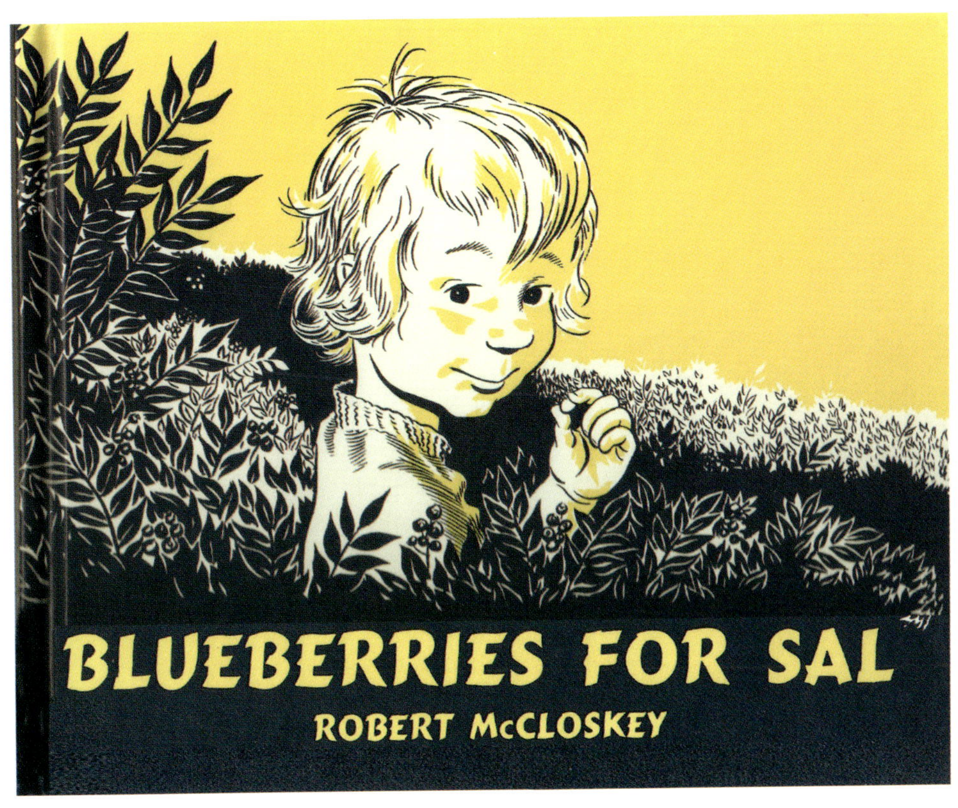

Blueberries for Sal, cover, Viking Press, 1948.

Blueberries for Sal

BY ROBERT McCLOSKEY

NEW YORK · THE VIKING PRESS

Blueberries for Sal, Frontispiece, Viking Press, 1948.

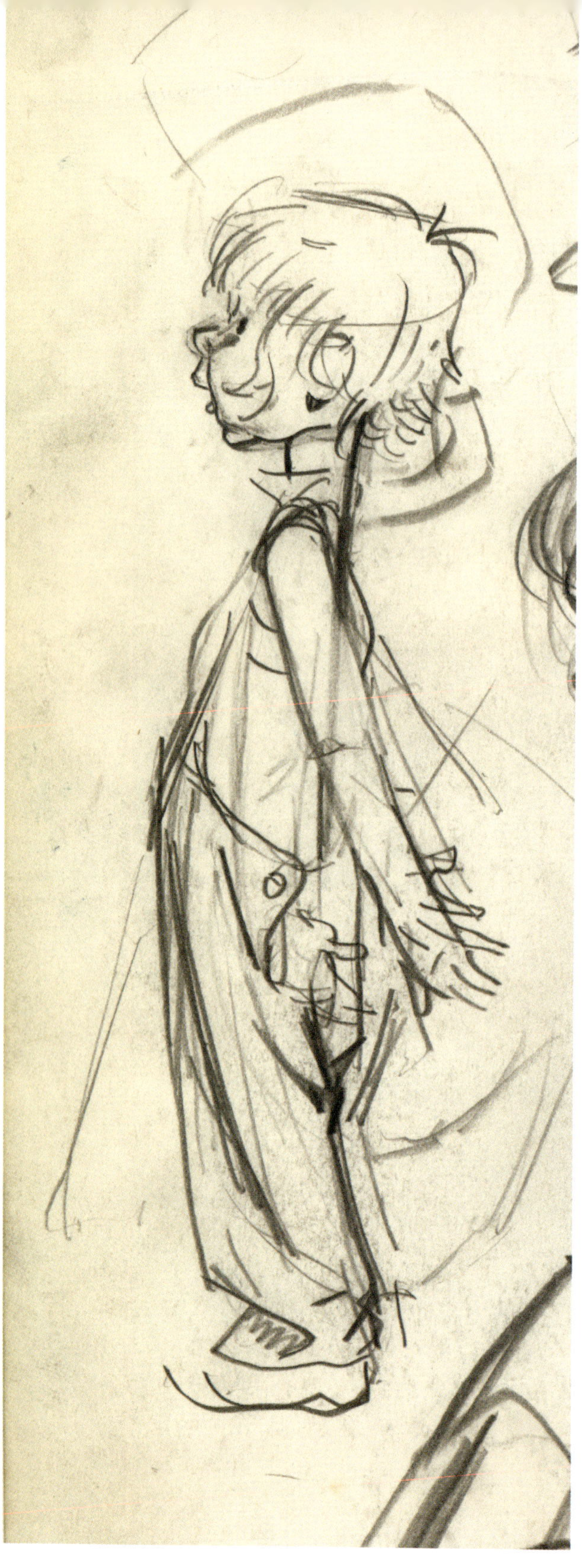

"Sketch of Sal for *Blueberries for Sal*," pencil on paper, ca 1947. Courtesy of May Massee Collection, Emporia State University.

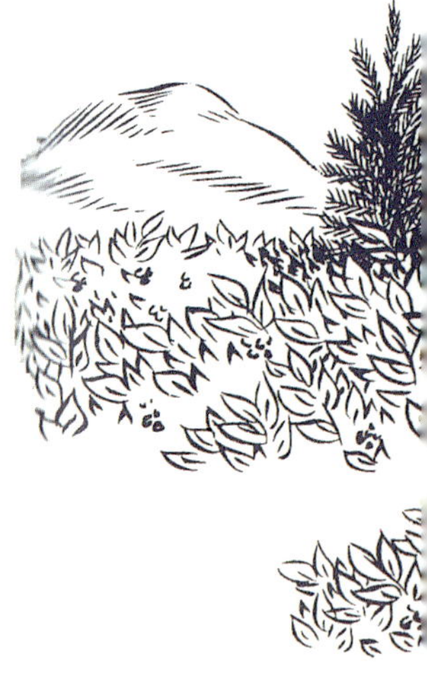

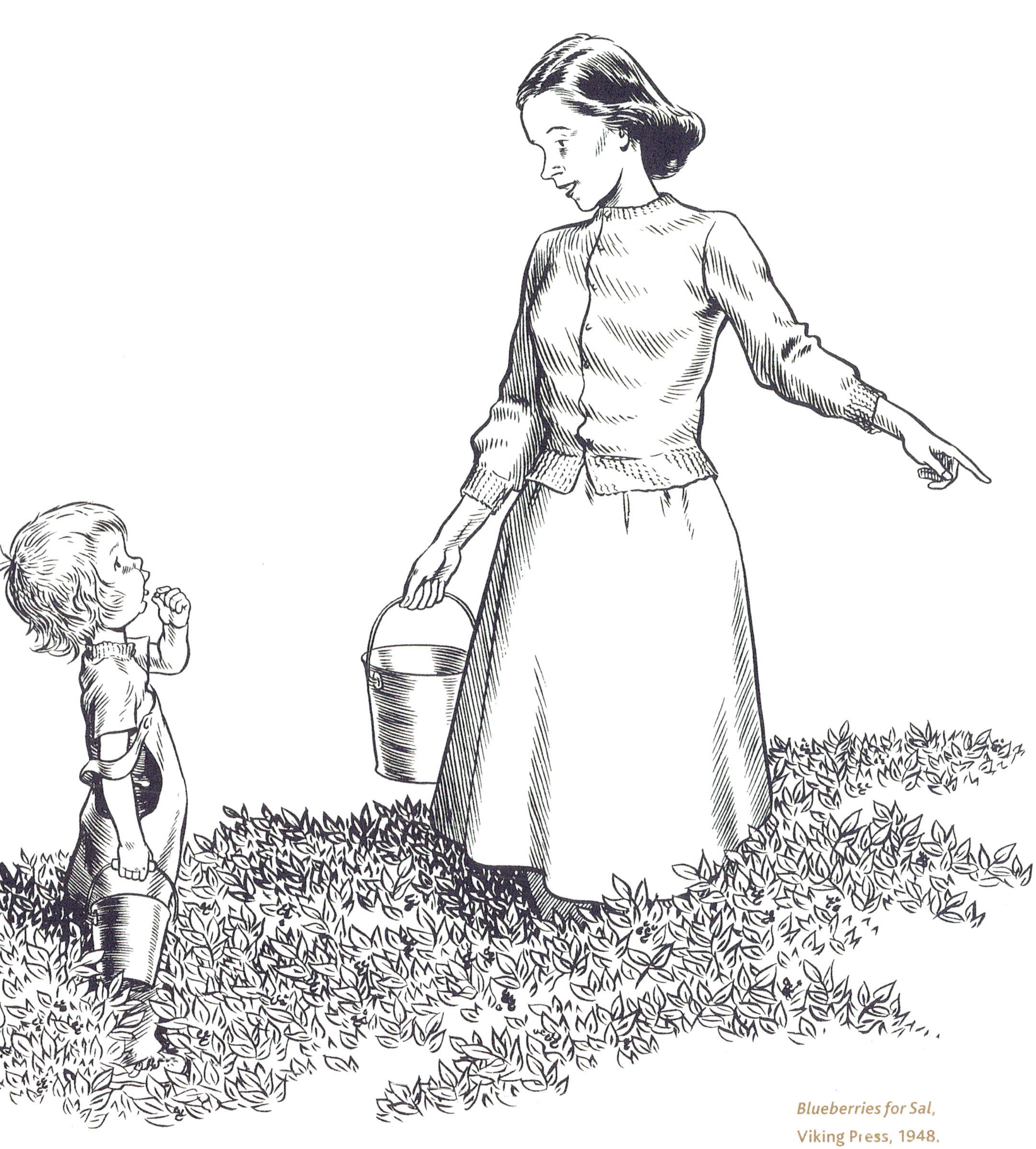

Blueberries for Sal,
Viking Press, 1948.

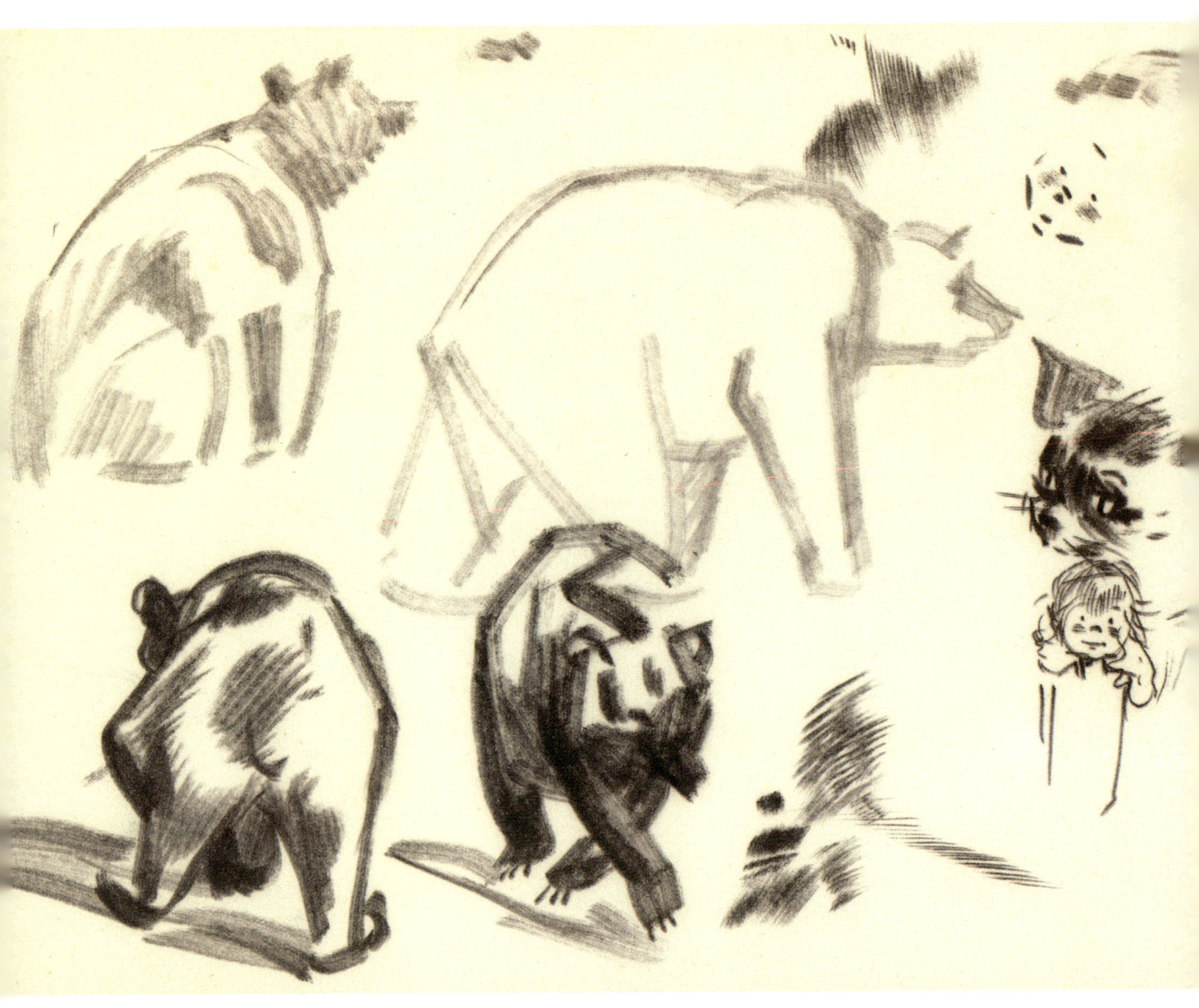

"Bear sketch for *Blueberries for Sal*," pencil on paper, ca. 1947. Courtesy of May Massee Collection, Emporia State University.

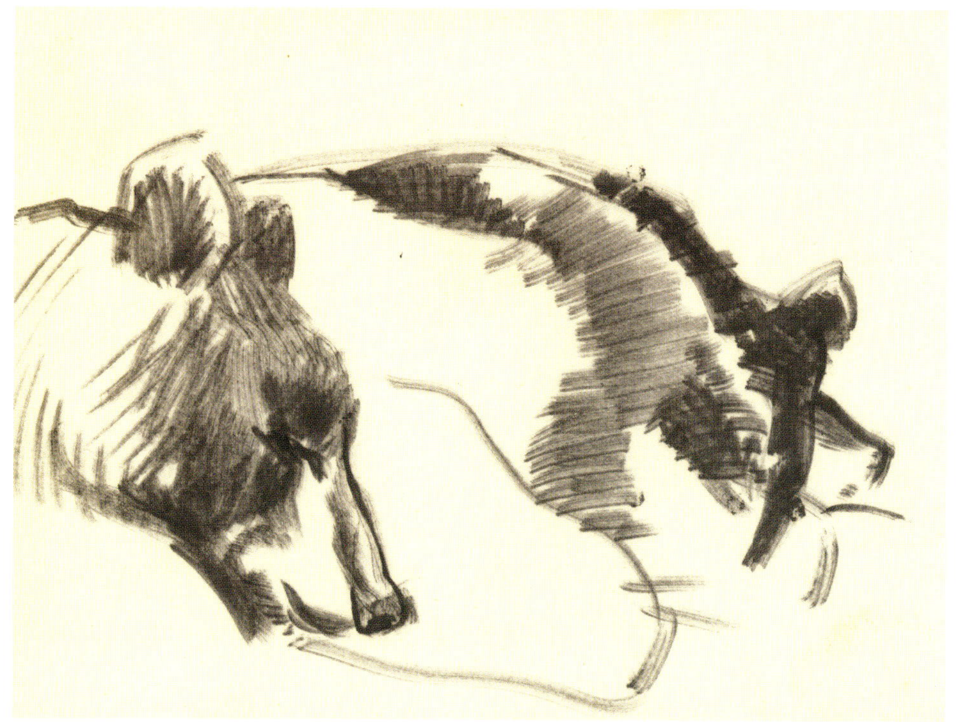

"Little Bear sketch for *Blueberries for Sal*," pencil on paper, ca 1947. Courtesy of May Massee Collection, Emporia State University.

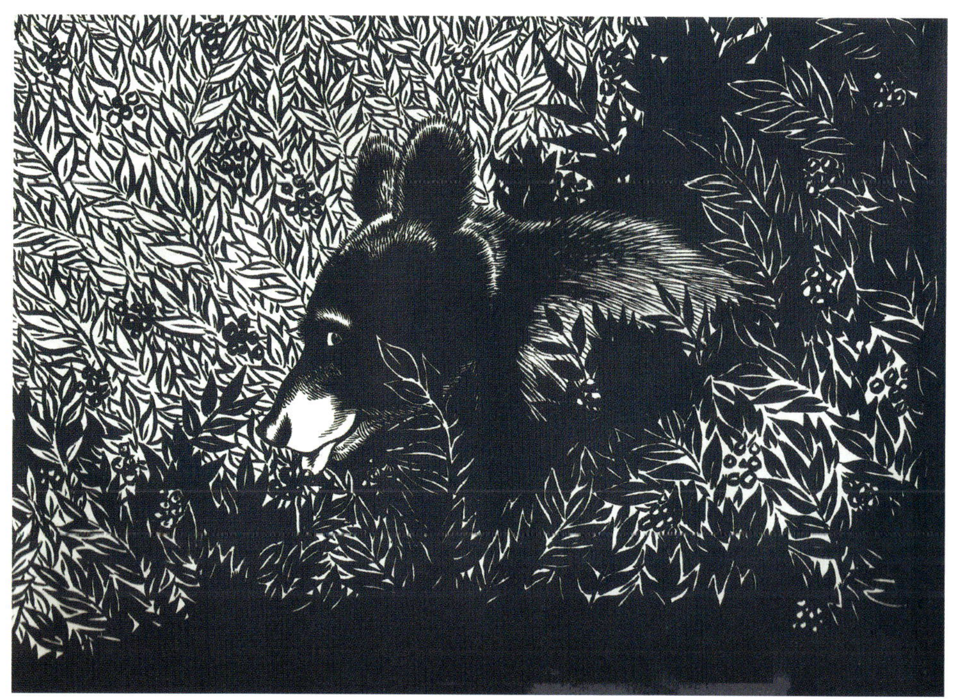

Blueberries for Sal, back cover, Viking Press, 1948.

Here are some pictures from *One Morning in Maine.*

"Sketch of Mom for *One Morning in Maine,*" pencil on paper, ca 1951.

One Morning in Maine, detail, "Mom and Sal," Viking Press, 1952.

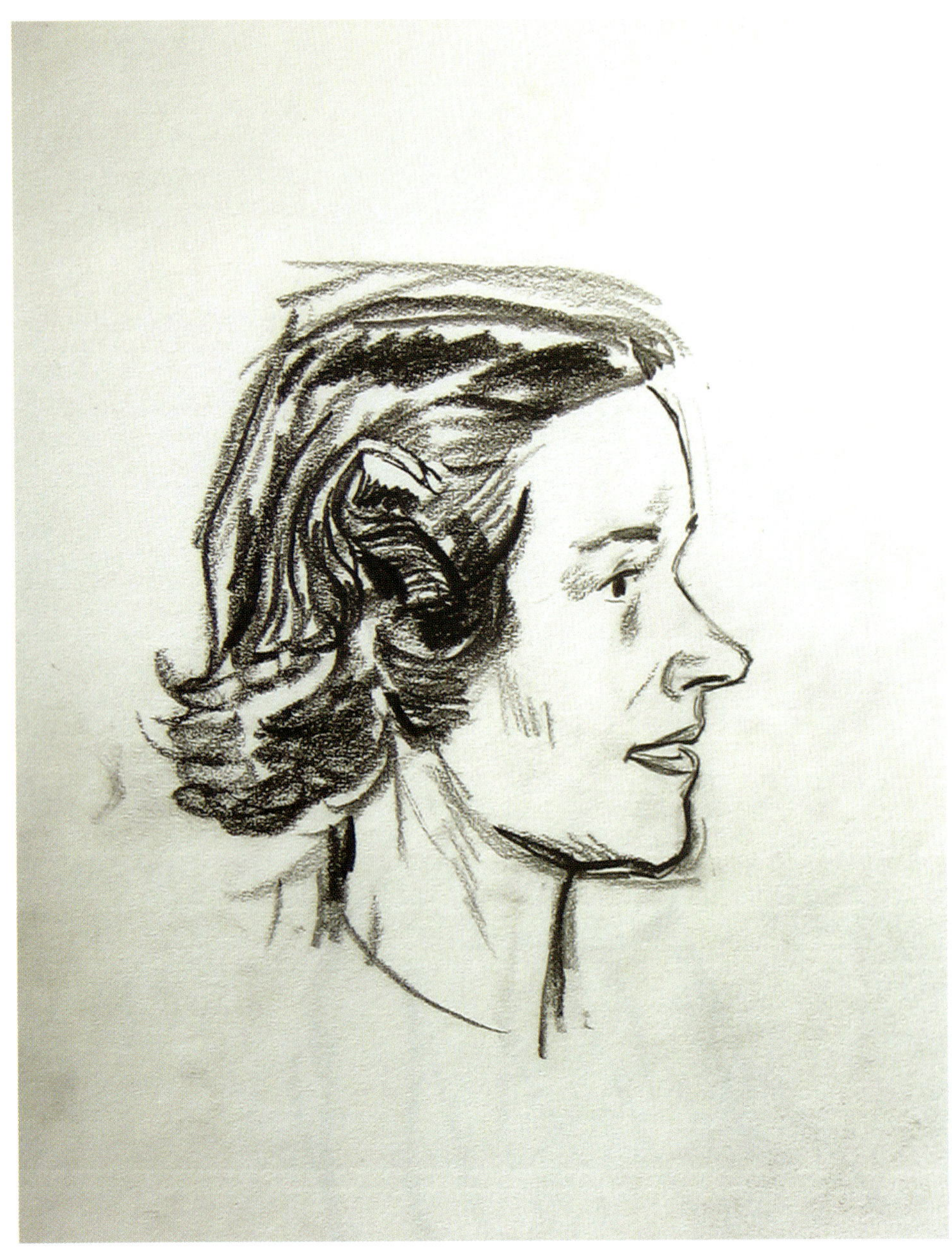

"Yes," said her mother. "But not for a long time, not until she stops being a baby and grows up to be a big girl like you. Jane is so young that she hasn't even grown all her baby teeth yet. Now let's all go upstairs and brush our hair and get dressed for breakfast."

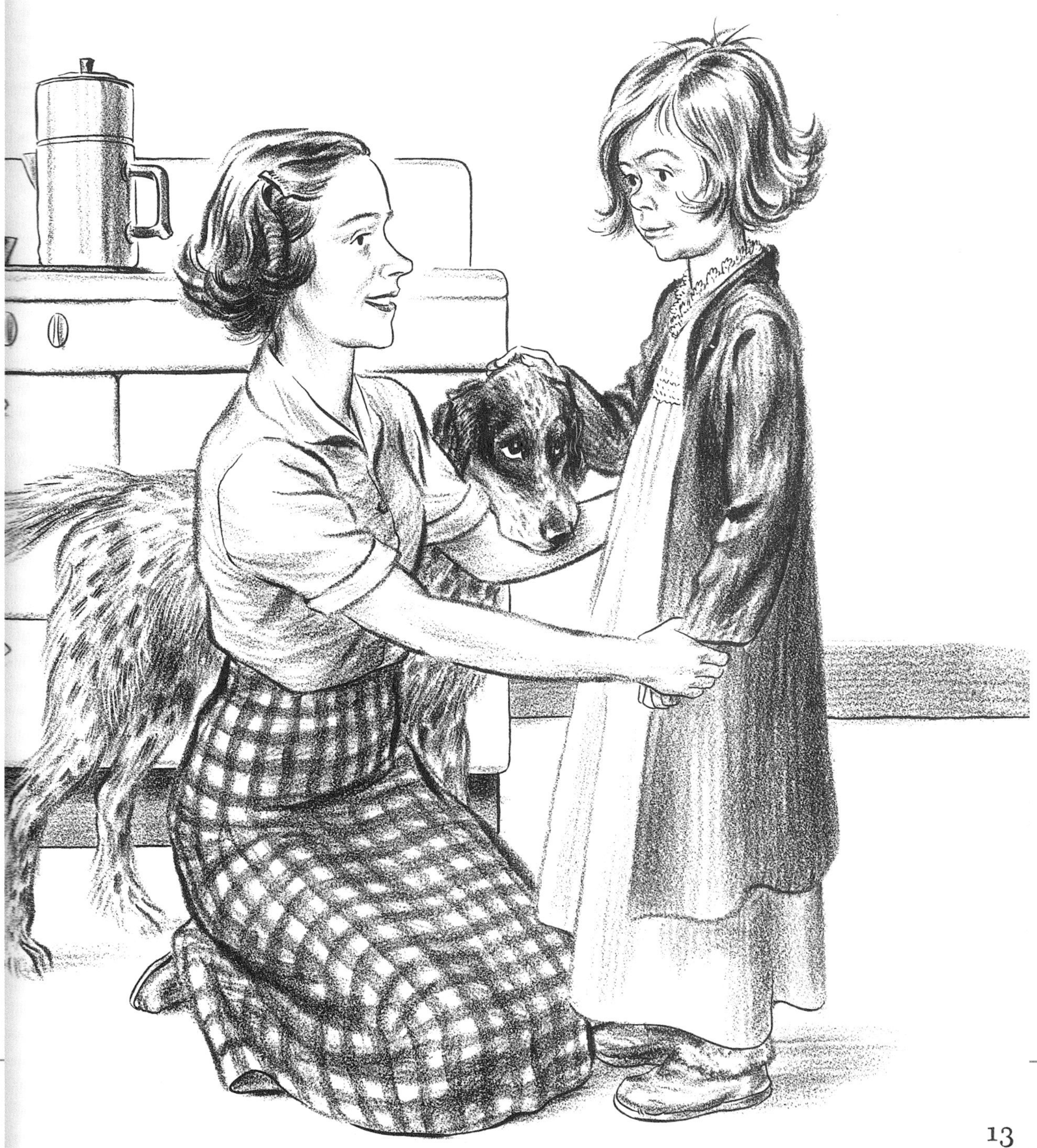

"Sketch of Sal showing her tooth," pencil on paper, ca 1951. Courtesy of May Massee Collection, Emporia State University.

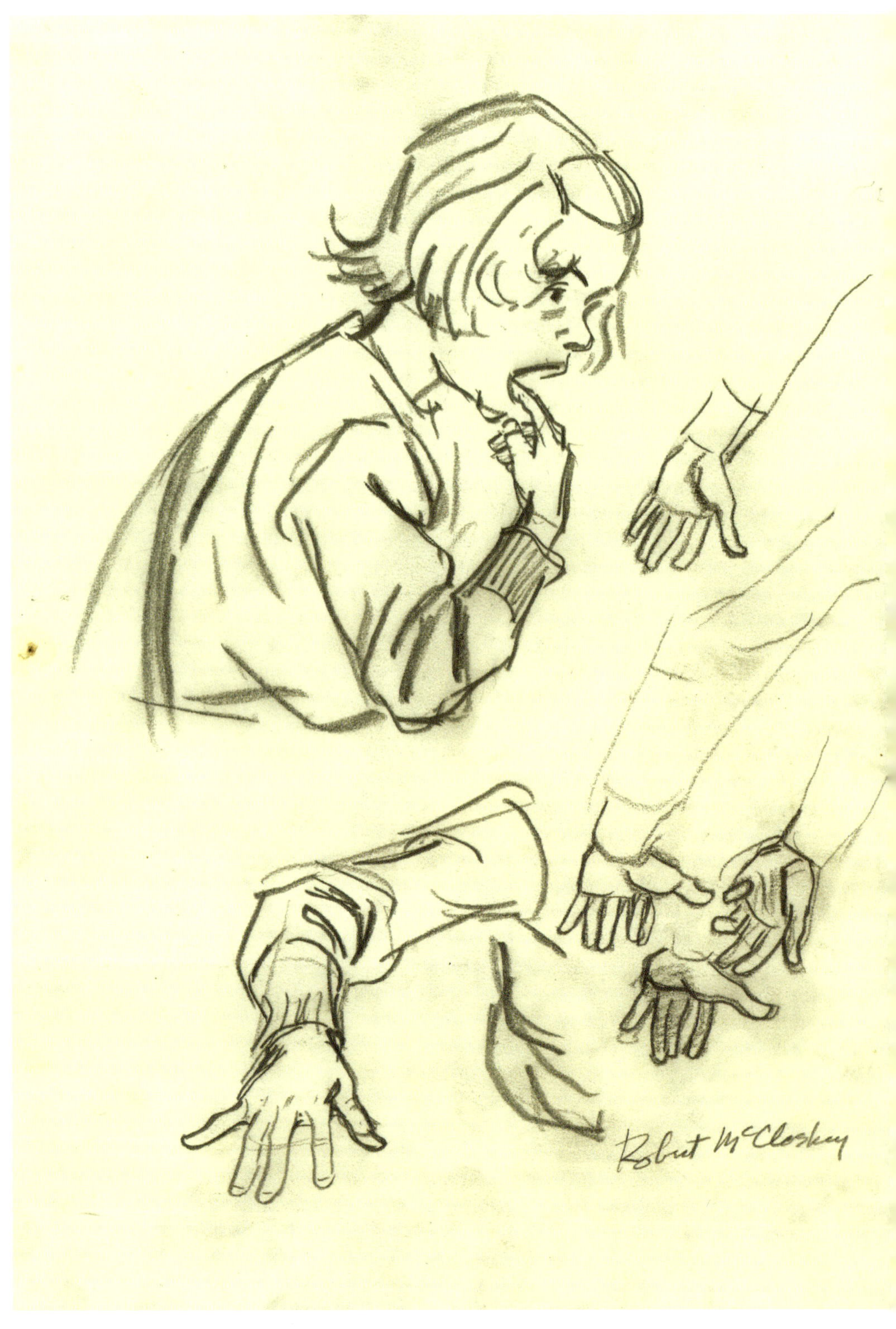

One Morning in Maine • 125

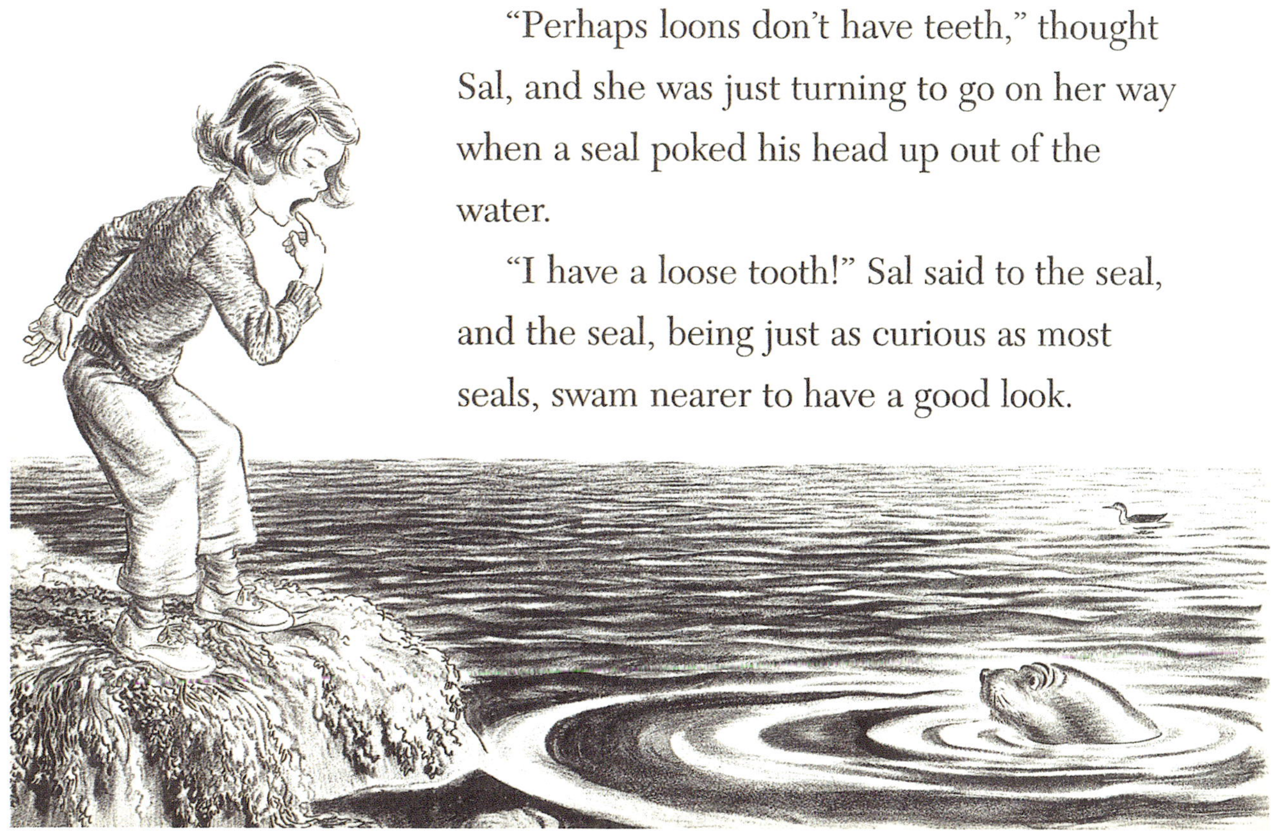

"Perhaps loons don't have teeth," thought Sal, and she was just turning to go on her way when a seal poked his head up out of the water.

"I have a loose tooth!" Sal said to the seal, and the seal, being just as curious as most seals, swam nearer to have a good look.

One Morning in Maine,
"Sal Showing her Tooth,"
Viking Press, 1952.

I don't think my father ever painted a Maine lighthouse. He could have included a lighthouse in *One Morning in Maine,* since we always passed within a hundred feet of the decommissioned Pumpkin Island Light on our way to Bucks Harbor. Instead, he drew the bell (light) buoy, which had replaced the light house as a navigational aid.

Here is the bell buoy in dream mode, with sirens perhaps singing sailors to their doom.

"Sirens on Bell Buoy," pencil on paper, date unknown.

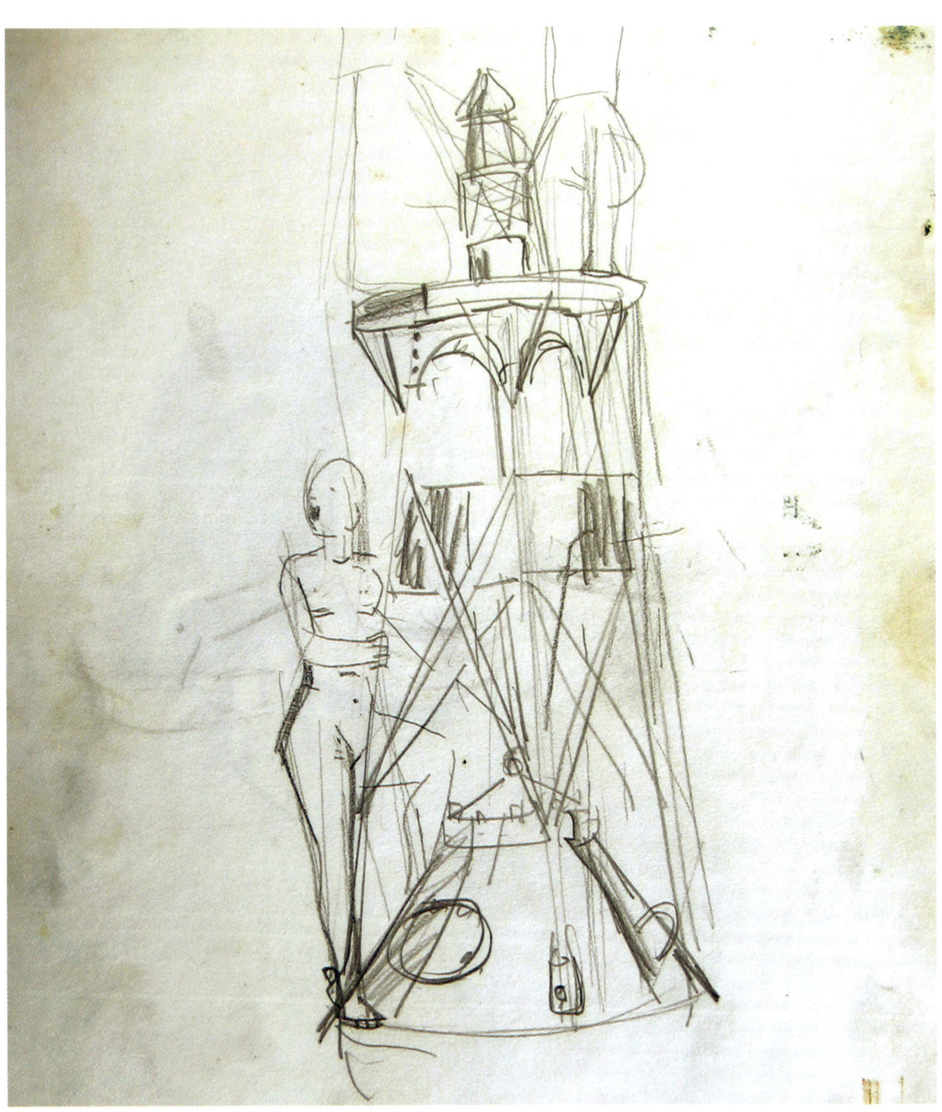

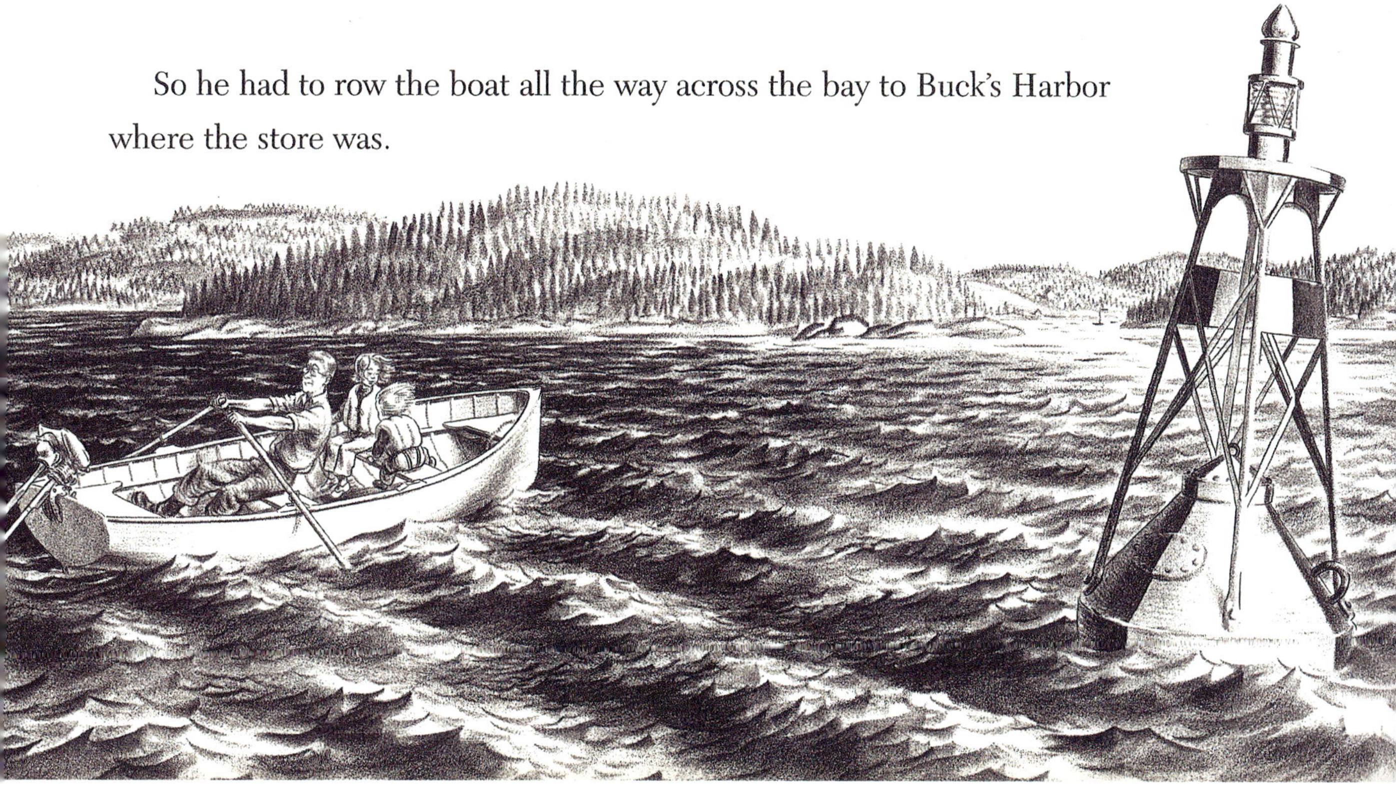

One Morning in Maine, "Rowing Past the Bell Buoy," Viking Press, 1952.

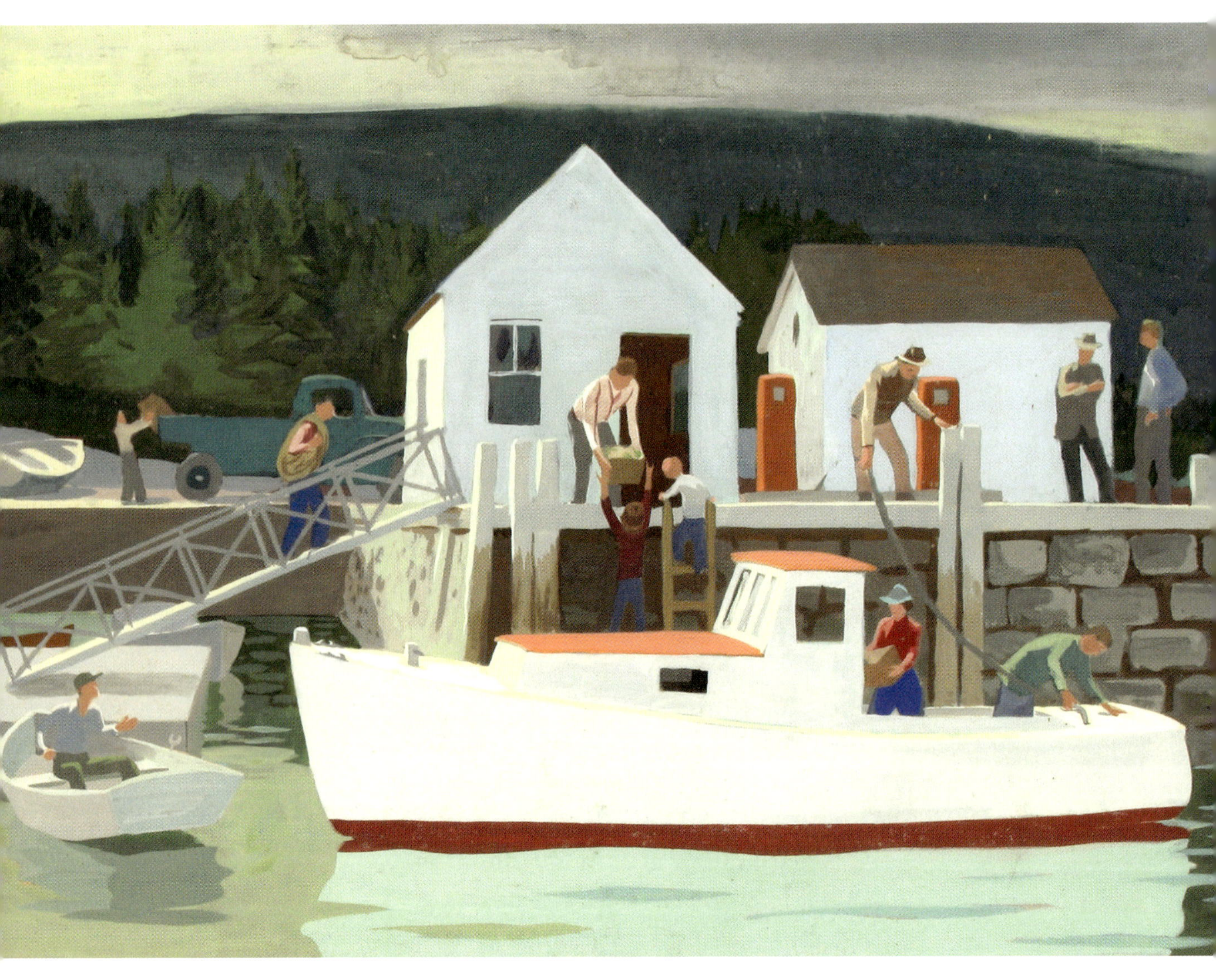

"Buying Gas and Supplies at Ray Gray's Wharf," book study for *Time of Wonder*, acrylic on cardboard, ca 1956.

This is one of the book studies for *Time of Wonder.* Ray Gray's Wharf is still there, now called Bucks Harbor Marine. The deck of our boat was really painted gray, not pink. She was built at Frankie Day's boatyard in the Benjamin River in Sedgwick about 1954. Junior Day bought her back from my father in the 1980s when she needed rebuilding, and kept her in top condition until he died a few years ago. The boat was rebuilt again and sold from the Great Island Boatyard in Harpswell, Maine, in 2014.

In this picture, my father, Sal, and I are getting gas and food to ride out the hurricane that is fast approaching. Hurricane Edna hit the Maine coast in 1954, and was the worst hurricane on our part of the coast in the last sixty years.

Here is the final version of the picture.

"Gassing Up at the Dock," acrylic on cardboard, 15" x 22", ca 1956.

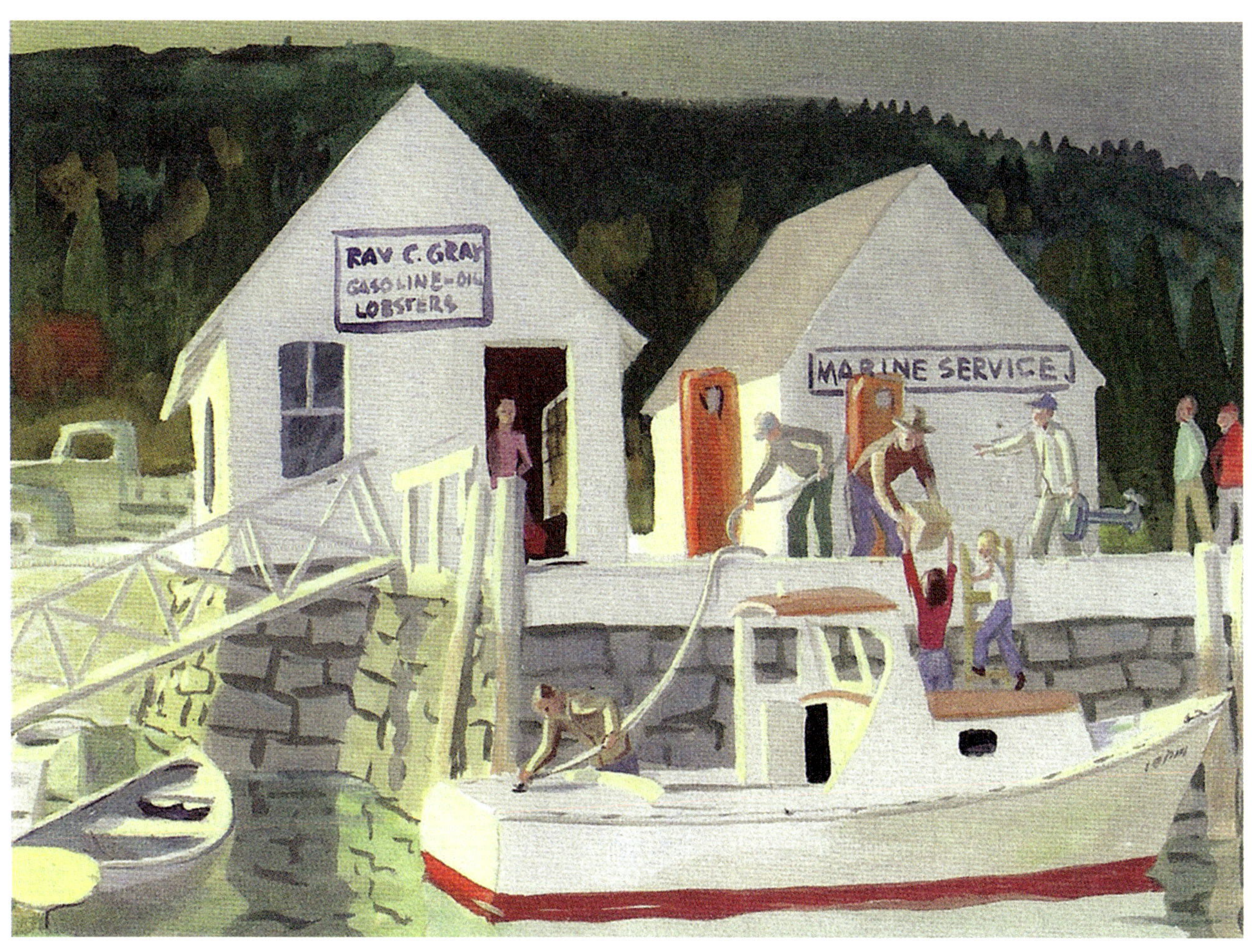

This sketch of the boat combines elements of the previous picture and the next picture. It is tied up to the wharf like the boat in the previous picture, but the angle of the bow is closer to that of the boat in the next picture.

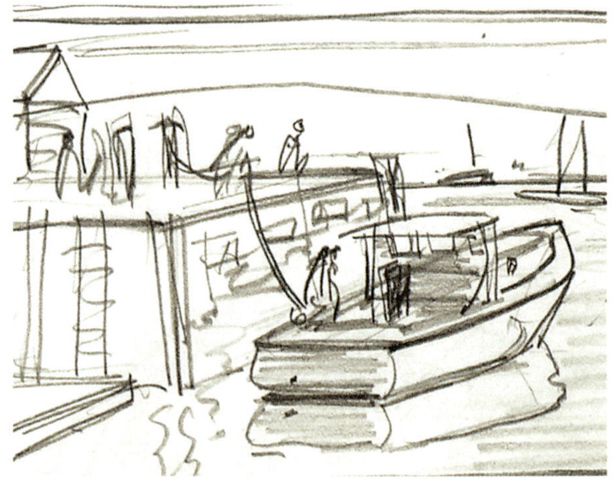

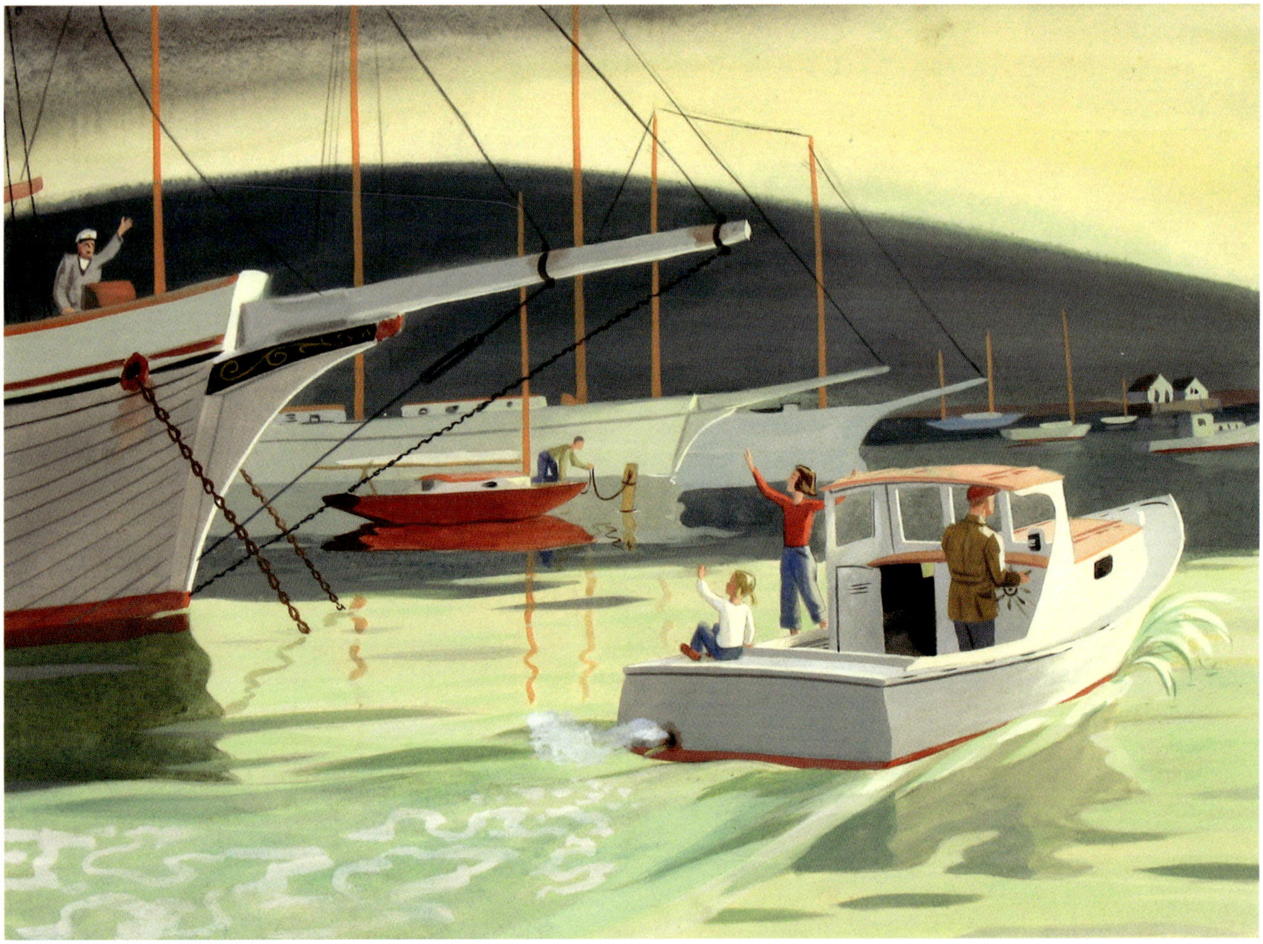

"Sketch, Gassing up at the Dock," pencil on paper, ca 1956.

"Waving to the Schooners in Bucks Harbor," book study for *Time of Wonder,* acrylic on cardboard, 15" x 22", ca 1956.

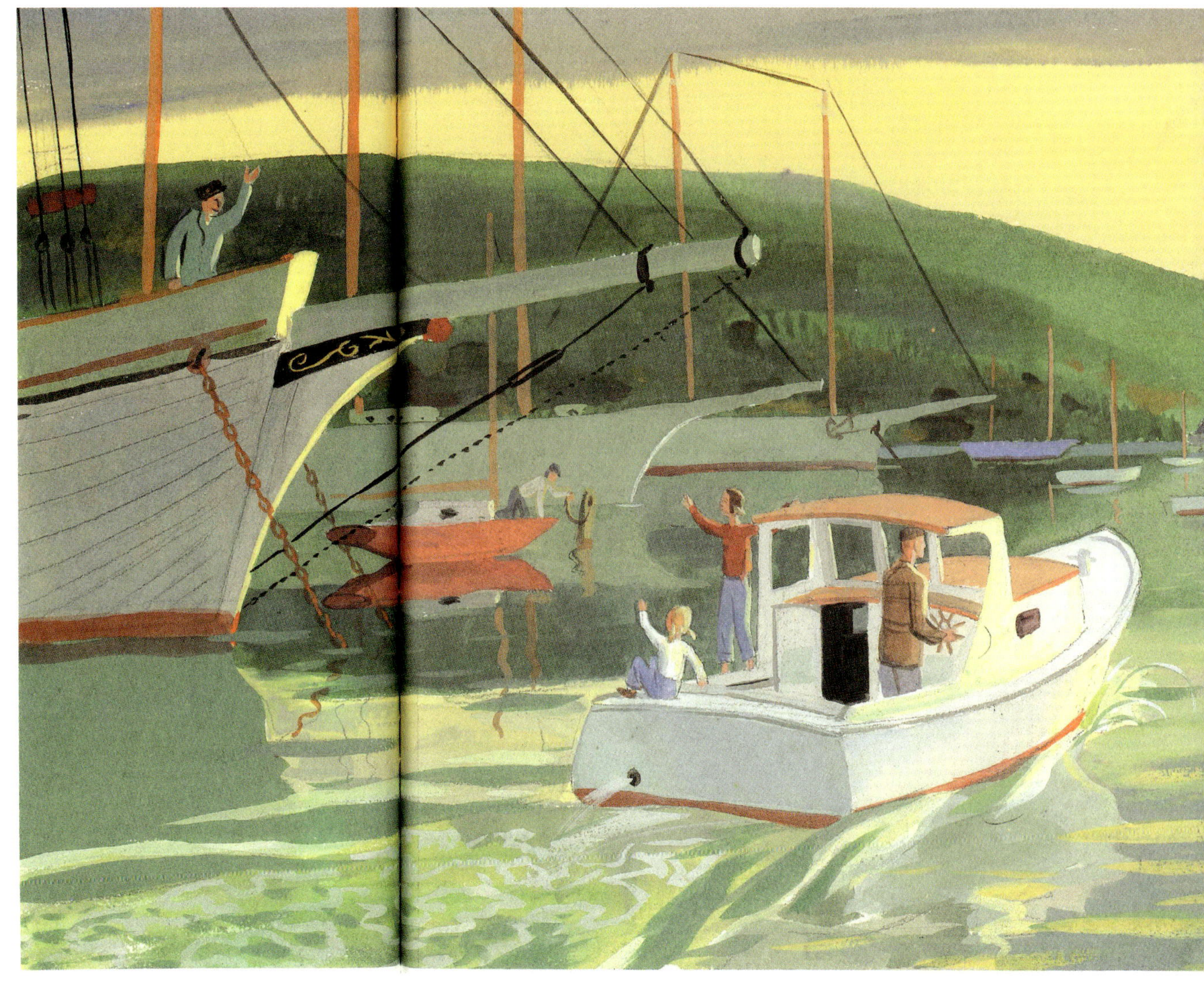

Time of Wonder, "Waving to the Schooners," Viking Press, 1957.

In the 1950s, the only gray schooner in the Penobscot Bay schooner fleet was the *Alice Wentworth*. In 1965, the *Alice Wentworth* was moved to Pier Four in Boston, where she was moored until 1974, when, at the age of 111, she was destroyed in a storm.

The picture changed again in the final version which appears in *Time of Wonder.* The final picture has somewhat more compact proportions and the bow of our boat is more rounded.

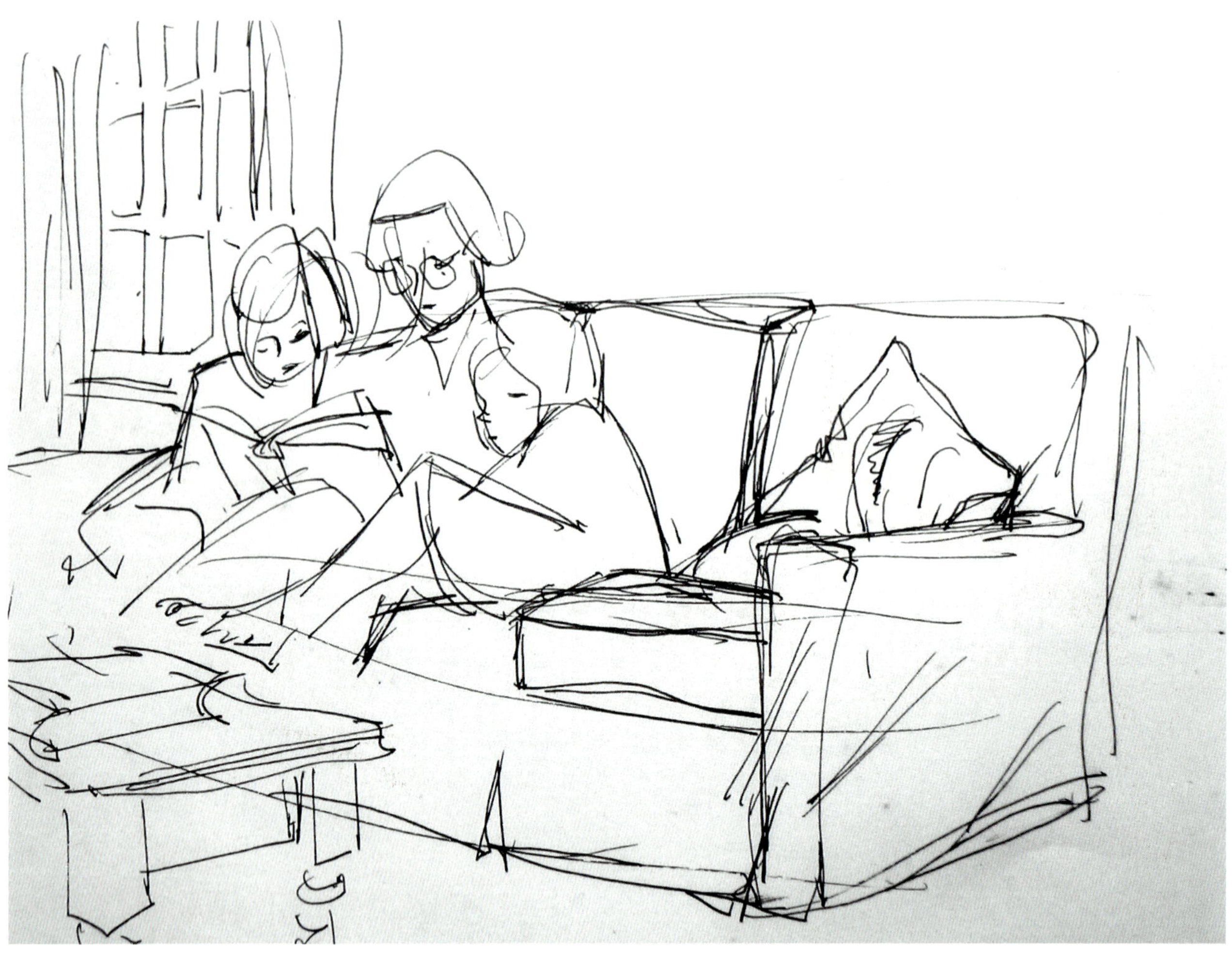

"Sketch of Mom, Sal, and Jane on the Couch," pencil on paper ca 1956.

Bob did a number of sketches of Mom reading to Sal and me on the couch.

The two sketches of Mom and Sal and me on the facing page show us in differing spirits. In the first, we are very focused on the story, and less on each other. In the second, there is more of a union of both family and story.

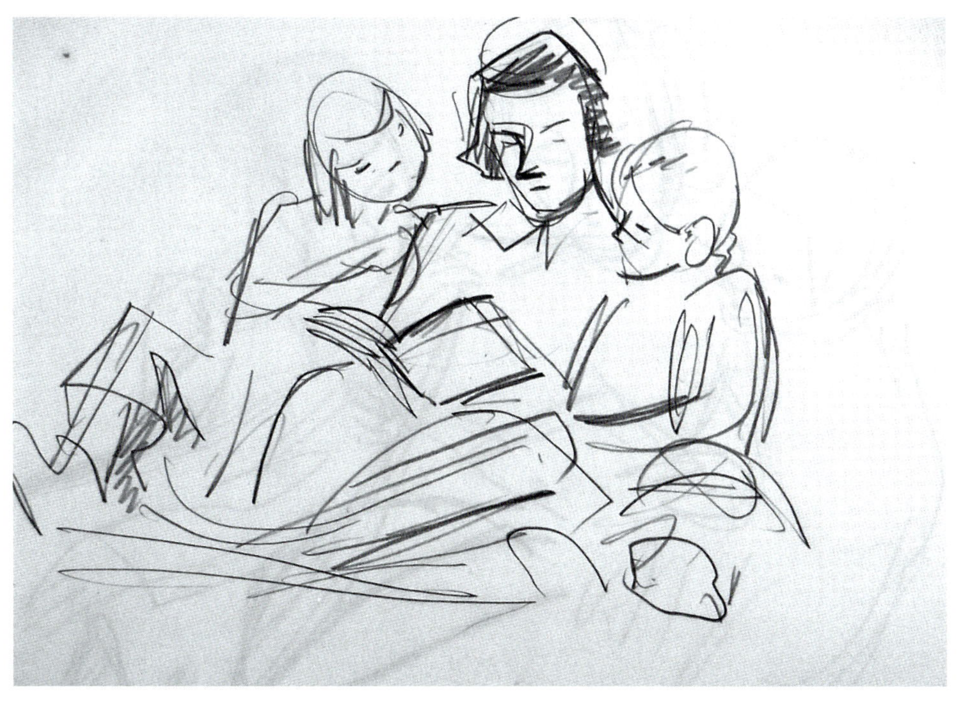

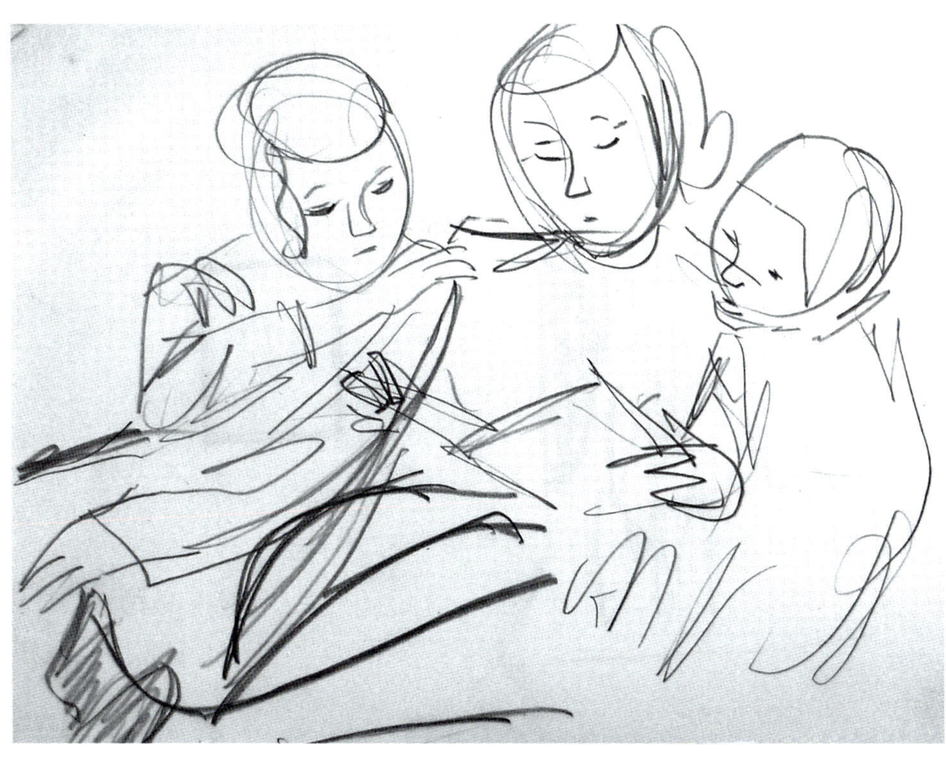

"Sketches of Mom, Sal, and Jane on the Couch," pencil on paper, ca 1956.

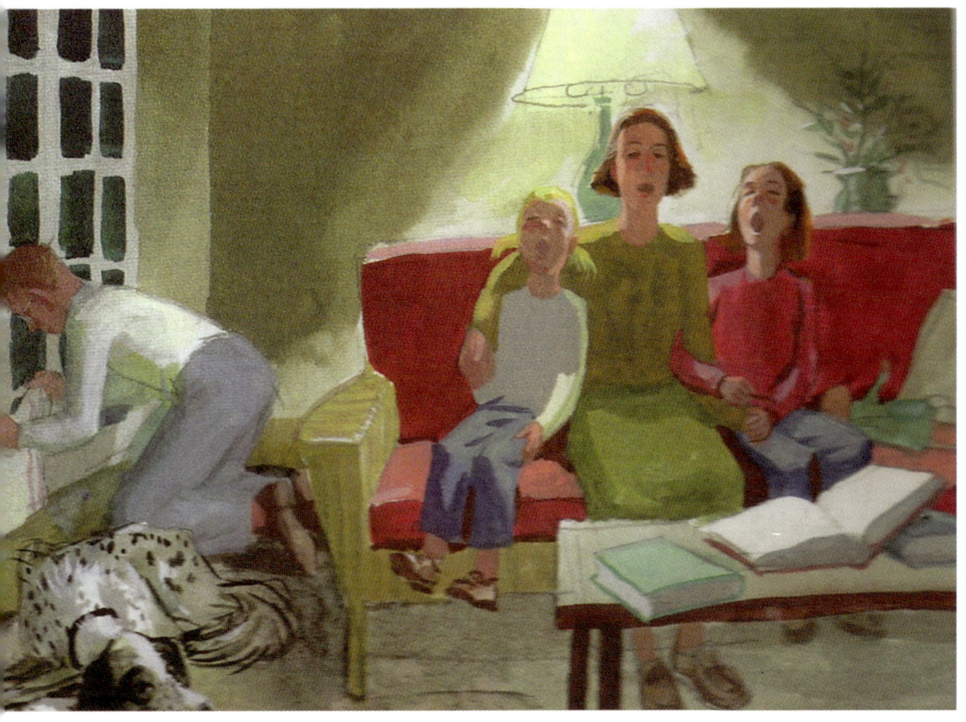

The finished picture appears in *Time of Wonder*, when we ride out the hurricane on the island. Mom read *Davey and the Goblin* to us to distract us from the scariness of the storm, while Bob paced the house and put towels against the doors to keep out the rain. And then we sang to keep up our courage.

Here, from one of Bob's sketchbooks is the birth of *Time of Wonder*.

Time of Wonder, "Singing in the Hurricane," Viking Press, 1957.

The text reads:

Berries Are Gone
Ferns Turn From Green To Yellow To Brown
End Of The Summer
Winds Come From The West And North West
Time When The Tides Are Highest And Lowest
**Low – Walk Way Out – Even Between Islands*
Winds Are Brisker – Washed Up Line Of Seaweed On Beach Grows
Larger And Higher
**Put Seaweed On The Garden*
The Robins Have Gone South. The
Swallows That Build Their Nests In The Boat
House Have Gone
Humming Birds Are Still Here.

The Gulls And Crows Are Around As Always,

Squawking And Fussing With Each Other –

But Banding Together To Chase

The Old Brown Eagle Back To Deer Island

When He Comes By Looking For Lunch . . .

(continuing on from the next page)

Time To Leave The Islands – Time To

Go To The Mainland. Time For Girl Scouts,

Music Lessons, School Busses, And Learning Things

From Books

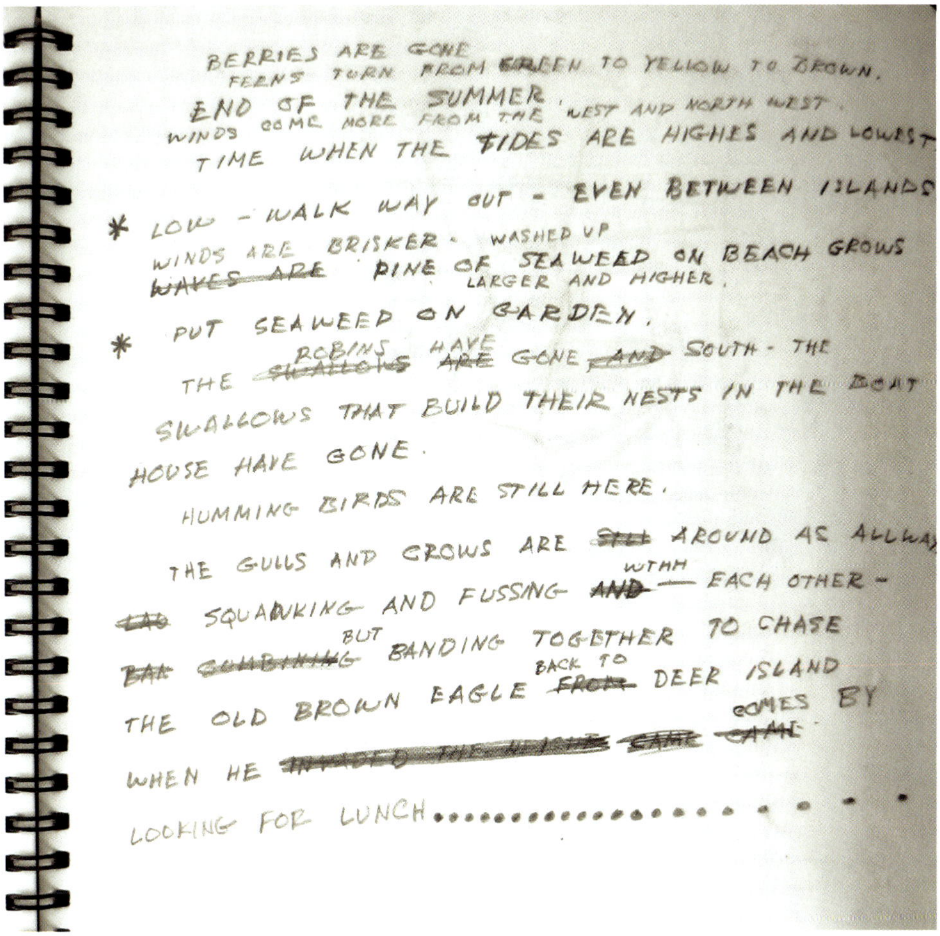

Original outline for *Time of Wonder.*

Here are some pictures of Burt Dow.

"Sketch of Burt Dow," pencil on paper, ca 1962. Courtesy of May Massee Collection, Emporia State University.

Burt Dow, Deep-Water Man, "Burt Watering the Flowers," Viking Press, 1963.

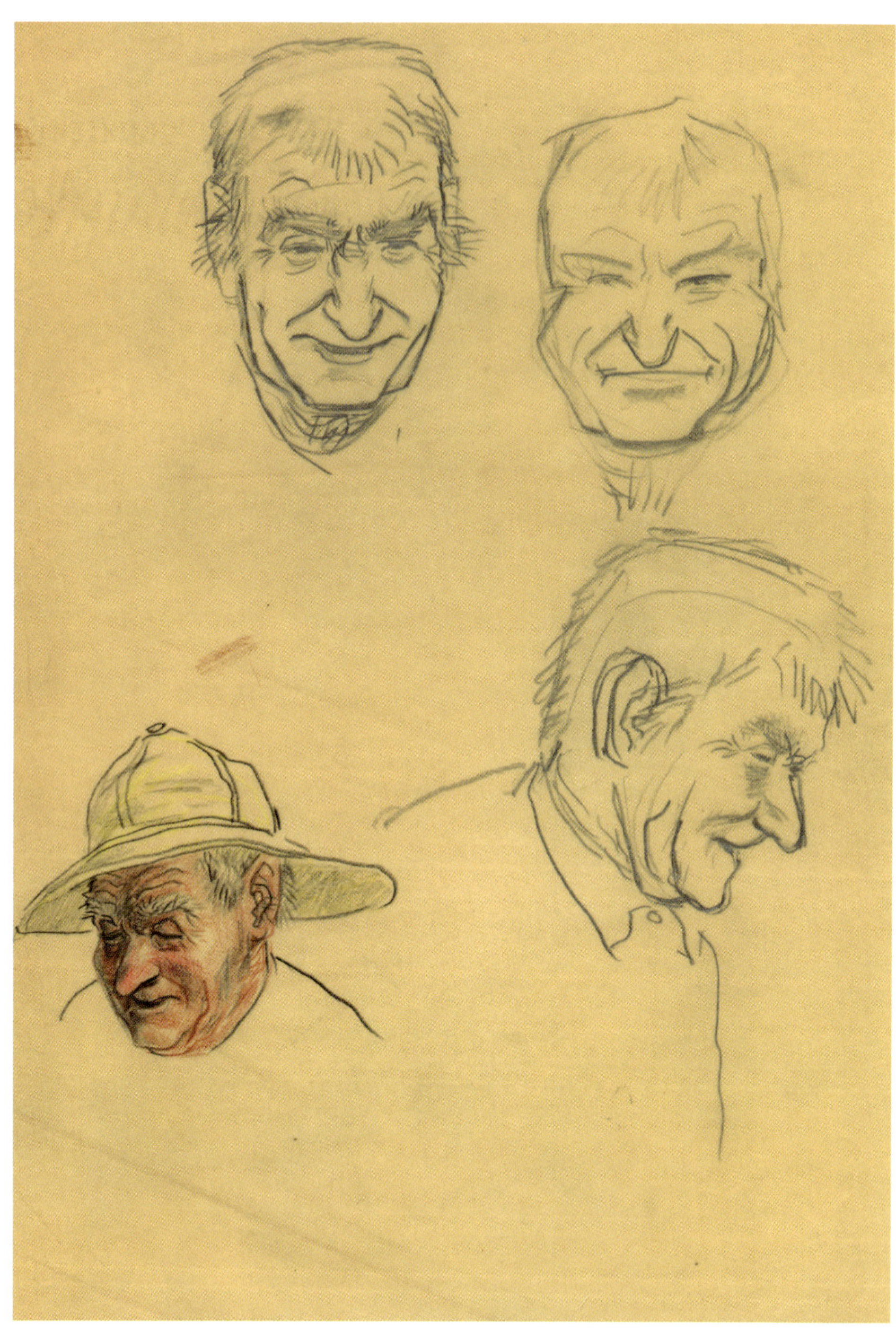

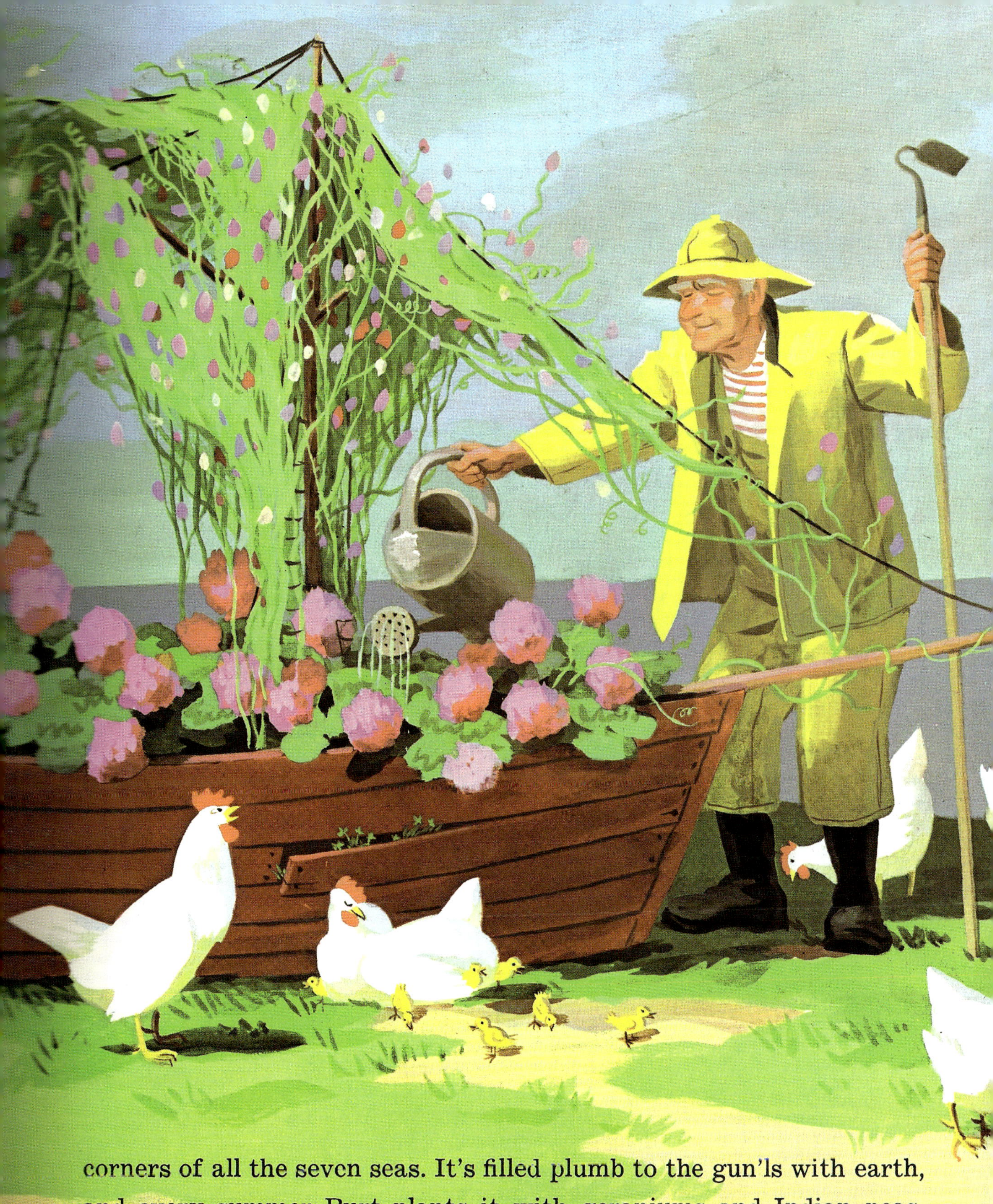

corners of all the seven seas. It's filled plumb to the gun'ls with earth, and every summer Burt plants it with geraniums and Indian peas. The geraniums brighten up the deck, and the Indian peas climb the rigging and sway this-a-way, that-a-way, in a smoky sou'wester.

Family 4

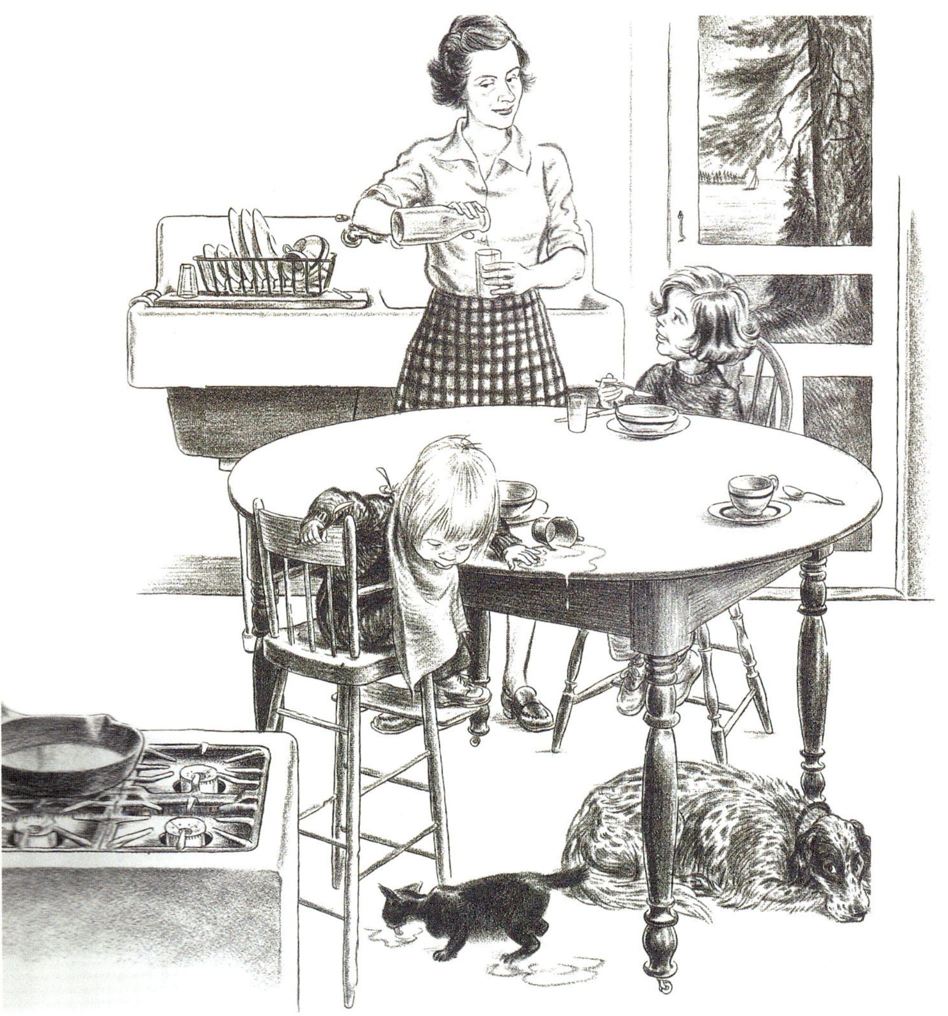

One Morning in Maine, "Breakfast," Viking Press, 1952.

This illustration from *One Morning in Maine* represents our family for me. Bob isn't in the picture, but he drew it. All the background is from our kitchen: the sink, table, stove, screen door, my high chair, which I still have upstairs, and the chair Sal sits on. Following is the sketch that preceded the picture.

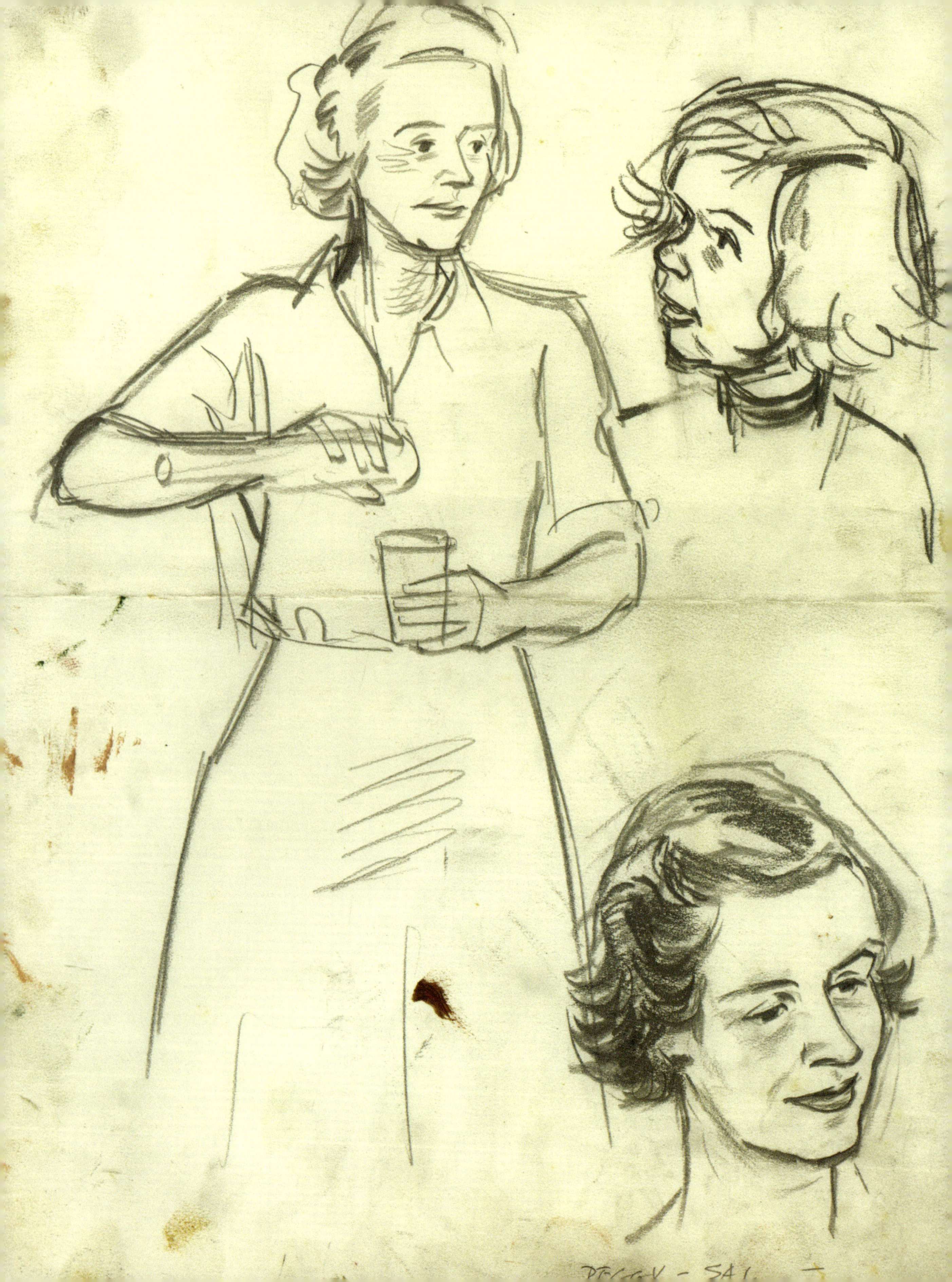

My mother was born Margaret Durand in 1917 in Ithaca, New York. Her father was an eye doctor and her mother was a storyteller and well known children's book writer, Ruth Sawyer. She wrote *Roller Skates,* about a girl in New York City who gains the freedom to explore the city when she receives a pair of roller skates for Christmas. Mom was known as Peggy and had a brother, David. She went to Mount Holyoke College, and then to business school, which she hated, and then to library school, where she found her calling as a children's librarian.

"Sketch of Sal and Mom for *One Morning in Maine,"* pencil on paper, ca 1951. Courtesy of May Massee Collection, Emporia State University.

Mom went to a cocktail party with Granny that Viking Press gave for their authors. She met my father there, and they were married in 1940. Then my father went into the army and was based in Anniston, Alabama, where his job was to draw pictures to train the troops. Mom joined him in Anniston and taught school during the war. Sal was born in 1945, and Bob was discharged in 1946. I was born in 1948. Mom quit work when Sal was born to become a full time mother and housewife.

I love the sweet, pensive expression on my mother's face in this painting.

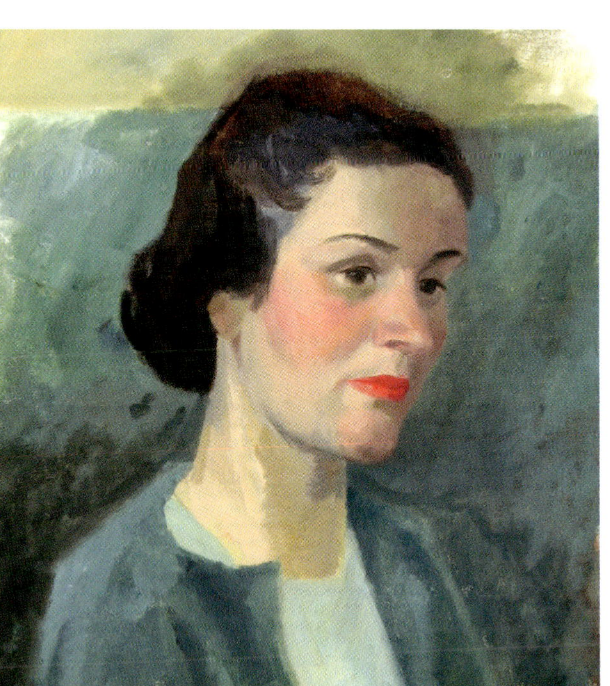

"Margaret McCloskey," oil on canvas board, 18" x 14", 1950s.

I thought that these were sketches of Sal. But then I see that, oops, in this sketch, it's a boy! I bet these are sketches of Doc, done while he and his parents, Marc and Bea Simont were visiting. Doc was

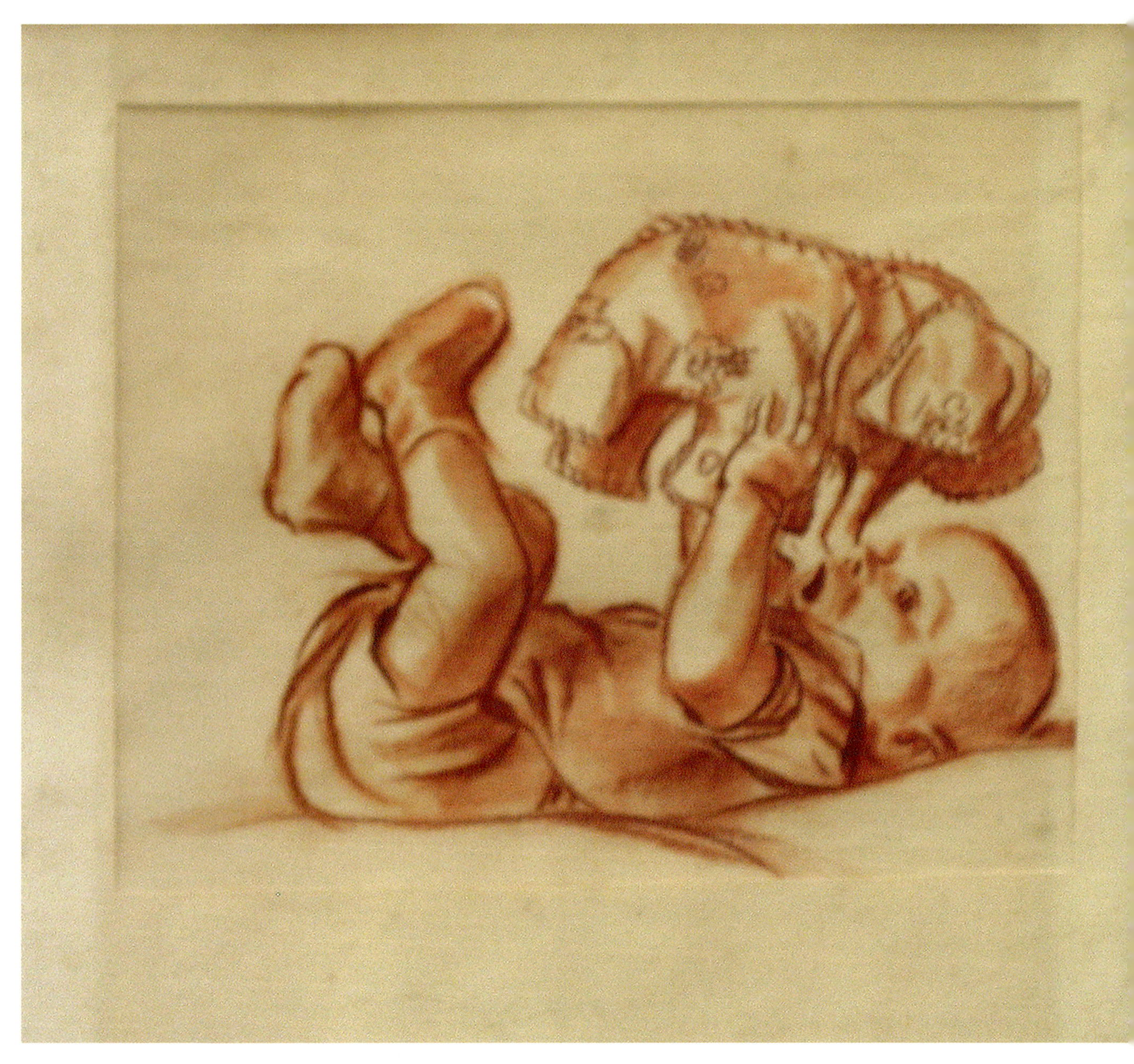

"Sal with Stuffed Elephant," chalk on paper, 14" x 17", ca 1946.

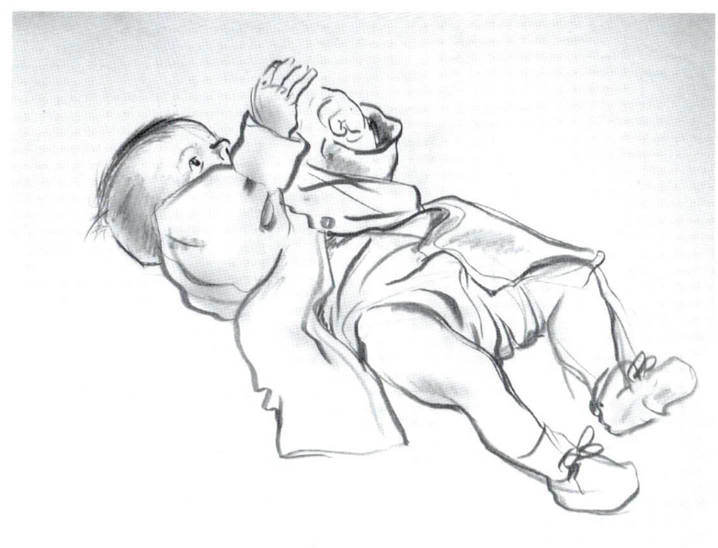

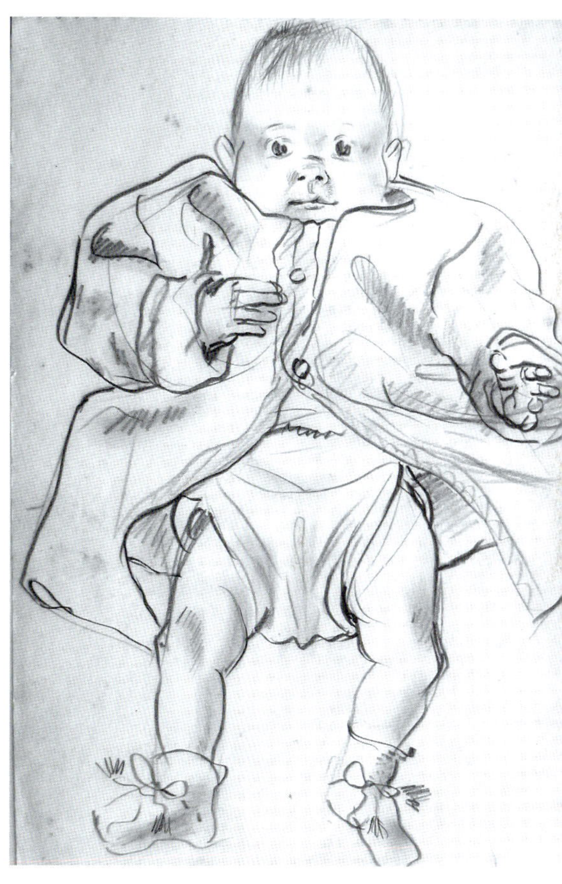

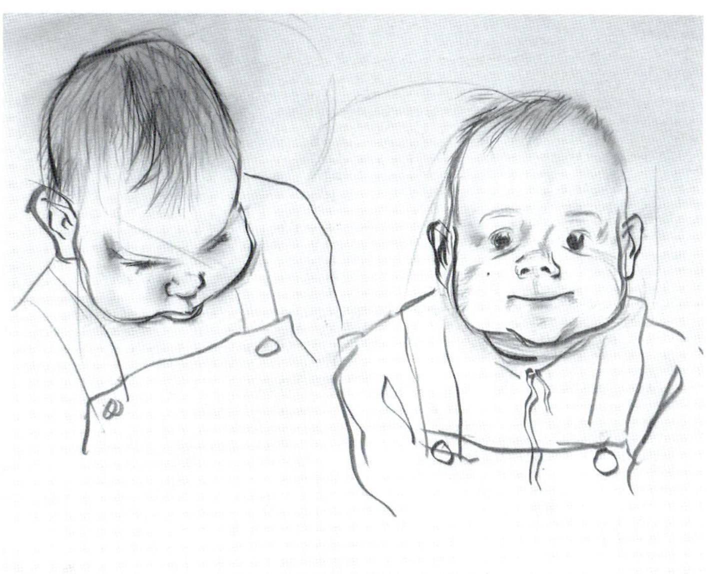

about a year younger than Sal. Marc Simont was Bob's art school roommate and the Simonts became life-long friends of our family. Marc also wrote and illustrated children's books and drew cartoons for magazines. His *A Tree is Nice* won the Caldecott Medal in 1957.

Three baby sketches, pencil on paper, dates unknown.

In this sketch of Sal, the bathrobe is given prominence. The pose is a mirror image of Sal's pose in the following painting.

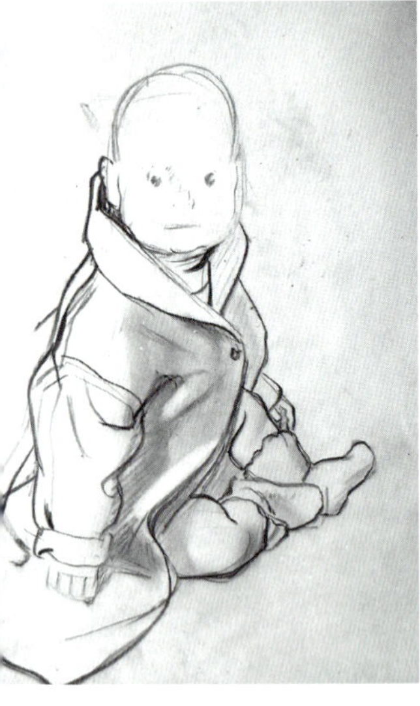

"Sketch of Baby with Robe," pencil on paper, date unknown.

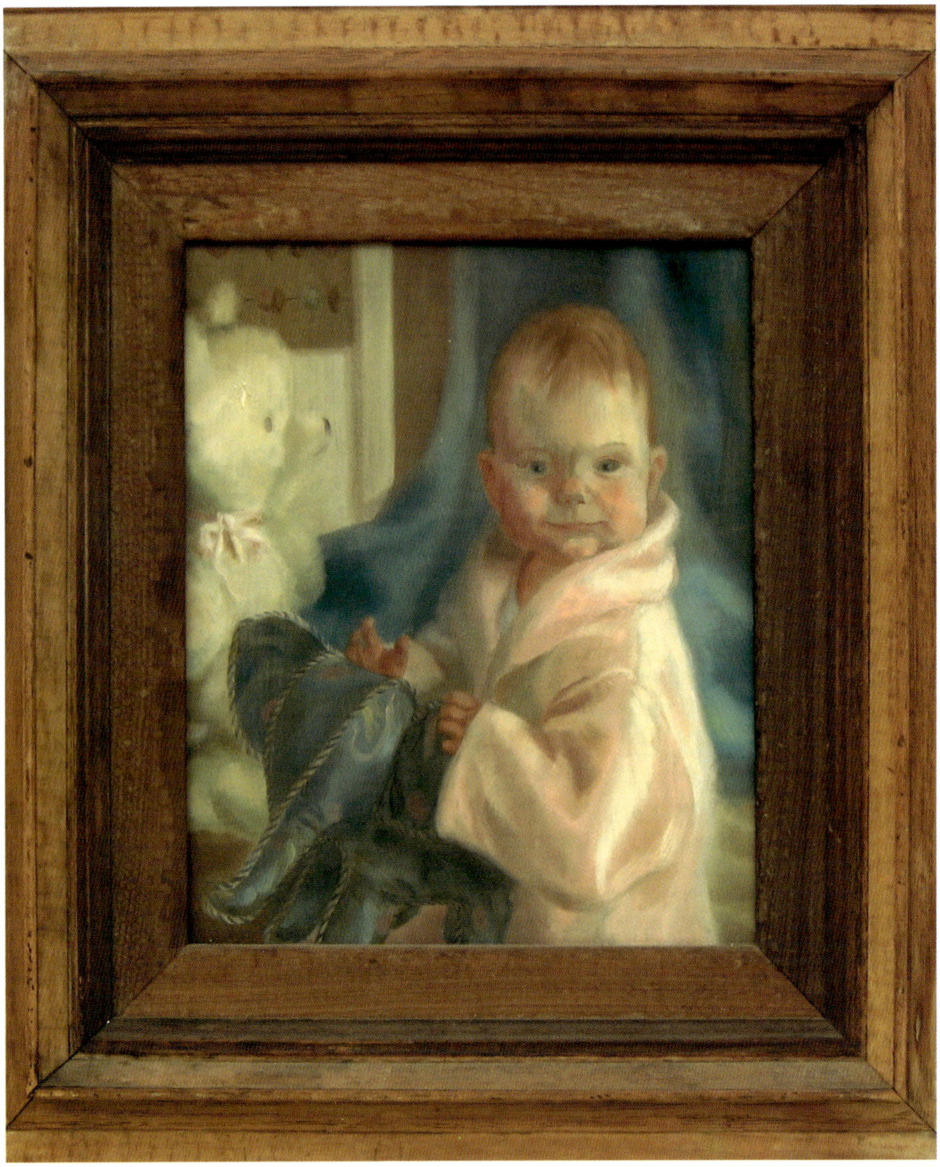

"Sal with Teddy Bear," oil on canvas board, 14" x 17", 1946.

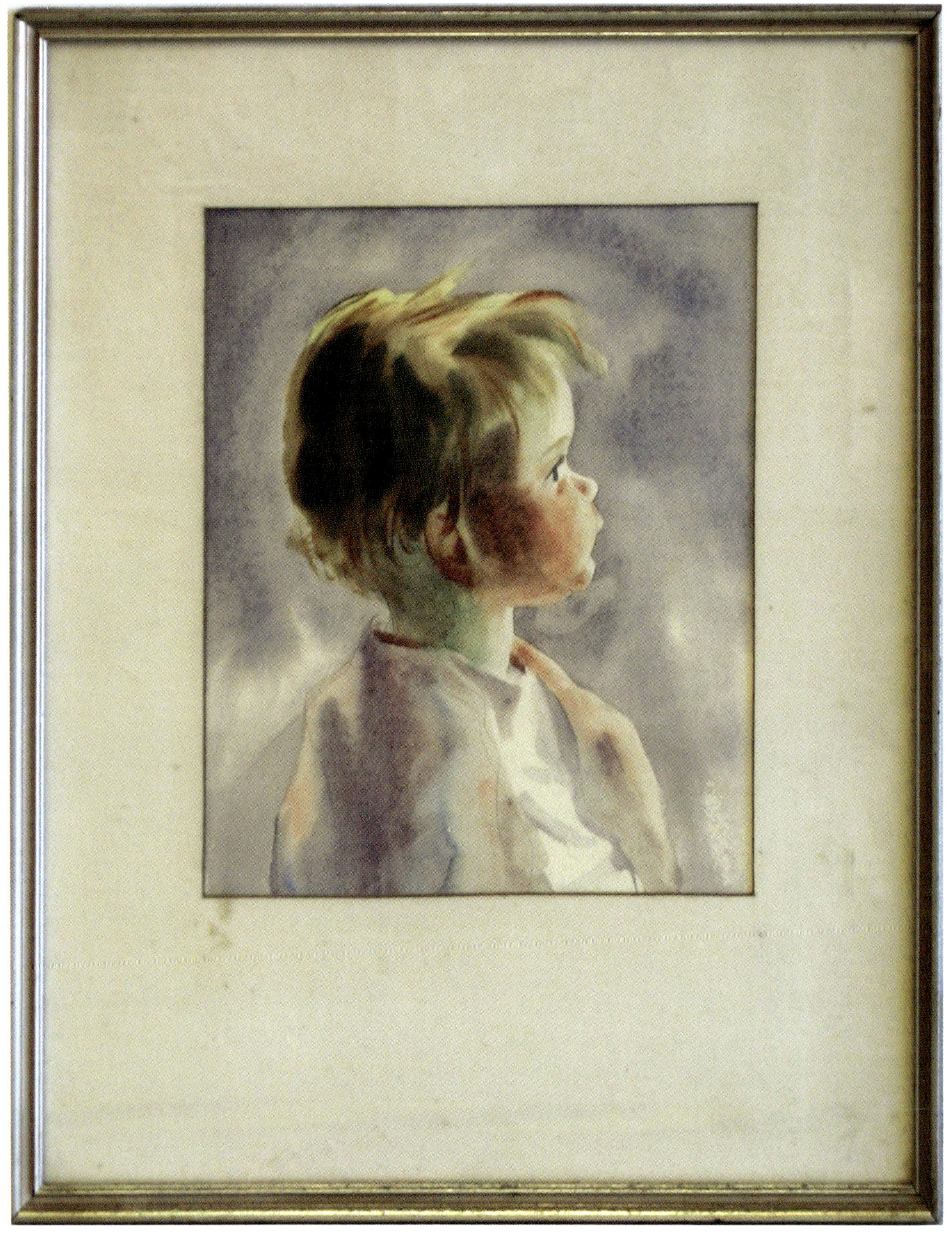

"Sal in Pink," casein or watercolor on paper, 21" x 17", ca 1947.

I love this painting of Sal. Bob may have done it around the time he wrote *Blueberries for Sal*. Sal says that Bob told her that he wrote *Blueberries for Sal* as a gift to her at the time when Mom was pregnant with me and was shifting her focus to include another baby.

"Sal and Penny," oil on canvas board, 20" x 16", ca 1947.

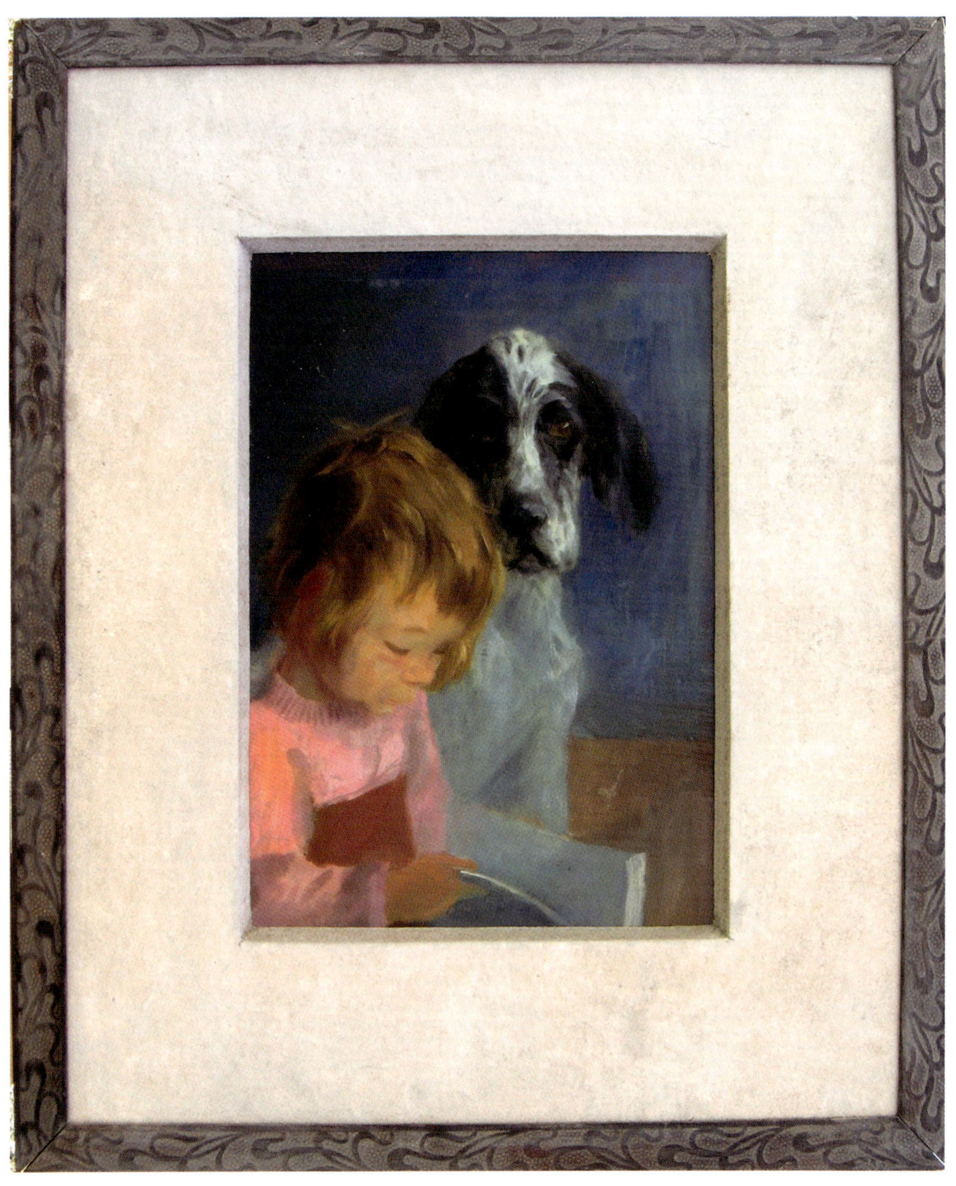

Here is Sal with our dog Penny. There are no baby pictures of me, but there are lots of sketches and paintings of me around the ages of four to eight.

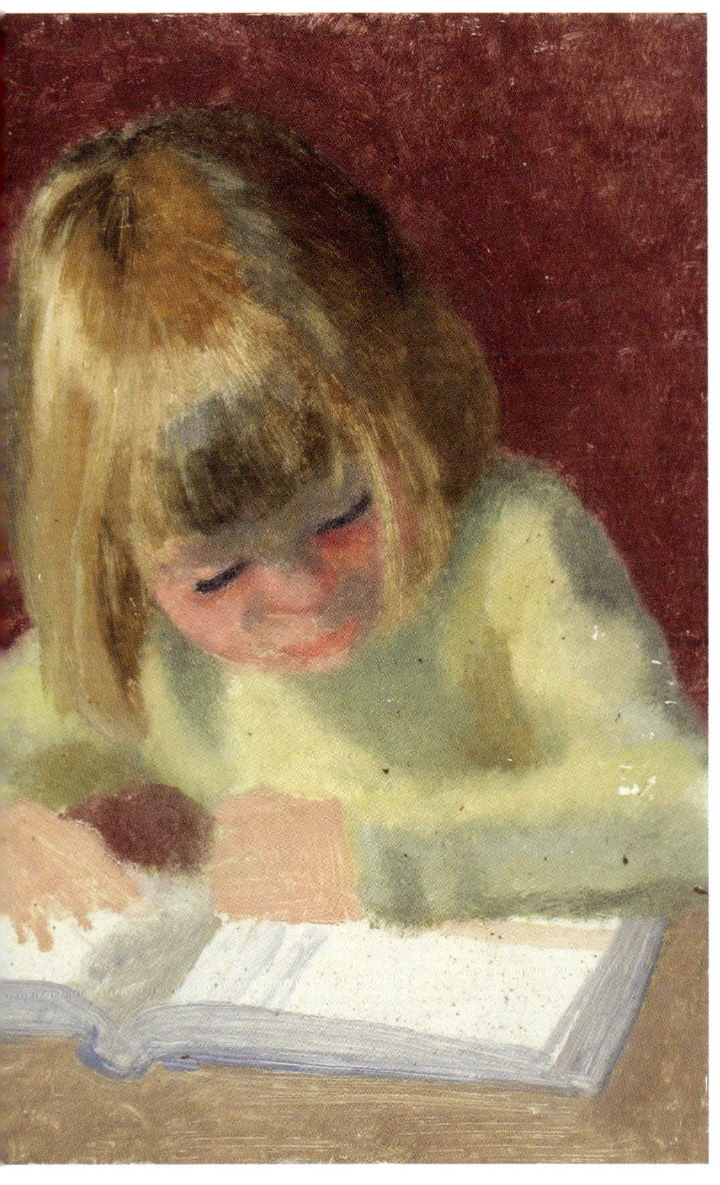

"Jane in Yellow with Book," oil on canvas board, 14" x 10", ca 1954.

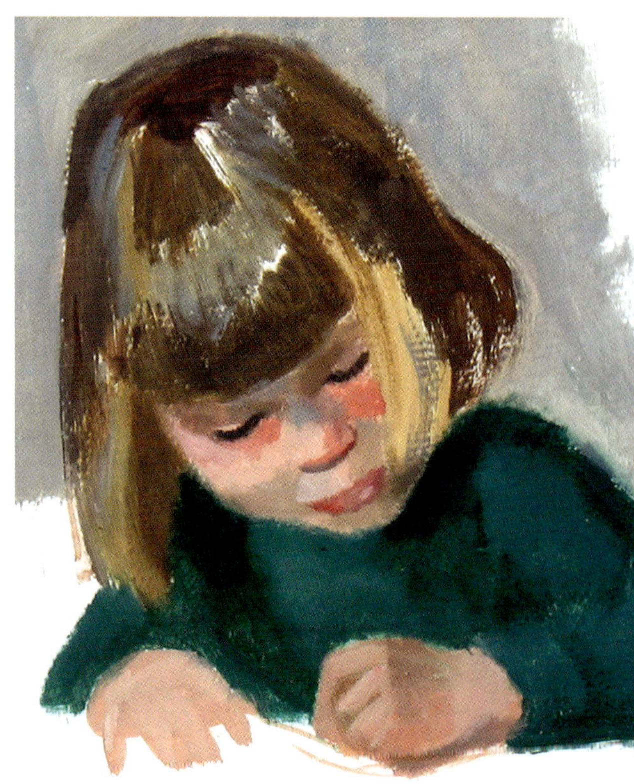

"Jane in Green Sweater," oil on canvas board, 14" x 10", ca 1953.

"Jane in Green with Overalls," oil on canvas board, 9" x 8", ca 1956.

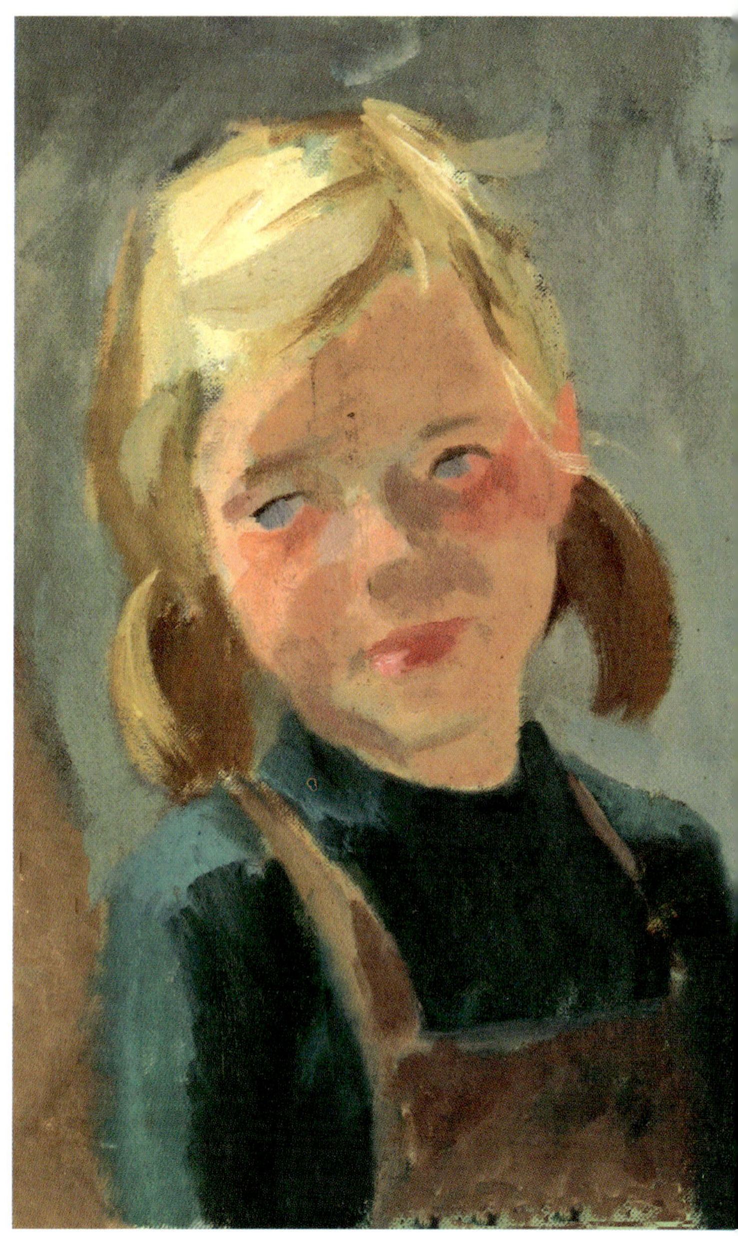

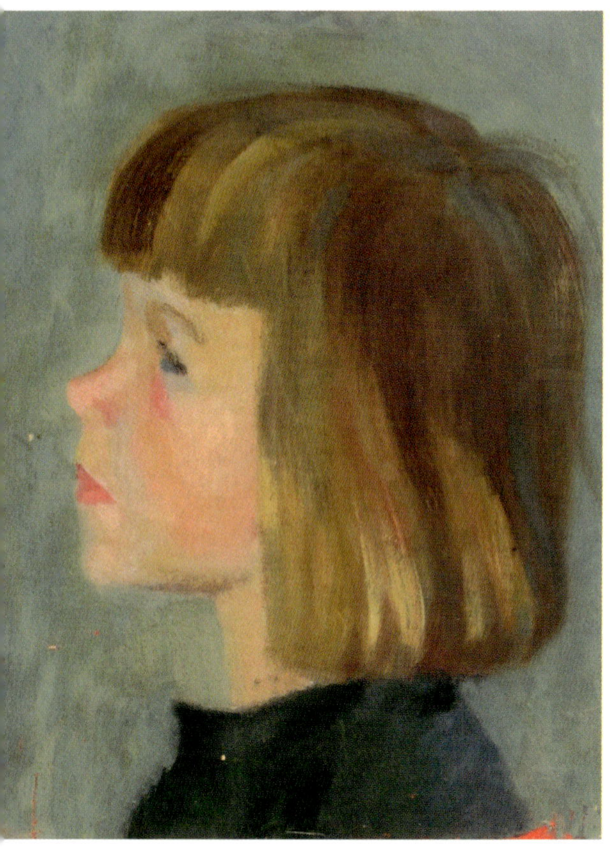

"Jane in Green in Profile," oil on Masonite, 8" x 9", ca 1955.

Mom sometimes nagged my father to do more portraits of Sal and me. It may be that these pictures are guilt pictures that he didn't have the heart to finish. Or perhaps he was just experimenting. Except for the framed one, all of these pictures were hidden in my father's studio for sixty years.

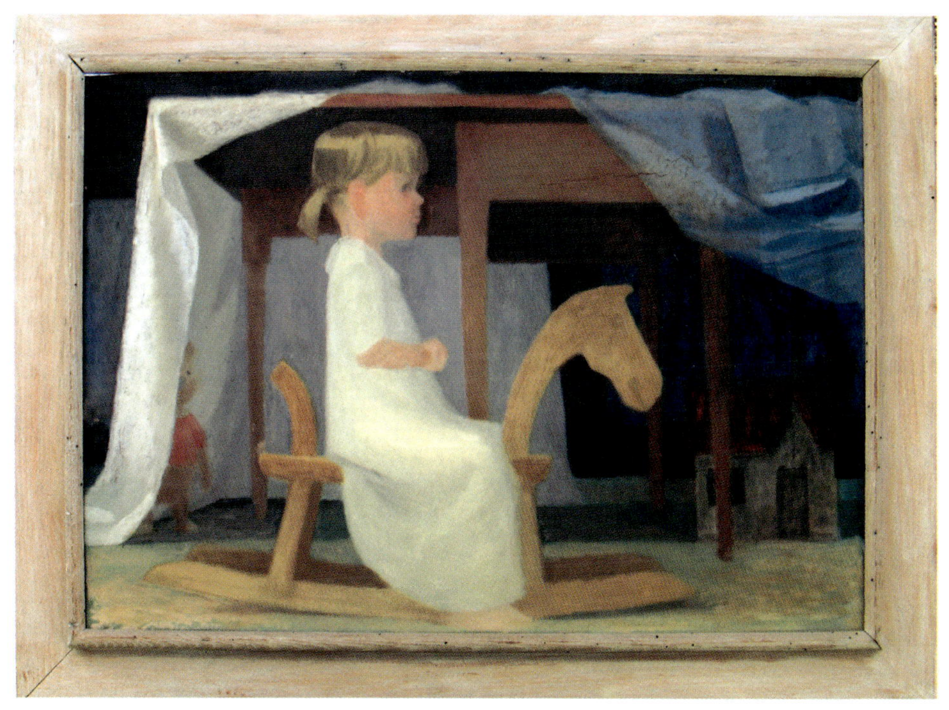

"Jane on a Rocking Horse," oil on Masonite, 22" x 32", ca 1953.

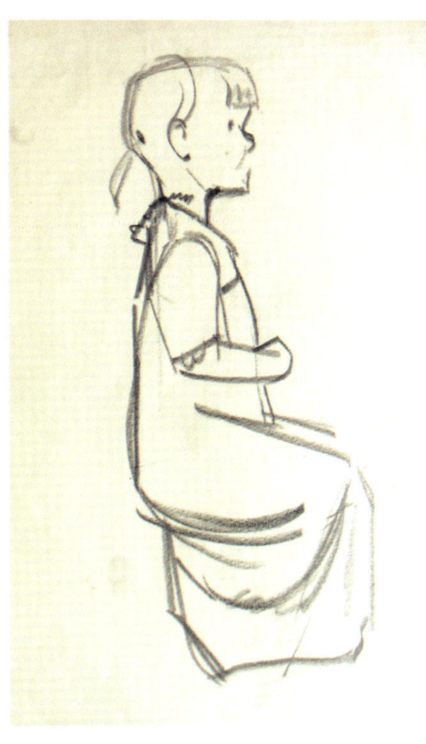

"Sketch of Jane on Rocking Horse," pencil on paper, ca 1953.

Here is a sketch and the painting of me in the living room in our home in Croton Falls, New York. We rented the house in the winter from May Massee, my father's editor at Viking Press. I was about four.

The table in the painting was the table that Mom used for sewing. The sheet may have been a way of saying that the table was a play house. Also, Bob got to demonstrate the drapery painting technique that he learned in art school. Piglet is on the left, peeking out from behind the sheet.

He was Sal's and when she outgrew him, he came to me. The rocking horse in the picture has a smile on his face, but the real horse, which my sister still has, looks serious. The doll house is imaginary, or who knows, may have been one my father remembered from his own childhood with his sisters, Dorothy and Melba.

This sequence of sketches illustrates me discovering that I am left handed. Following is a series of sketches and paintings of Sal.

"Sketch of Jane Painting Right Handed," pencil on paper, ca 1953.

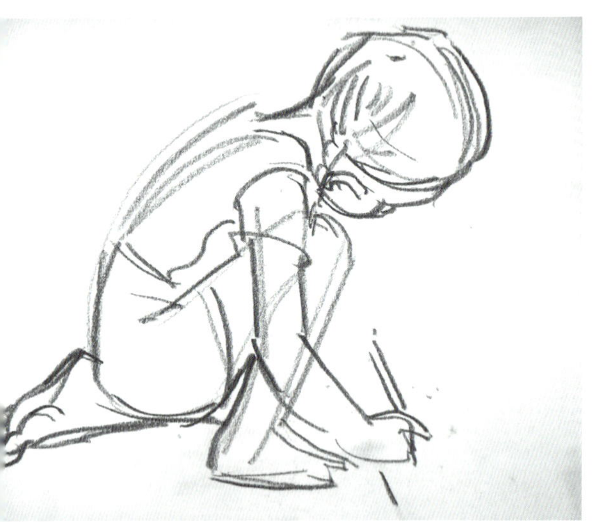

"Sketch of Jane Painting Left Handed," pencil on paper, ca 1953.

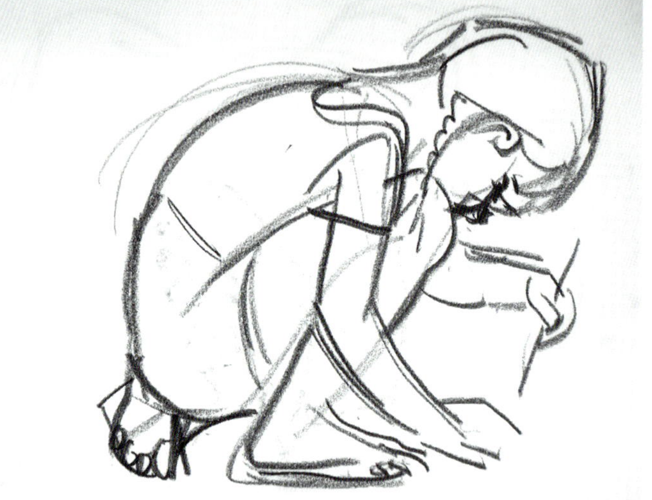

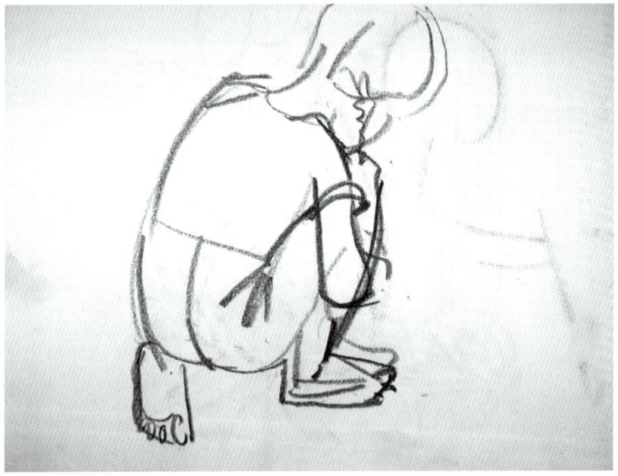

"Sketch of Jane Considering," pencil on paper, ca 1953.

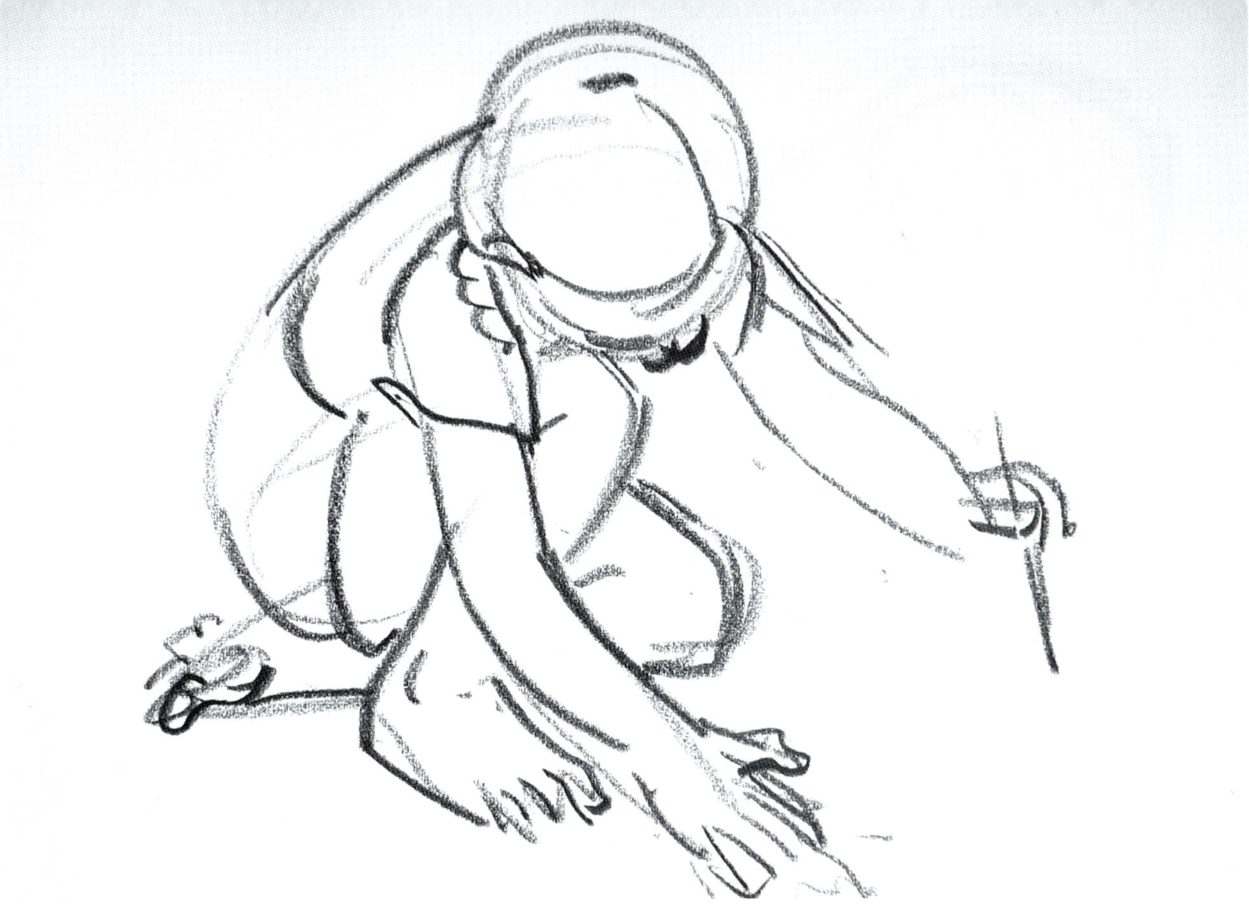

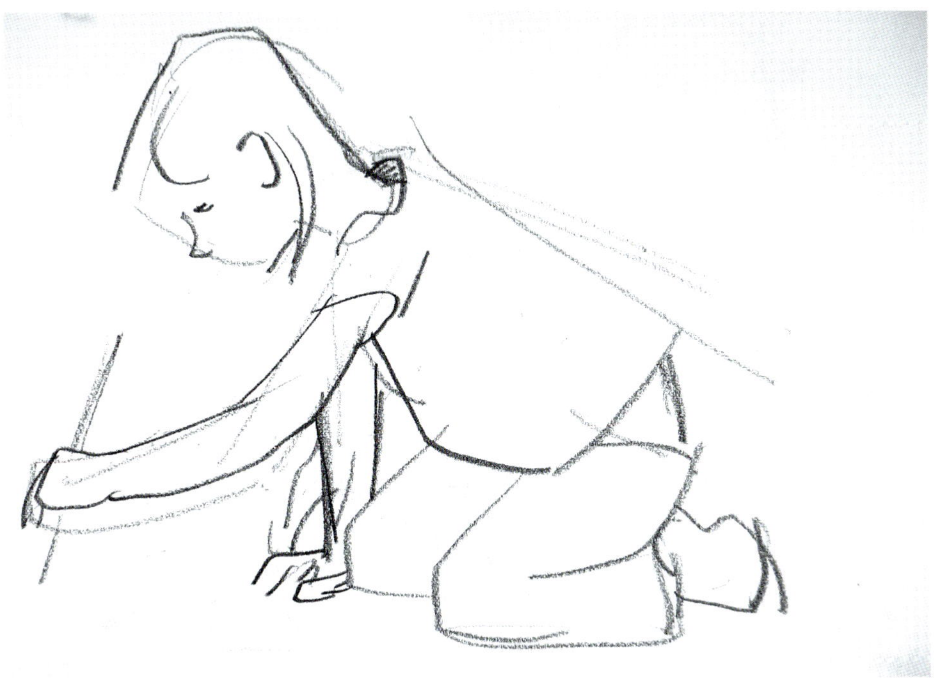

"Second Sketch of Jane Painting Left Handed," pencil on paper, ca 1953.

"Third Sketch of Jane Painting Left Handed," pencil on paper, ca 1953.

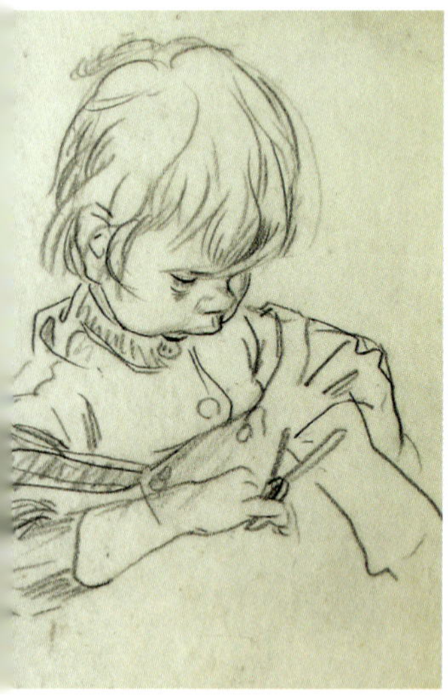

"Sketch of Sal with Scissors," pencil on paper, ca 1948.

"Sketch of Sal, Pensive," pencil on paper, ca 1950.

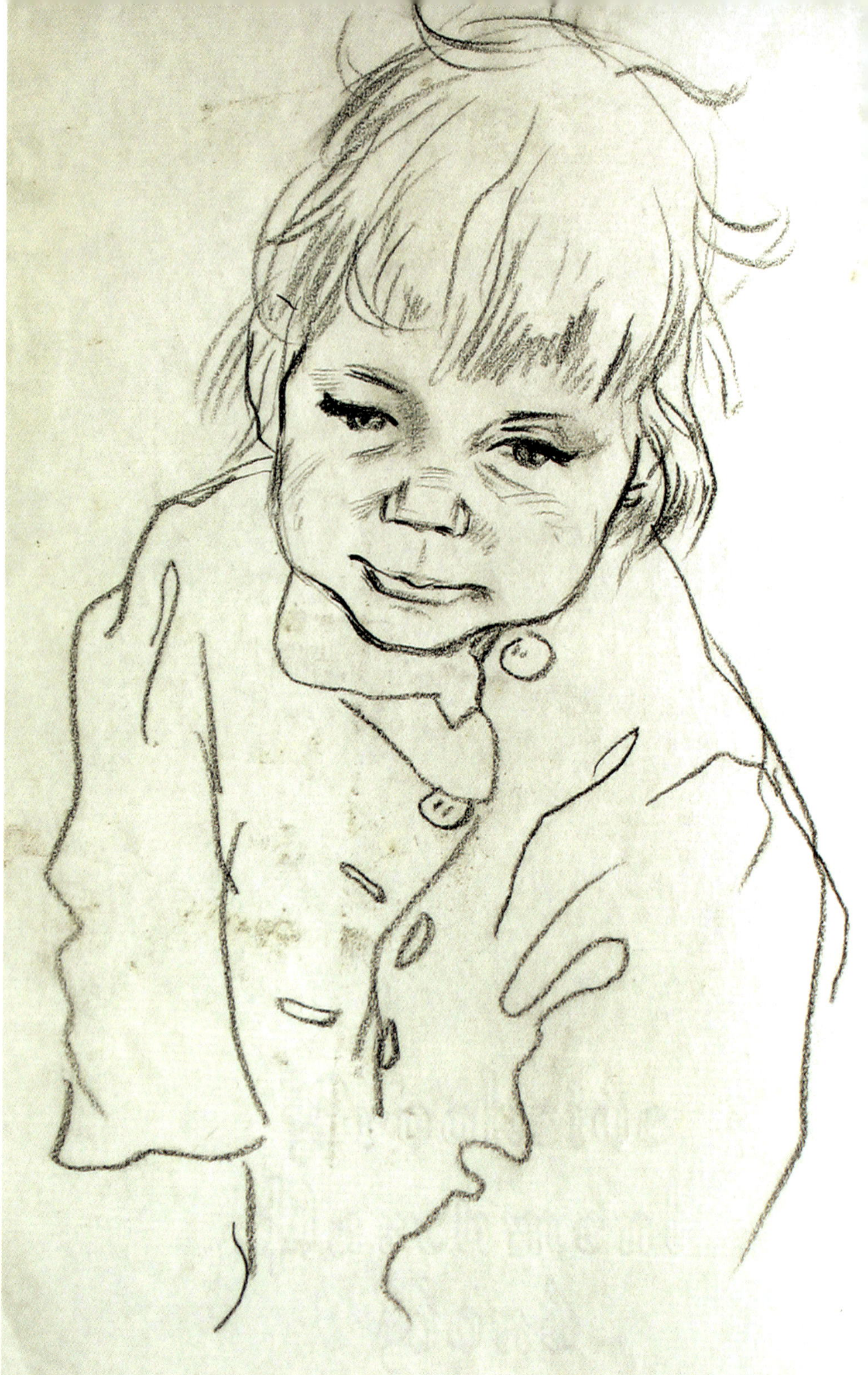

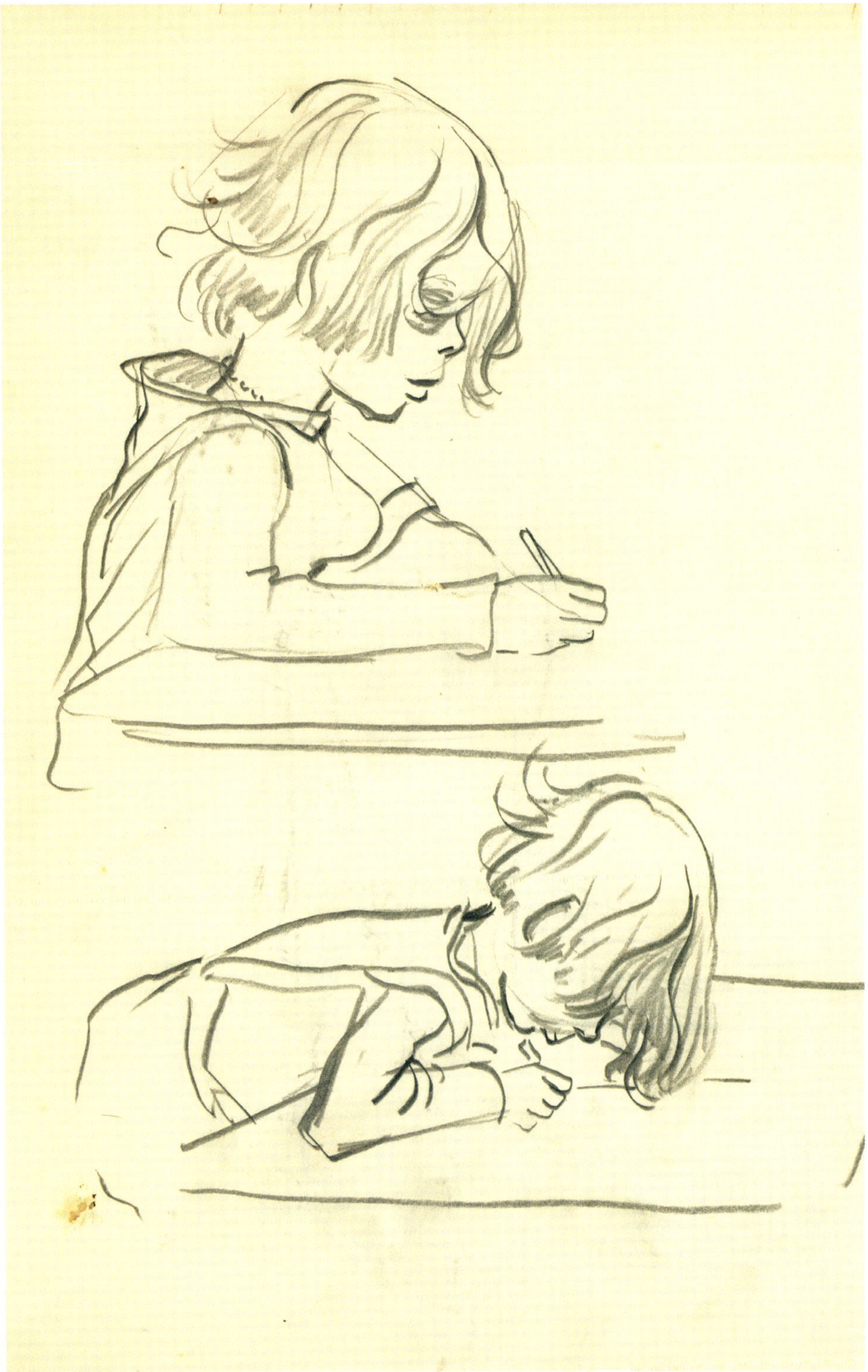

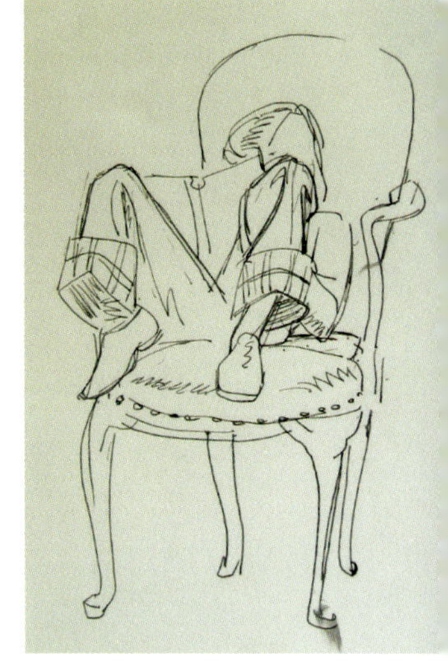

"Sketch of Sal Drawing," pencil on paper, ca 1952. Courtesy of May Massee Collection, Emporia State University.

"Sketch of Sal Reading in Chair," ink on paper, ca 1954.

"Sal in Red," oil on canvas board, 16" x 12", ca 1953.

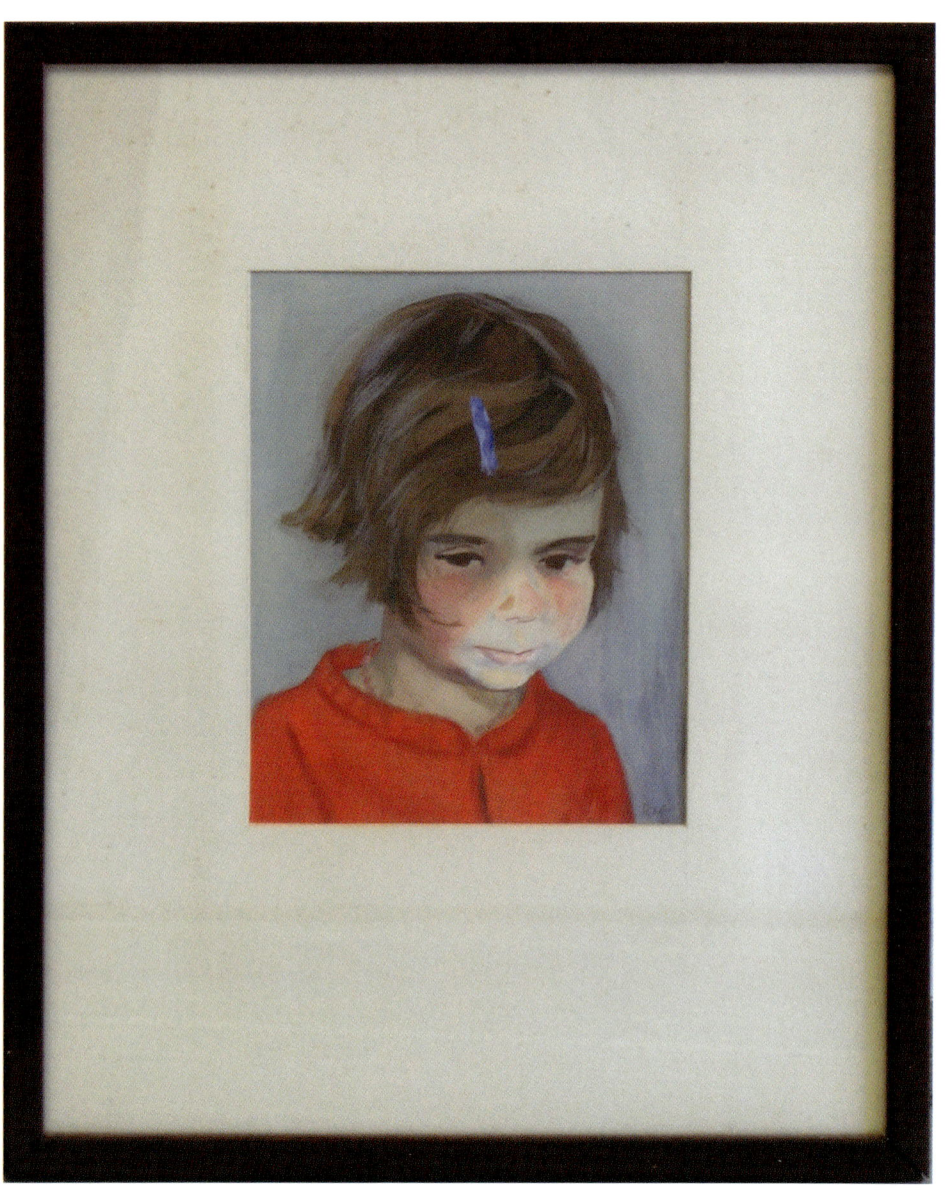

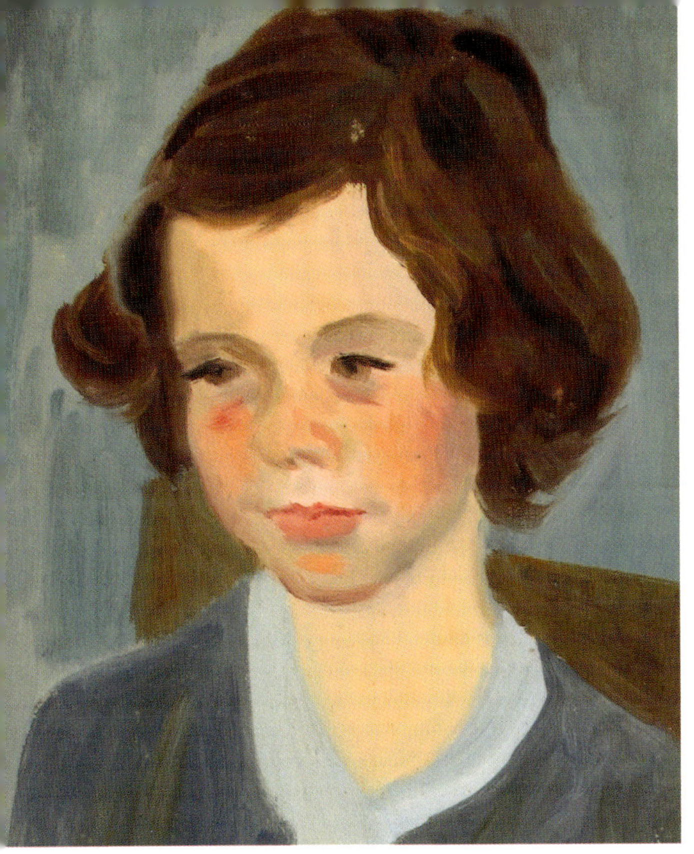

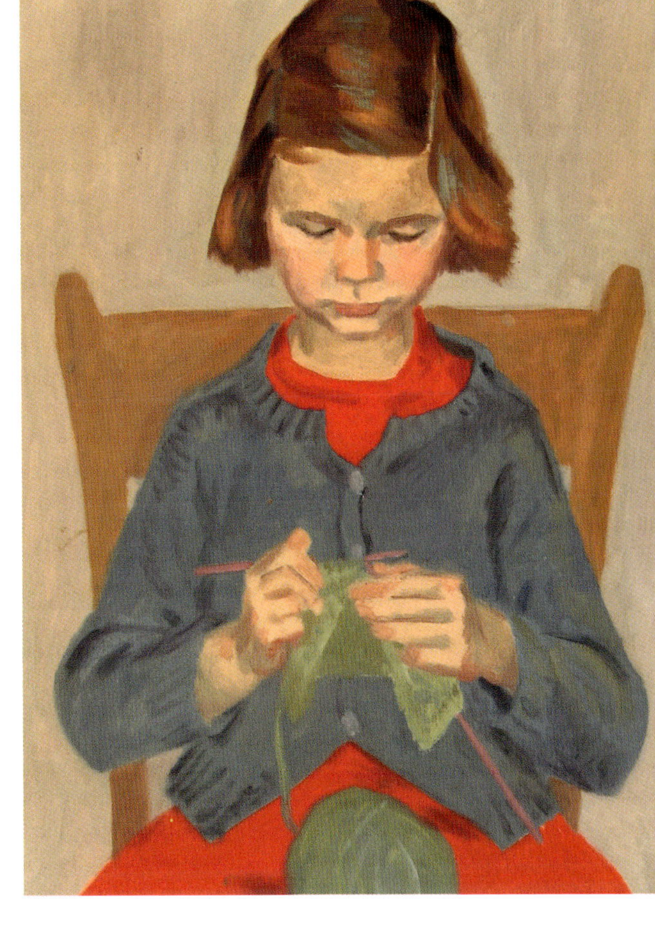

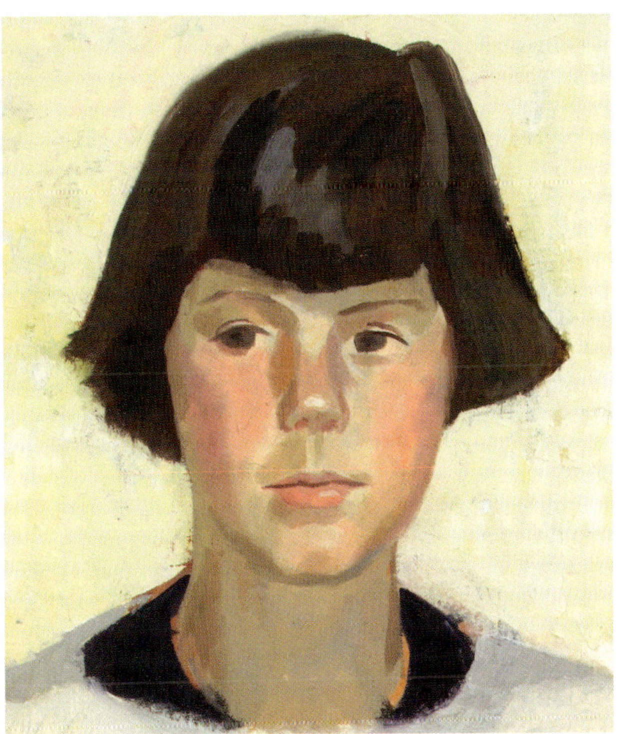

"Sal in Blue," oil on canvas board, 12" x 9", ca 1954.

"Sal in Red and Grey," oil on Masonite, 10" x 8", ca 1953.

"Sal Knitting," oil on Masonite, 20" x 16", ca 1954.

"Sal in Blue and White,
oil on Masonite,"
14" x 10", ca 1956.

"Jane in Pink and Blue,"
oil on canvas board,
14" x 10", ca 1960.

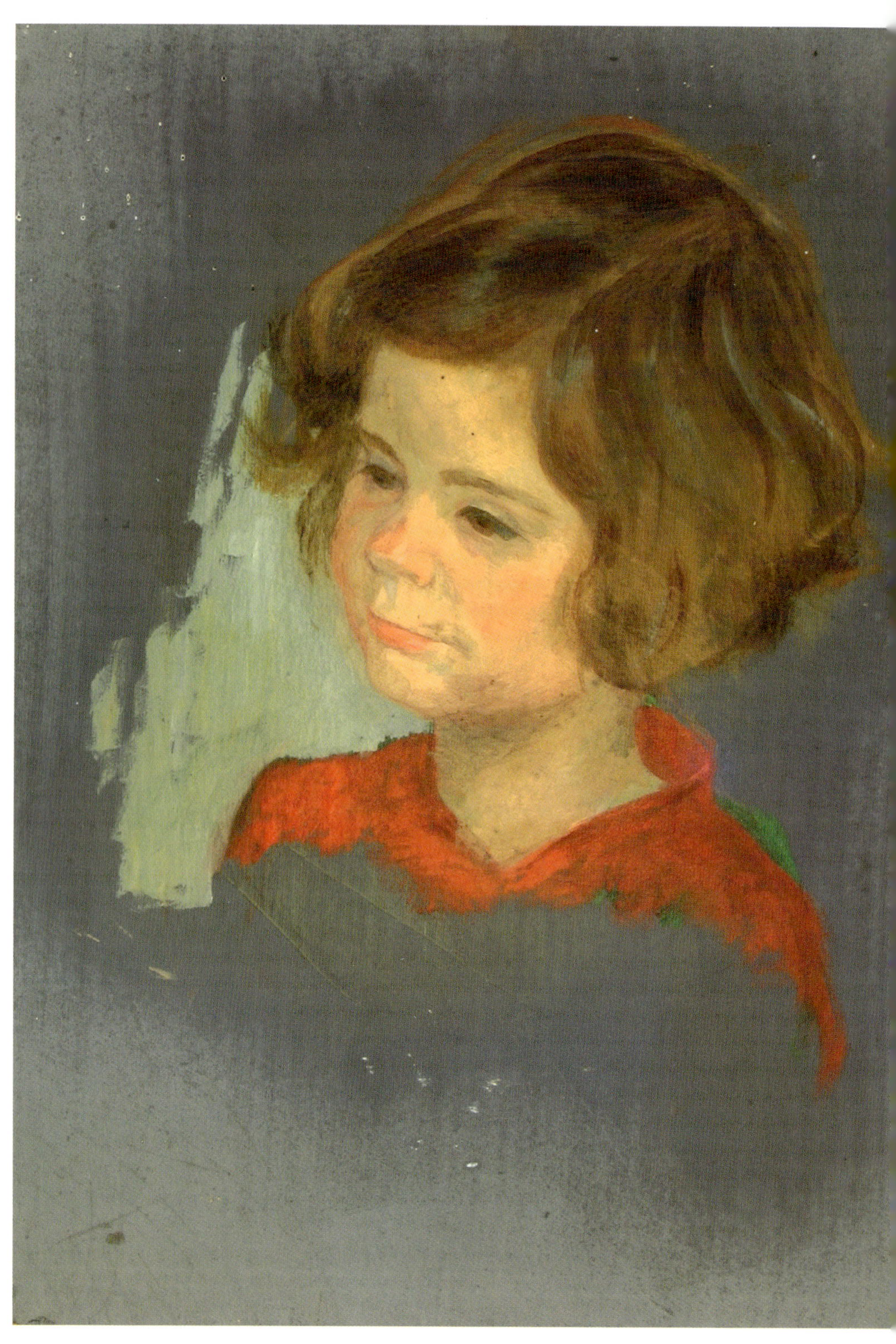

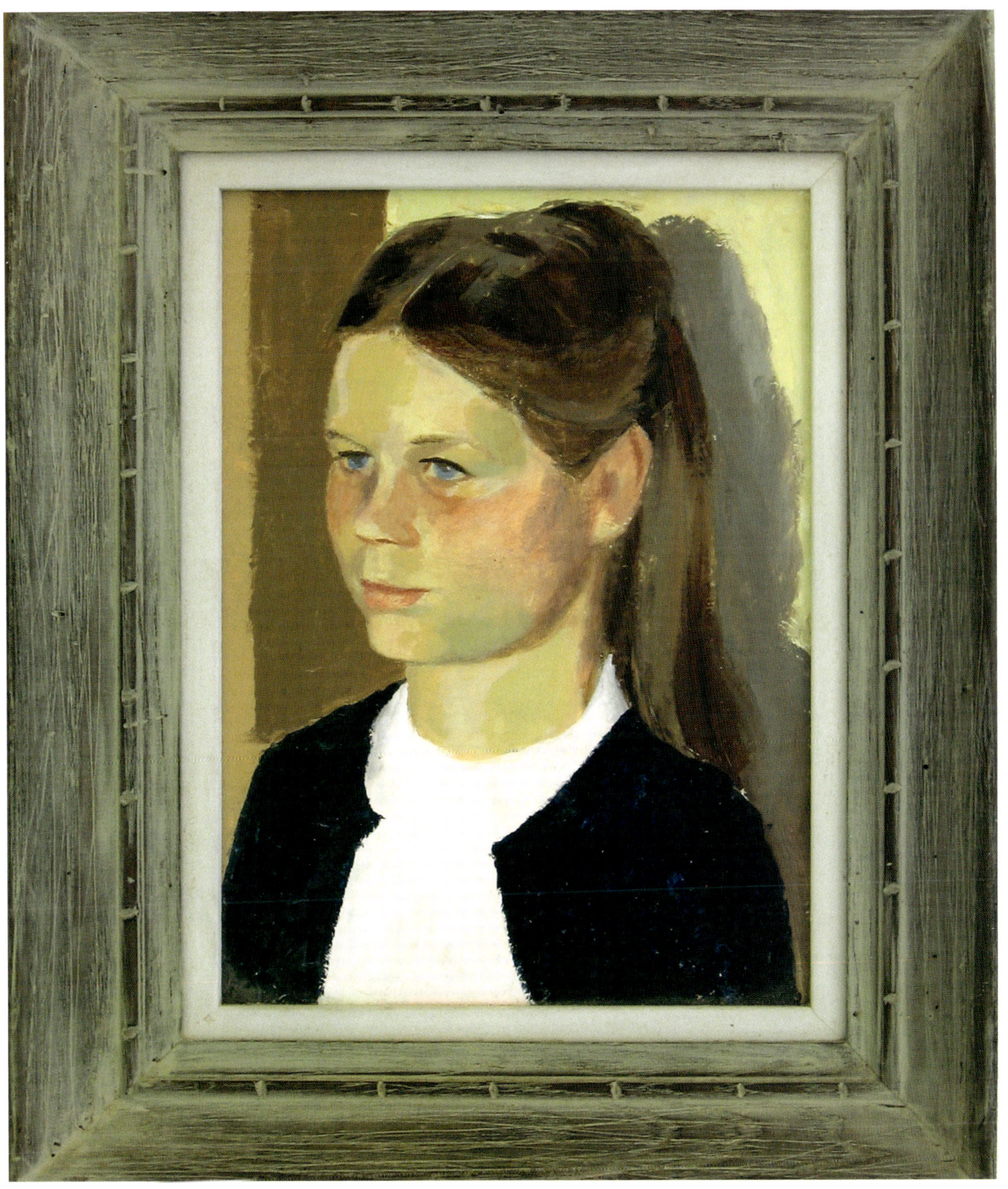

This picture of me in blue and pink is the last portrait Bob did of Sal and me. He did a number of paintings of Sal and me playing.

"Sal and Jane Painting," oil on canvas board, 16" x 12", ca 1954.

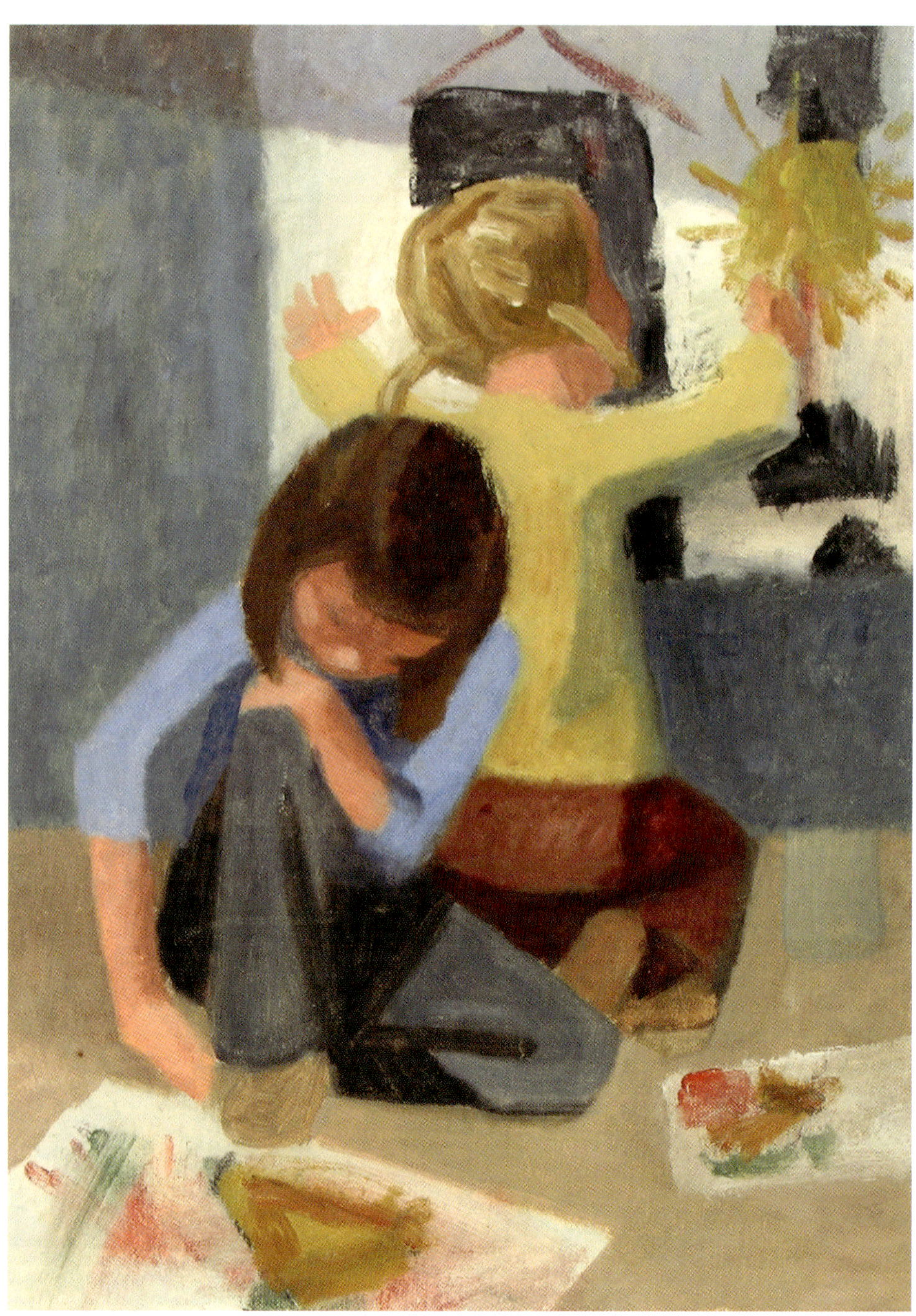

"Sal and Jane on the Beach," oil on Masonite, 24" x 28", ca 1954.

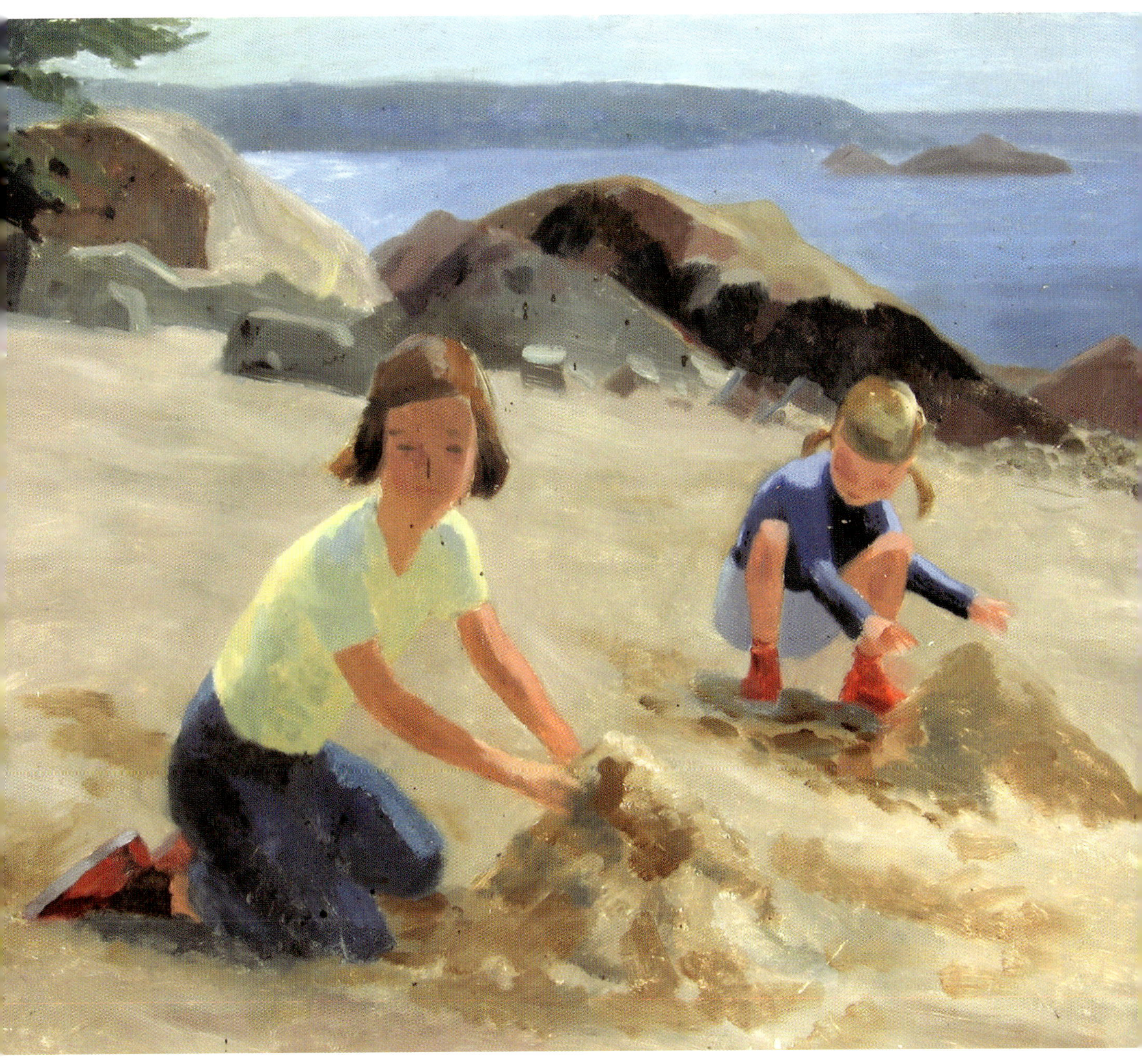

In the chapter on Maine, there were several pictures of Sheep Island. In this painting, Bob has greatly reduced Sheep Island to the size of a large ledge, and brought it closer to our island.

"Sal and Jane with Tinker Toys and Blocks," oil on Masonite, 18" x 30", ca 1954.

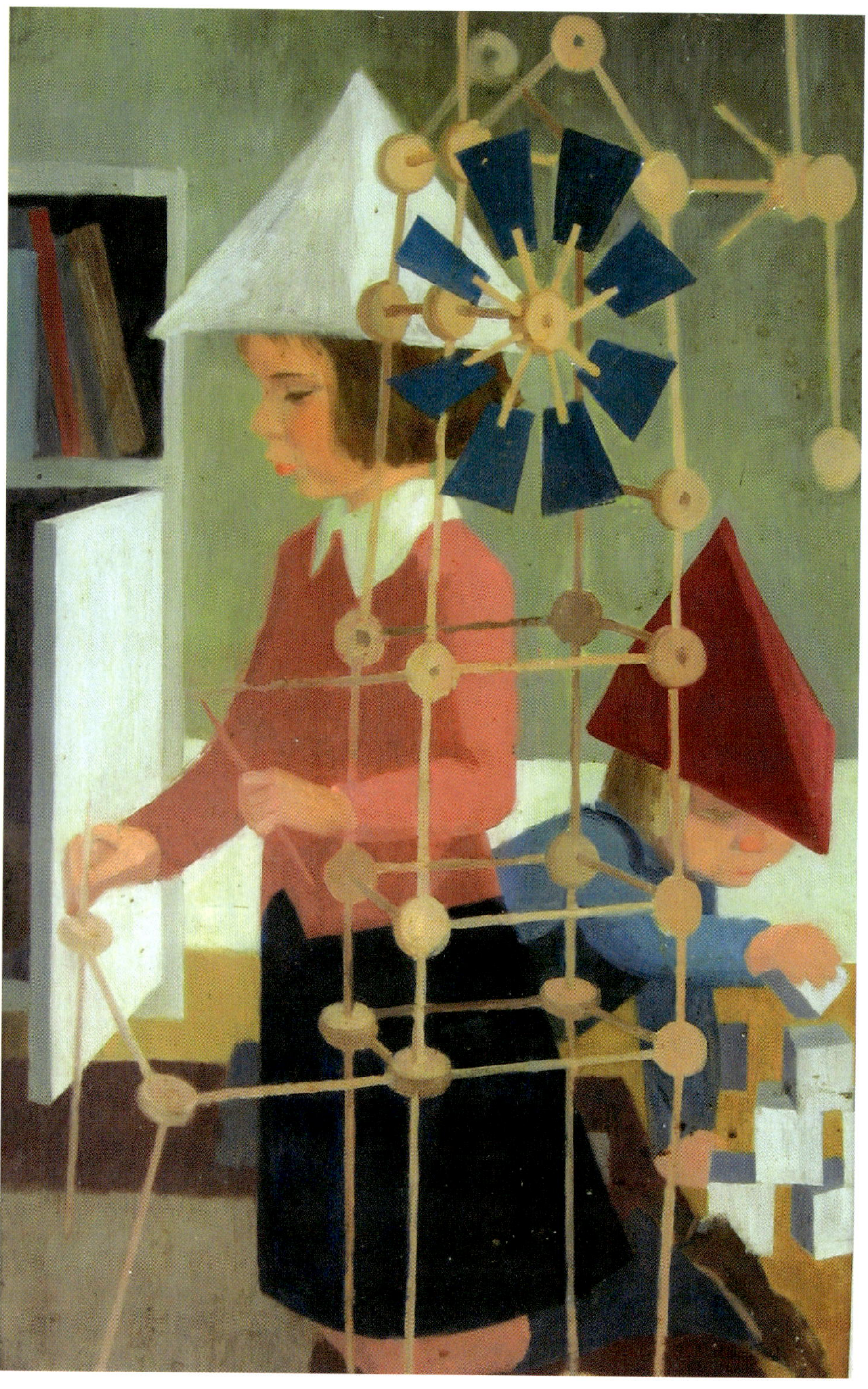

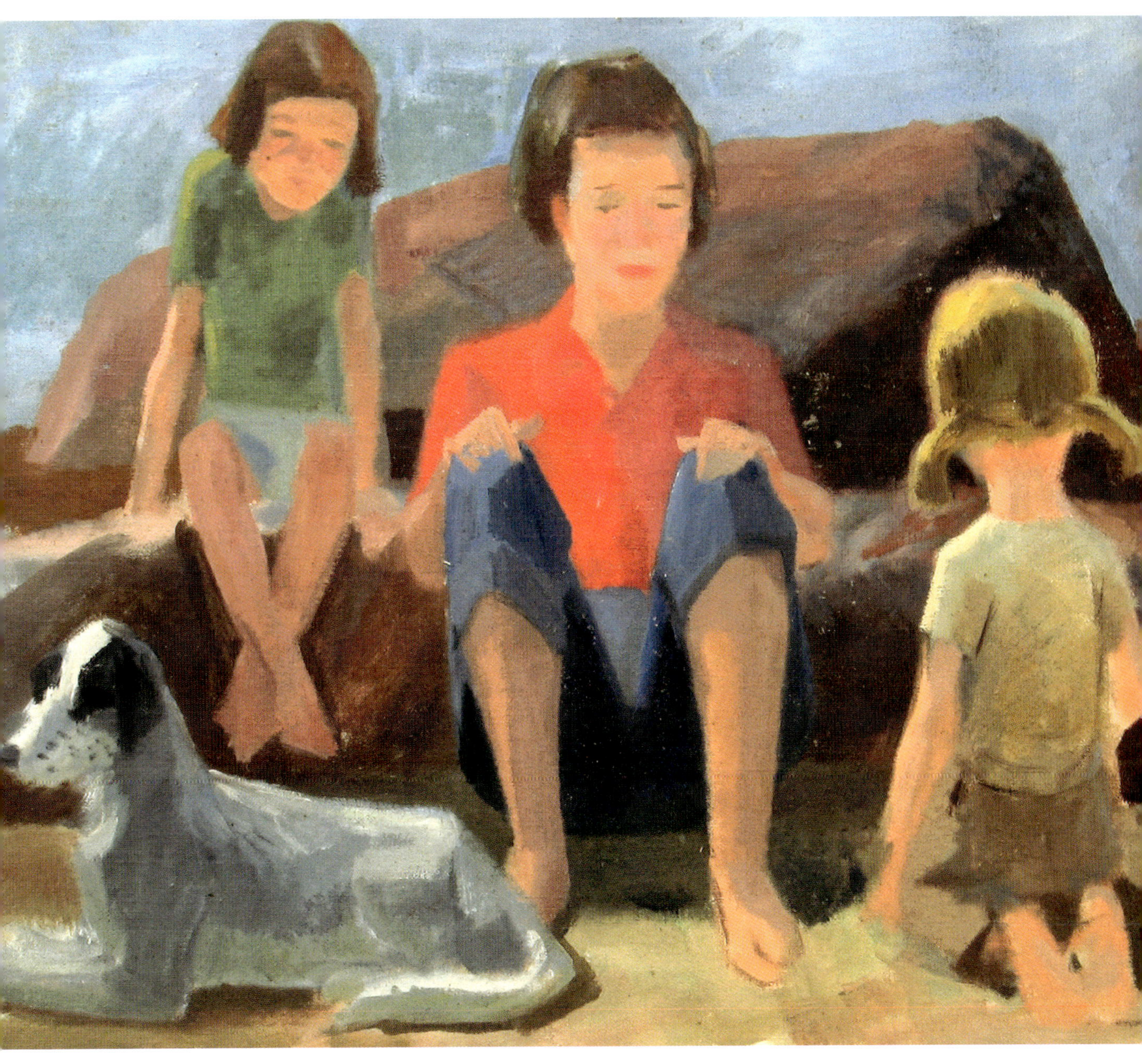

This is the last portrait my father did of our family.

"Mom, Sal, Jane and Penny on the Beach," oil on Masonite, 16" x 20", 1950s.

Mom took guitar lessons in Taxco, Mexico, in 1959, and Bob made a number of sketches of her.

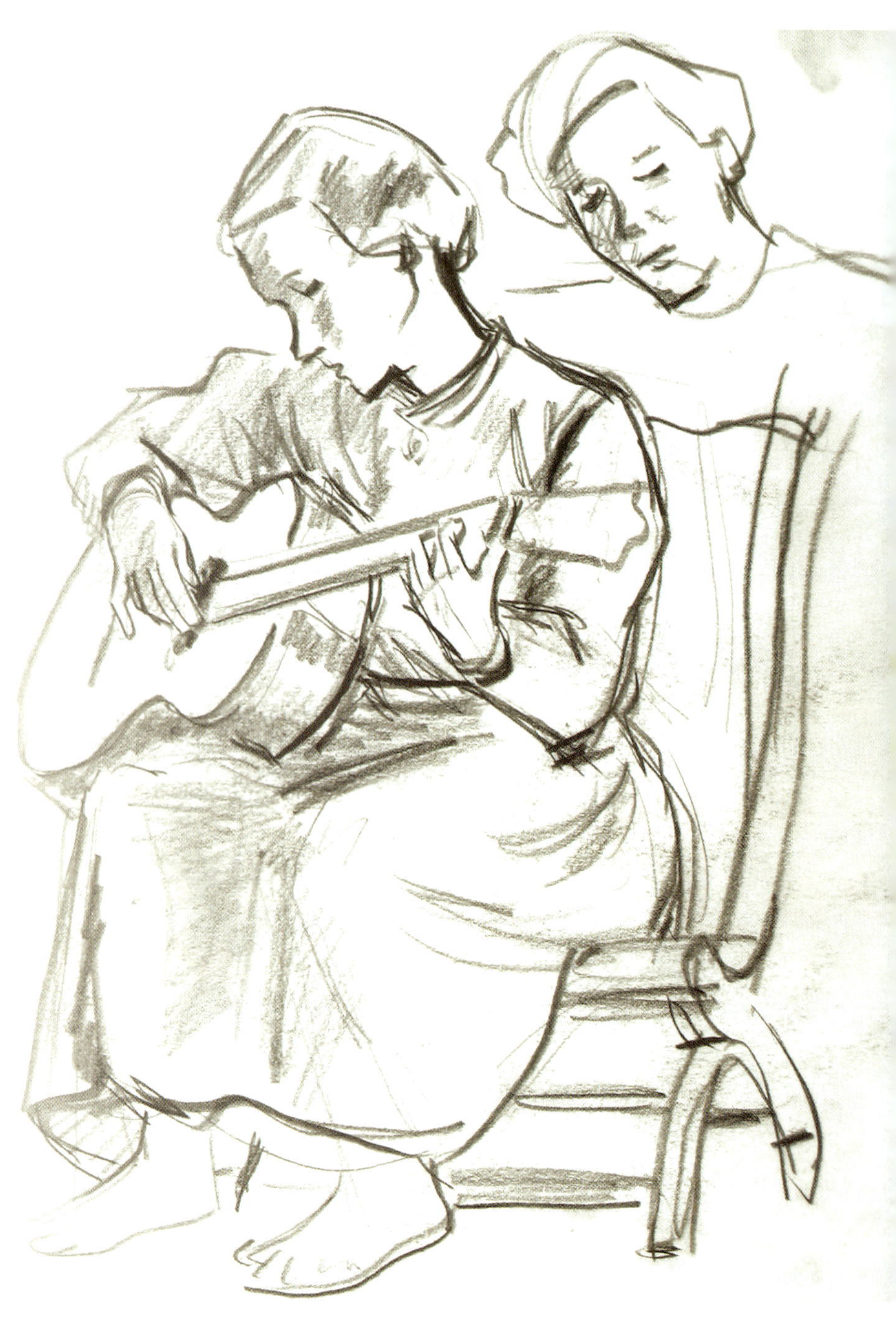

"Sketch of Mom with Guitar," pencil on paper, 1959.

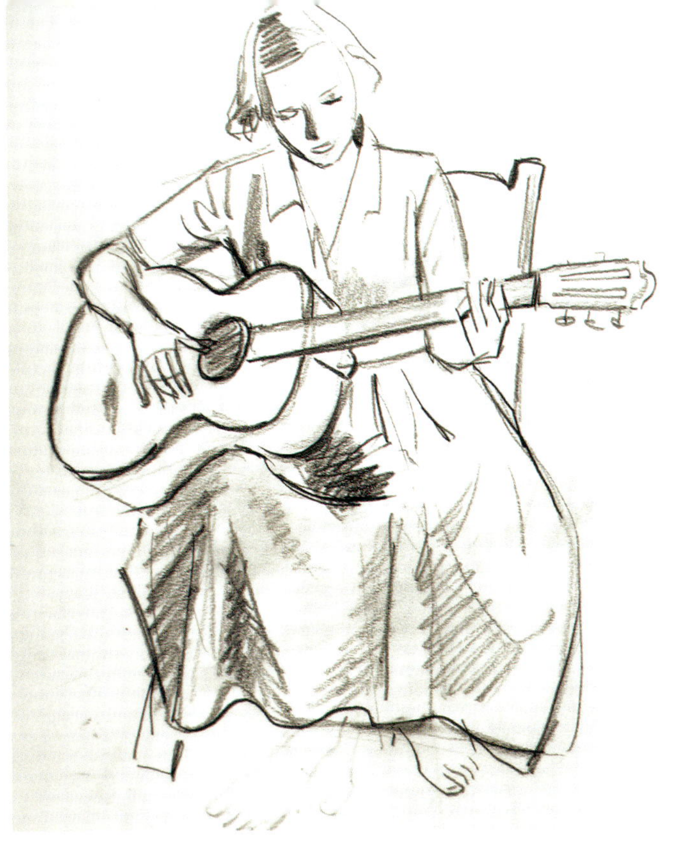

"Sketch of Mom with Guitar II," pencil on paper, 1959.

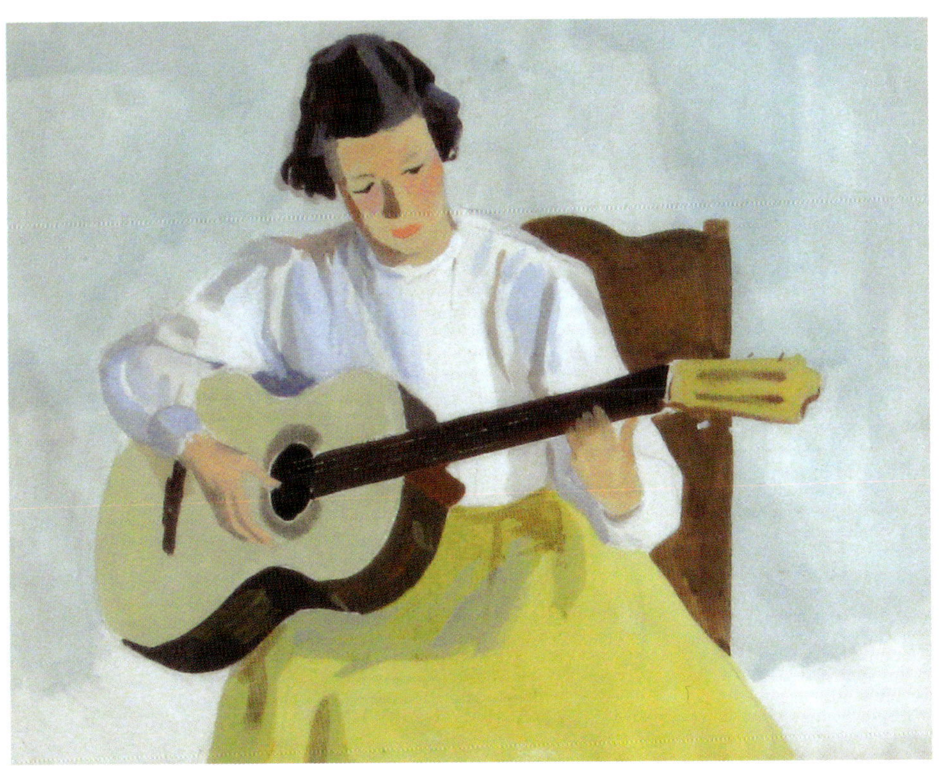

"Mom Playing the Guitar," from sketches done in 1959, acrylic on paper, 11" x 14", 1980s.

New York 5

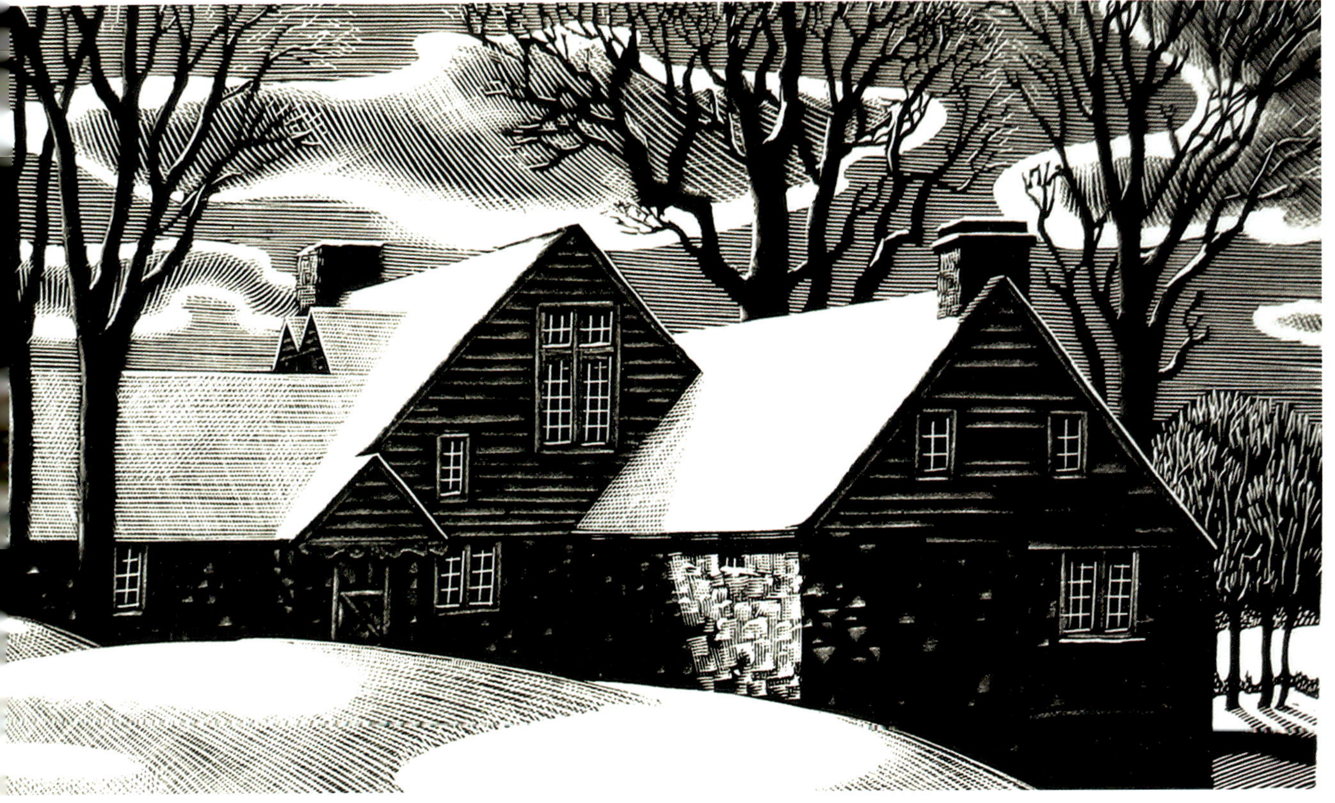

"Winter Home," linoleum cut, 4" x 6", 1950s.

My father did not make many pictures that are clearly from New York. This is one of several lineoleum cut cards he sent to May Massee, his long-time editor, friend, and mentor at Viking Press. I thought it was a picture of her summer home, where our family stayed in the winter. But my sister Sal thinks it was the home of Morton Schindel, in nearby Weston, Connecticut. Looking at it again, the house does not look quite like our New York home, so maybe Sal is right.

Anyway, May wrote to thank him, using one of the note cards, which he saved. Otherwise, we would never have known he did the picture.

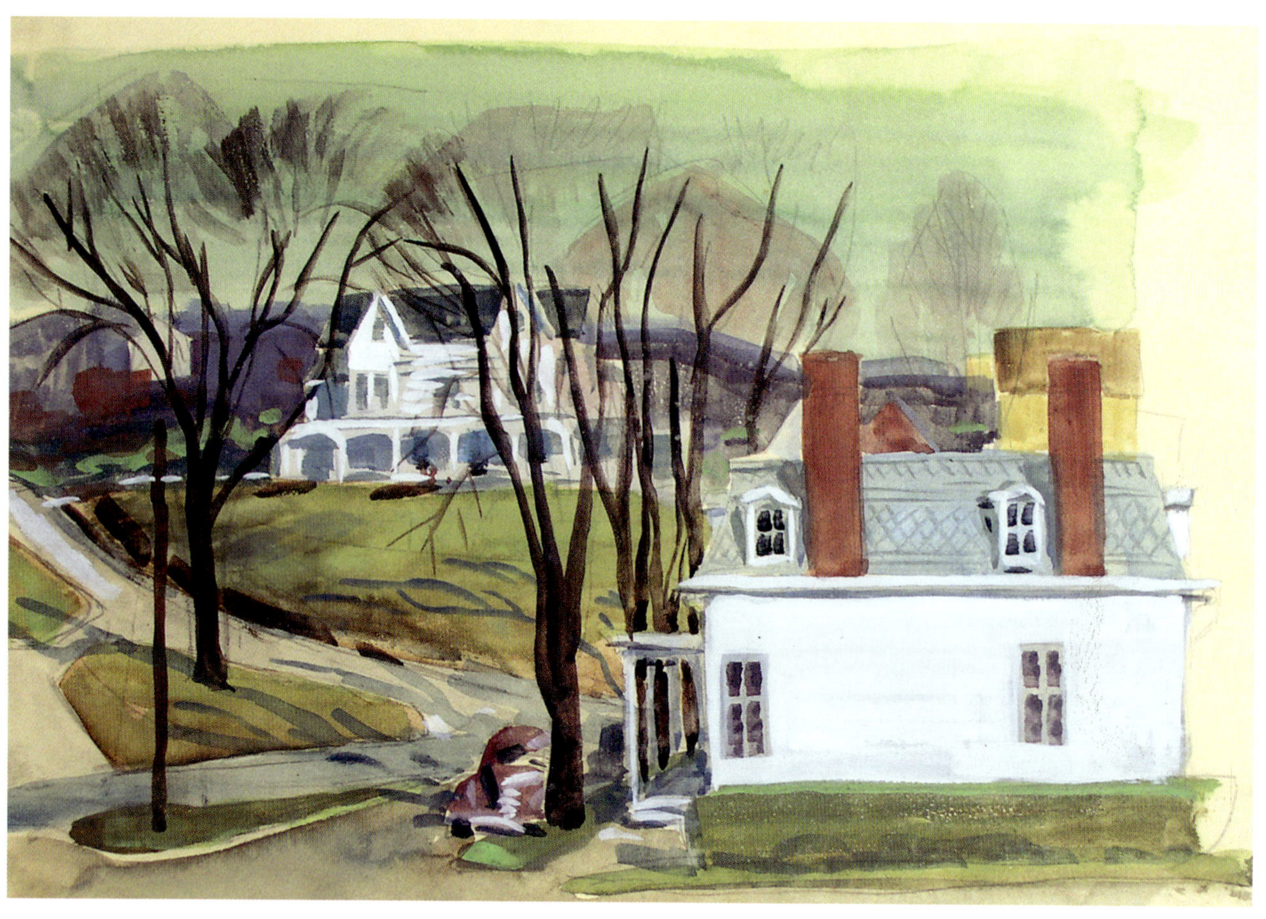

"Croton Falls Village," watercolor on paper, 7" x 11", 1950s.

I think the painting above is of Sal's and my nursery school, run by Mrs. Taylor. Maybe Bob made this painting, or the sketch for this painting, while waiting to pick Sal and me up at school.

I believe Bob did the facing painting in New York in the 1950s. My parents bought some land behind a dairy farm. The pastures were slightly hilly and dotted with trees and stone walls, though I don't remember the stone wall enclosure shown here. We had a right of way through the cow pastures, but there was no road. When we visited our land, sometimes with a picnic, we picked our way among the cow patties. My parents thought of building a house there, and even worked with an architect on the design, but the estimated cost was too high, so they gave up the idea.

While we were in New York, Bob illustrated a number of books, including *The Man Who Lost his Head, Yankee Doodle's Cousins, Journey Cake, Ho!* and the *Henry Reed* series.

On the next pages are sketches and illustrations for *The Man Who Lost His Head,* which Bob probably did at the Central Park Zoo in New York City.

"Cows in Field," oil on Masonite, 12" x 16", 1950s.

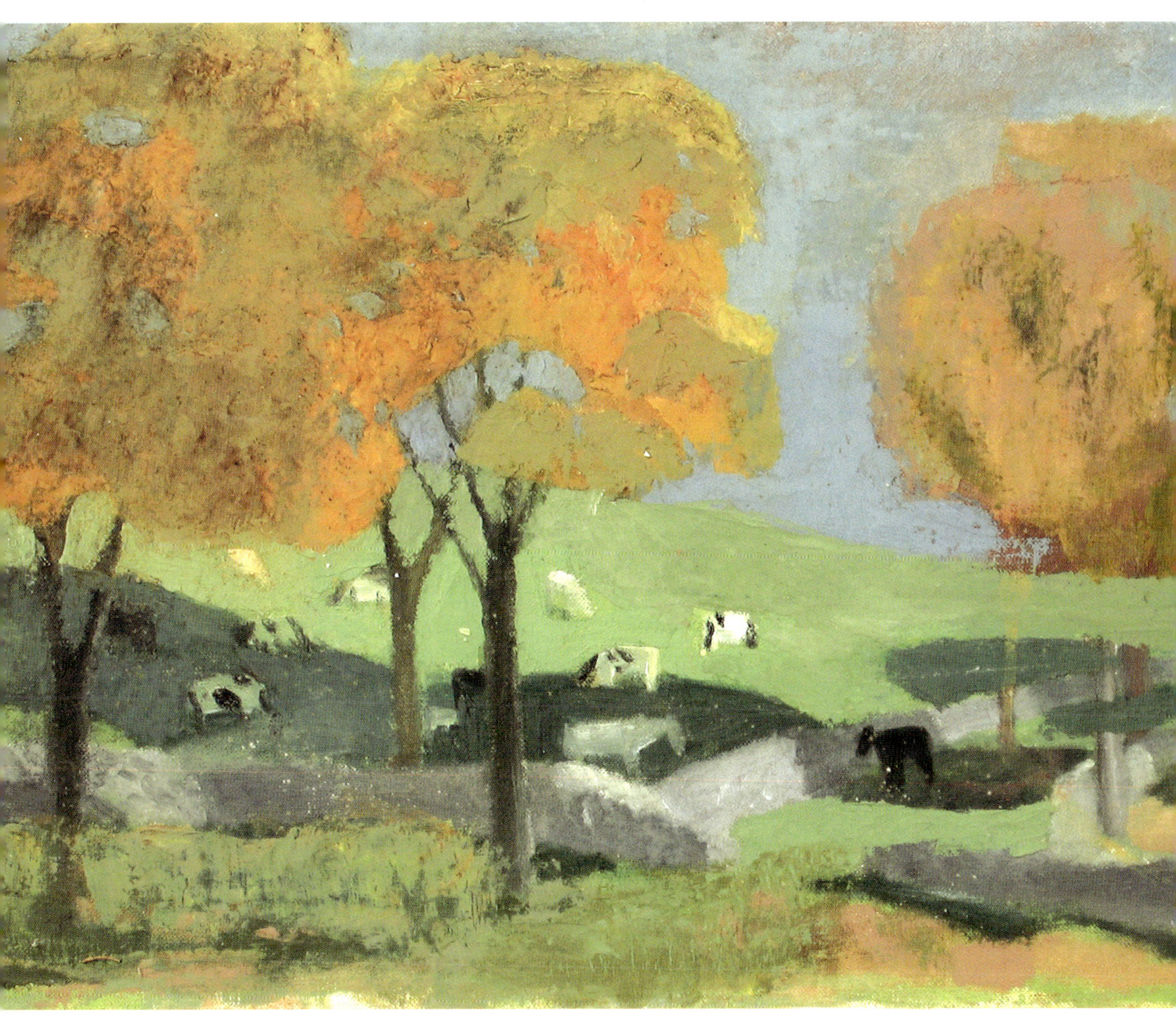

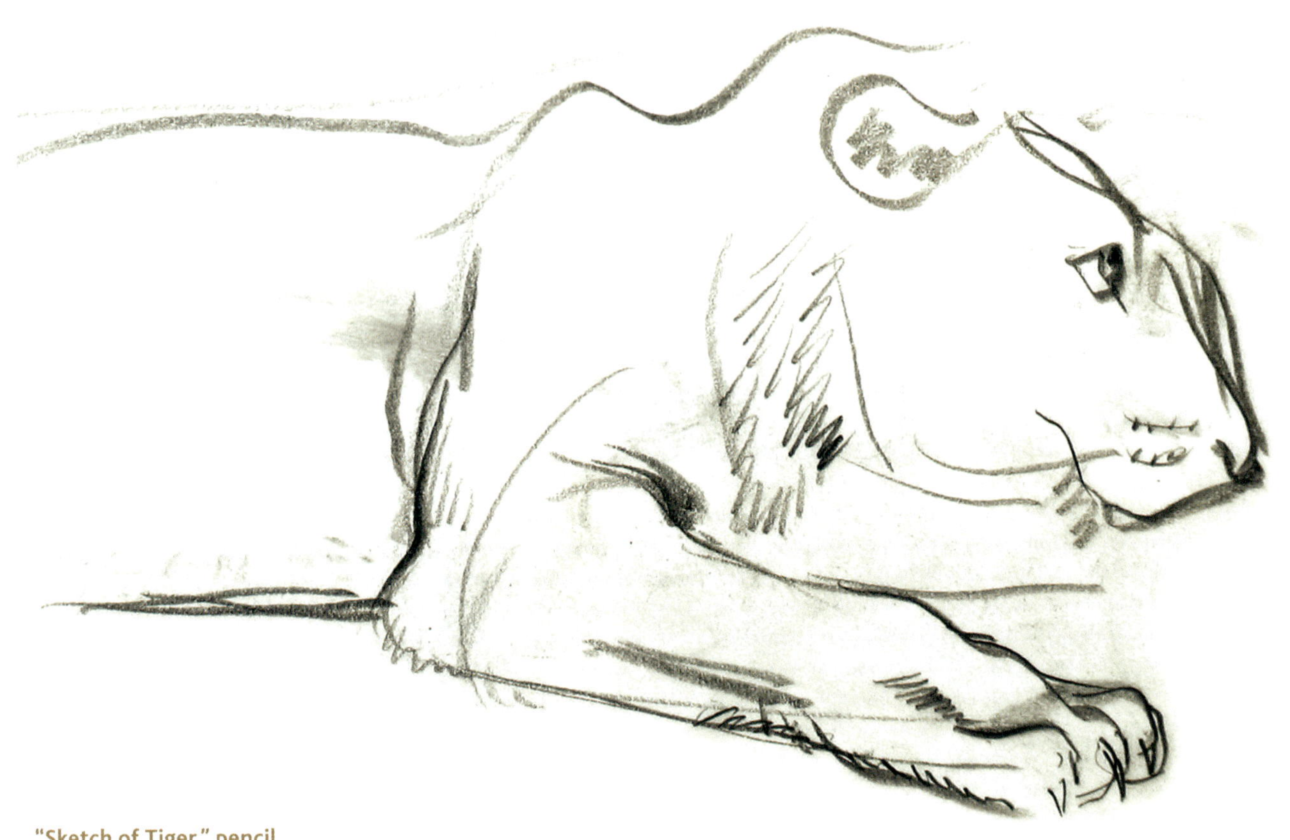

"Sketch of Tiger," pencil on paper, ca 1941.

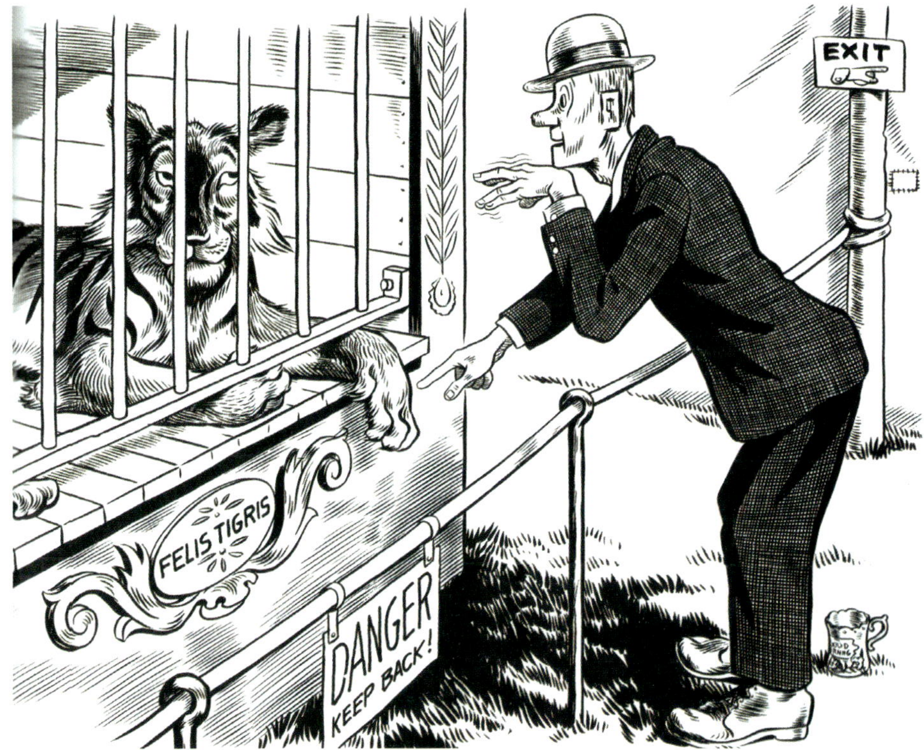

The Man who Lost His Head, by Claire Bishop, illustrated by Robert McCloskey, Viking Press, 1942.

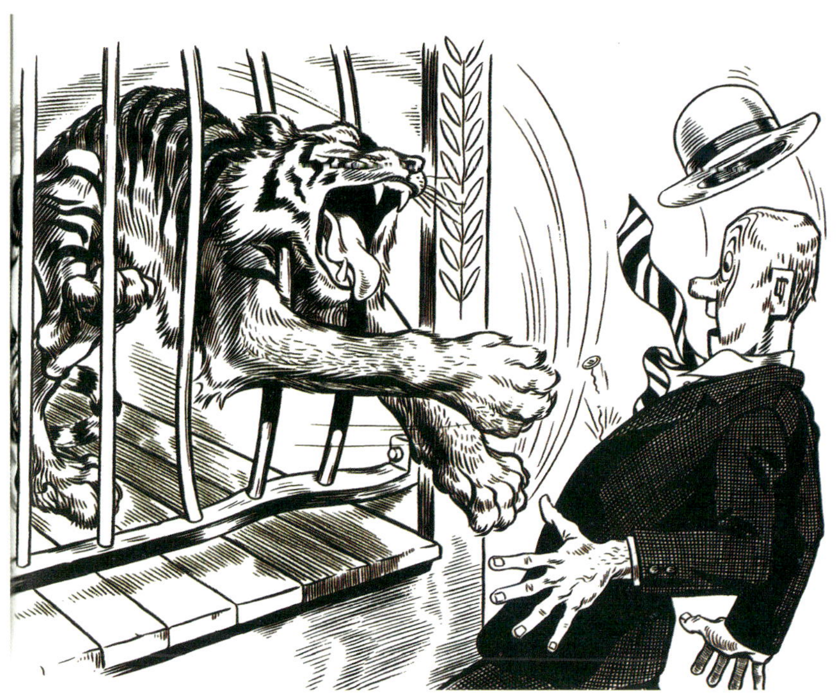

The Man who Lost His Head by Claire Bishop, illustrated by Robert McCloskey, Viking Press, 1942.

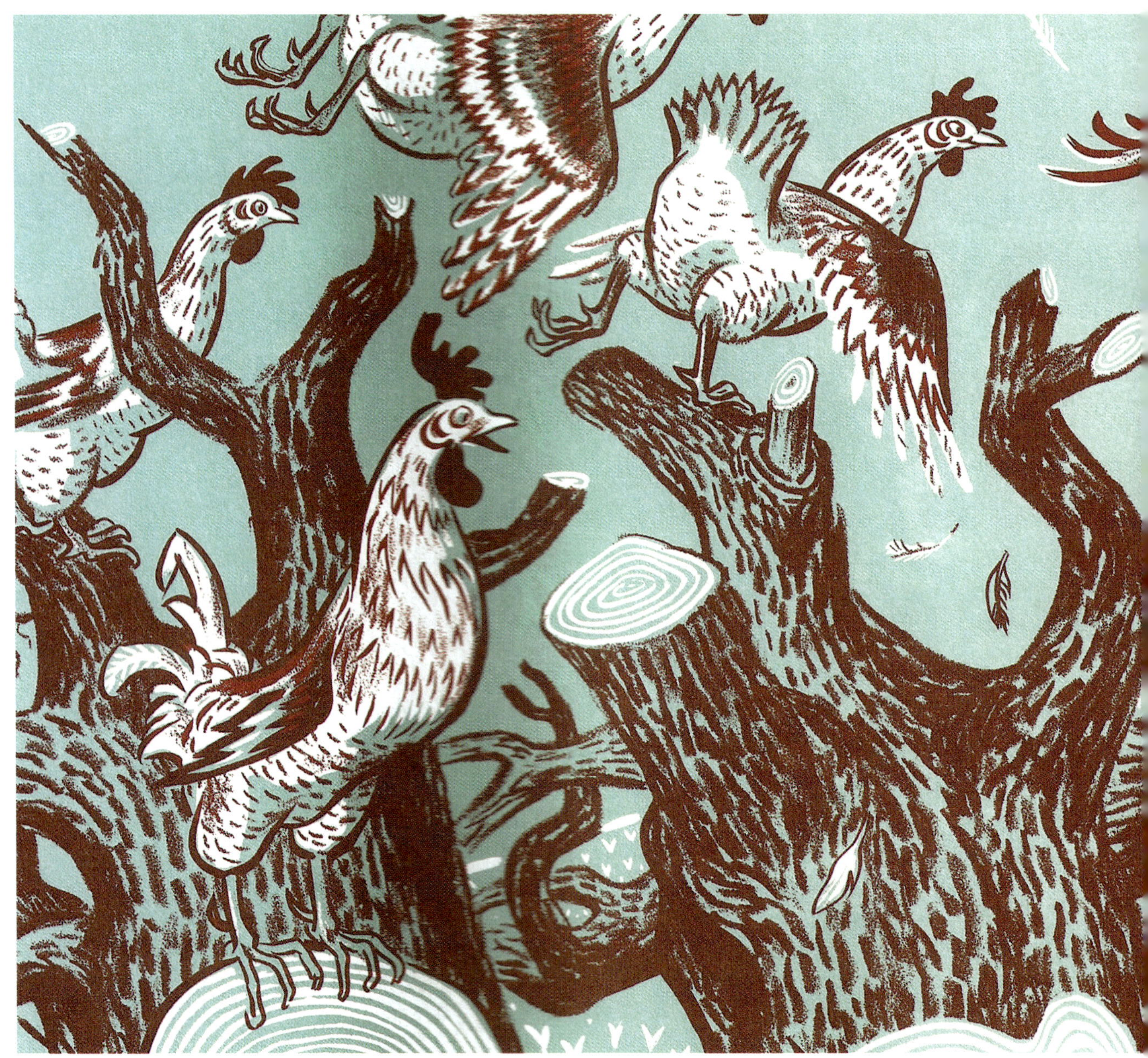

In 1953, my mother's mother, Ruth Sawyer, wrote *Journey Cake, Ho!* about a boy who is forced to seek his fortune because his family can't support him. They send him on his way with a journey cake, and the results are surprising.

Journey Cake Ho! by Ruth Sawyer, illustrated by Robert McCloskey, Viking Press, 1953.

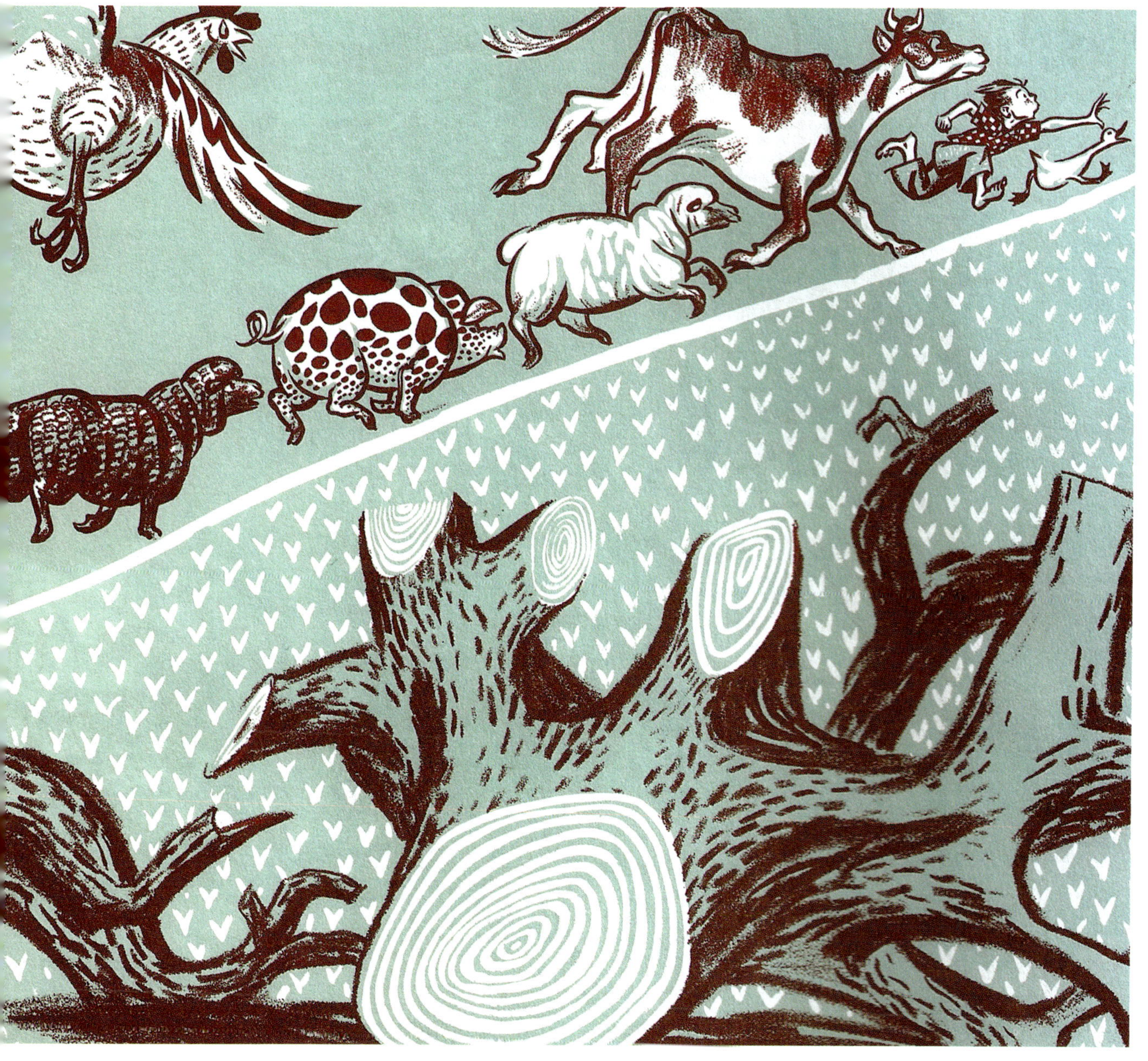

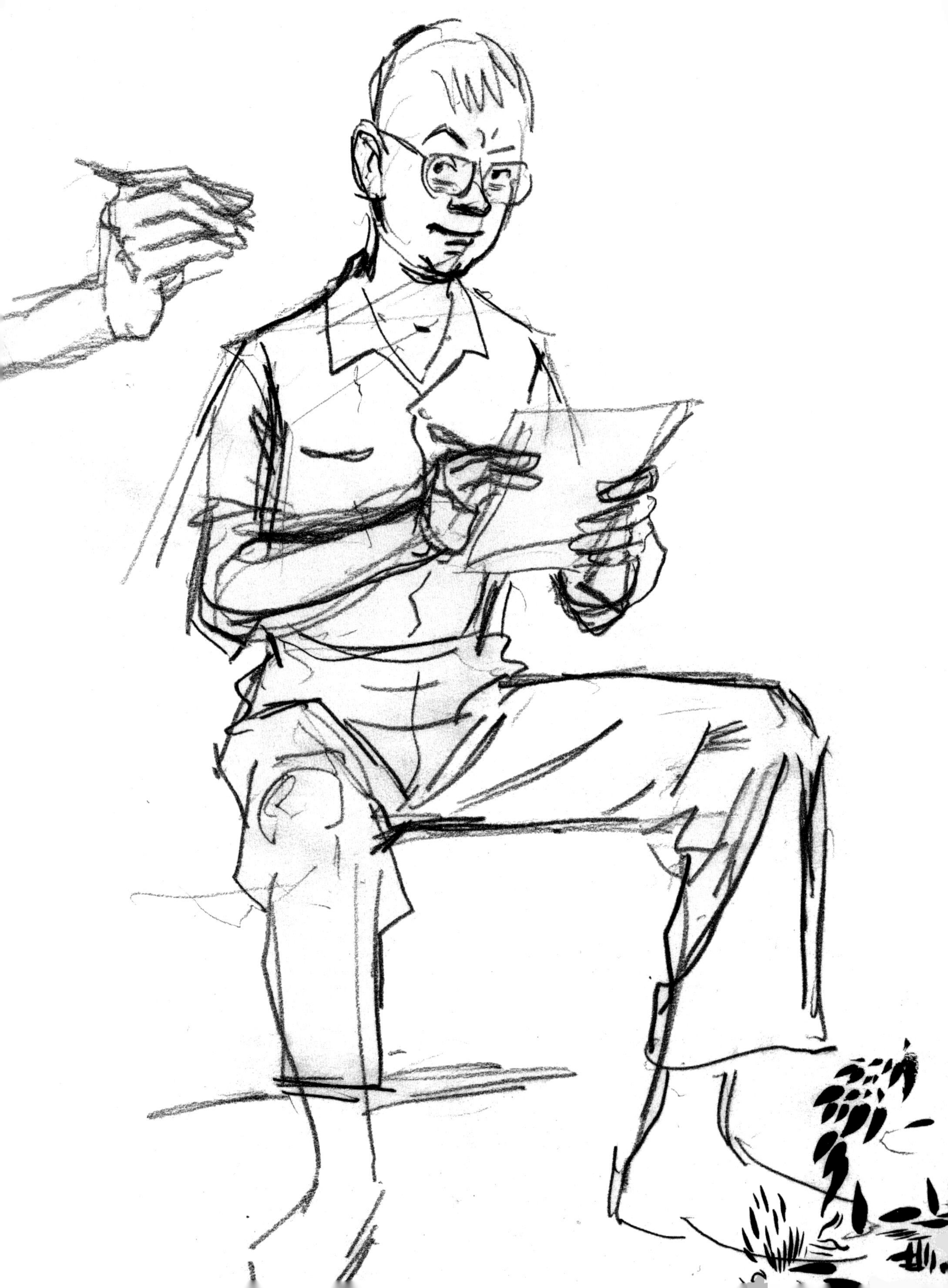

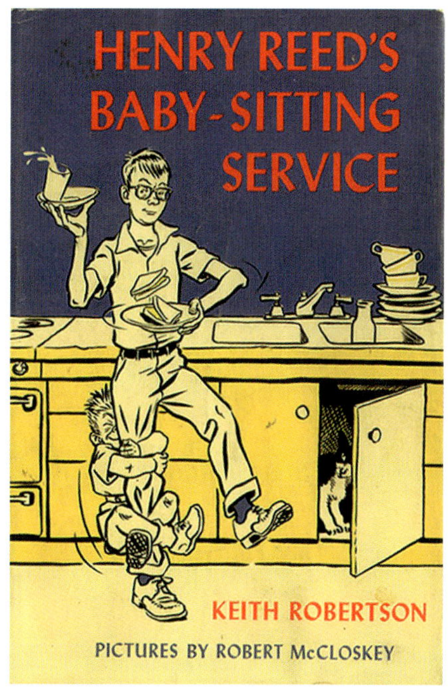

The year after my parents decided not to build the house, we moved from Croton Falls. Sal and I went to school in Switzerland for a year, while our parents traveled around Greece and Italy. The next year we moved to Bedford, New York, which was supposed to have excellent schools.

Henry Reed's Baby-Sitting Service, by Keith Robertson, illustrated by Robert McCloskey, Viking Penguin, 1966.

"Sketch for *Henry Reed,*" pencil on paper, ca 1963.

Bob did no sketches of Bedford. He wrote and illustrated *Burt Dow: Deep-Water Man* while we were there (and in Maine in the summers), but of course, the country he painted for *Burt Dow* was Maine, not New York. After he finished *Burt Dow,* he illustrated several of the Henry Reed books.

While we lived in Bedford, my mother worked as the children's librarian at the nearby Katonah Library. During her time there, the Westchester Library System planned a children's summer reading drive, and Mom persuaded Bob to make a publicity illustration for all the libraries in Westchester County. For many years, I had one of these free standing prop-up pictures, but it was eventually lost in the shuffle.

A couple of years ago, I met James Noble, and he said that he had another print of the same picture.

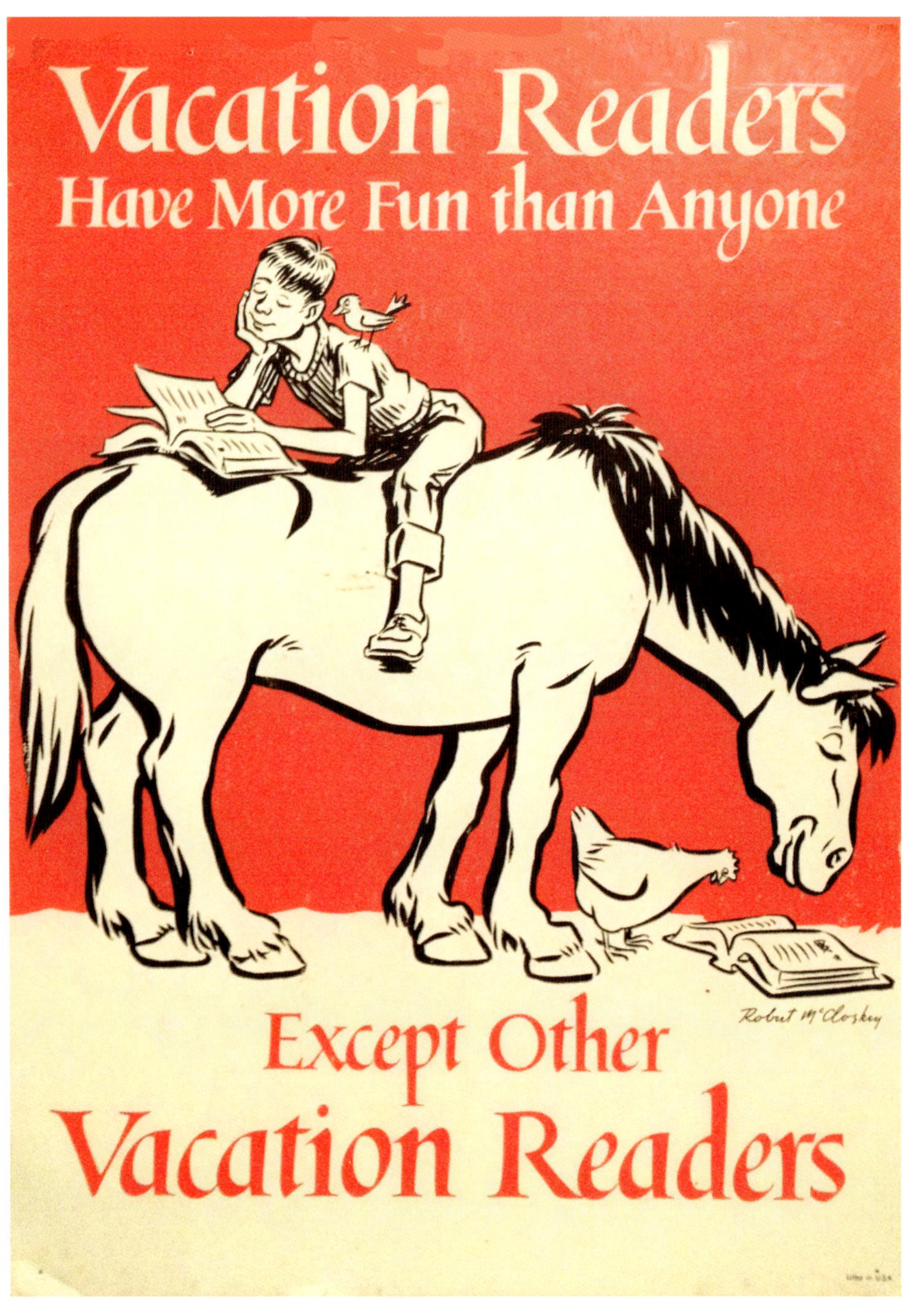

"Vacation Readers," reproduction of acrylic on cardboard, 12" x 9", ca 1963. Courtesy of James Noble.

Mexico

6

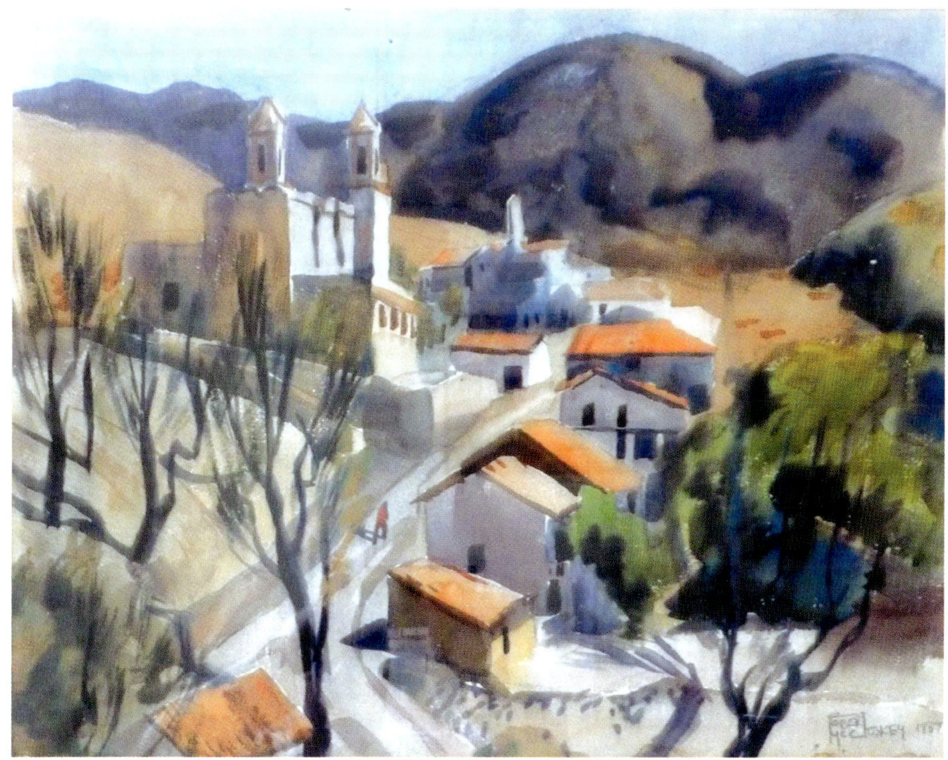

"Mexican Town" (probably Taxco,) watercolor on paper, 18.5" x 23.5", 1930s. Courtesy of the McCloskey Museum, Heritage Hall, Hamilton, Ohio. Photo by Janet Sohngen.

In 1958 and 1959, when Sal was twelve and thirteen years old, and I was nine and ten, our family spent a couple of winters in Taxco, Mexico. Bob was forty- four and forty-five years old.

Because my father was self employed, and could work wherever he was, they were not tied to a particular place, except by us children. In 1955, my parents went to Mexico, while Sal and I stayed with our neighbors, the Mortensens. In 1958, when Sal was in seventh grade and I was in the fourth grade, my parents decided that we were old enough to go to Mexico, too. We went for two months that year, and then again in 1959, for six months. We rented houses in Taxco, a town halfway between Mexico City and Acapulco.

Taxco was known as the silver capital of Mexico. In the 1700s, Jose de la Borda founded the town, and made a fortune from Taxco's silver mines. The silver languished in the twentieth century until an American artist and craftsman, William Spratling, came and set up a silver shop. Spratling trained almost all the silversmiths in Taxco, and they in turn trained the next generation. His design, which made extensive use of native Indian design, became the dominant design of Taxcanian and Mexican silver. One of his first and most talented apprentices, Hector Aguilar, was our landlord at the Casa Borda. His shop, the Taller Borda, was downstairs from our apartment.

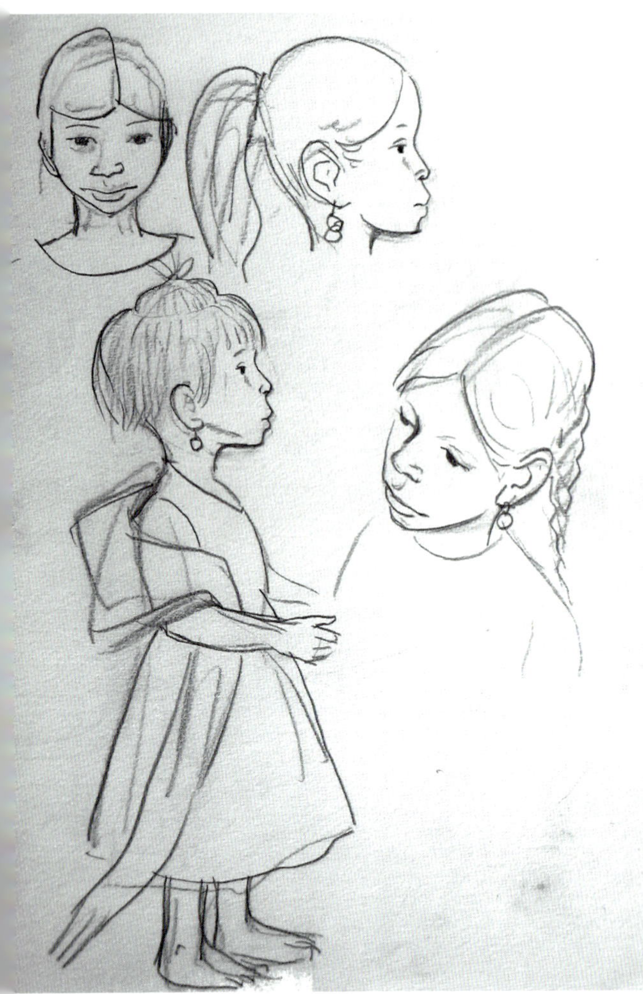

"Sketch of Four Girls," pencil on paper, ca 1958.

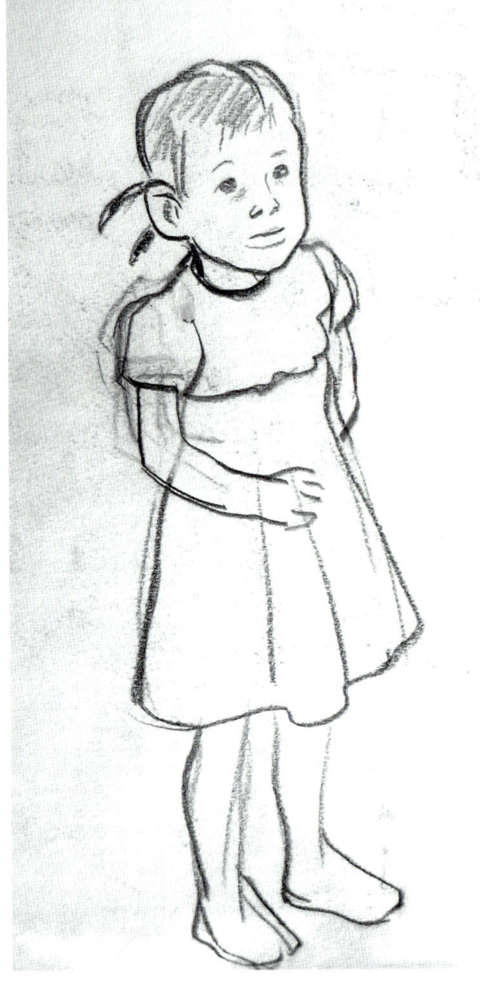

"Sketch of Little Girl Looking Up," pencil on paper, ca 1958.

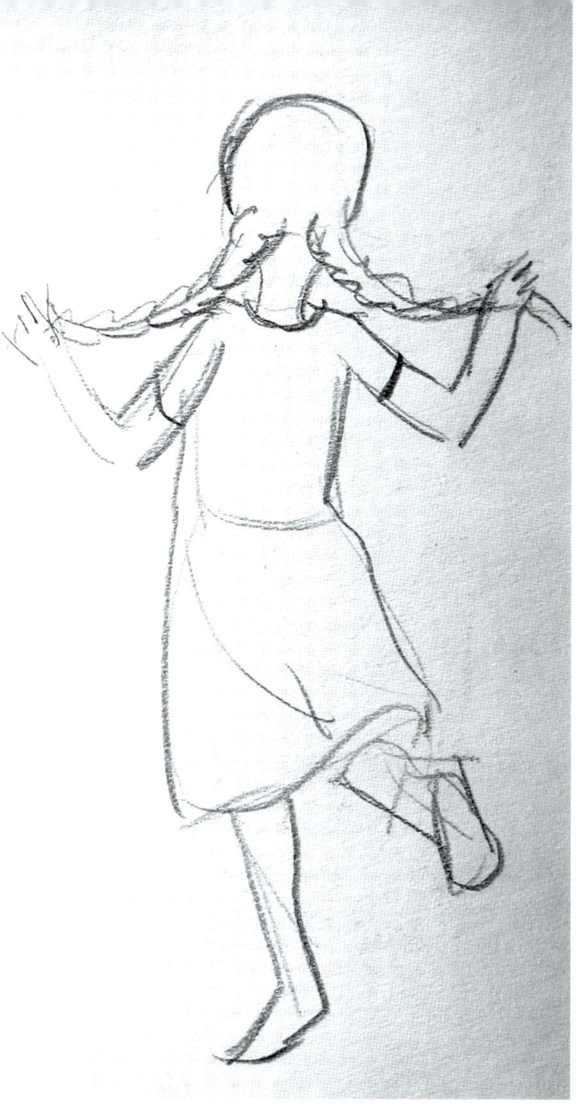

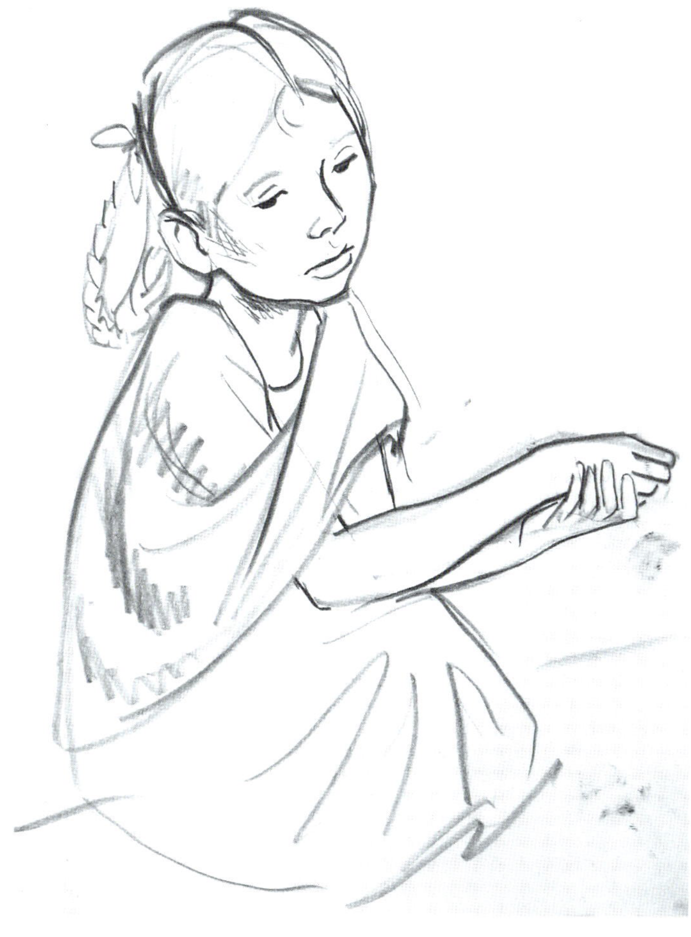

"Sketch of Little Girl Running Holding Pigtails," pencil on paper, ca 1958.

"Sketch of Sad Older Girl," pencil on paper, ca 1958.

William Spratling was from New Orleans and was friends with William Faulkner and Sherwood Anderson. When he came to Mexico, he became friends with Diego Rivera, and was instrumental in getting Rivera a commission to paint a mural at Rockefeller Center. When Sherwood and Elizabeth Anderson divorced, she came to live with Spratling in Taxco Viejo.

My parents knew William Spratling slightly. They were part of the Mexican-American group of arts and crafts people in Taxco. Spratling himself had moved out of town to Taxco Viejo, ten miles away, where he had more privacy. I never met him as a child, but in 1967, when my friend Edee and I went down from college over spring vacation to visit my parents in Taxco, Mom had arranged a trip for us to visit Spratling's shop and museum, where he talked with us briefly. Five months later, Spratling was killed in a car crash.

Sal and I went to Mexican schools, which was a wonderful adventure. Mom volunteered at the Taxco orphanage and took guitar lessons. Bob did many sketches around town, hoping to make them into a children's book about Mexico. He did write a children's book when we returned to the States, but decided not to publish it. He said that he didn't know Mexicans well enough to portray them as he wanted to, and thought the book might be patronizing. Still, he did many sketches in Mexico, and made some paintings from the sketches after we returned home. He drew many children. All of these sketches were from 1958 or 1959.

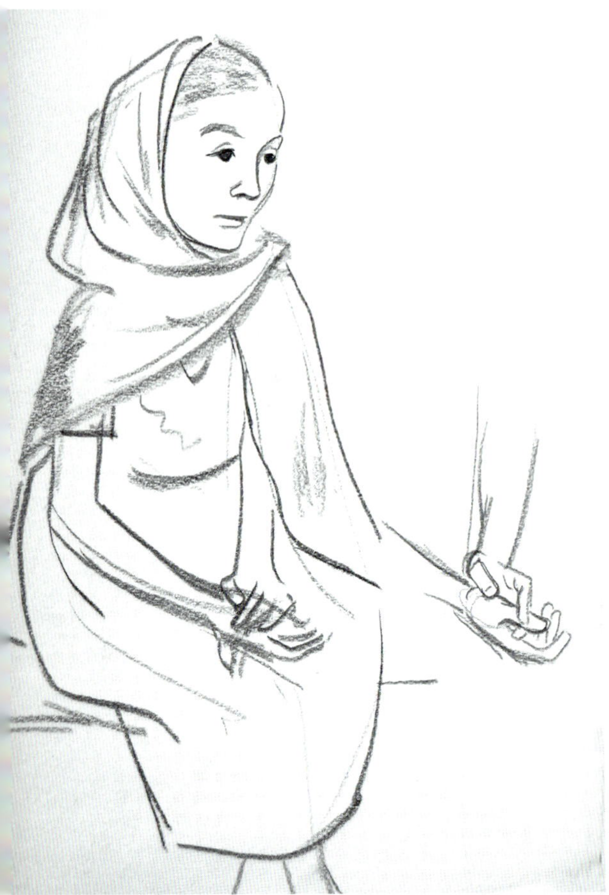

"Sketch of Woman with Folded Hands," pencil on paper, ca 1959.

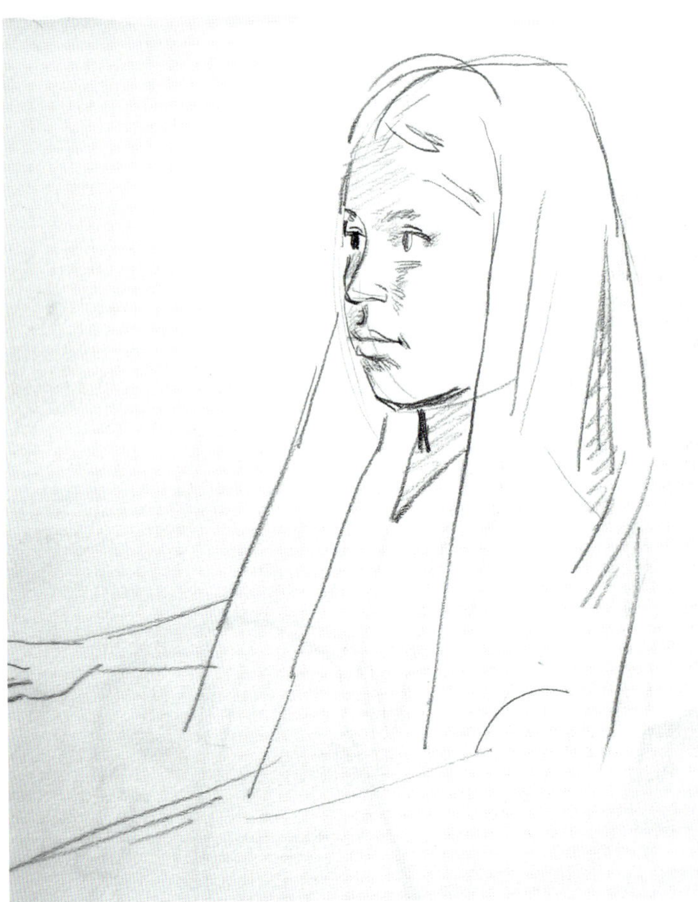

"Sketch of Beautiful Young Woman," pencil on paper, ca 1959.

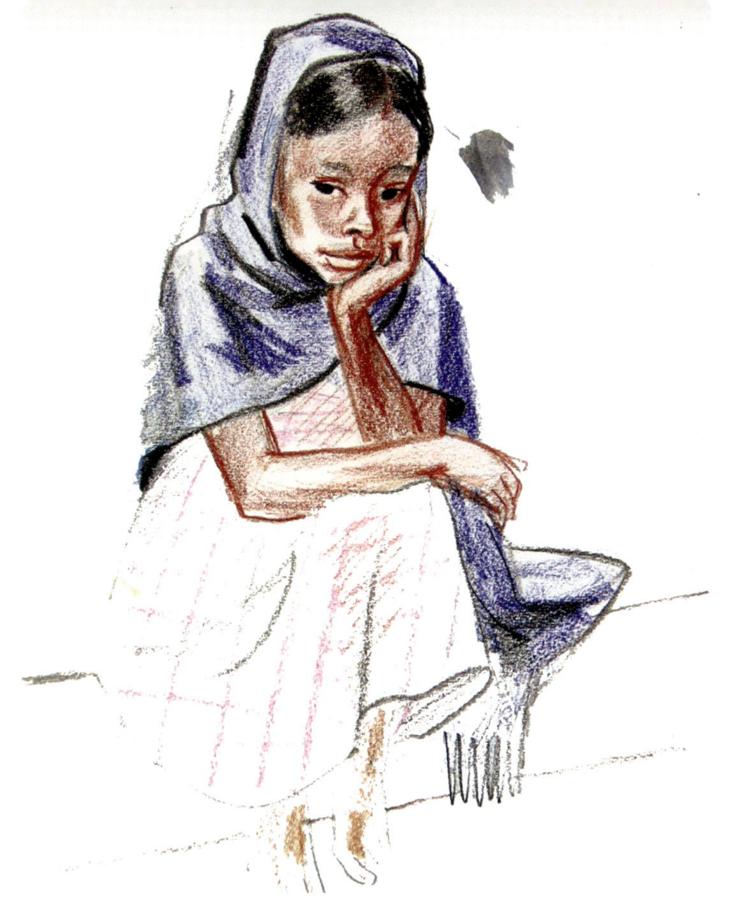

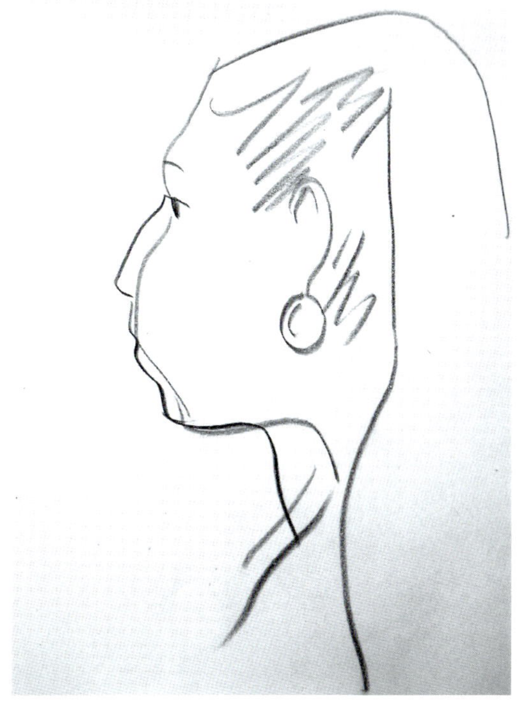

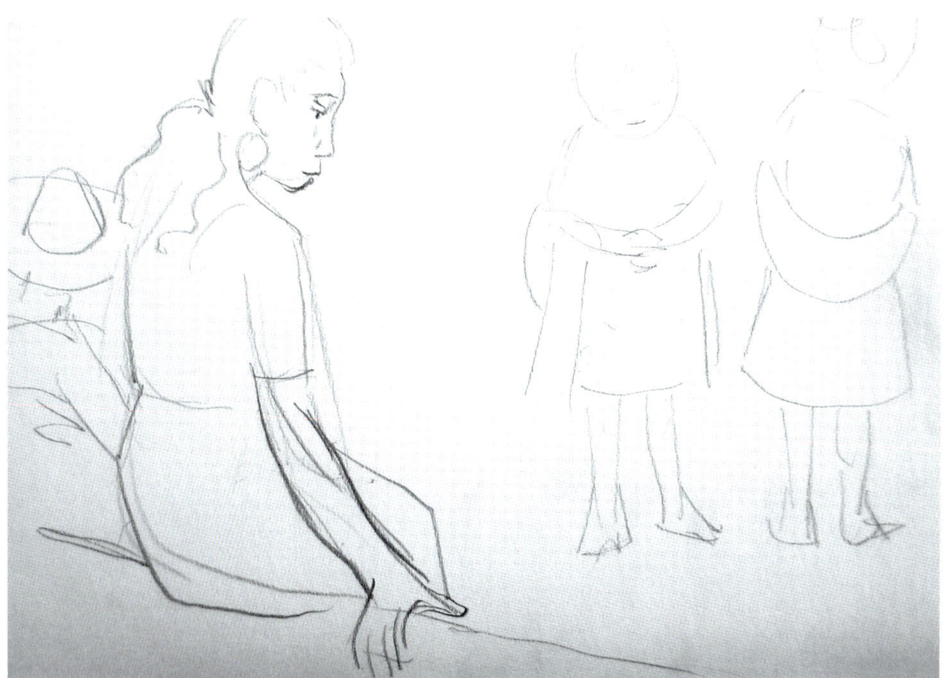

"Sketch of Woman with Chin on Hand," colored pencil on paper, ca 1958.

"Sketch of Woman with Pure Indian Features," pencil on paper, ca 1959.

"Sketch of Older Woman Facing Away," pencil on paper, ca 1958.

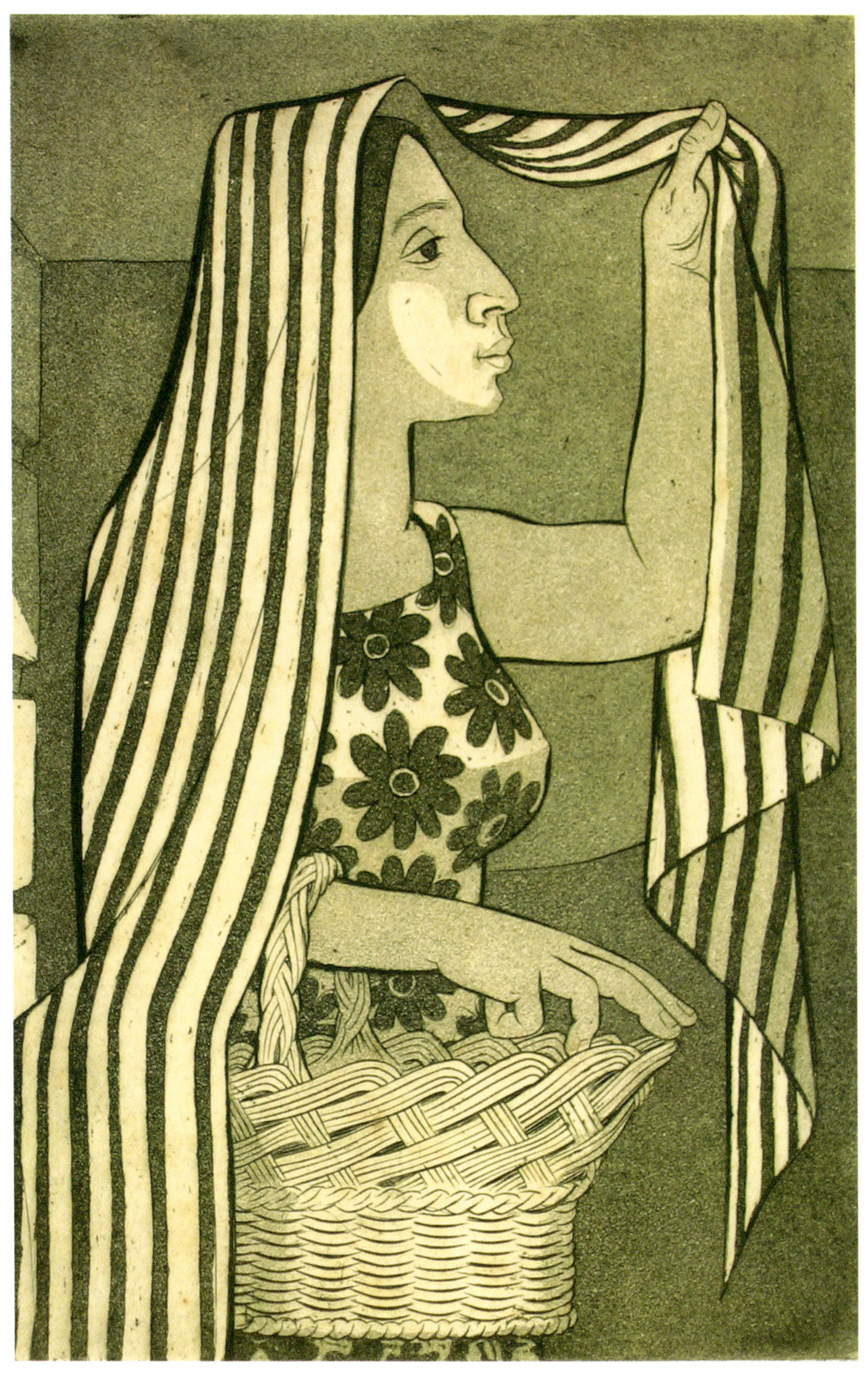

"Woman with Rebozo and Basket," copper etching on paper, 17" x 13", 1958.

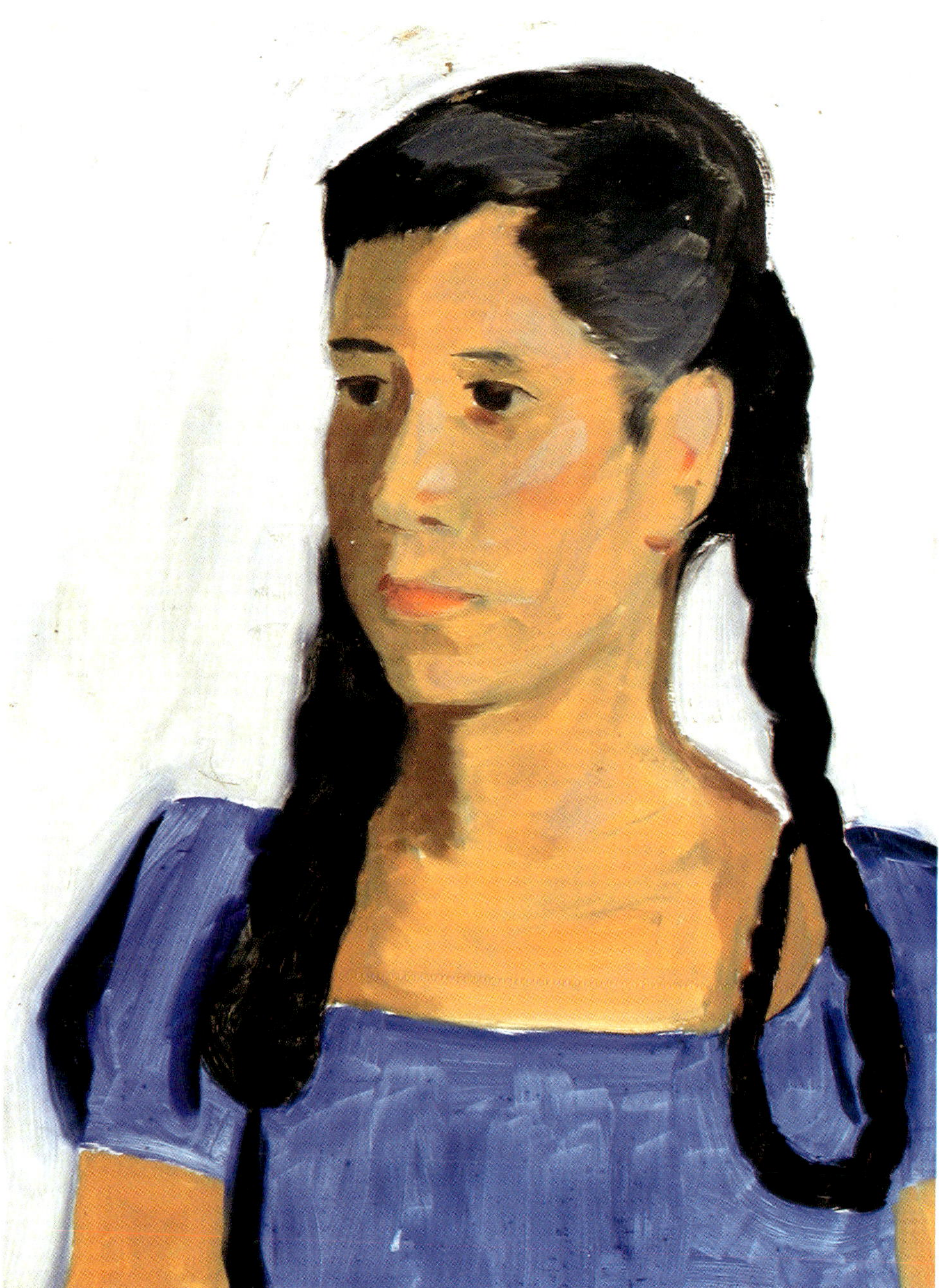

"Portrait of Norma," oil on Masonite, 16" x 12", 1959.

Bob liked to sketch people—women, children, babies, all kinds of people. Above is a picture of Norma, who was a friend of Sal's from school. She was thirteen years old, the same age as Sal when we were at the Casa Borda.

"Sketch of Woman with Baby," pencil on paper, ca 1958.

"Sketch of Woman with Baby and Child," pencil on paper, ca 1958.

"Sketch of Woman Holding Child with Another Child," pencil on paper, ca 1958.

In 1958, we lived at the Casa Scott, next door to Dr. Phil Platt, who was a retired army doctor. He had been a doctor in the cavalry in the Spanish American War in the Philippines. Dr. Platt was also an artist and taught my father how to etch.

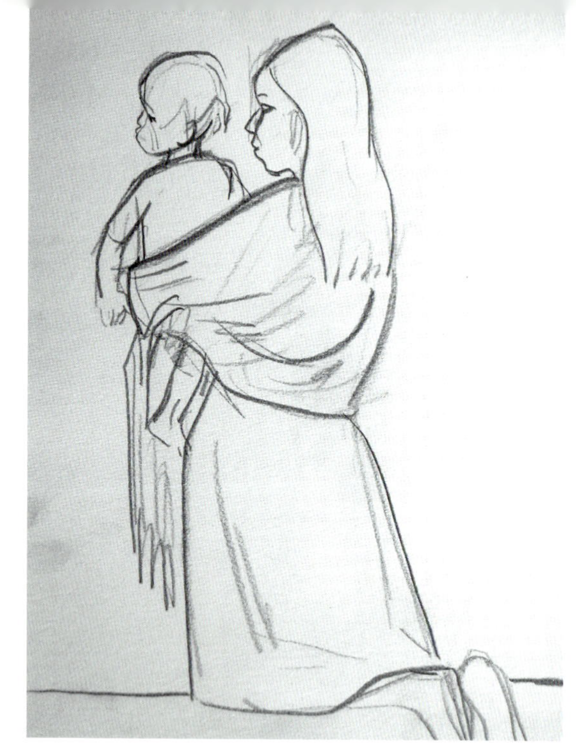

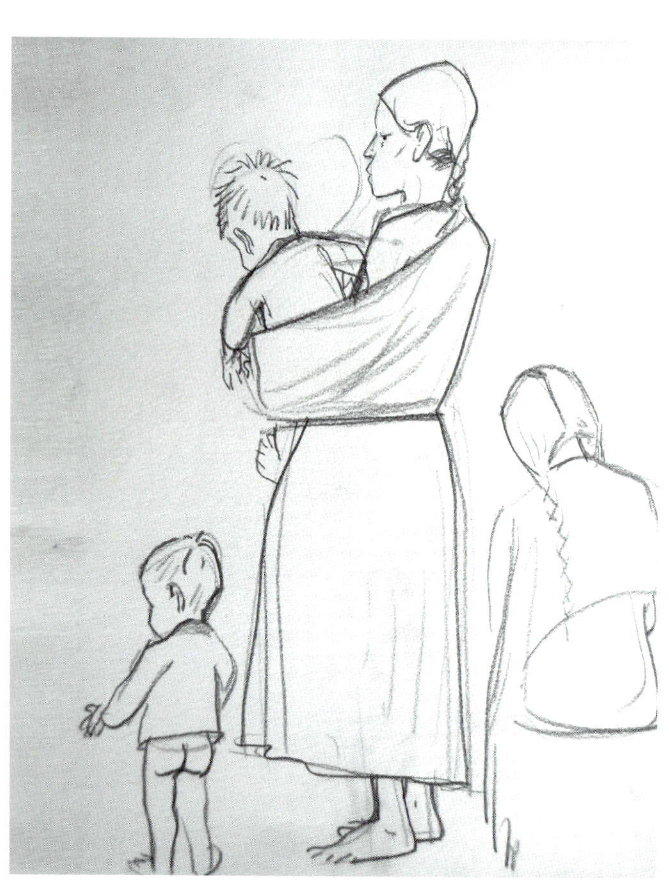

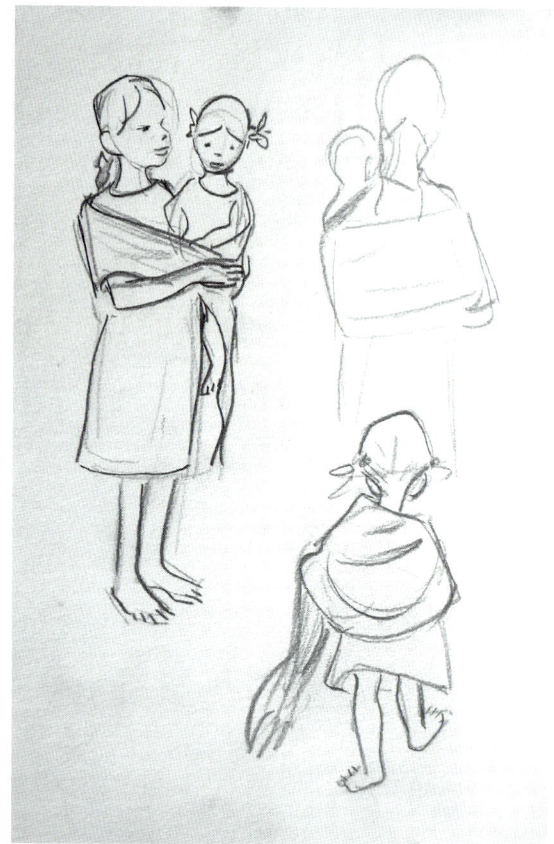

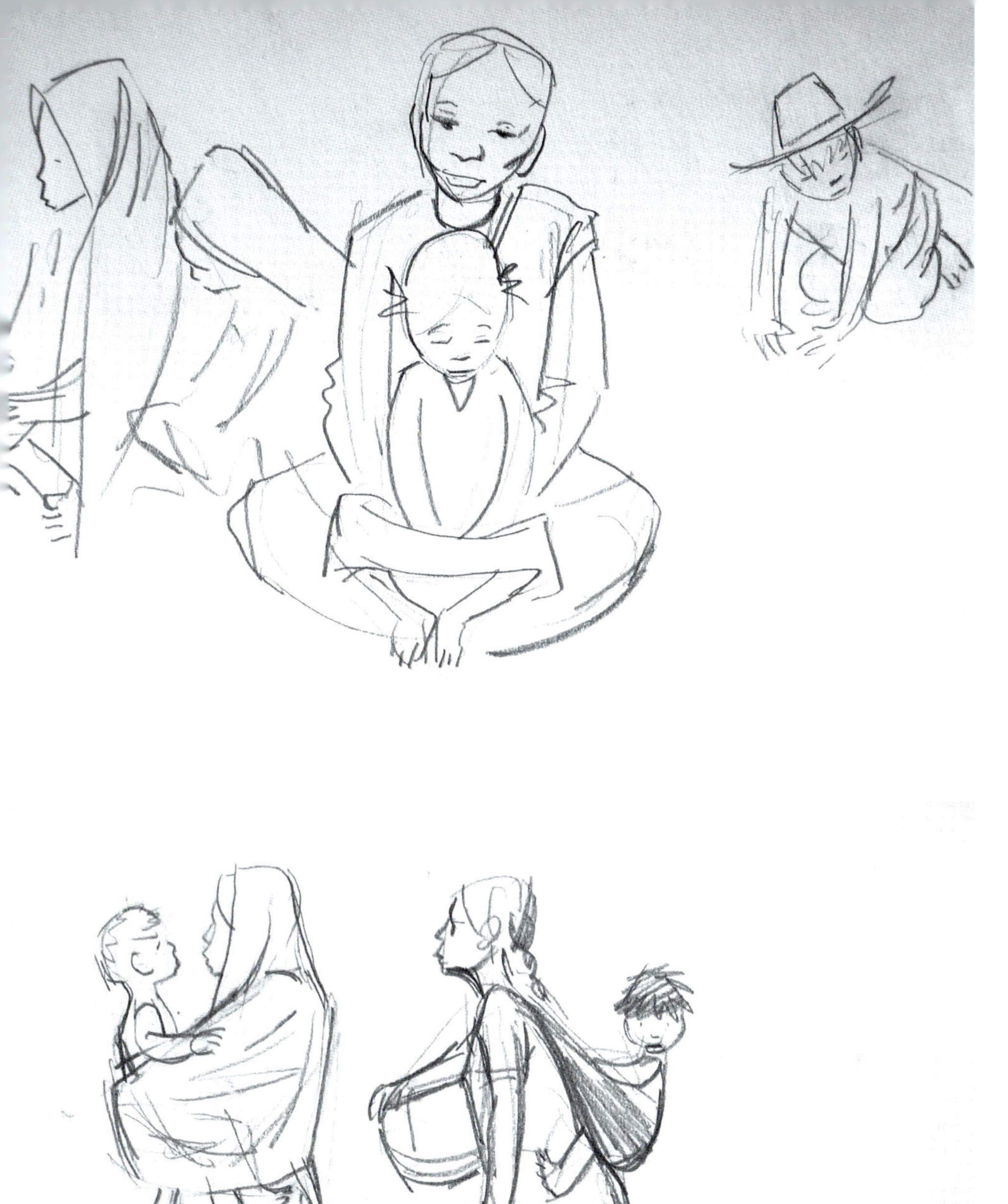

"Sketch of Woman Cross-Legged with Young Child," pencil on paper, ca 1958.

"Sketch of Two Women with Kids," pencil on paper, ca 1958.

"Sketch of Pig, Boy, and Woman Holding a Baby," pencil on paper, 1959.

"Woman with Young Child with Rebozo and Post," oil on Masonite, 28" x 16", 1960s.

"Sketch of Sad Girl in Chair with Baby," pencil on paper, ca 1959.

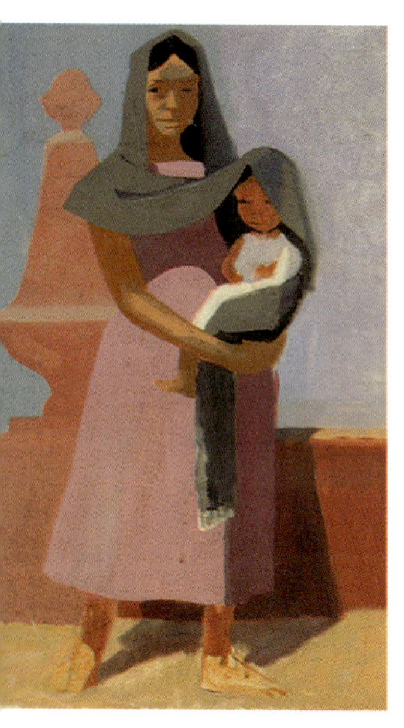

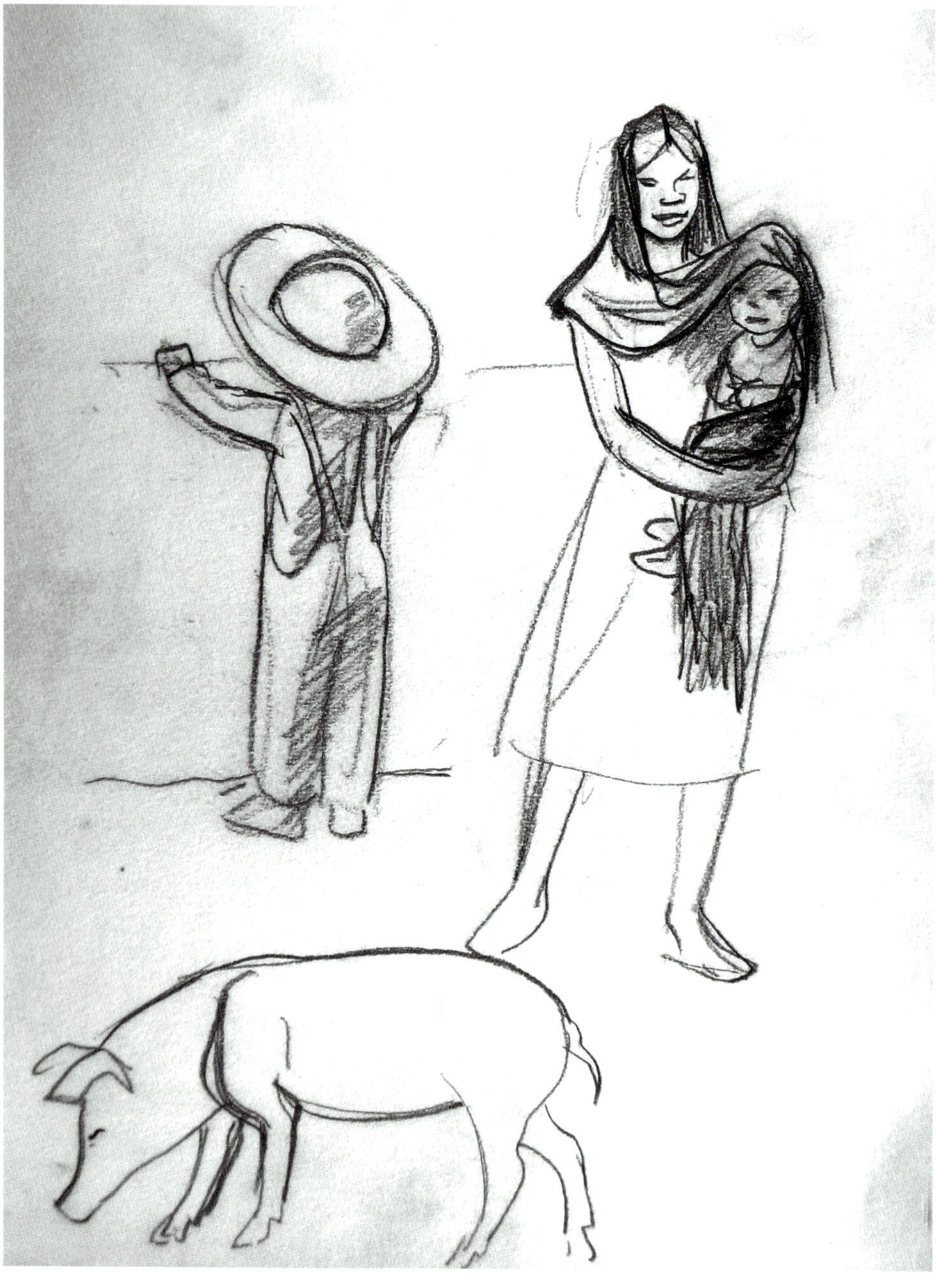

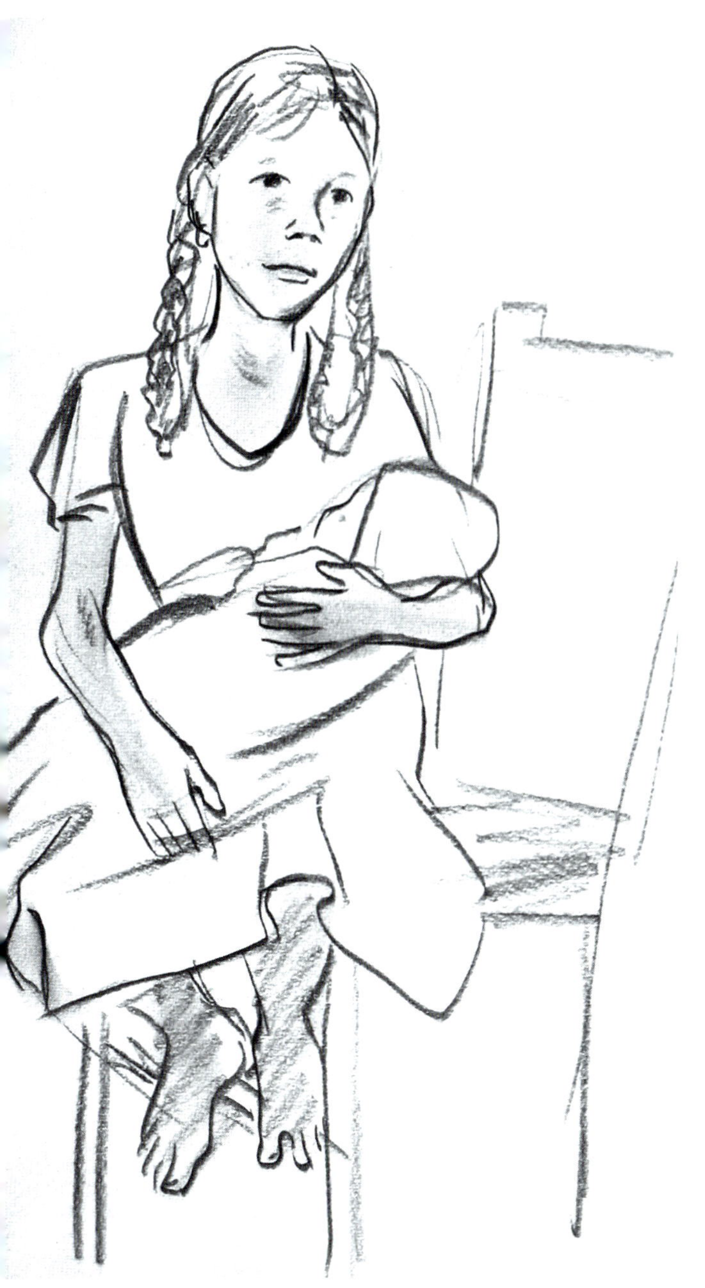

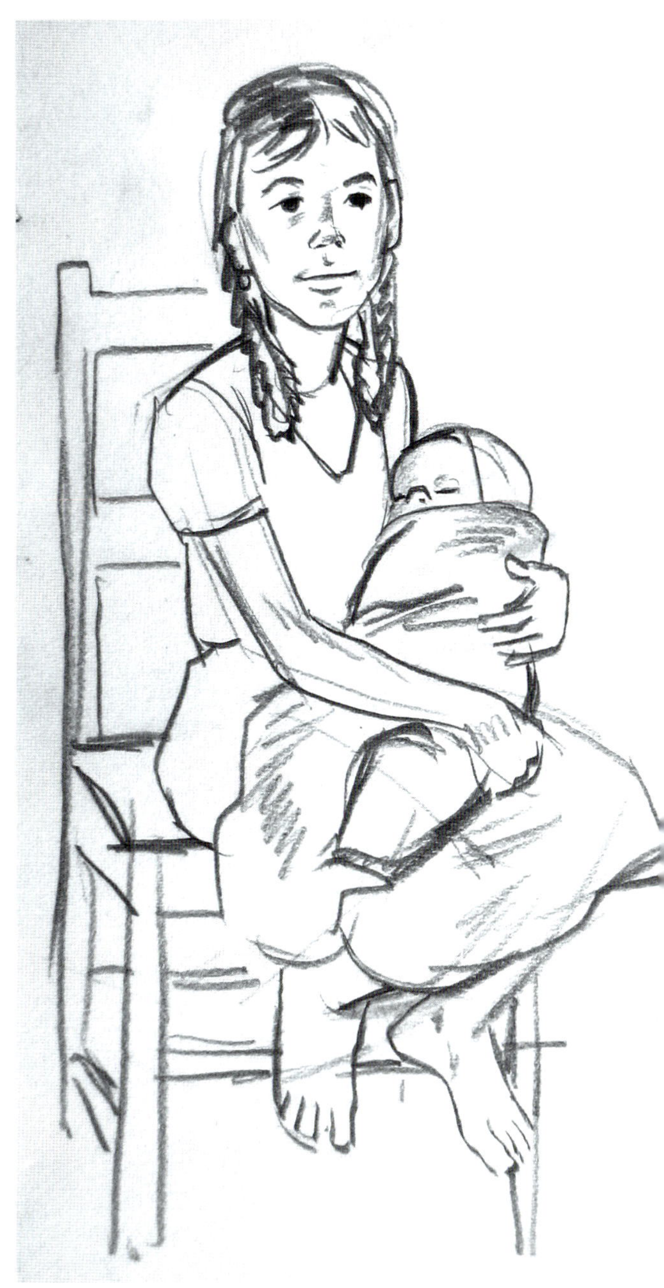

"Sketch of Happy Girl in Chair with Baby," pencil on paper, ca 1959.

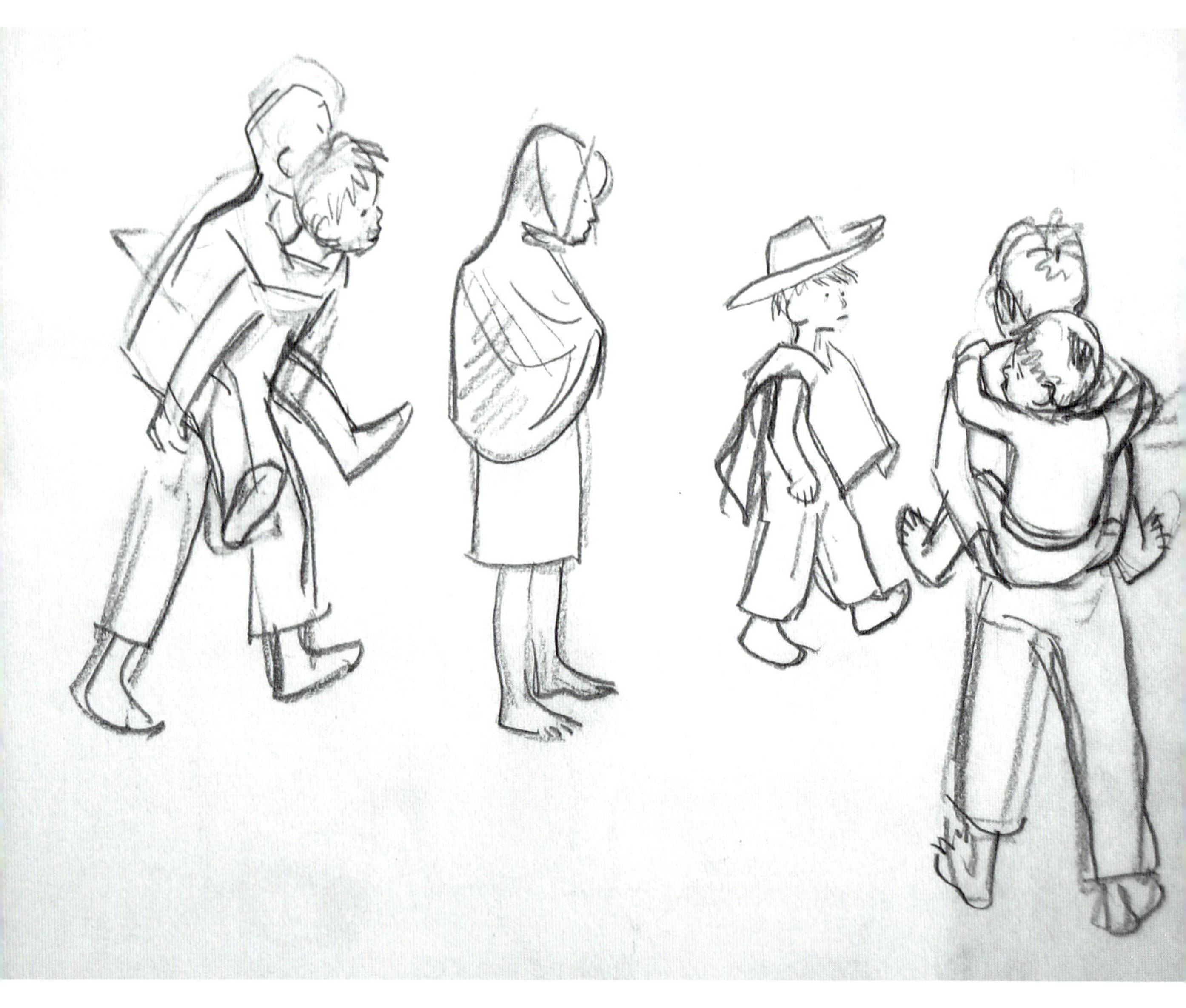

"Sketch of Boys with Babies," pencil on paper, ca 1959.

I can't figure out why my father left blank areas on some of his paintings. Did he want to push the boundaries of what it meant for a painting to be "finished?" Or was he attempting some experiment, and when he had succeeded, lost interest in finishing the painting? Or perhaps he was attempting some painterly experiment, and when he found his experiment wouldn't work, put the painting aside? I think he only left blank canvas in his portraits.

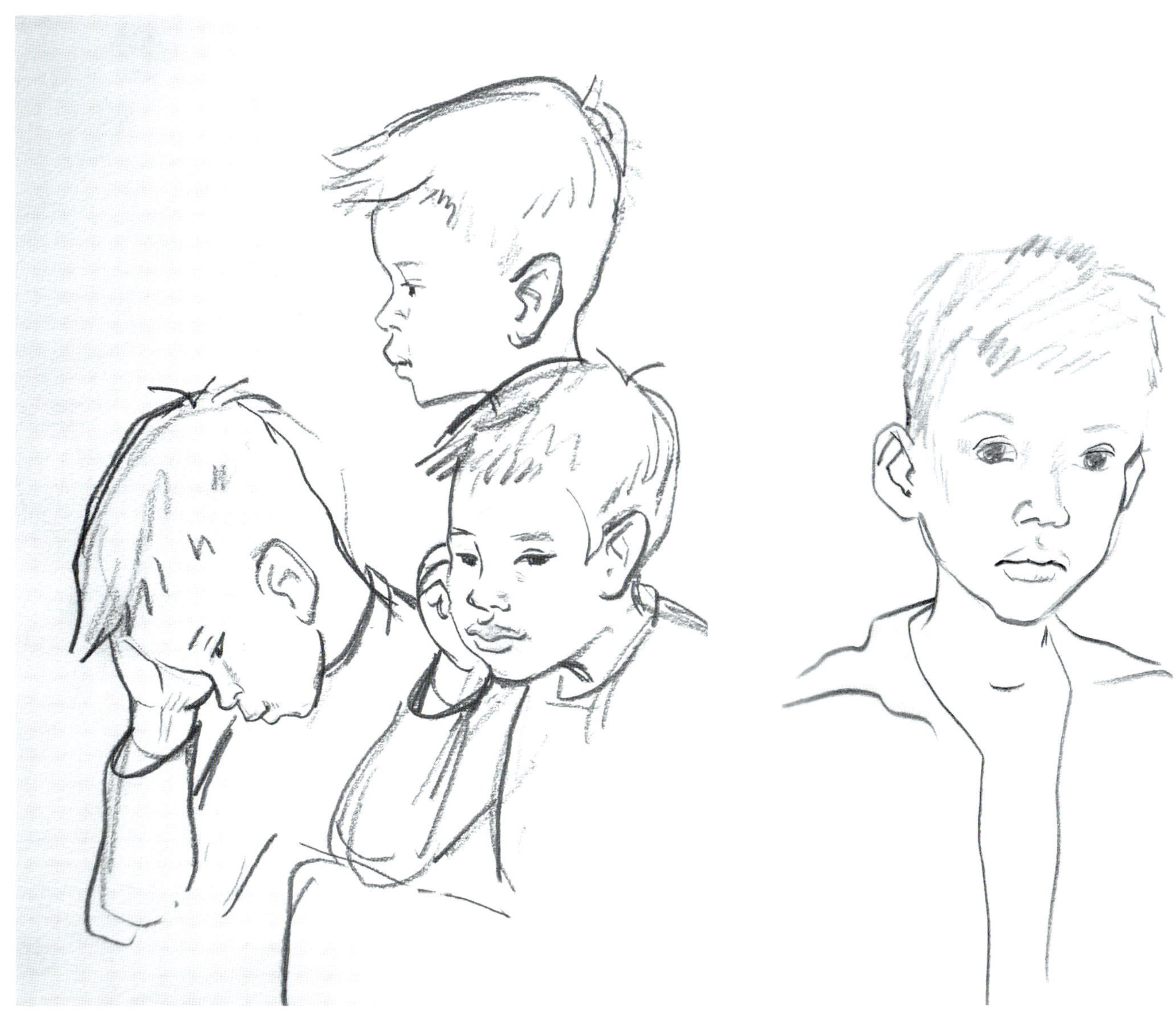

"Sketches of Angel," pencil on paper, ca 1959.

Angel was a boy in Taxco who washed cars, shined shoes, ran errands, and did whatever he could to make money. He posed for my father to make money, and introduced his younger brother, Jesus, so that he could pose and make money, too.

Bob sketched only a few portraits of men, but mostly he drew men at their work. He also drew women at work, and he drew people socializing and people who were alone. He drew churches, buildings, and street scenes, too. He sketched what he saw around him.

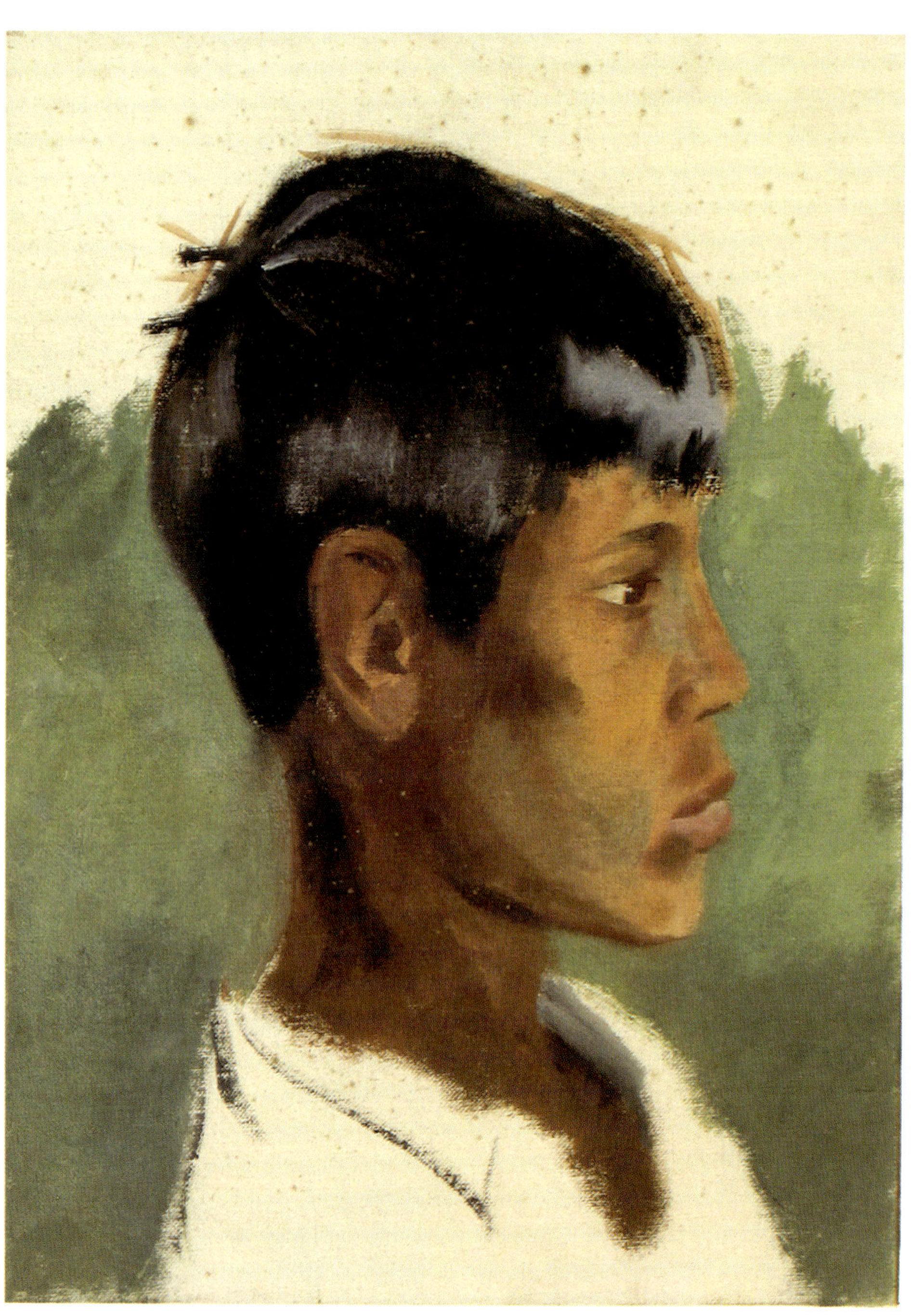

"Angel," oil on canvas board, 14" x 10", 1959.

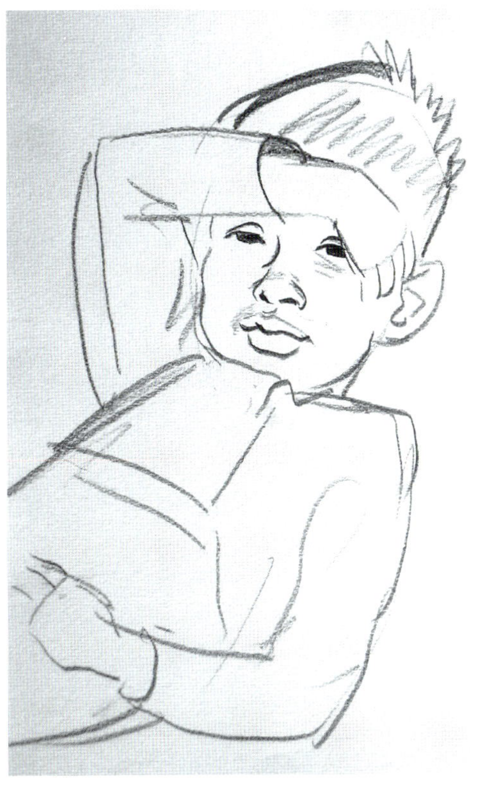

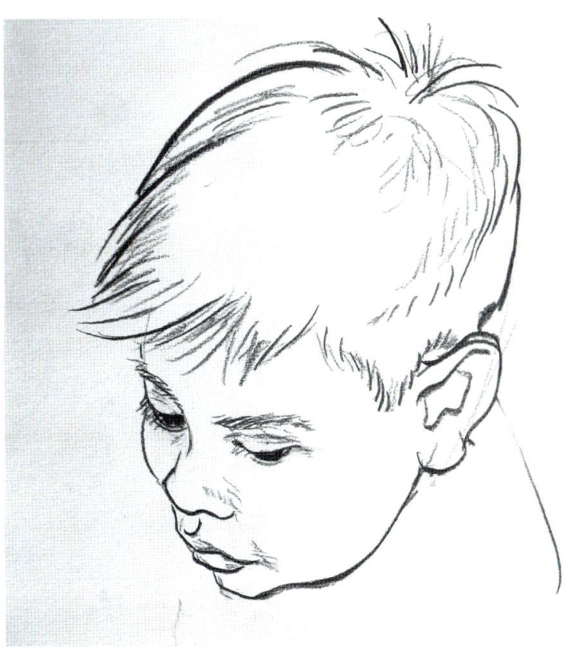

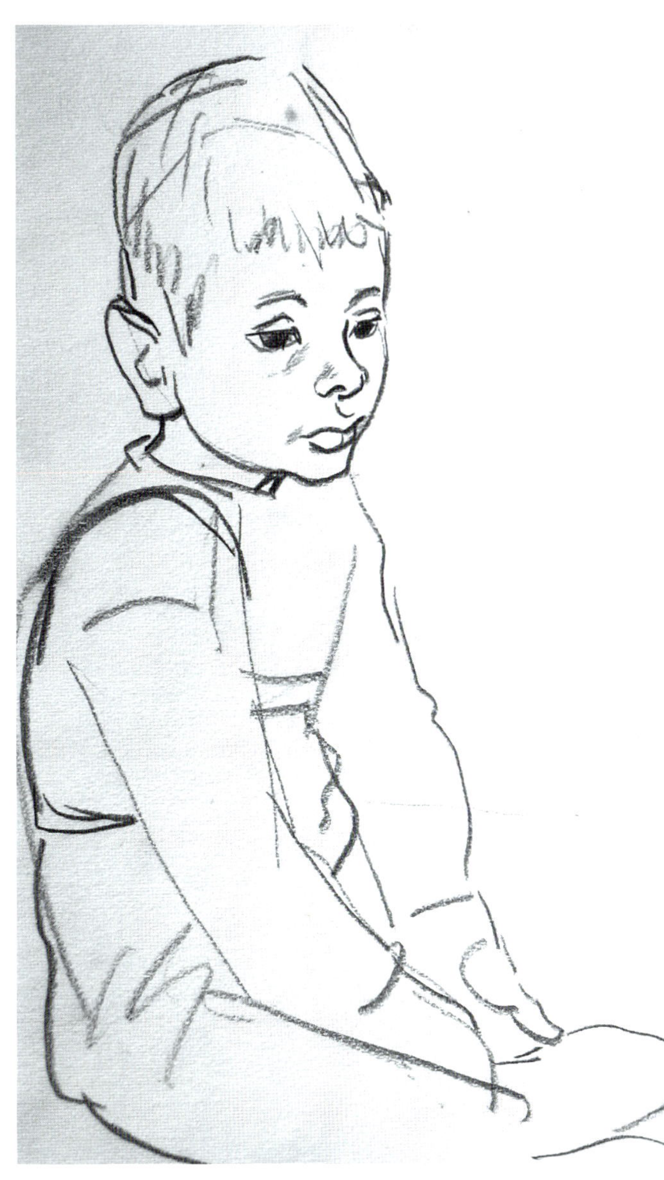

"Sketches of Jesus," pencil on paper, ca 1959.

"Boys on Pilings," oil on Masonite, 24" x 48", 1980s, from a sketch done in the 1950s.

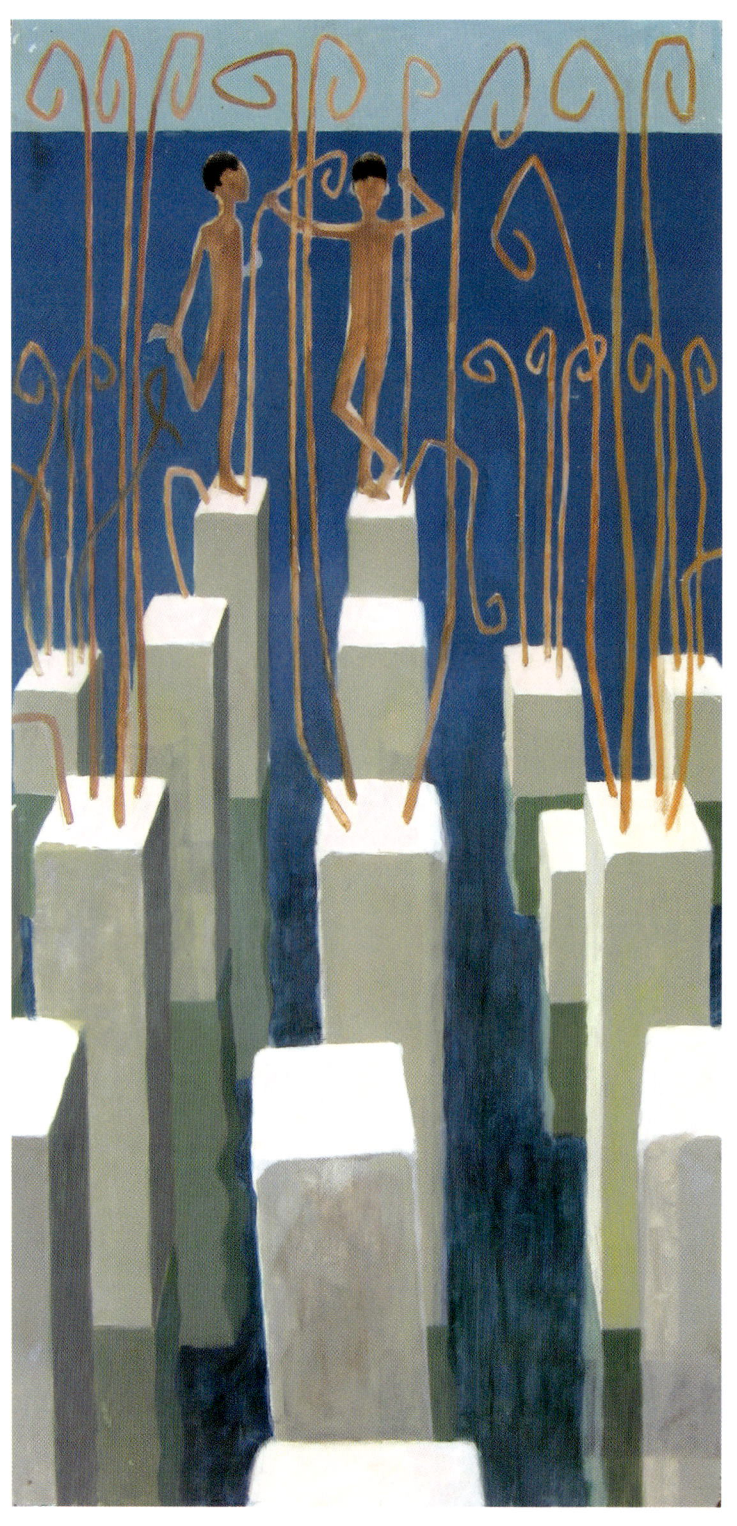

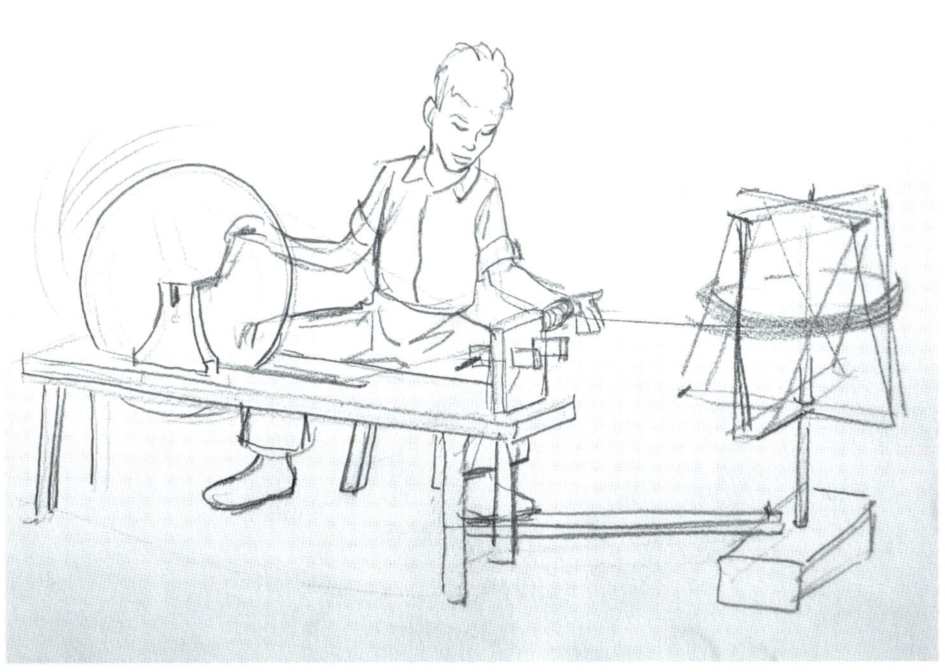

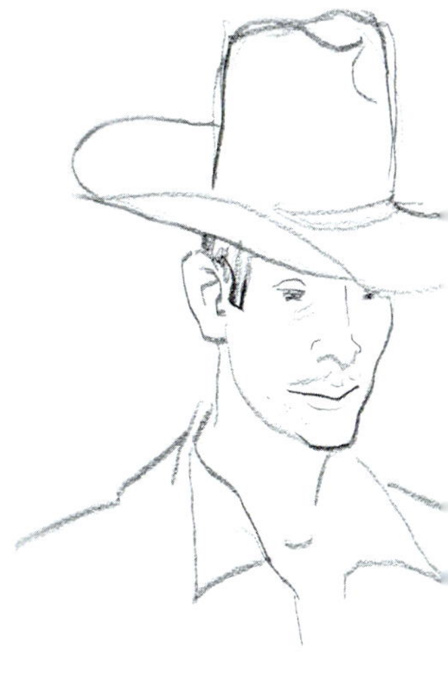

"Sketch of Man in Sombrero," pencil on paper, 1950s.

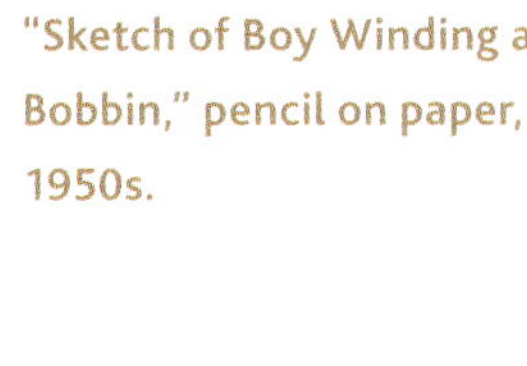

"Sketch of Boy Winding a Bobbin," pencil on paper, 1950s.

"Sketch of Man Weaving," pencil on paper, 1950s.

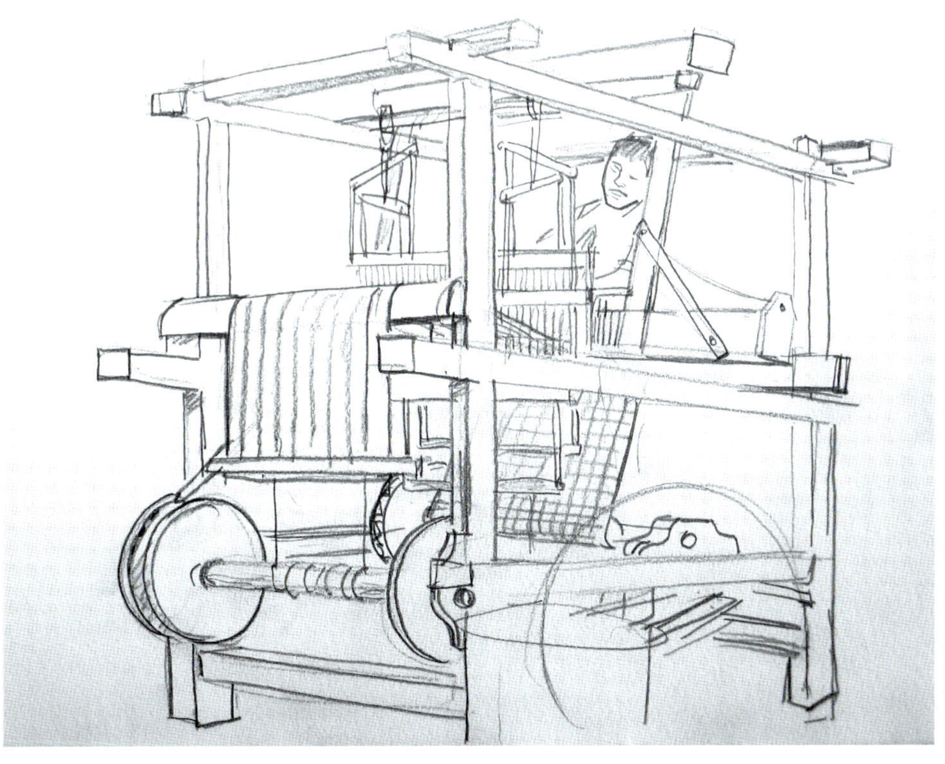

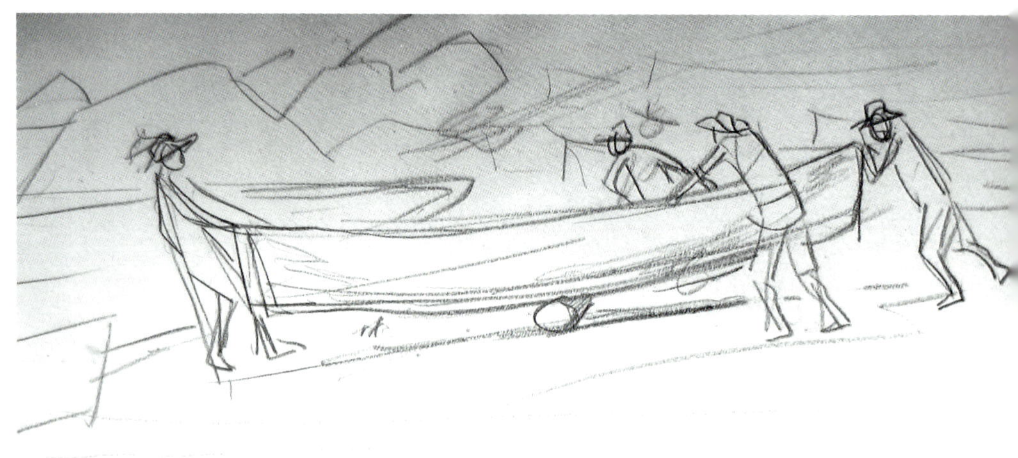

"Sketch of Men Launching a Boat," pencil on paper, 1959.

"Men Launching a Boat, Zihuatinejo," acrylic on paper, 6" x 8", 1959.

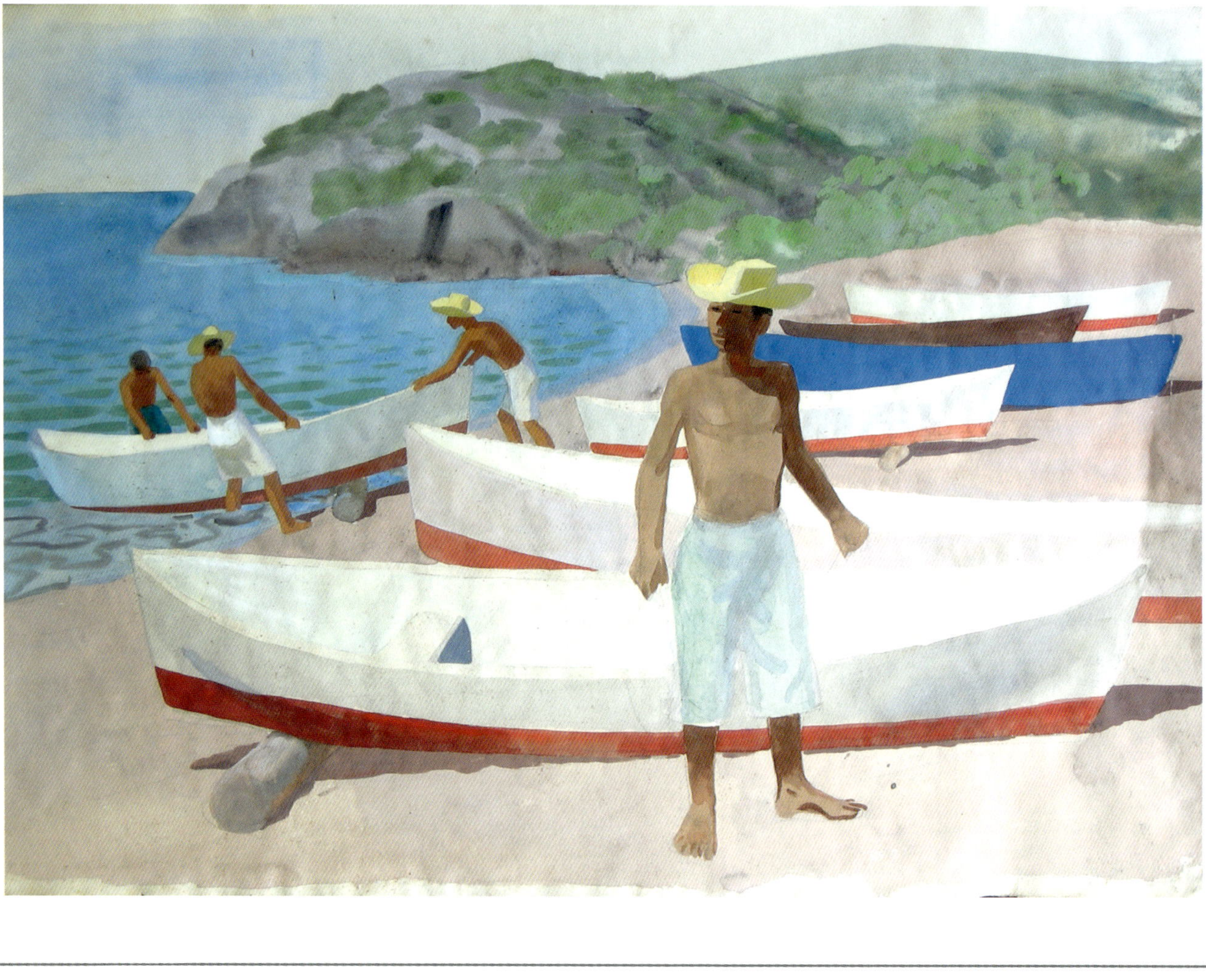

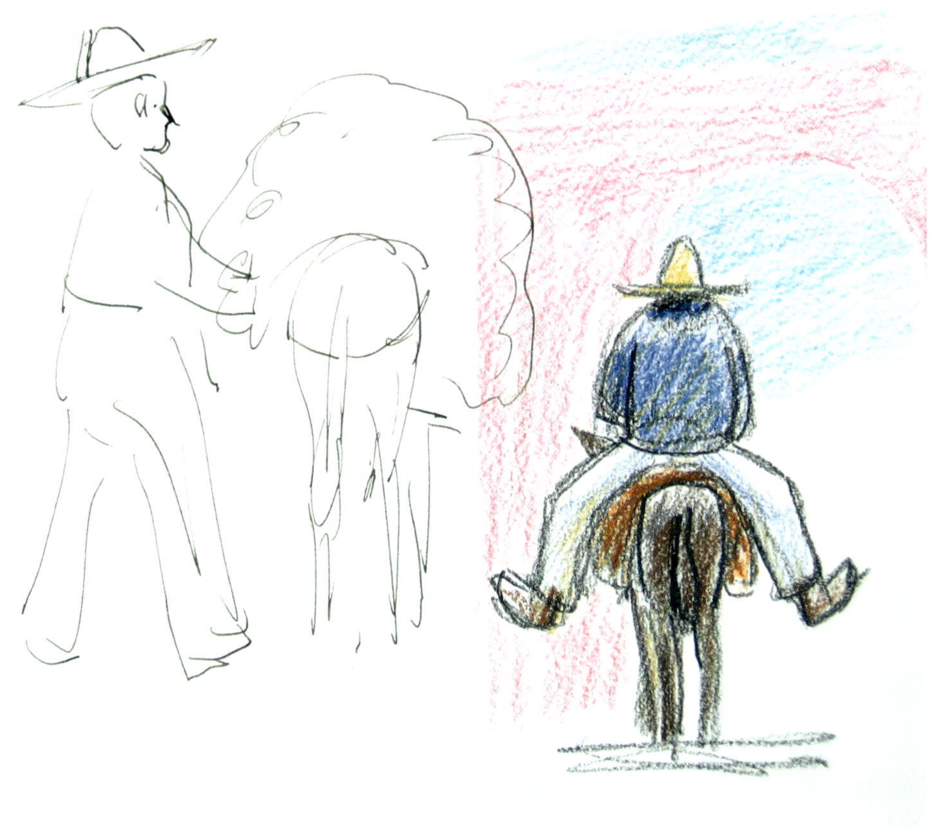

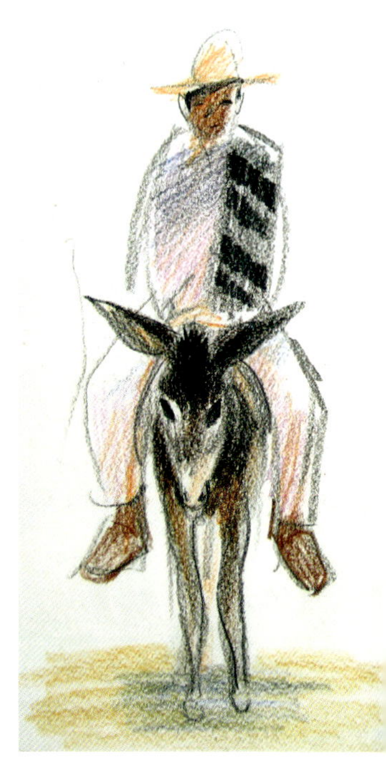

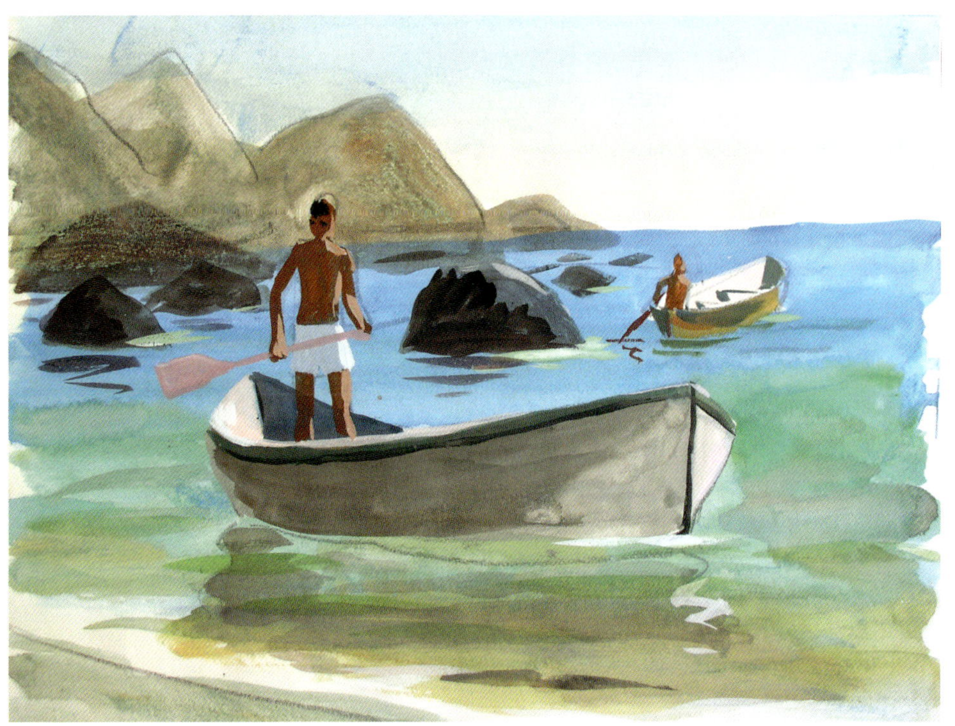

"Sketch of Man Approaching on Burro," colored pencils on paper, 1959.

"Sketch of Man Leaving on Burro," colored pencils on paper, 1959.

"Men Paddling Boats, Zihuatinejo," acrylic on paper, 6" x 8", 1959.

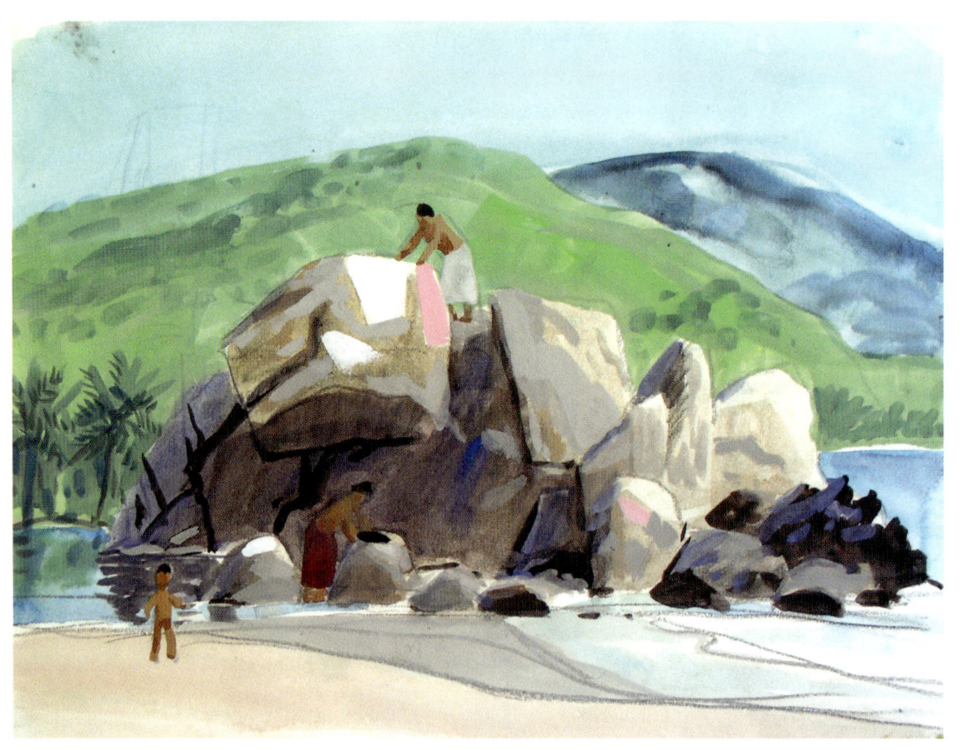

"Women Washing Clothes on Big Rock," acrylic on paper, 9" x 12", 1959.

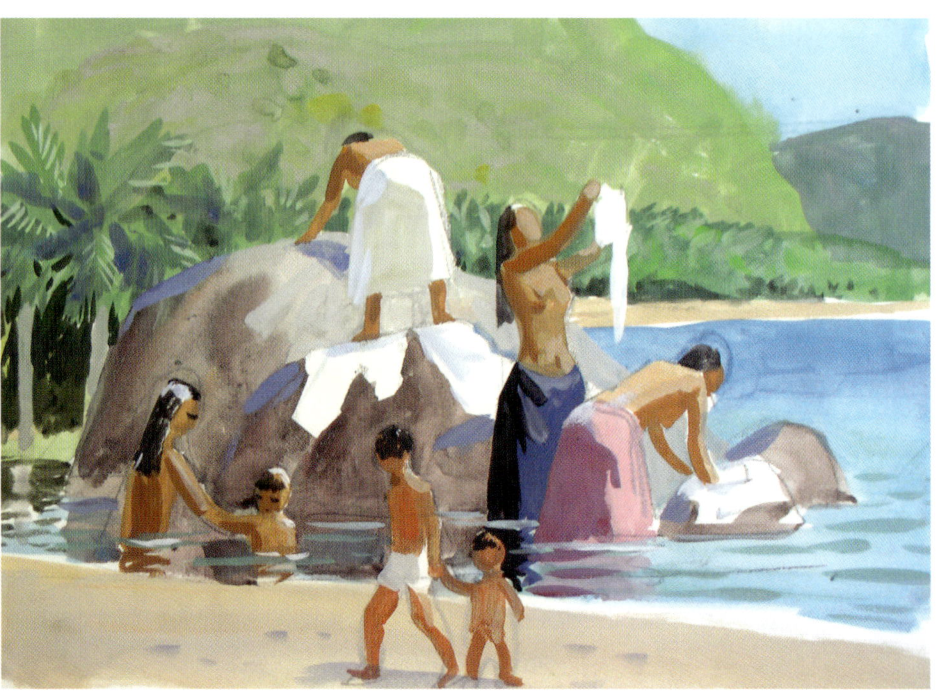

"Women Washing Clothes on Small Rock," acrylic on paper, 9" x 12", 1959.

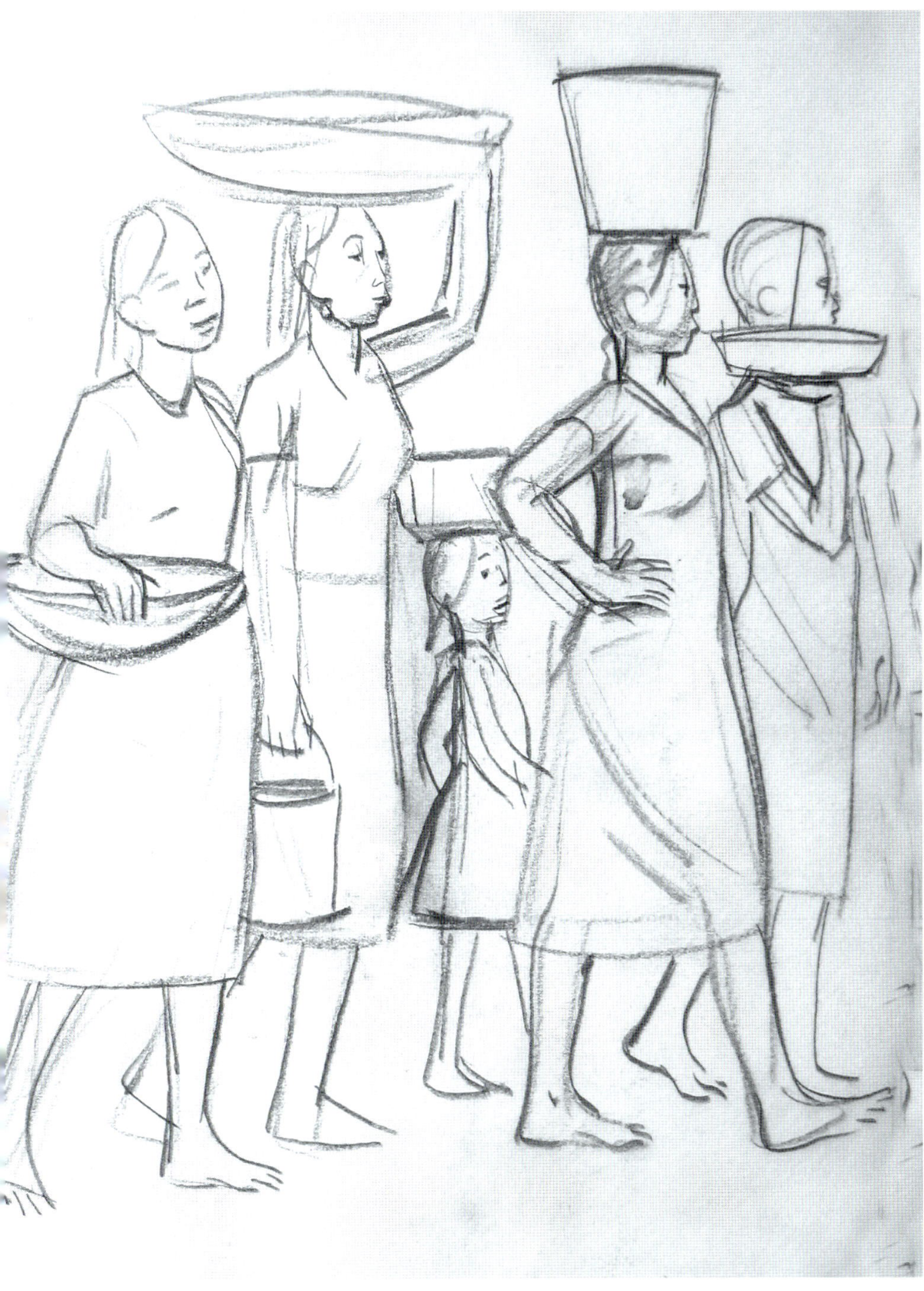

"Sketch of Women Carrying Baskets," pencil on paper, ca 1959.

"Sketch of Woman on Stone Bench," pencil on paper, 1959.

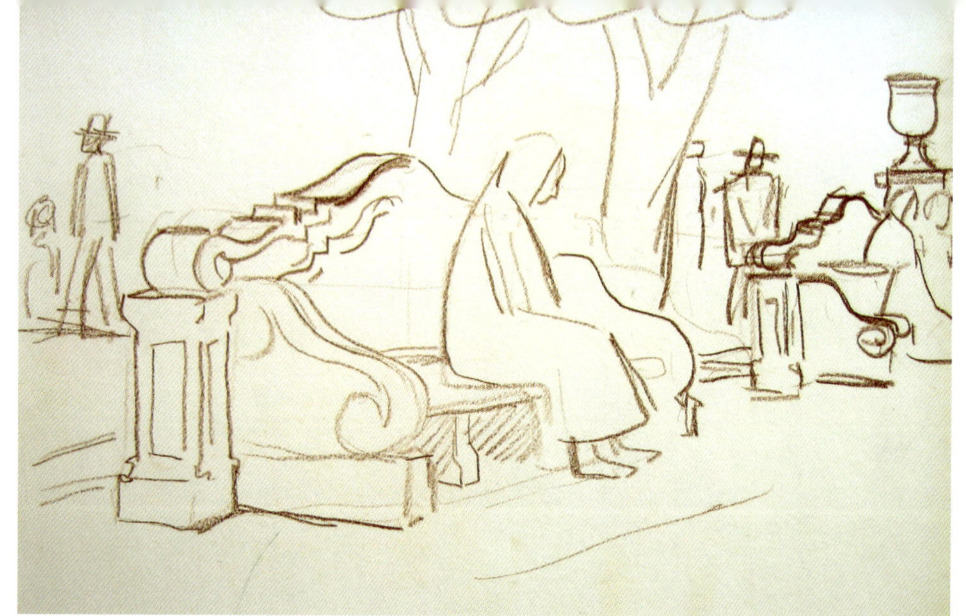

"Sketch of Man on Stone Bench and Woman with Tray," colored pencil on paper, 1959.

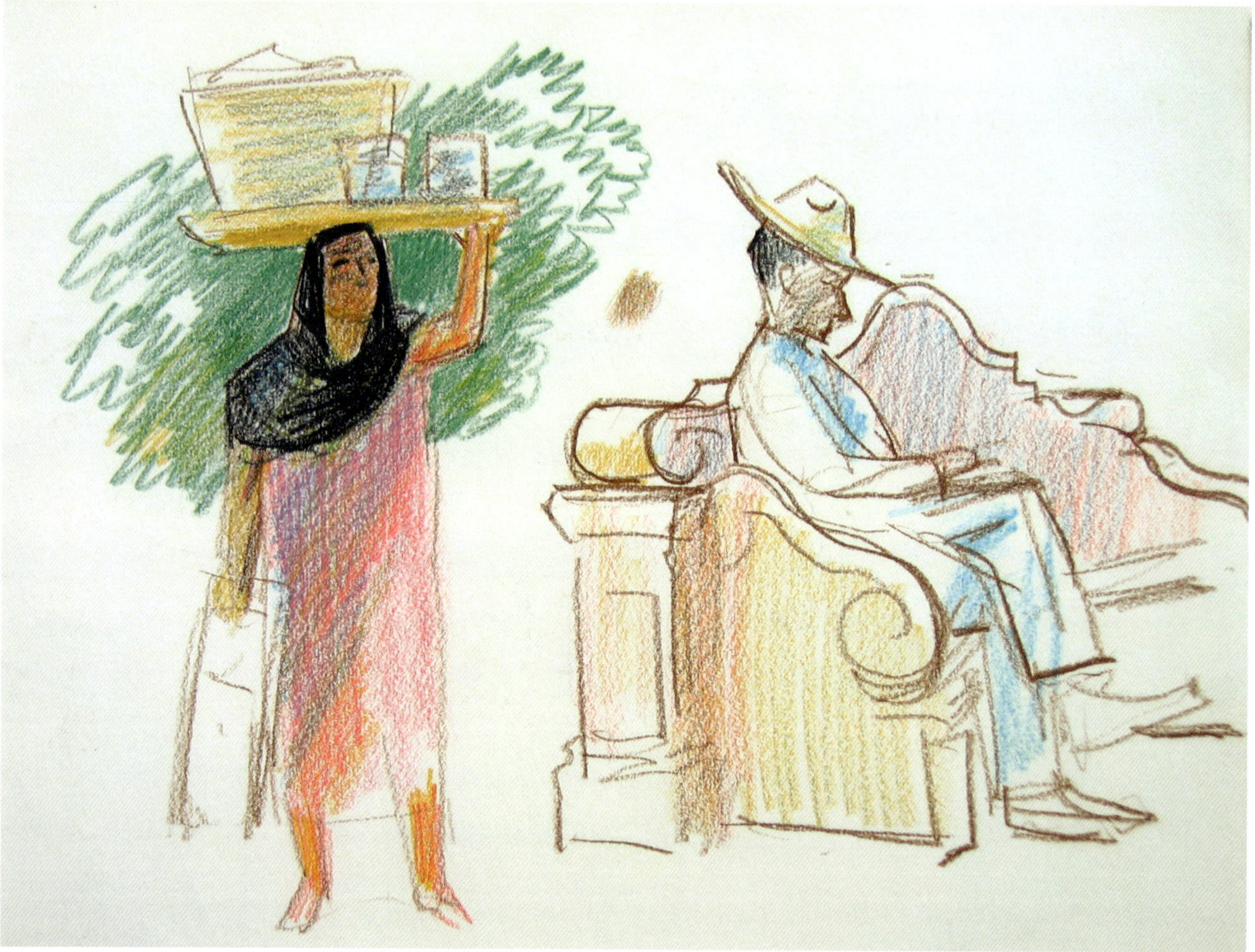

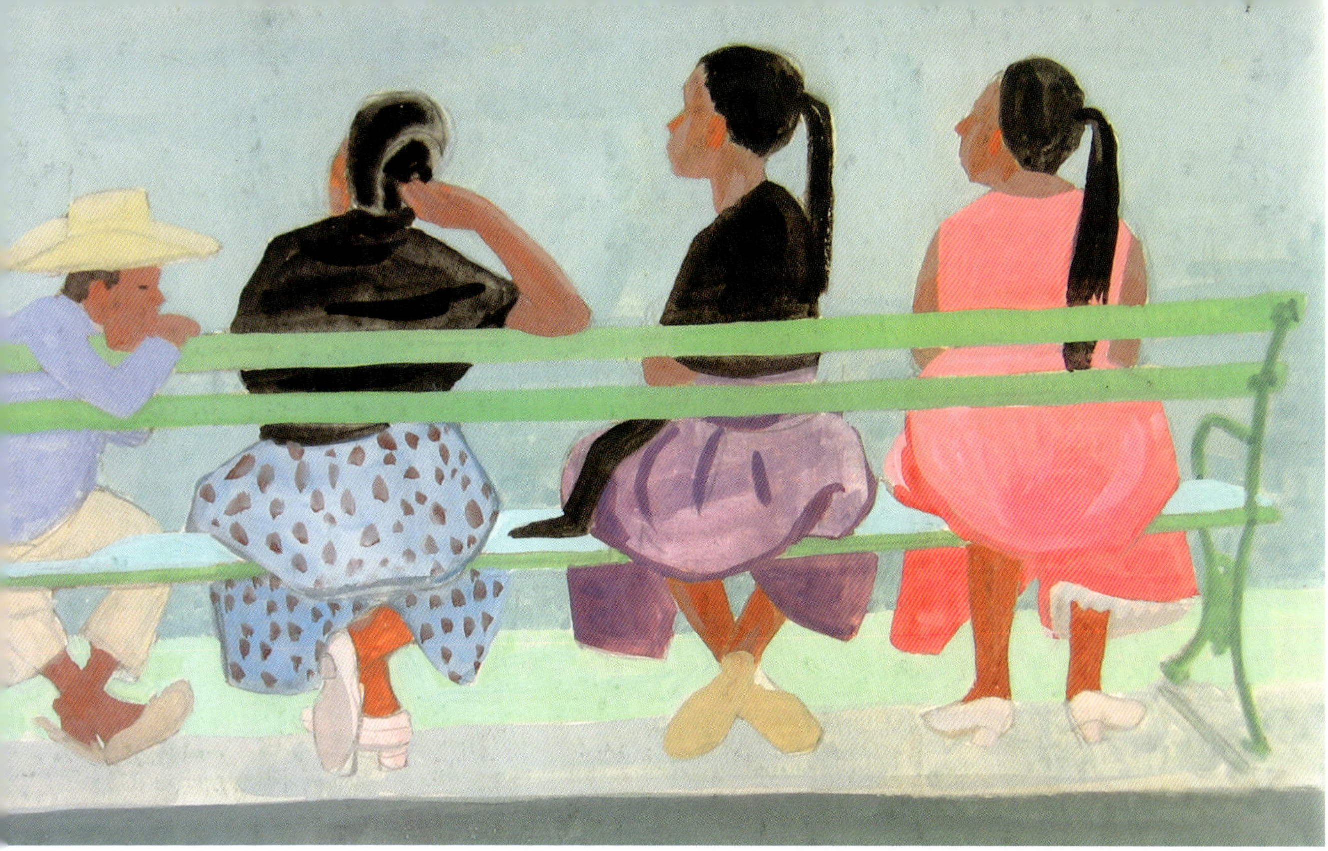

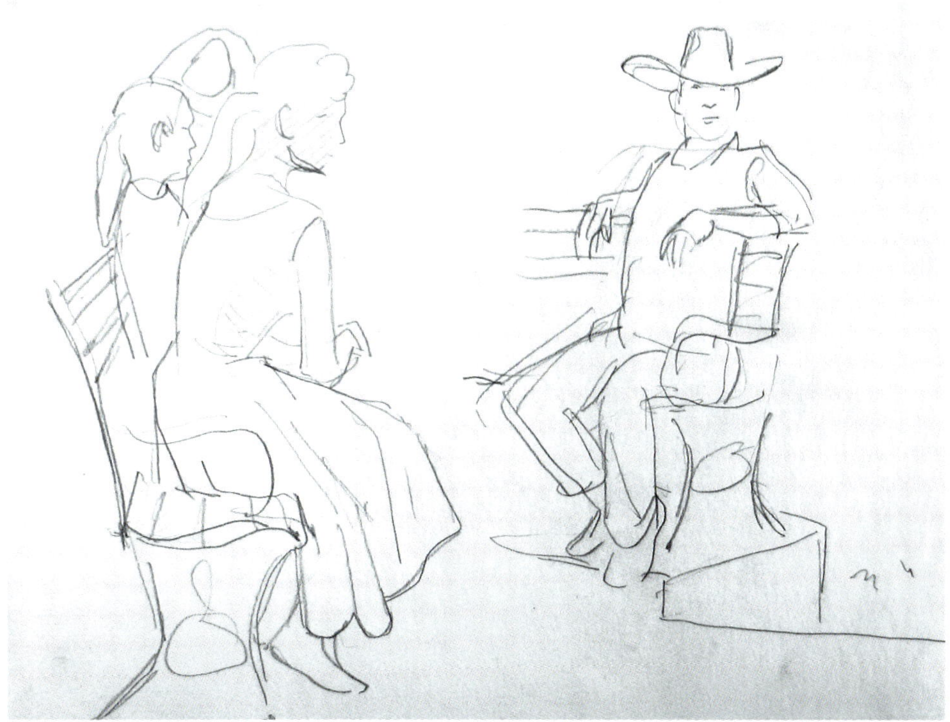

"Women and Man on Bench," acrylic on paper, 8" x 10", 1959.

"Sketch of Women and Man on Benches," pencil on paper, 1959.

"Sketch of Men Around a Table," pencil on paper, 1959.

"Sketch of Woman Walking by Women Braiding Hair," pencil on paper, 1959.

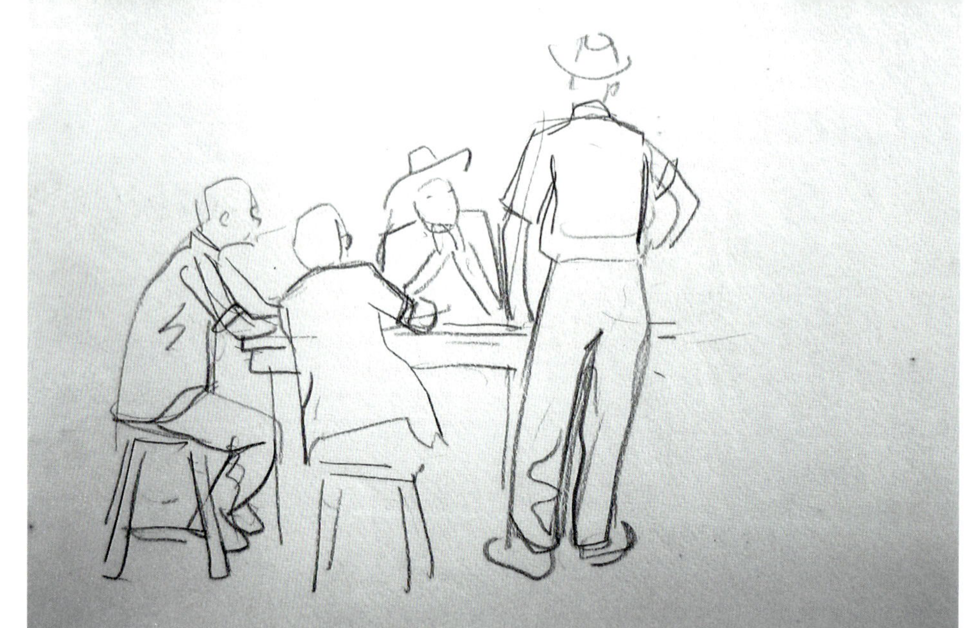

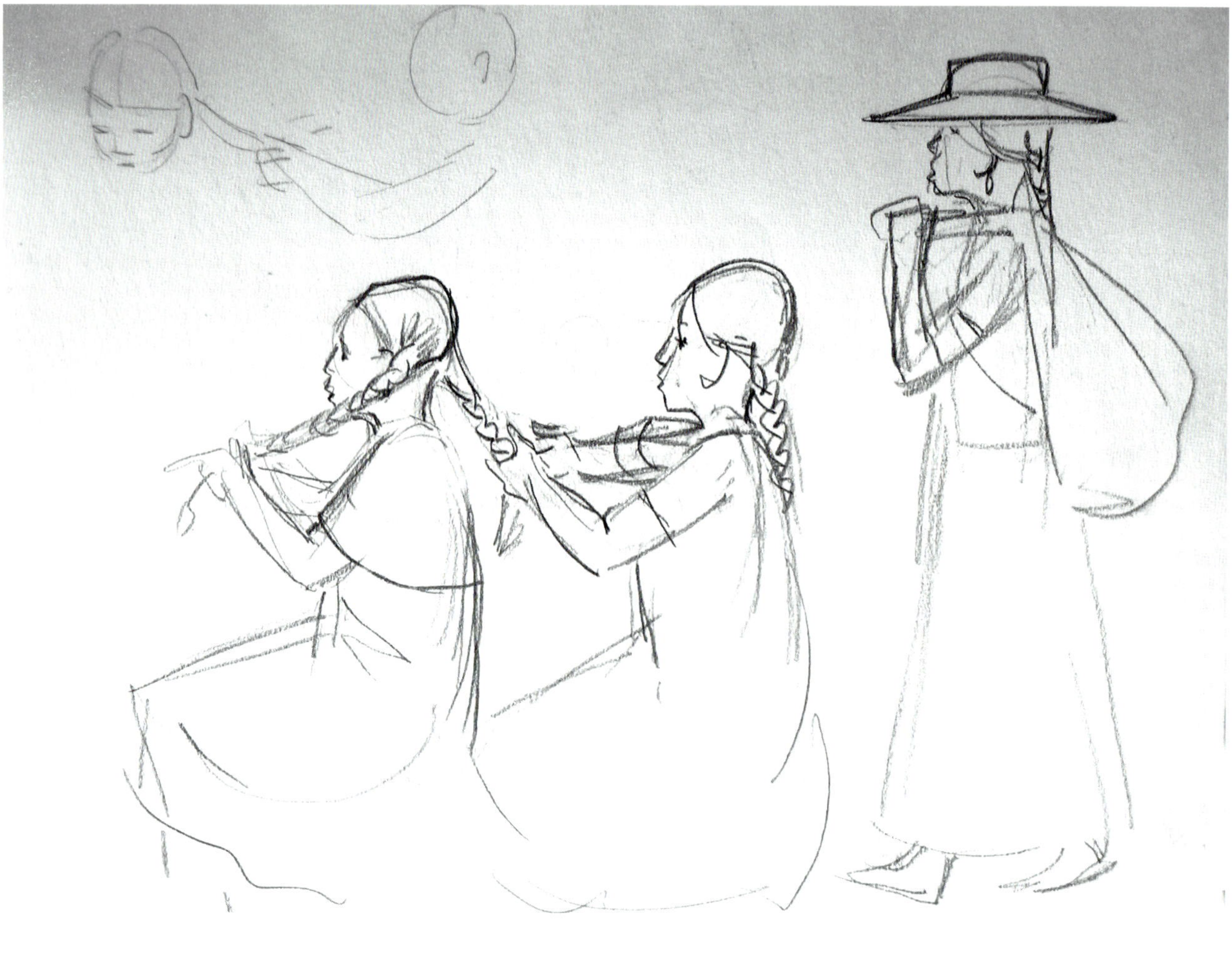

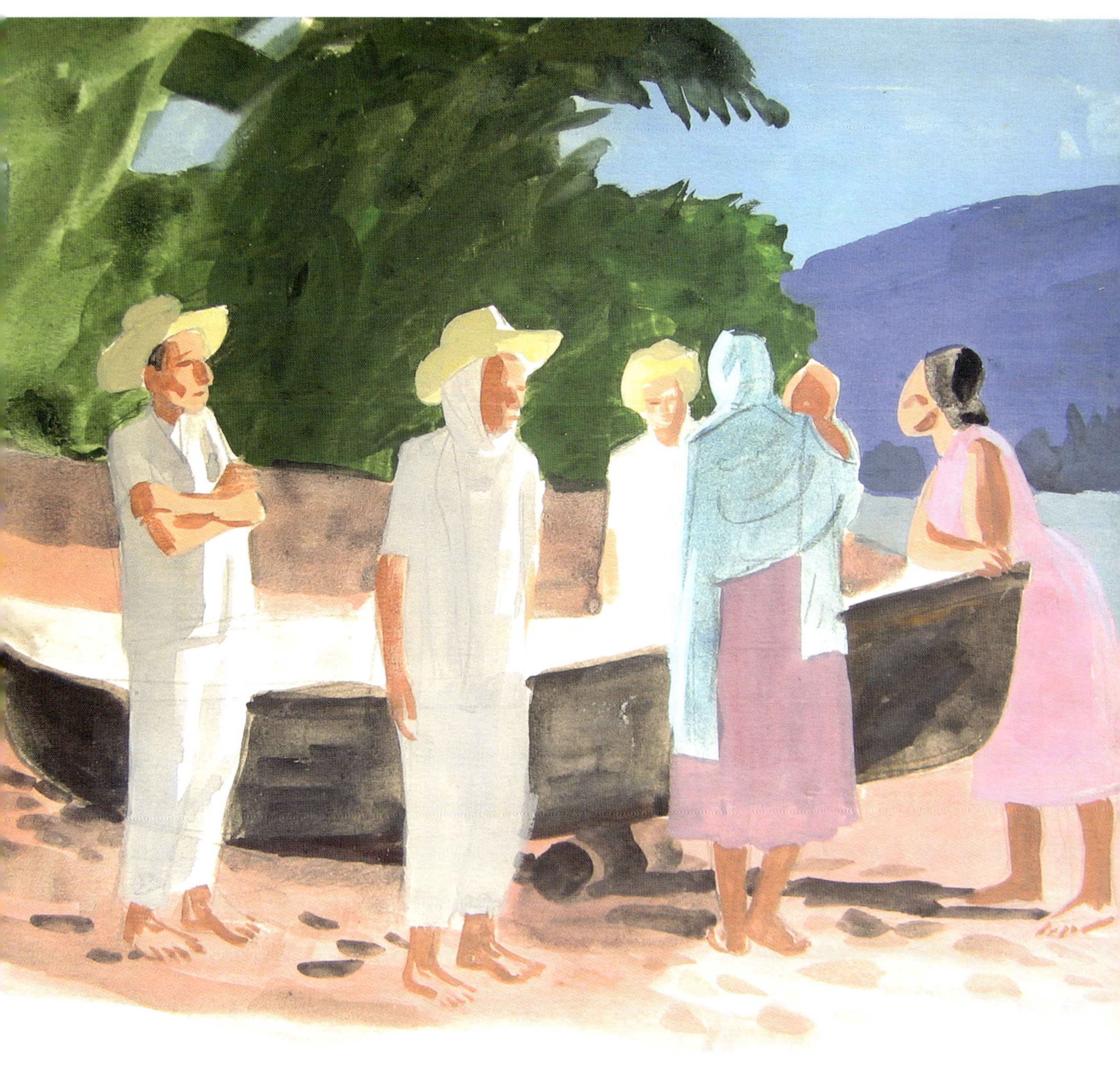

"Men and Women Around a Boat," acrylic on paper, 9" x 12", 1959.

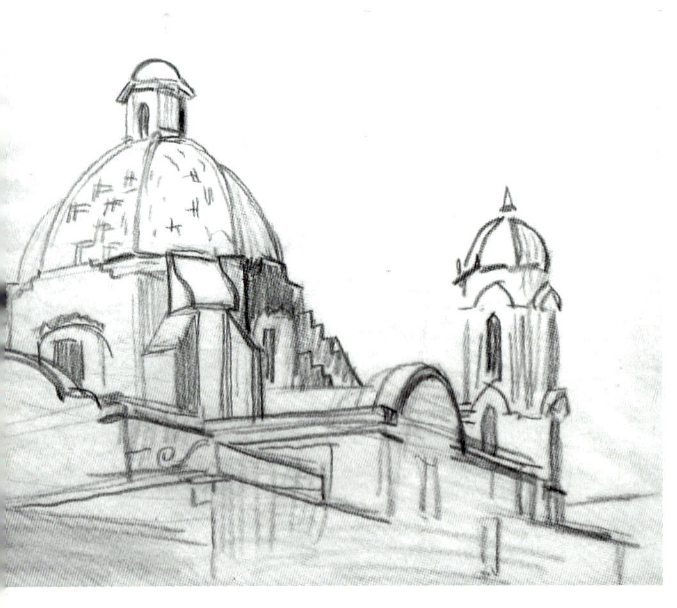

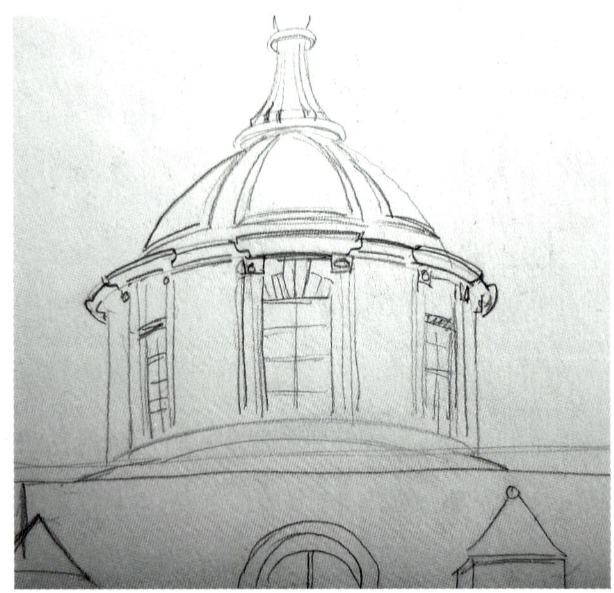

"Sketch of Church Domes," pencil on paper, 1959.

"Sketch of Dome of San Bernadino, Taxco," pencil on paper, 1959.

"Sketch of Arches and Flying Buttresses," pencil on paper, 1959.

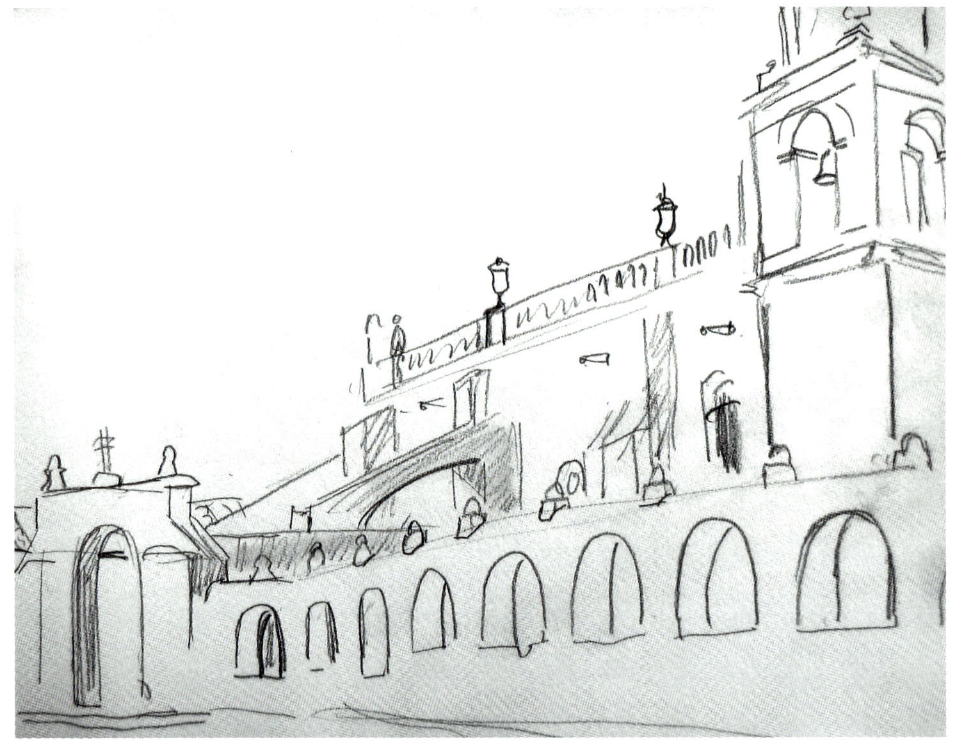

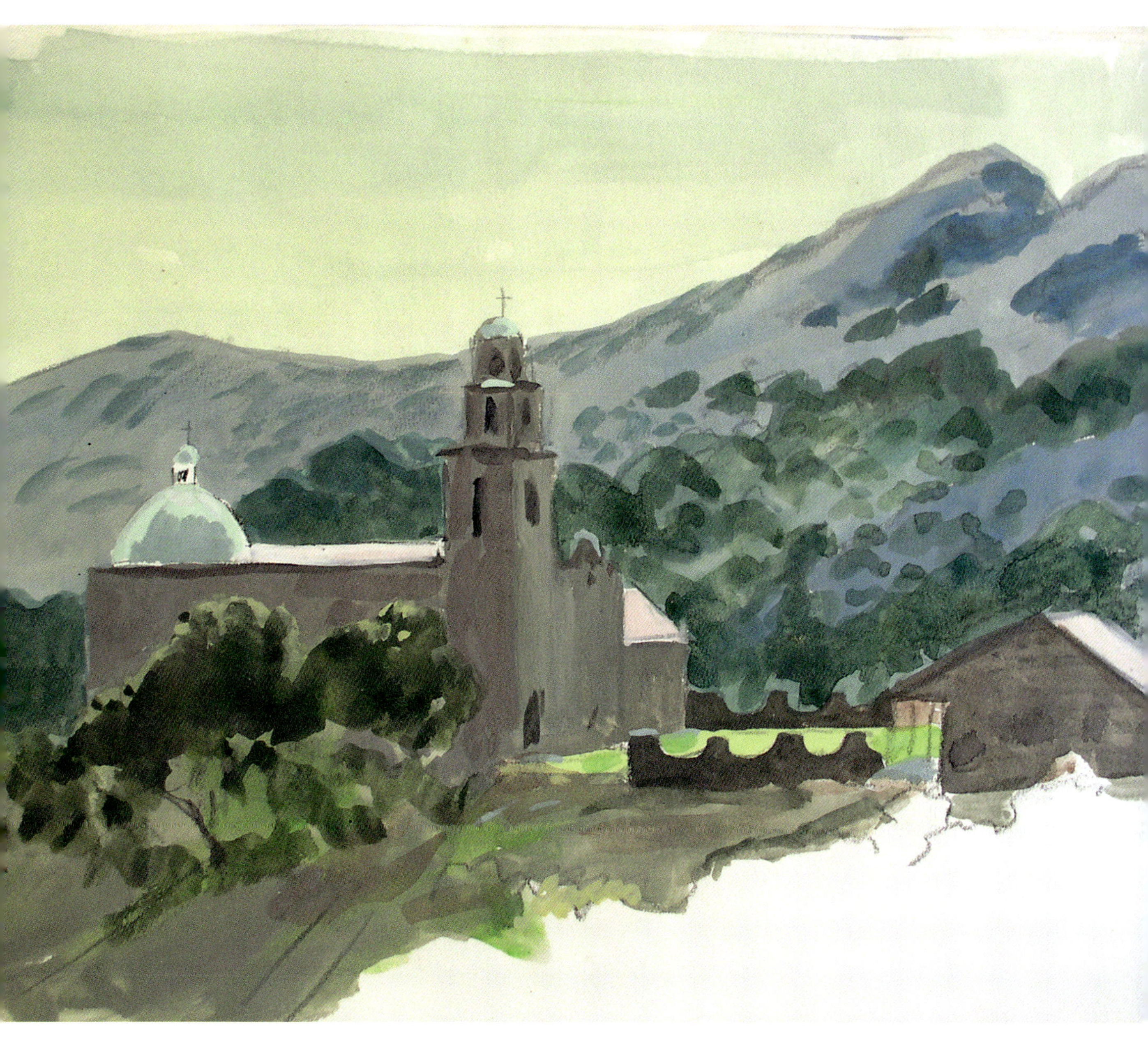

"Church in the Country,"
acrylic on paper,
19" x 12", 1959.

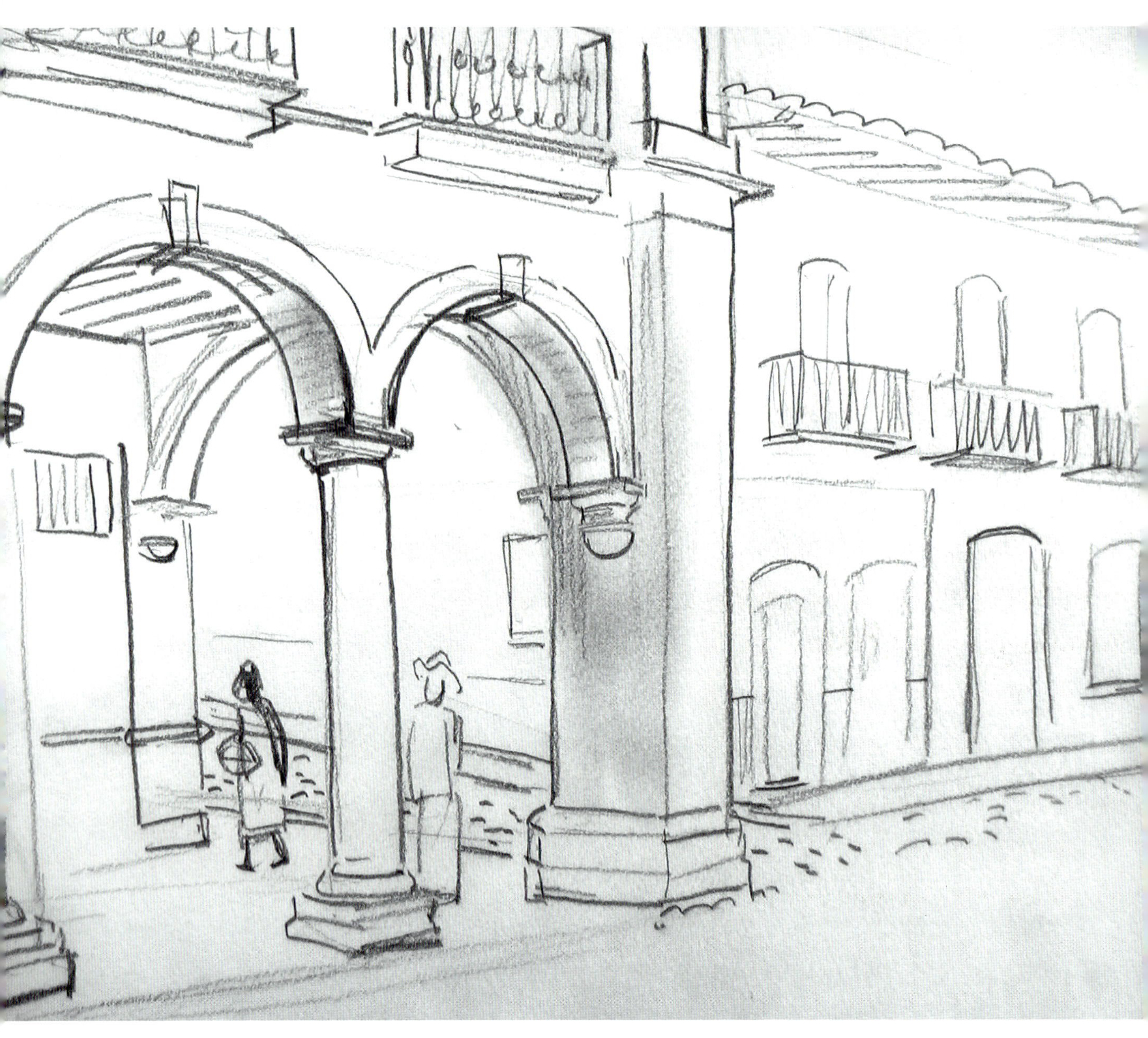

"Sketch of Entry Through Arches," pencil on paper, 1959.

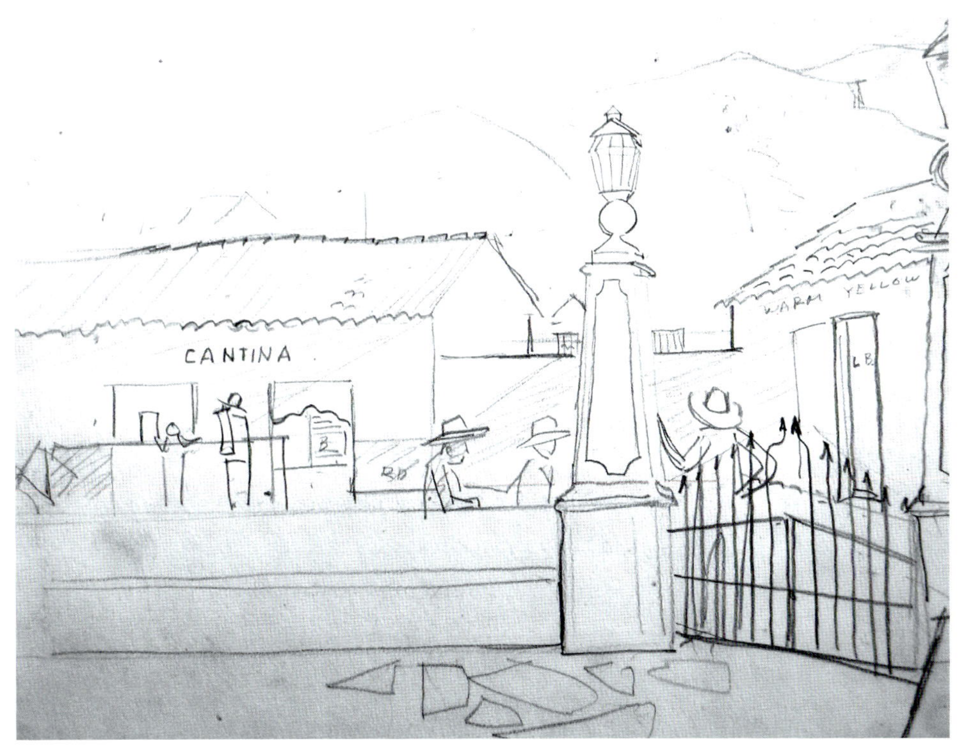

"Sketch of Cantina with Post and Gate," pencil on paper, 1959.

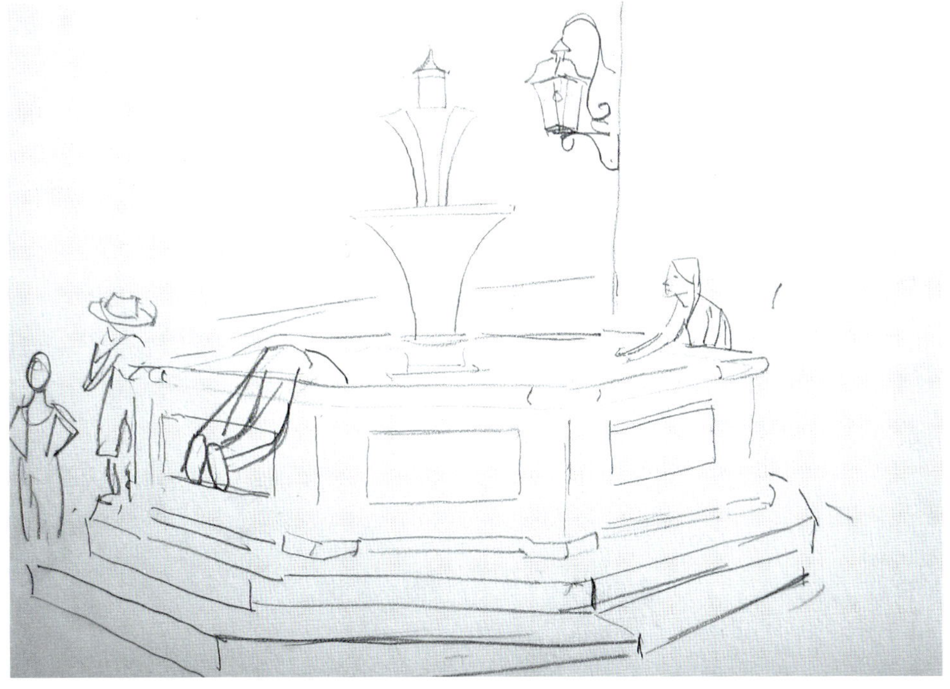

"Sketch of Public Fountain, Taxco," pencil on paper, 1959.

These sketches start out with what looks like a sketch of me (my hair was long and straight, Sal's was short and curly) on our living room balcony, drawn by my father sitting on the balcony of my parent's bedroom.

The rest of the sketches show a fantasy of a woman on the balcony while a man with a guitar walks the streets below. In Mexico, this would mean a serenade and romance.

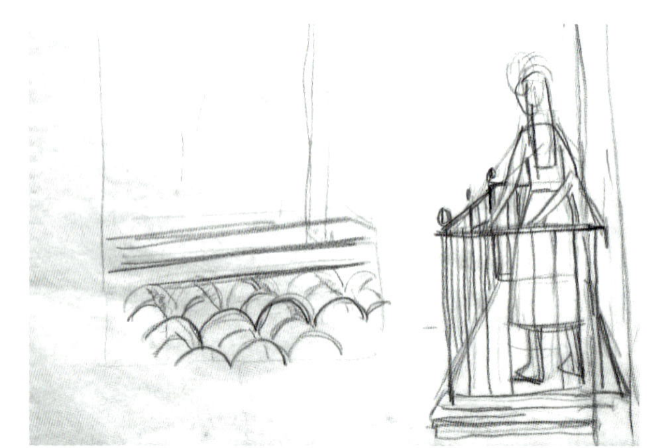

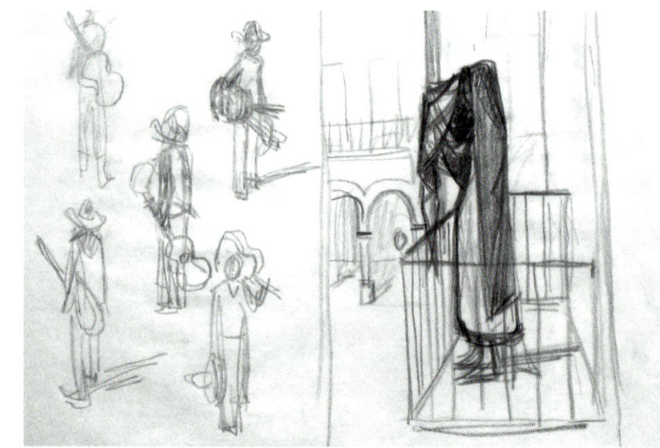

"Sketch of Jane on Balcony, Casa Borda, Taxco," pencil on paper, 1959.

"Sketch of Woman with Rebozo and Man with Guitar," pencil on paper, 1959.

"Sketch of Woman Peeking from Her Balcony at a Man in the Street," pencil on paper, 1959.

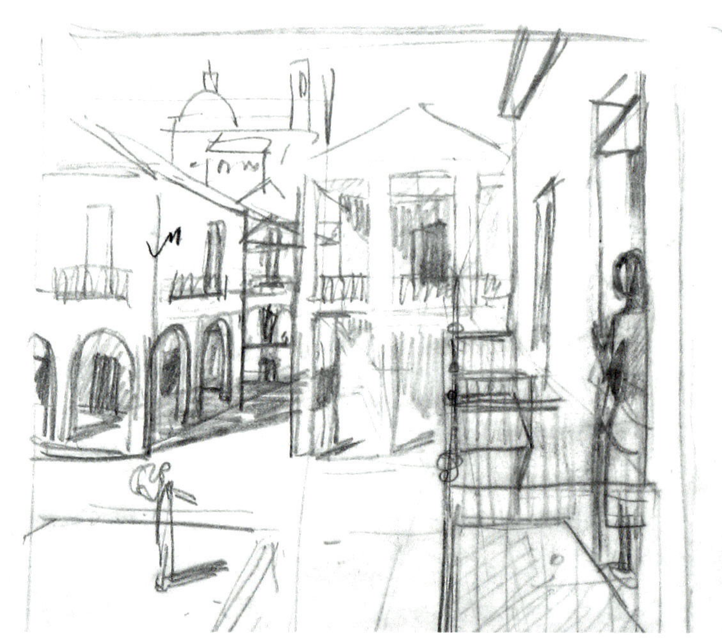

In the final painting, all the drama is hidden in an architectural scene.

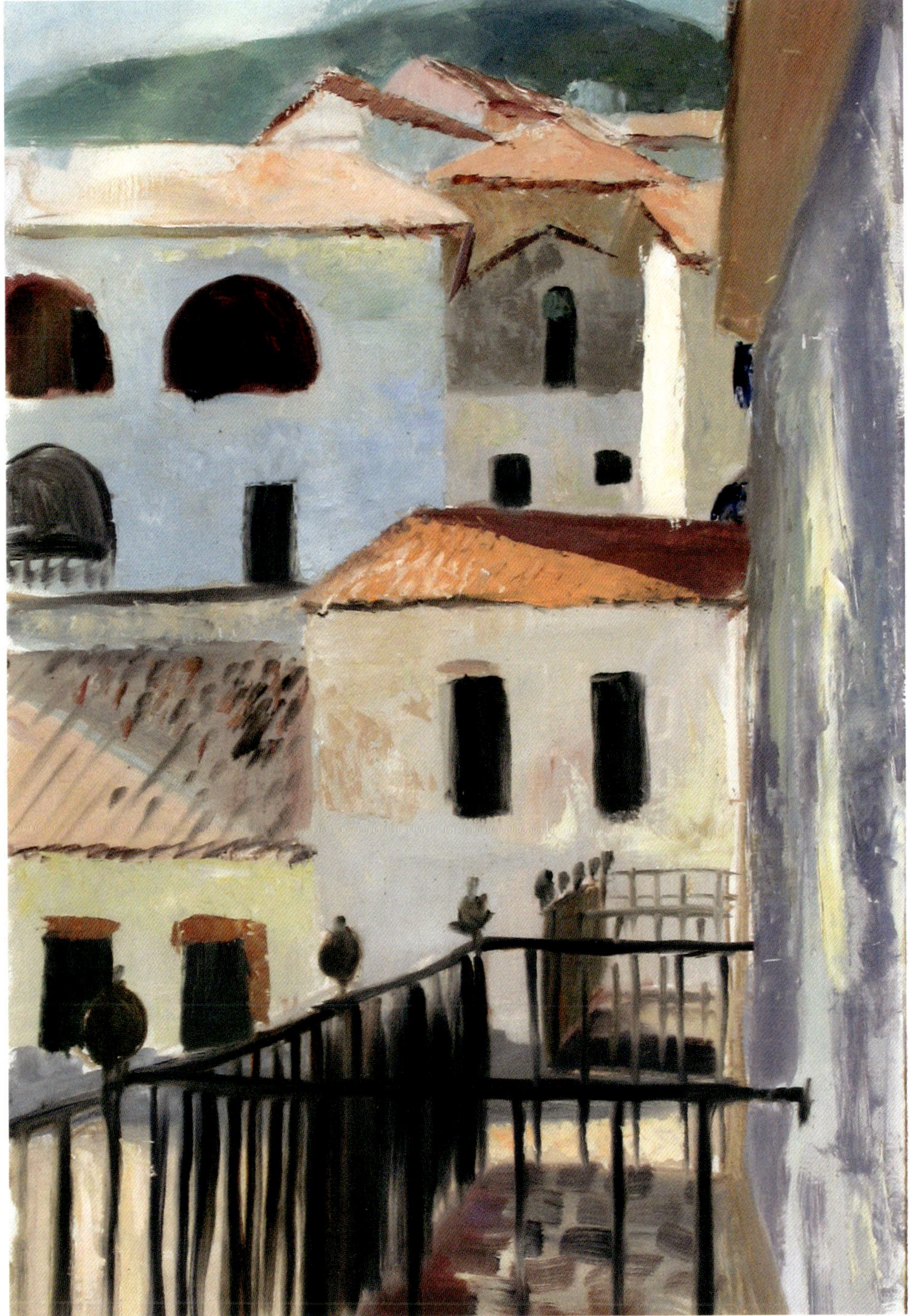

"Balconies of the Casa Borda, Taxco," oil on Masonite, 18" x 12", 1959.

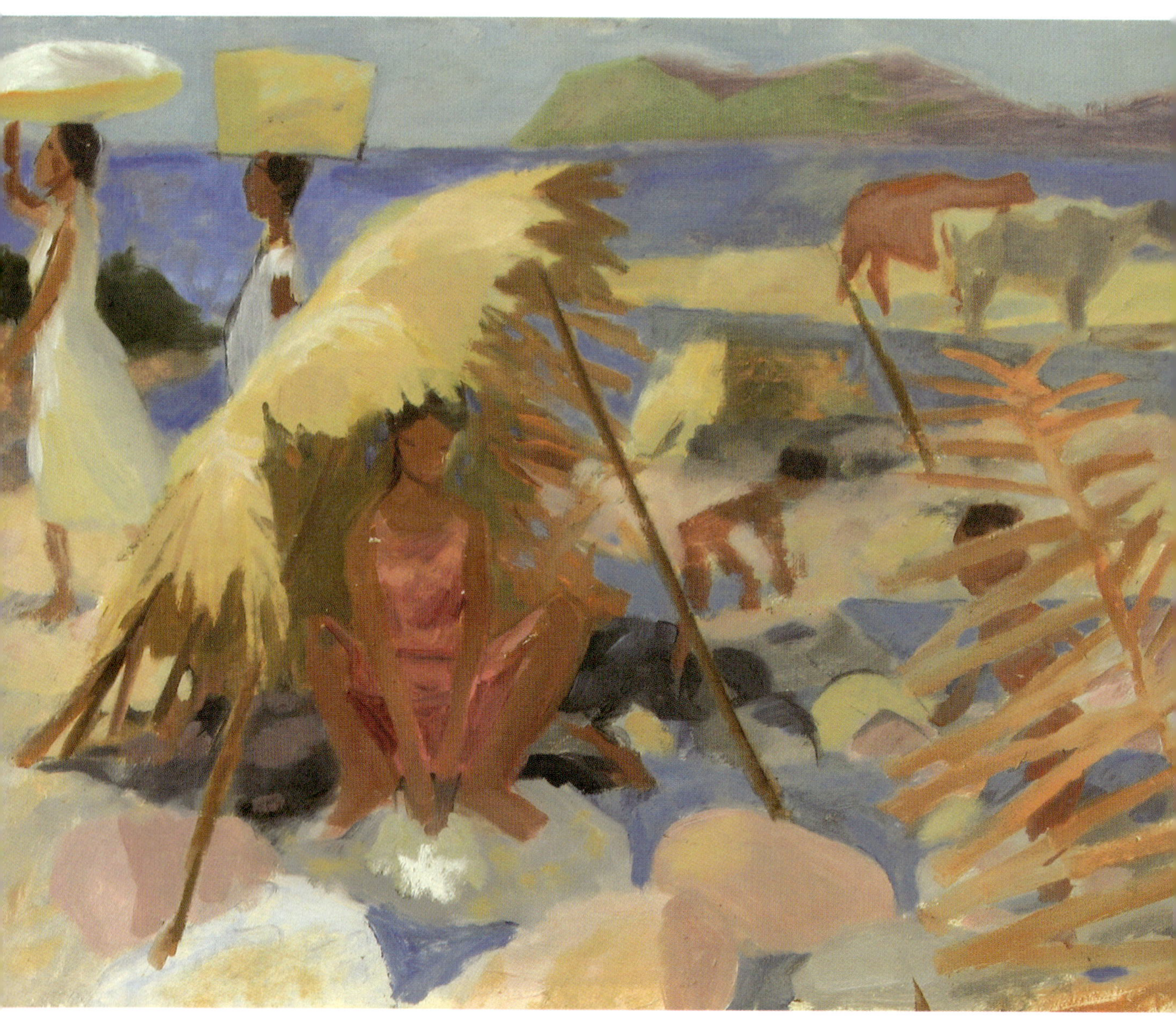

"Beach Scene, Zihuatinejo," oil on canvas board, 18" x 24", 1960s.

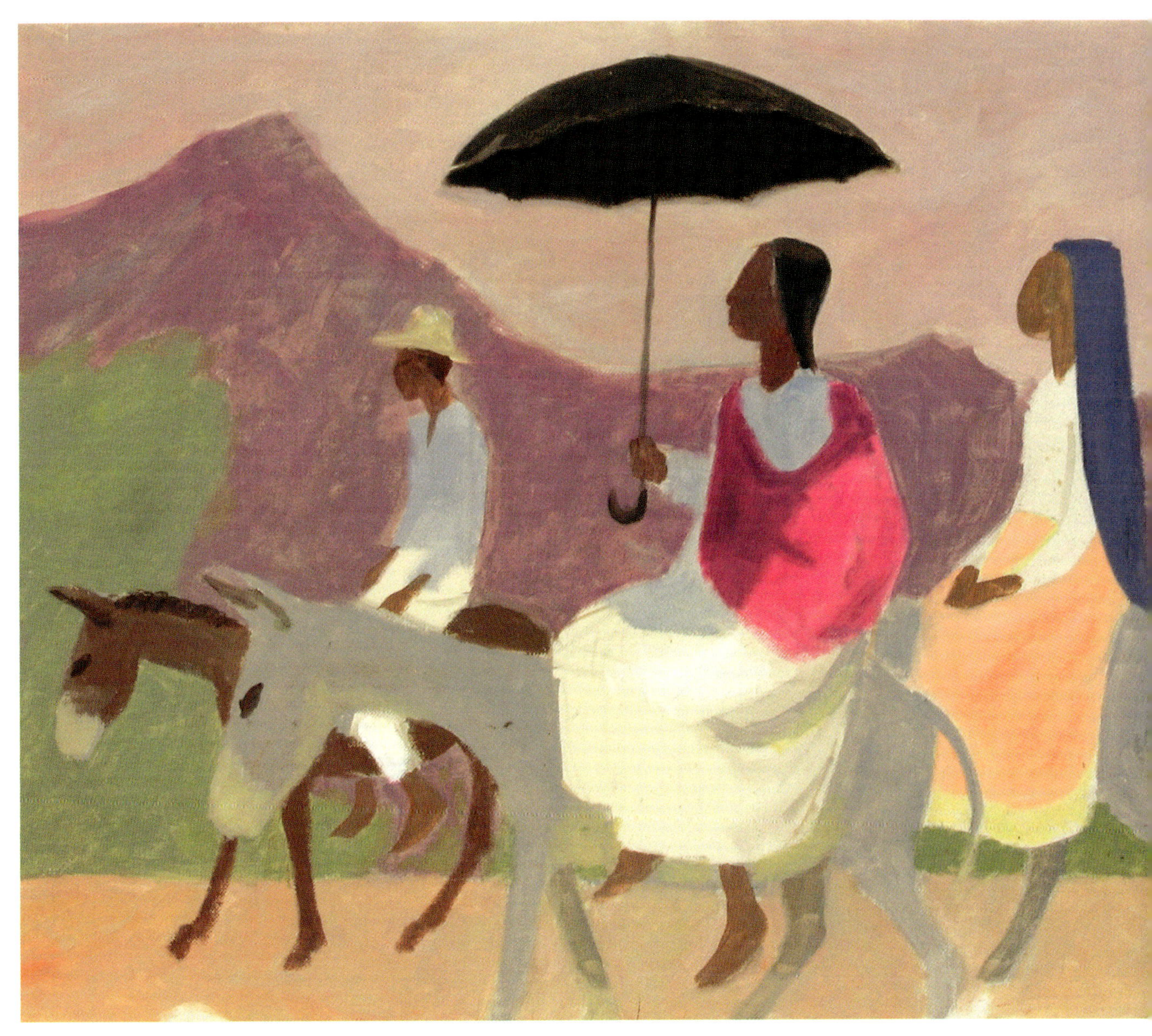

"People, Umbrella, and Burros," oil on canvas board, 14" x 18", 1960s.

Europe

7

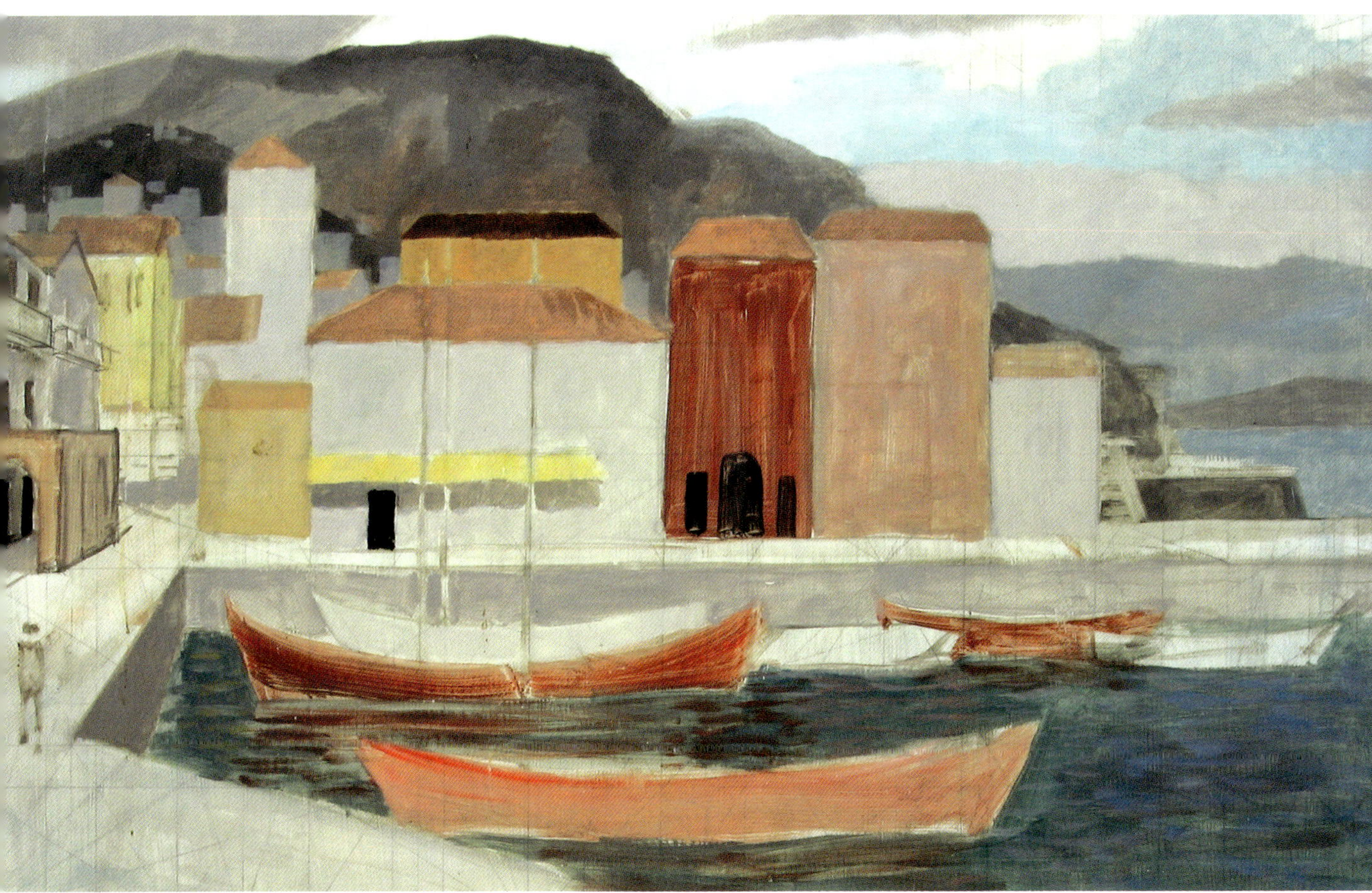

"Waterfront in Greece or Italy," oil on Masonite, 20" x 32", 1960s.

Bob won the Prix de Rome (now called the Rome Prize) during World War II, which included a year's study at the American Academy in Rome. However, because of the war, my father's year in Rome was postponed until 1948, when Rome had recovered enough for the Academy to reopen.

My family sailed to Rome when Sally was three and a half and I was just one month old. My father was thirty-four and Mom thirty-one. We lived in an apartment, and had the help of Maria, who was our cook, maid, and babysitter.

Maria helped my mother navigate the shopping, housekeeping, cooking, and childcare logistics in a foreign language and city.

During my father's year at the American Academy in Rome, he took lessons in mosaics and made three pieces. When we came home from Italy, two of these mosaics sat on the mantle of our living room in Maine. The chimney area was dim and the mosaics were somber and very high up, so it was hard to see them. Sal said that when she asked Bob about this mosaic, he replied that it was a baby carriage. It was only when I was a teenager and helped take the mosaic down for cleaning, that I saw that it was also a unicorn.

"Unicorn Baby Carriage," mosaic, 15" x 15", 1948–49.

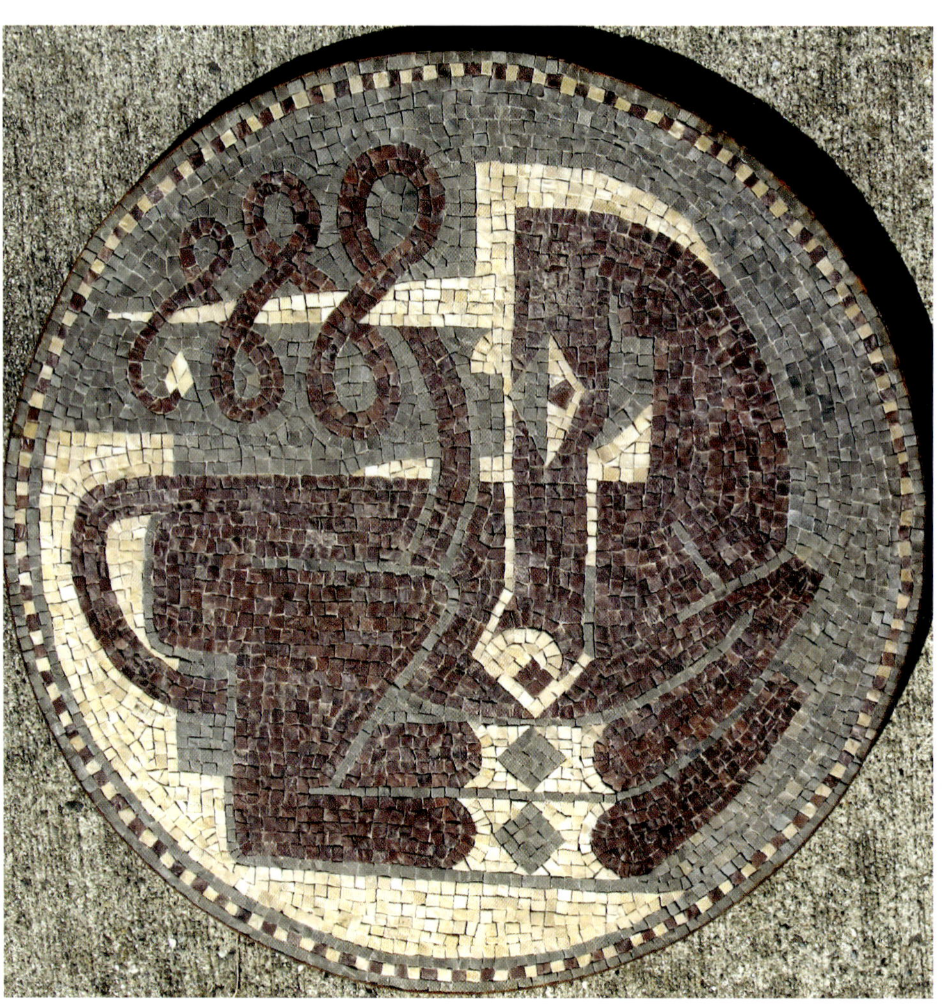

The unicorn was a magical beast, which could only be caught by a virgin. The virgin girl went into the forest alone and sat down in a clearing. By and by, a unicorn came to her, laid his head in her lap and went to sleep. While he was asleep, the people of the town crept up on the pair and threw a net over them, bound the unicorn, and returned with him to town, where he was given to a "worthy couple."

The unicorn legend is surely a story of the transformation of a young man into a responsible husband and family man, and of the transmutation of a wild but innocent girl into a responsible wife and mother. The virgin and the unicorn become the Worthy Couple, and the myth culminates with the arrival of a baby and a baby carriage. My father had become a father for a second time when I was born just before we went to Italy. My arrival must have brought home to my father his family role and responsibilities, which he showed in his mosaic.

The baby carriage may also have been in memory of my father's grandfather on his mother's side, who died in 1913, a year before my father was born. A runaway baby carriage was rushing toward the railroad tracks with a train fast approaching. My great grandfather, Christian Wismeyer, raced to the tracks and managed to pull the carriage to safety, but he himself was killed.

As is often the case in my father's world, things are not what they seem: A baby carriage, which seems like the epitome of security, became an instrument of death to his grandfather, near death to the baby his grandfather rescued, and the entrapment of a free, young, unicorn man.

When I asked Bob about this mosaic, he said, "She is smoking a cigarette." But later I saw that she is also playing the old game with a daisy: he loves me, he loves me not...

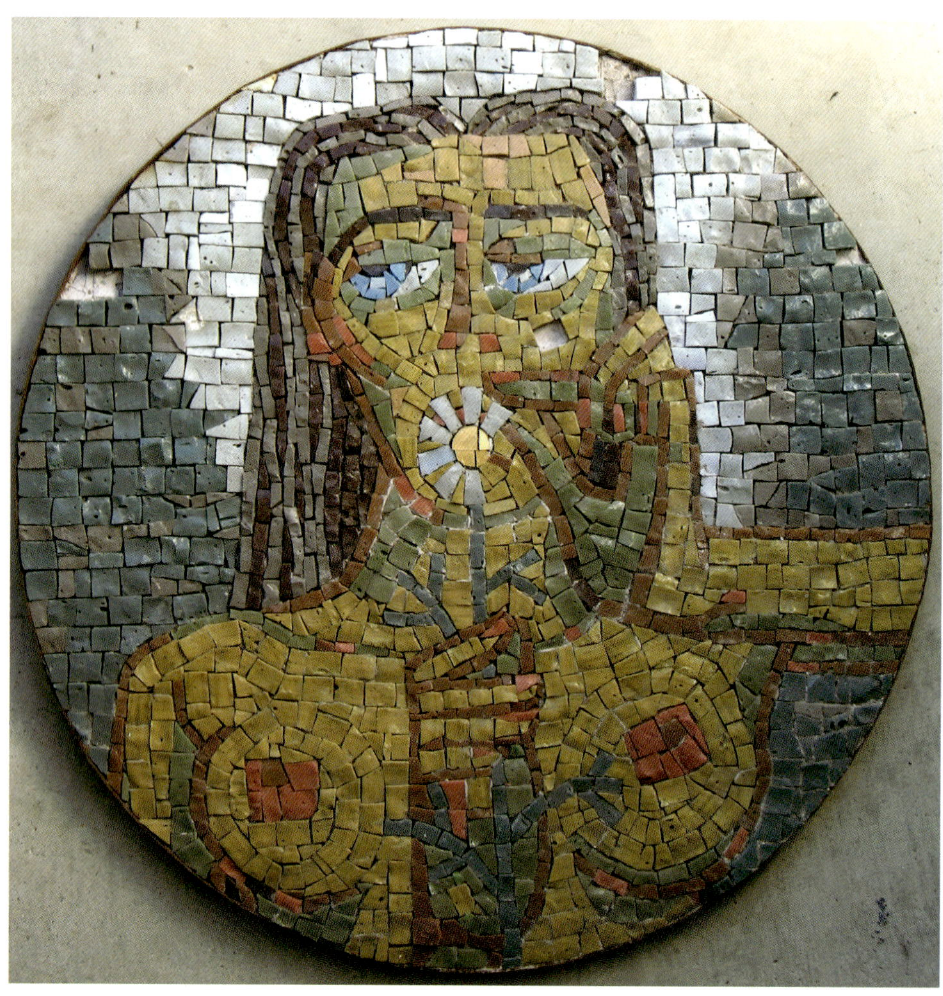

"Woman Pulling Petals from a Daisy (or Smoking a Cigarette,)" mosaic, 15" x 15", 1948–49.

My father did a mosaic of a seagull, which we already saw in the Maine chapter.

Back in Italy, Sal caught scarlet fever, and we were put in quarantine. After she recovered and we escaped from quarantine, my father cut short his year of study and our family came home to the States.

Twelve years later, in the winter of 1960-61, we returned to Europe. My parents put Sal and me in school in Switzerland, while they traveled around Greece and Italy. The following pictures are from that time. Bob made sketches that winter, and then did the paintings over a number of years after my family returned home.

"Sketch of Village on Promontory," pencil on paper, 1960.

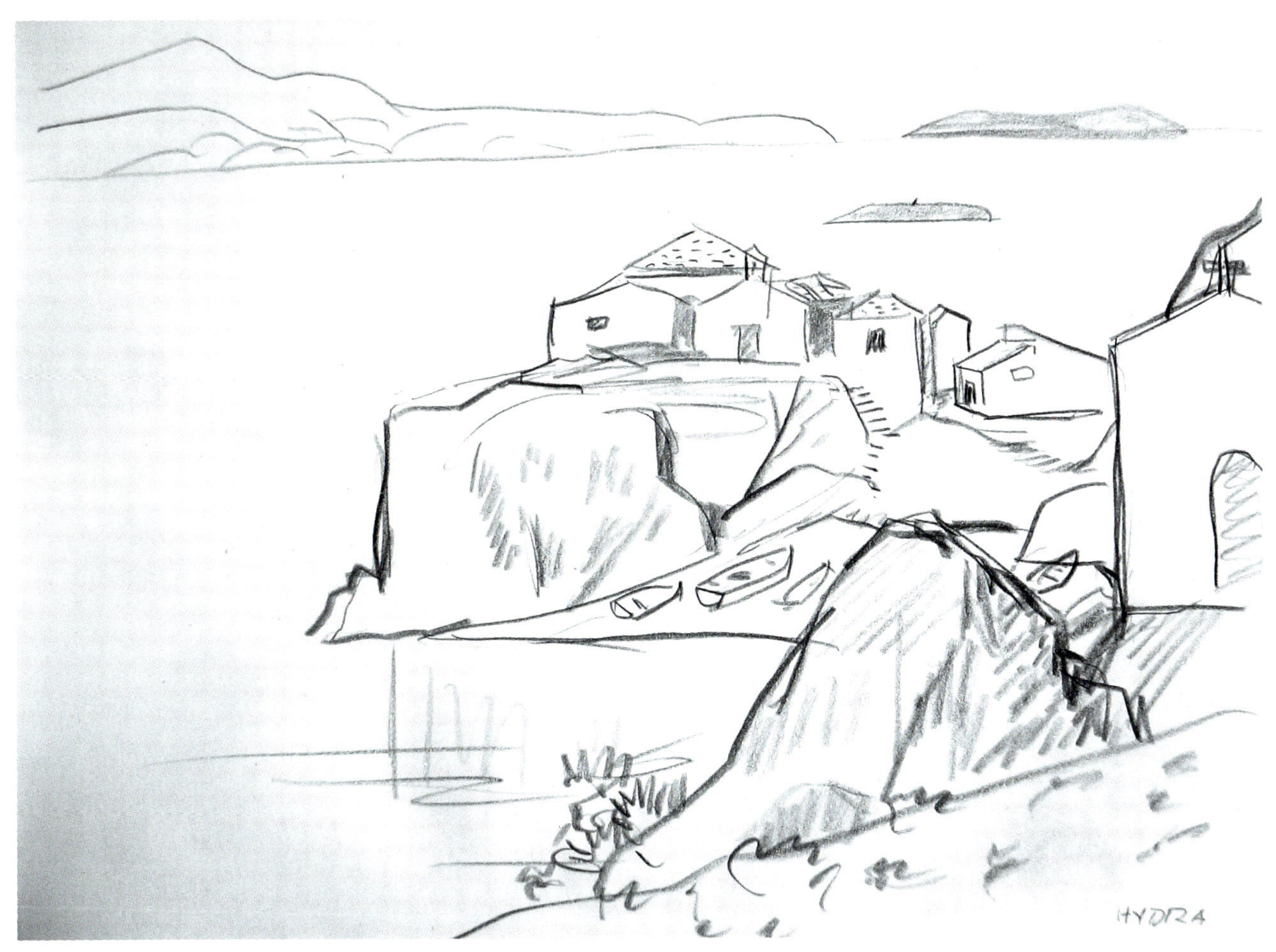

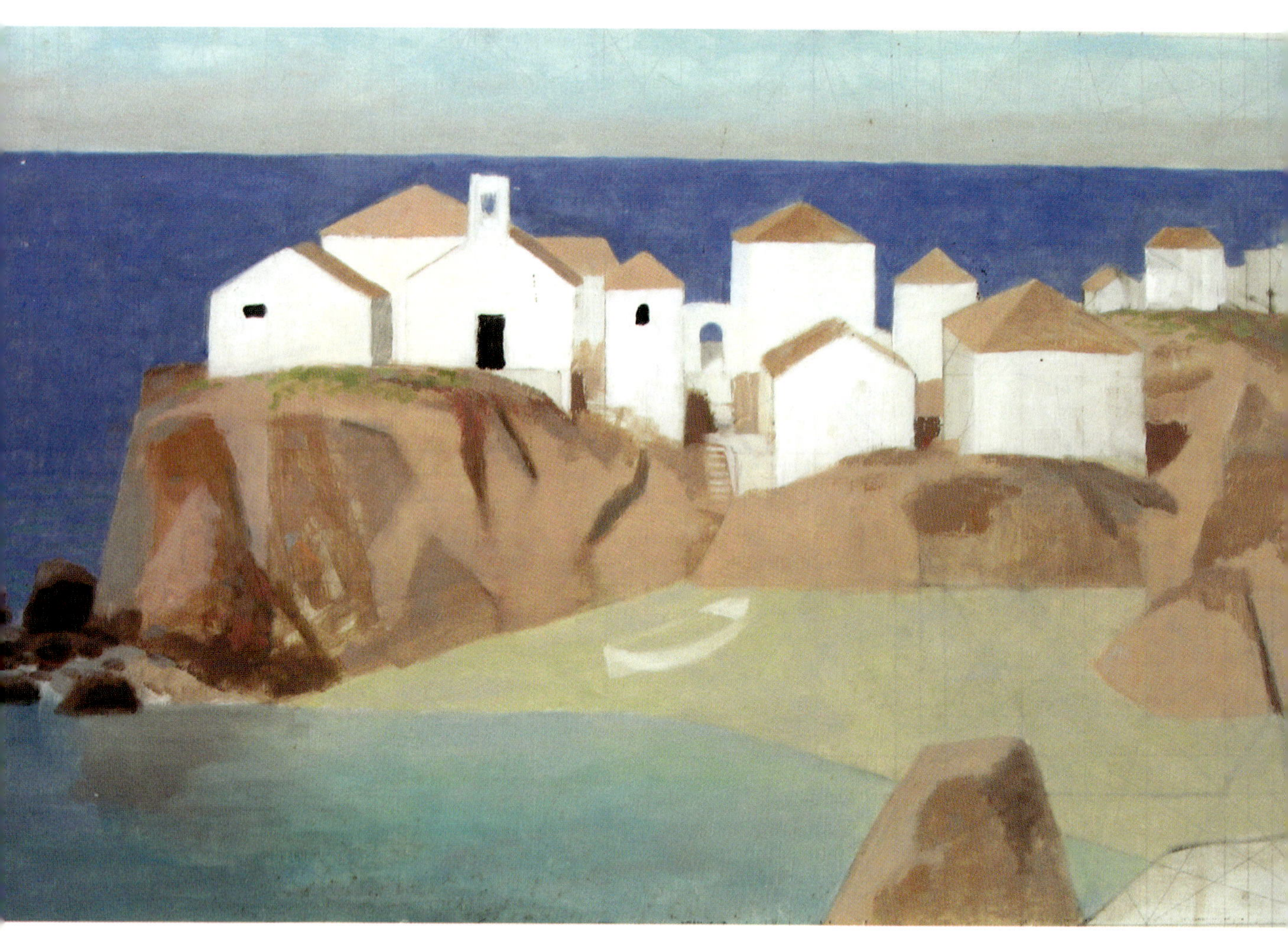

"Village on Promontory in Greece or Italy," oil on Masonite, 20" x 32", 1960s.

"Town on Water in Greece," oil on Masonite, 20" x 32", 1960s.

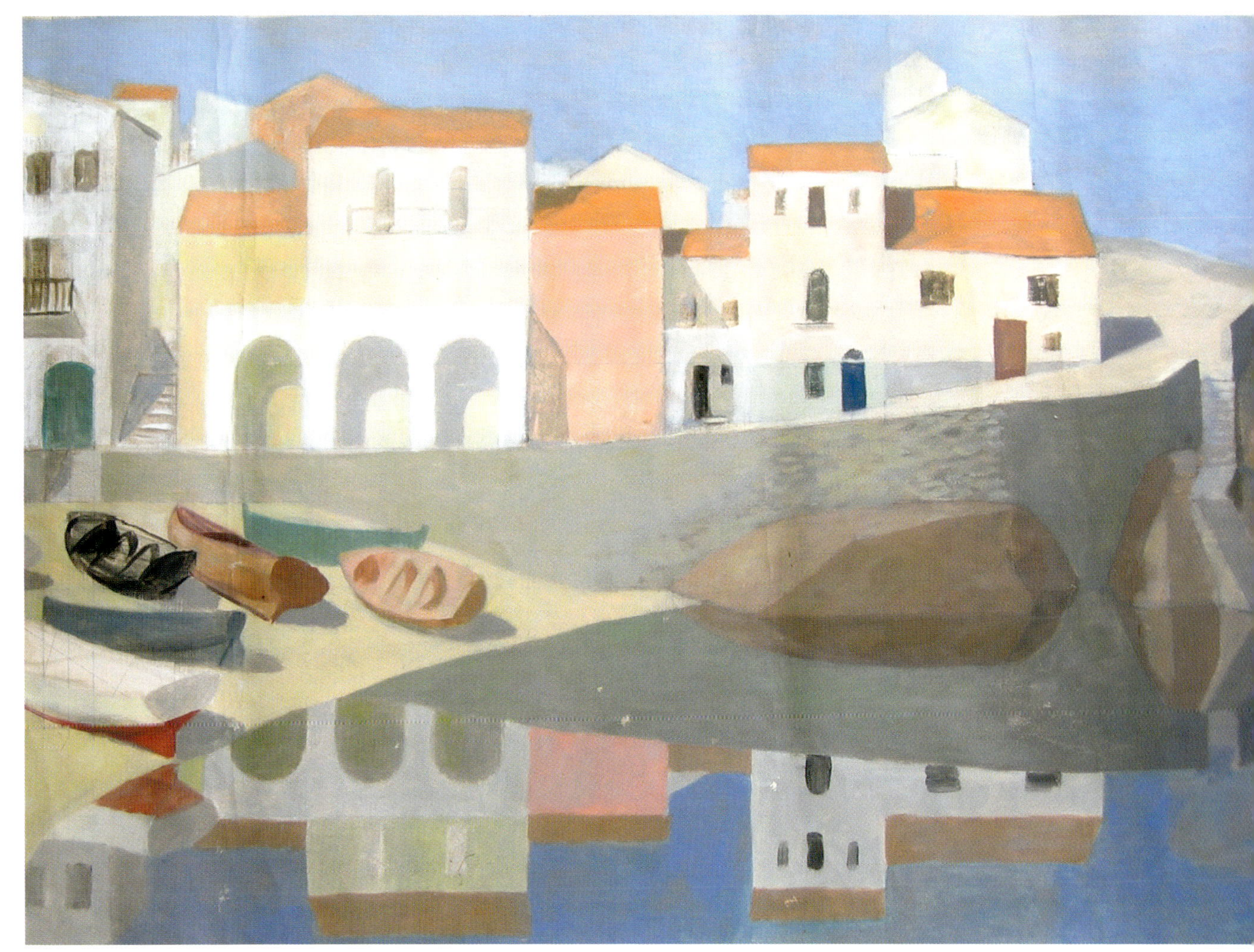

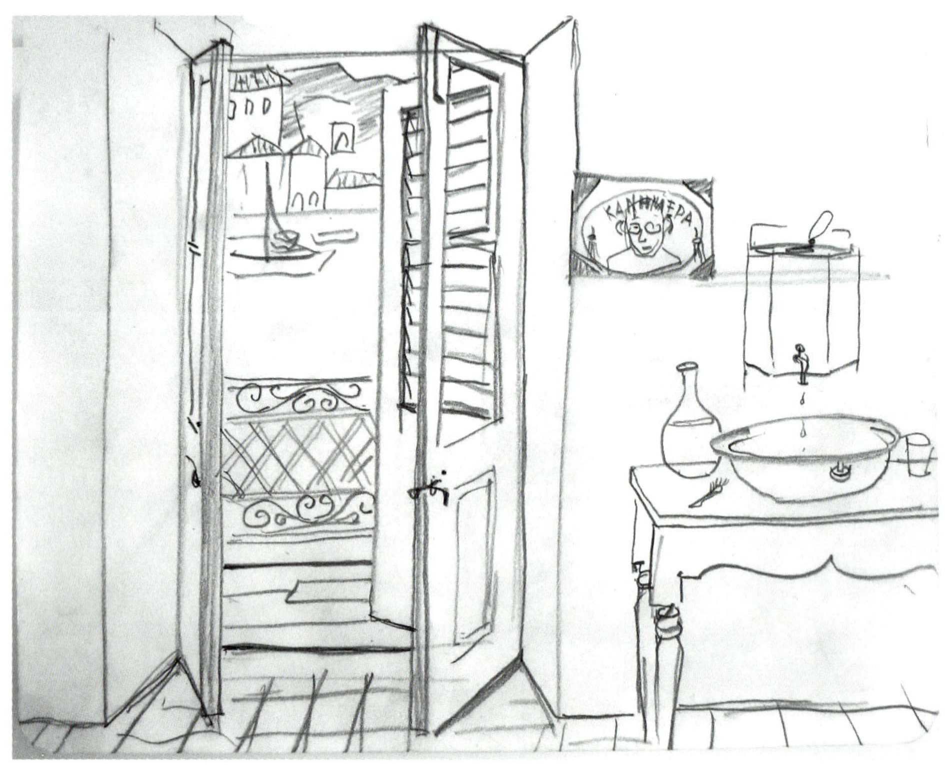

"Sketch of Bedroom," pencil on paper, 1960.

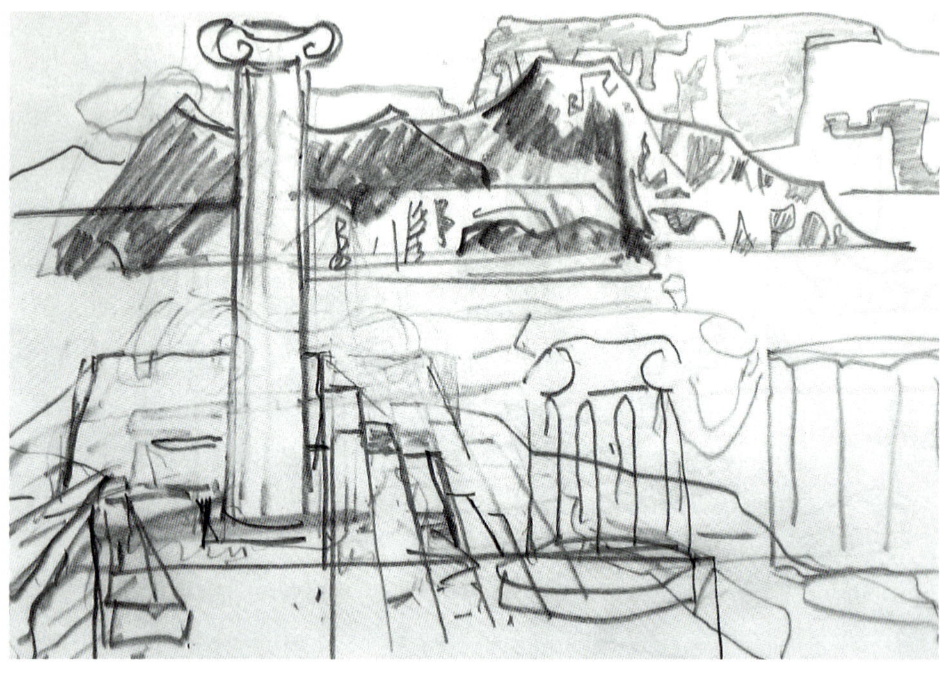

"Sketch of Pillar and Steps," pencil on paper, 1960.

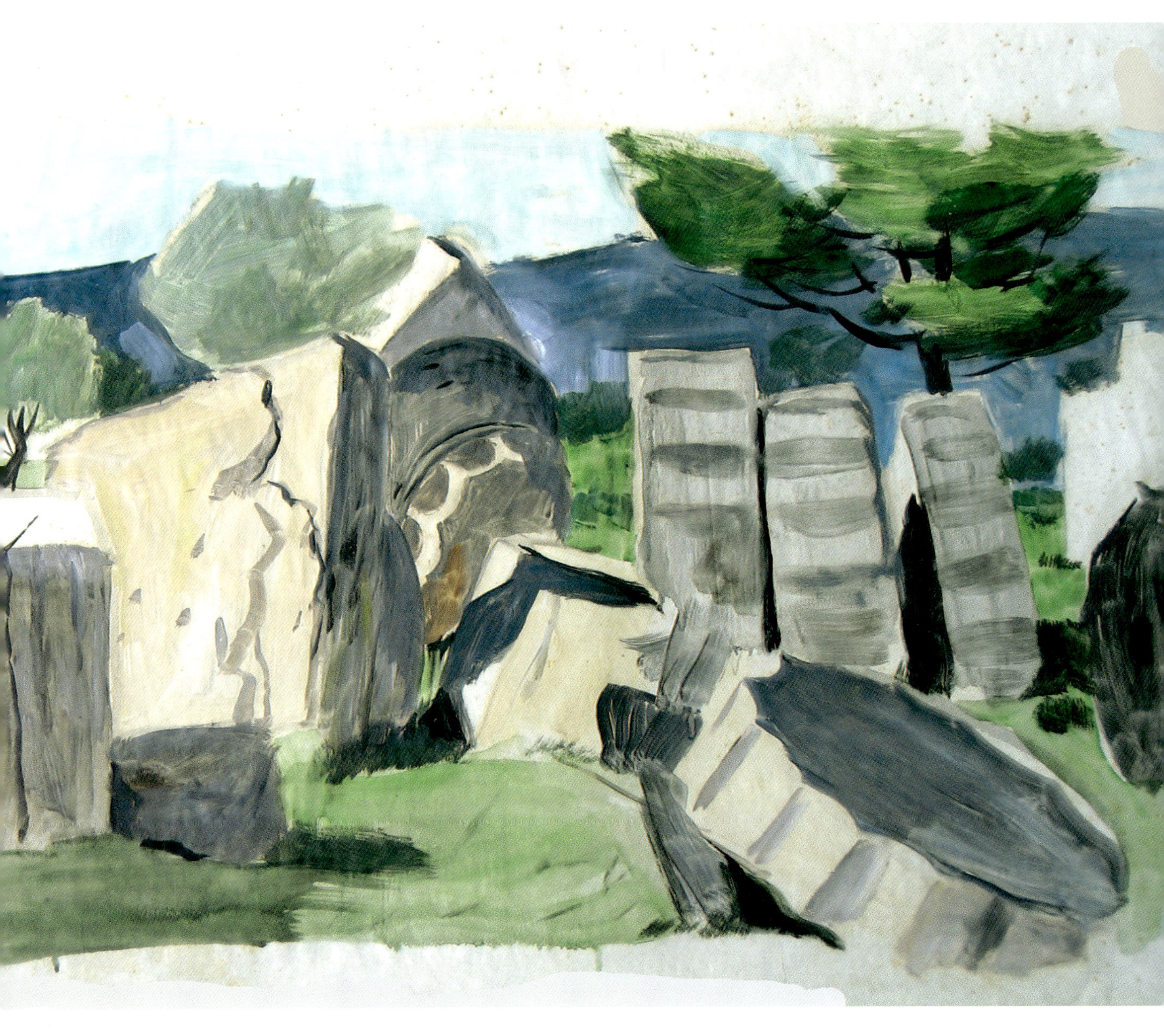

"Greek Ruins," acrylic on paper, 8" x 12", 1960.

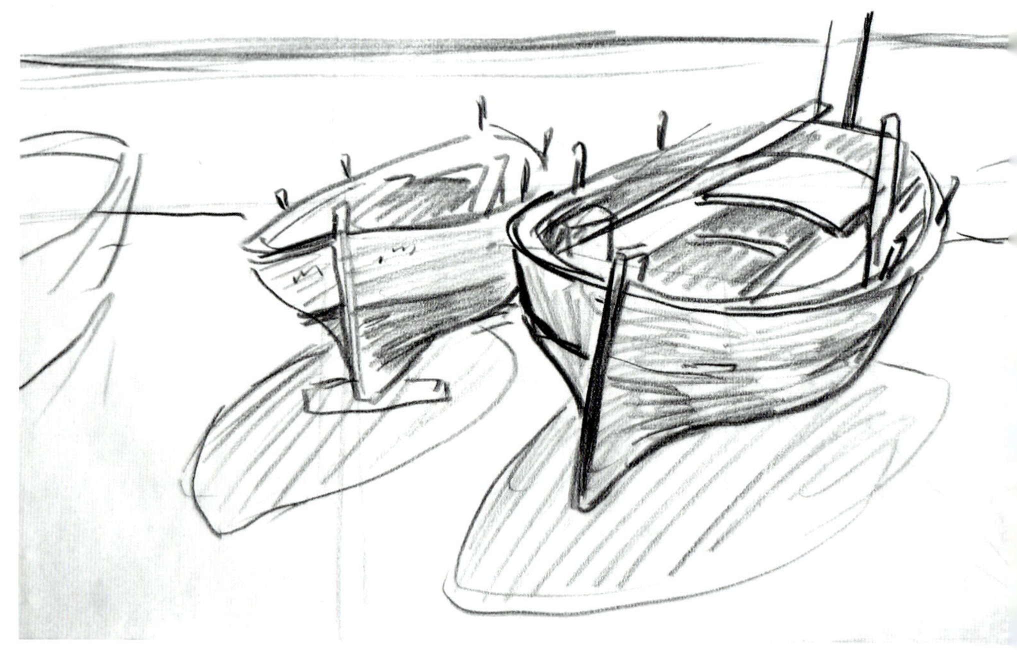

"Sketch of Boats on Beach," pencil on paper, 1960.

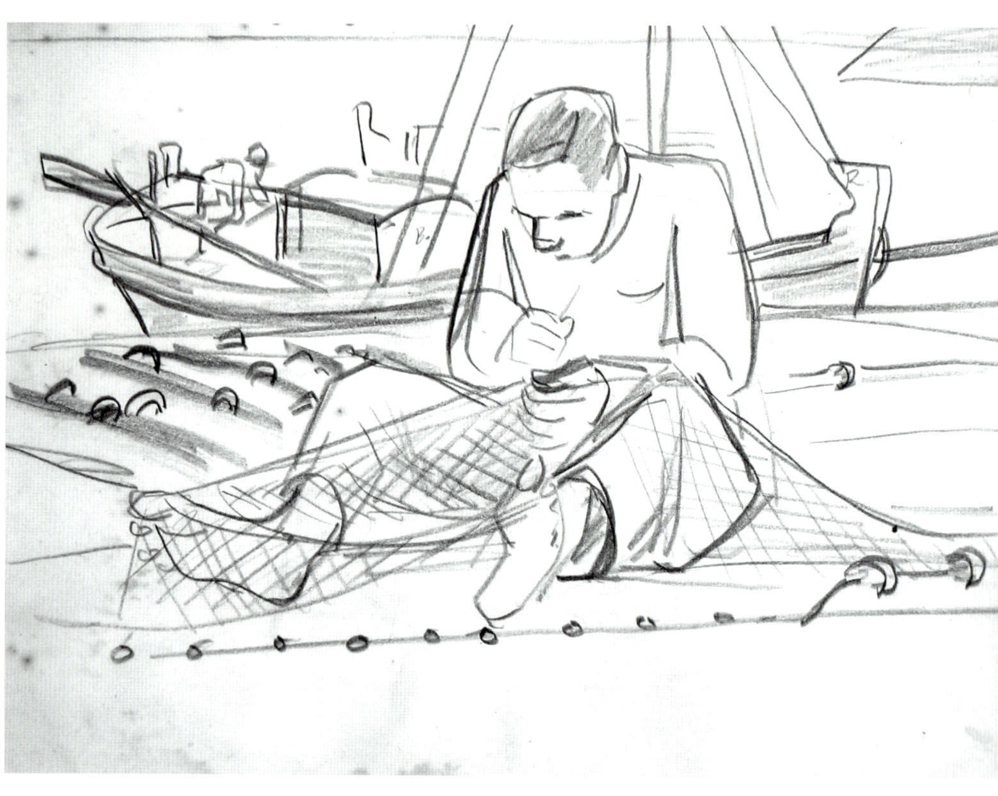

"Sketch of Fisherman Mending Nets," pencil on paper, 1960.

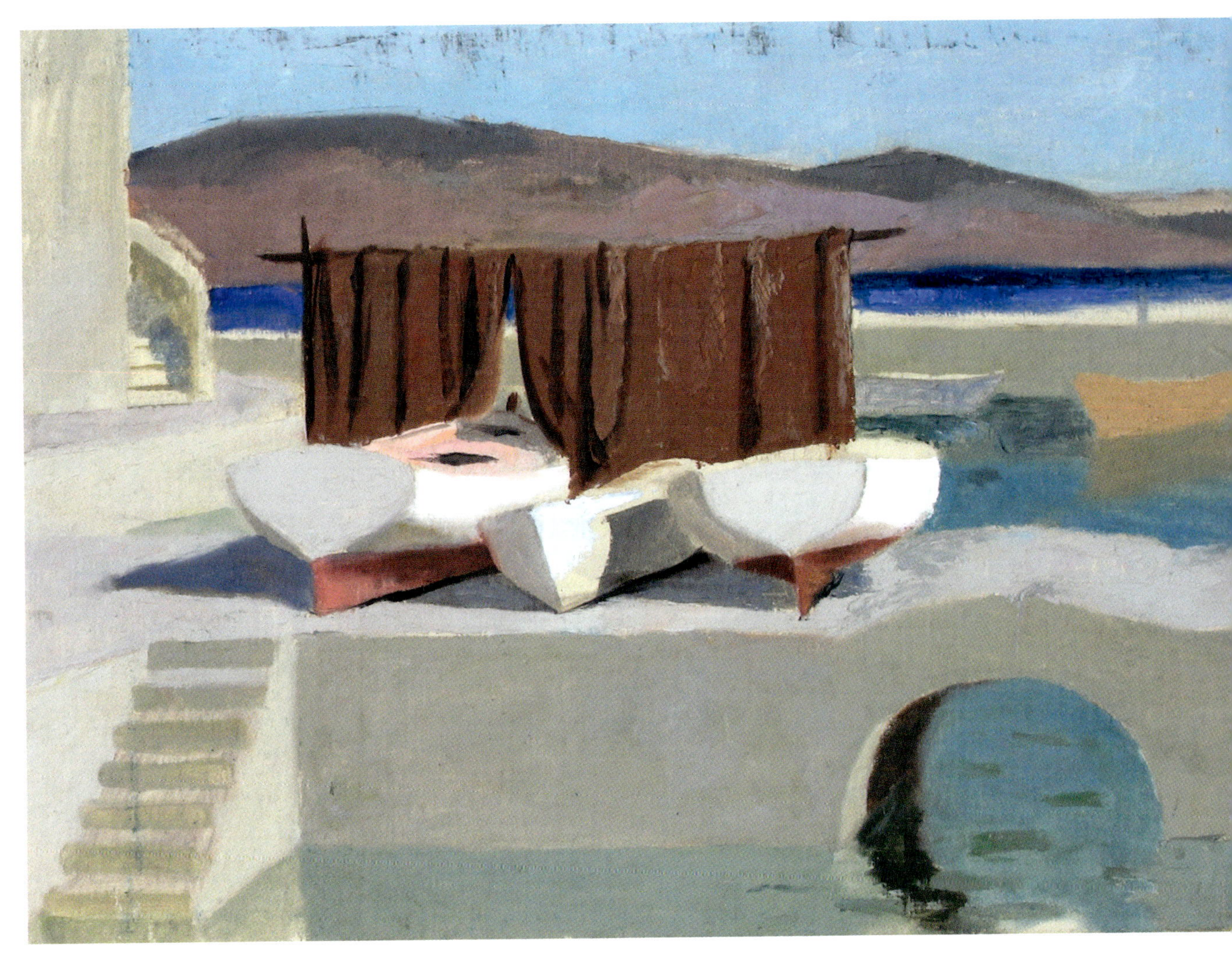

"Three Boats and One Arch," oil on Masonite, 15" x 25", 1960.

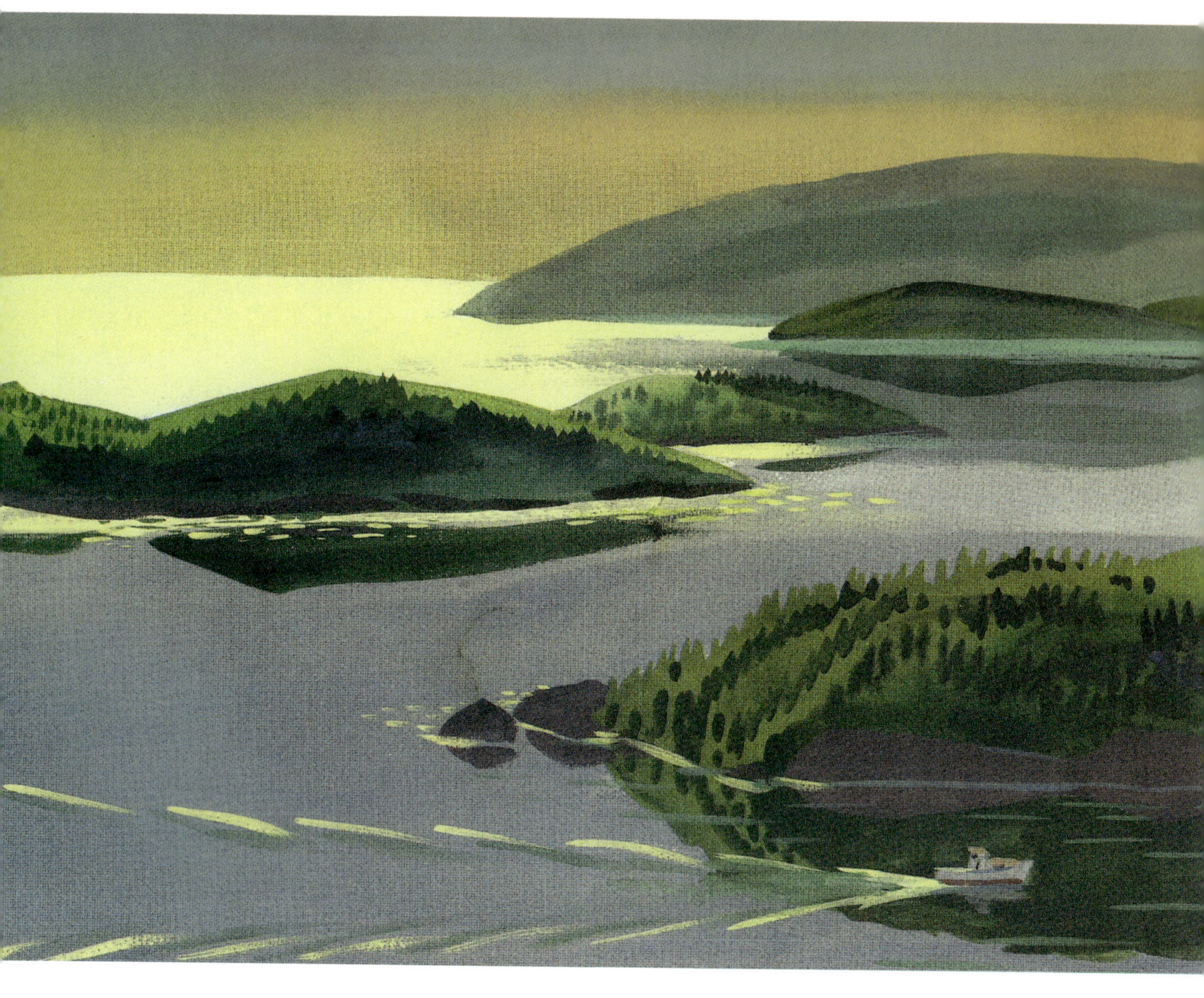

"Morning Light on the Harbor," from *Time of Wonder*, Viking press, 1957.

My father loved the patterns of mountains and the sea, especially with the shadows of the clouds on them. *Time of Wonder* features patterned islands in the sea, but islands are just mountains submerged. He continued drawing mountains in Mexico, and then Europe.

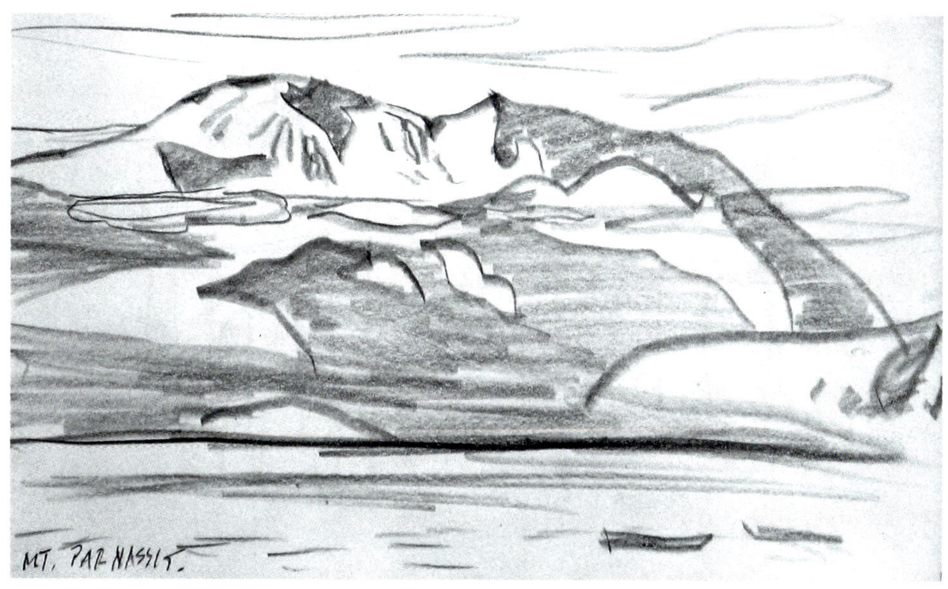

"Sketch of Mount Parnassos," pencil on paper, 1959.

"Mountains and the Sea, Mexico," acrylic on paper, 12" x 19", 1959.

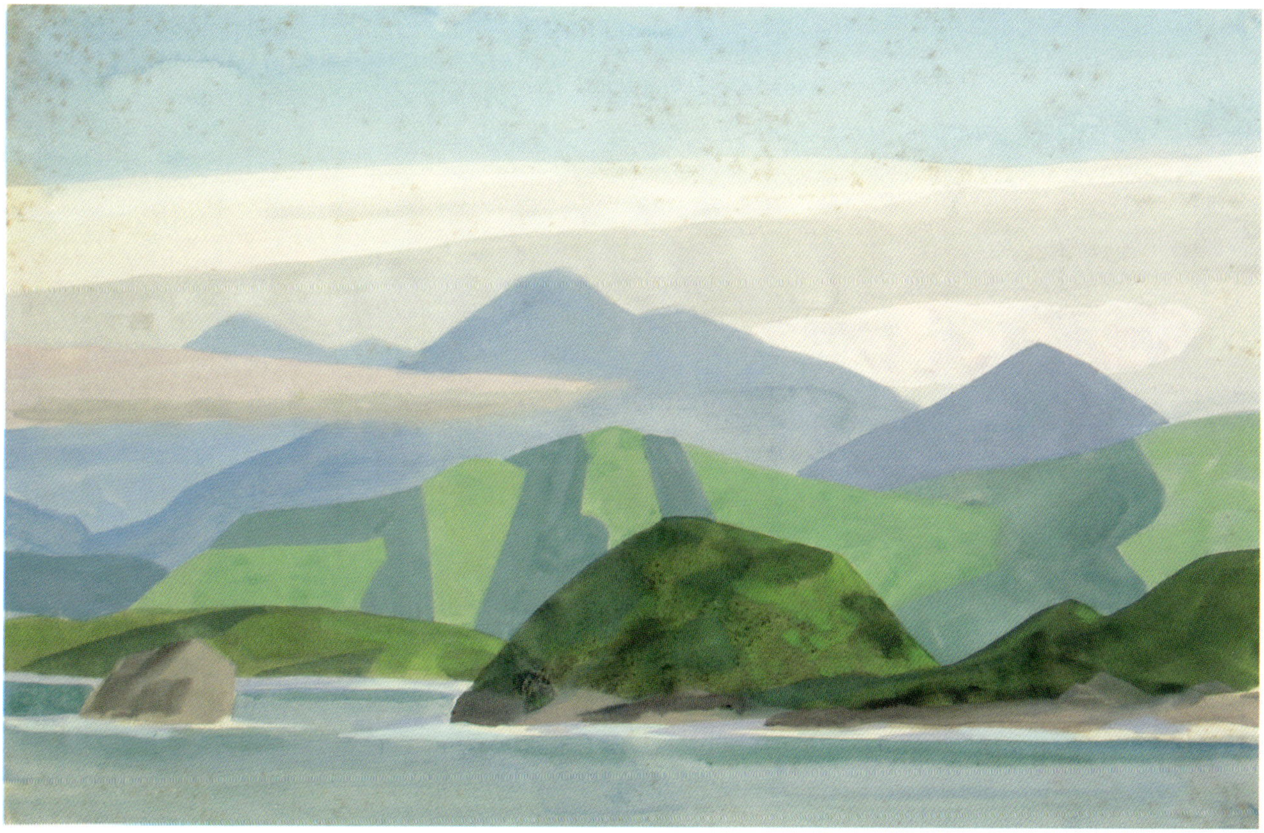

According to myth, Orpheus spent his youth on Mount Parnassos, and while he was there, Apollo gave him a lyre. Pan and Dionysus were supposed to have lived on the mountain and, so, too, did the Muses, who oversaw art, poetry, music, and dance. The winged horse Pegasus lived on Mount Parnassos, too. My father loved classical art and mythology and was surely aware of the mythological history of the mountain.

In Greek myth, Europa was carried off by Zeus in the form of a bull. Below is a sketch of mountains and a bull, possibly Zeus.

"Sketch of Mountain and Bull," pencil on paper, 1960.

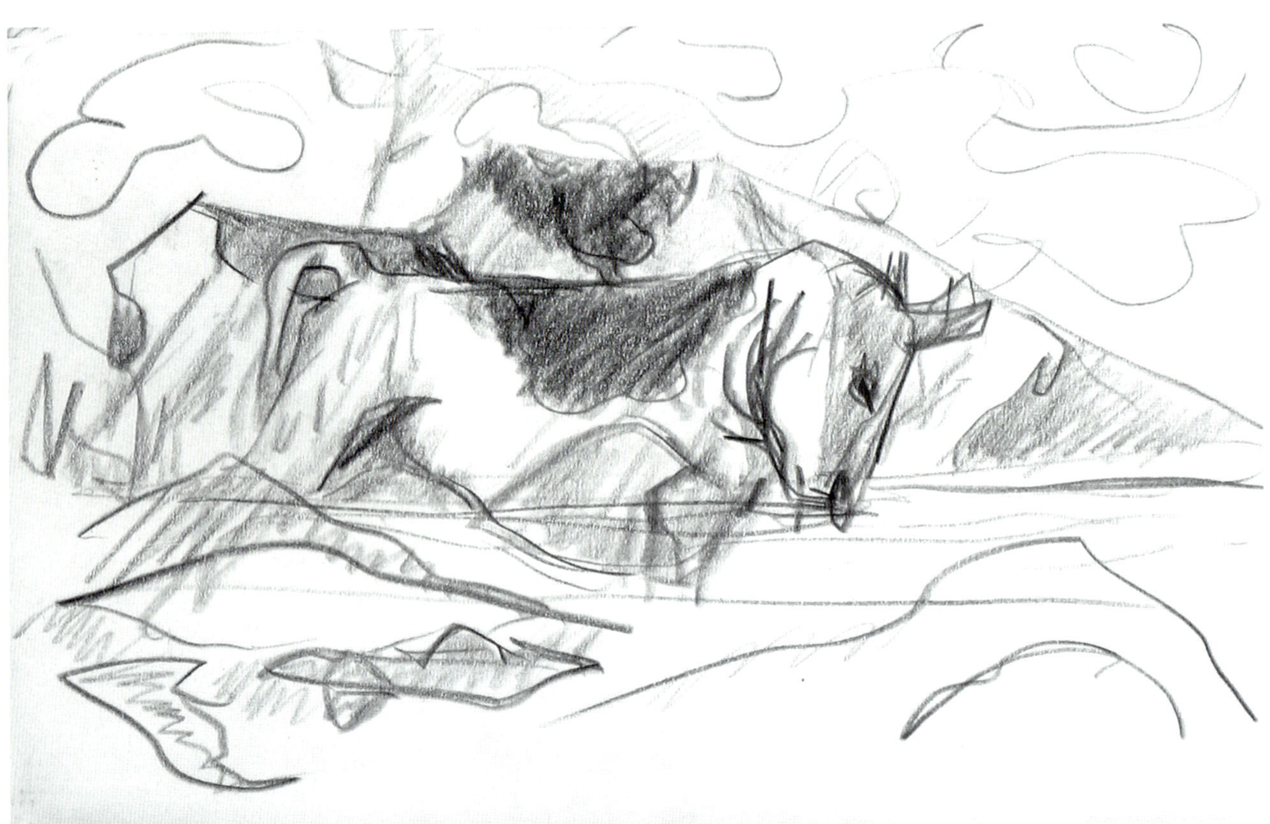

St. Thomas 8

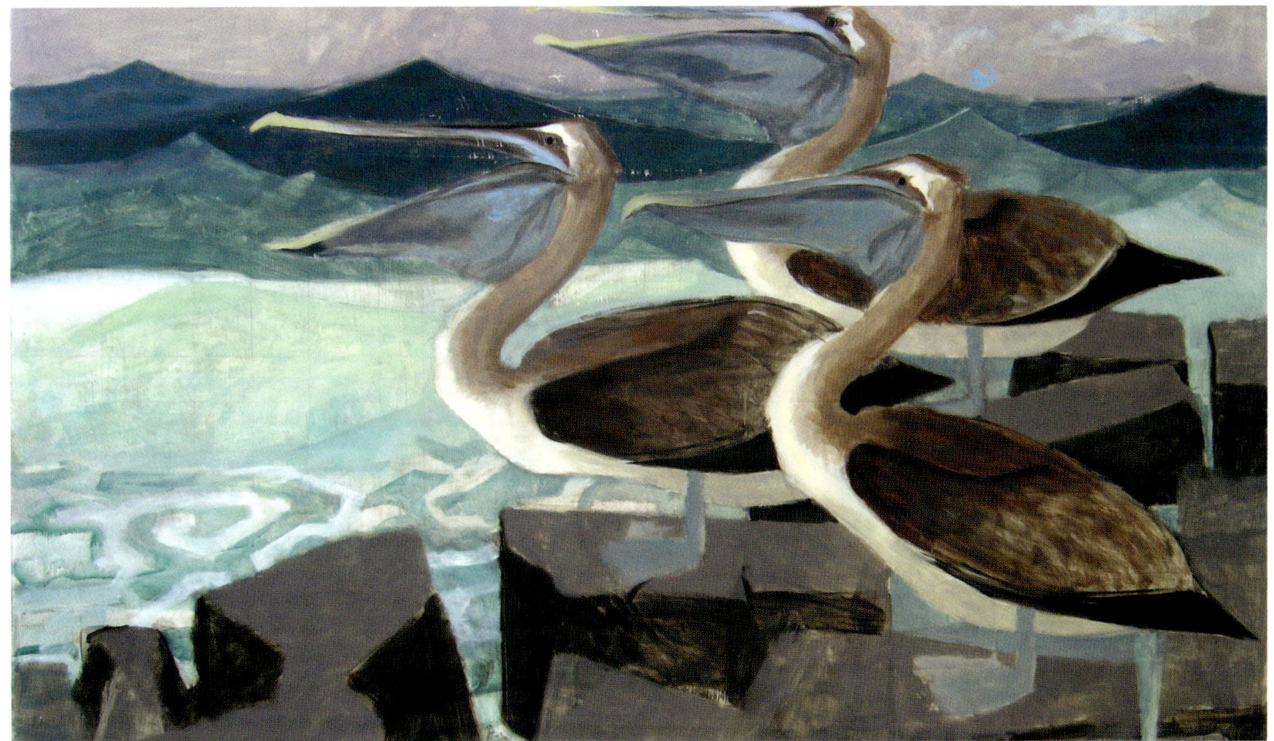

"Pelicans on Rocks," oil on Masonite, 30" x 48", 1980s.

After I went off to college, there was nothing to keep my parents in Bedford, New York, where we had lived during the winter for six years while Sal and I went to high school. They rented a house in Taxco for several years, and even considered buying a house, but that can be complicated in Mexico. During that time they visited their friend Morton Schindel in St. Thomas and decided to buy a house there instead.

They lived in St. Thomas during the winter for about a dozen years, until Mom came down with emphysema, when they decided to leave St. Thomas and spend their winters in Florida. Maine was always their home from May to November.

"Sketch of Woman in Scarf," pencil on paper, 1980s.

"Woman in Scarf," acrylic on paper, 1980s.

"Woman with Bare Shoulders," acrylic on paper, 1980s.

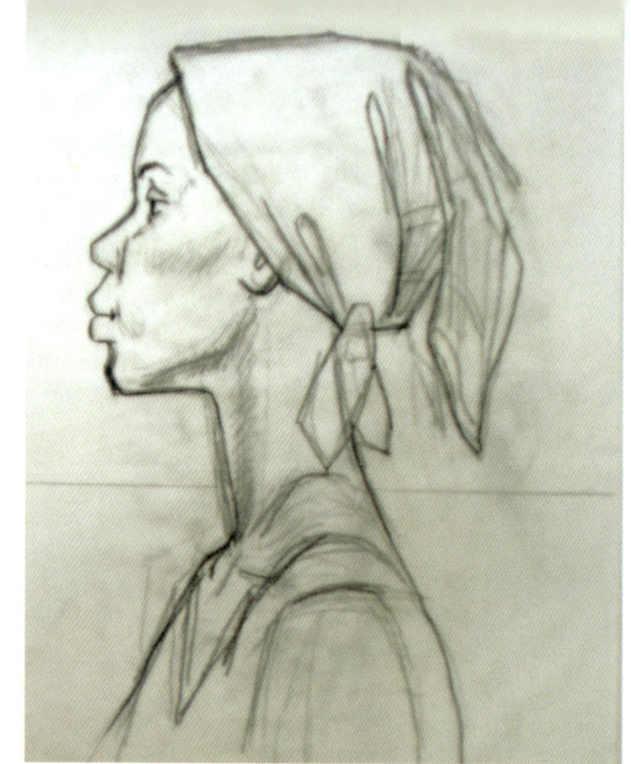

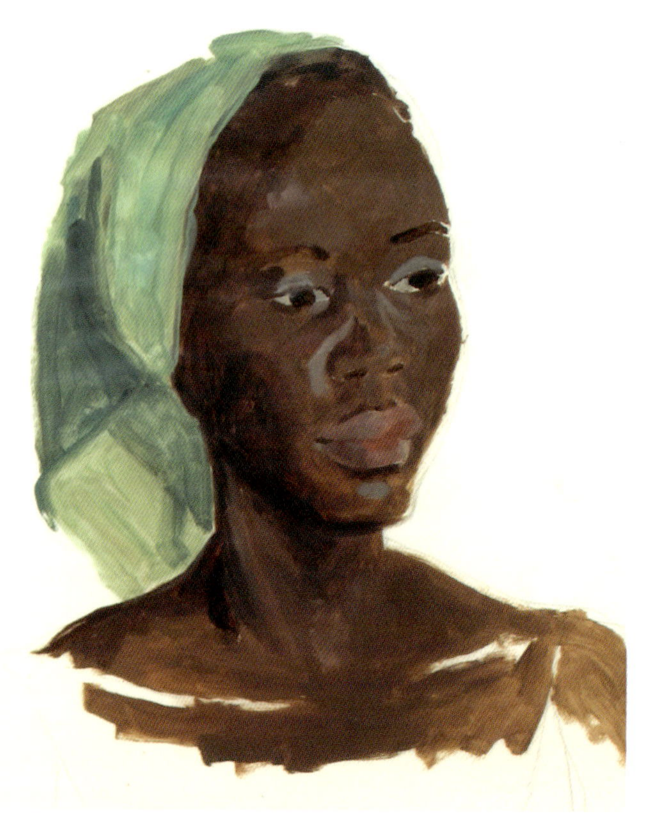

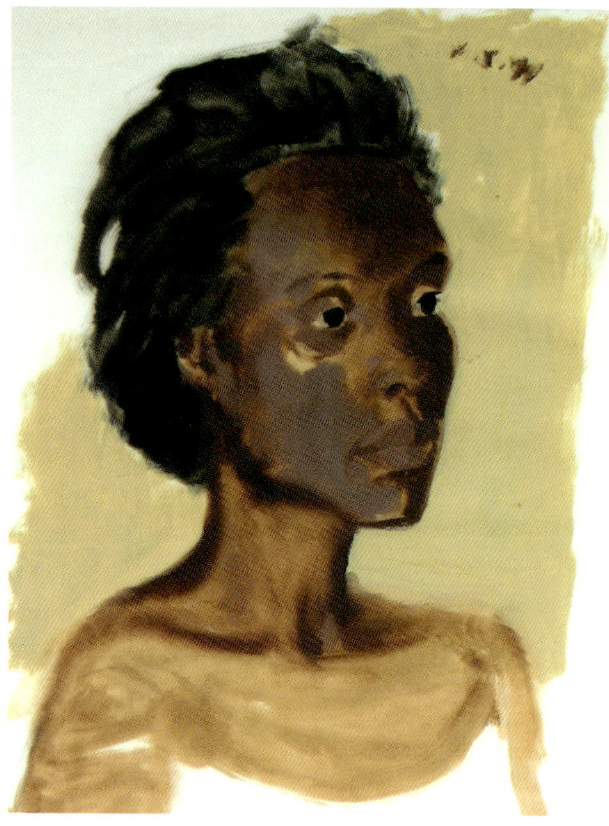

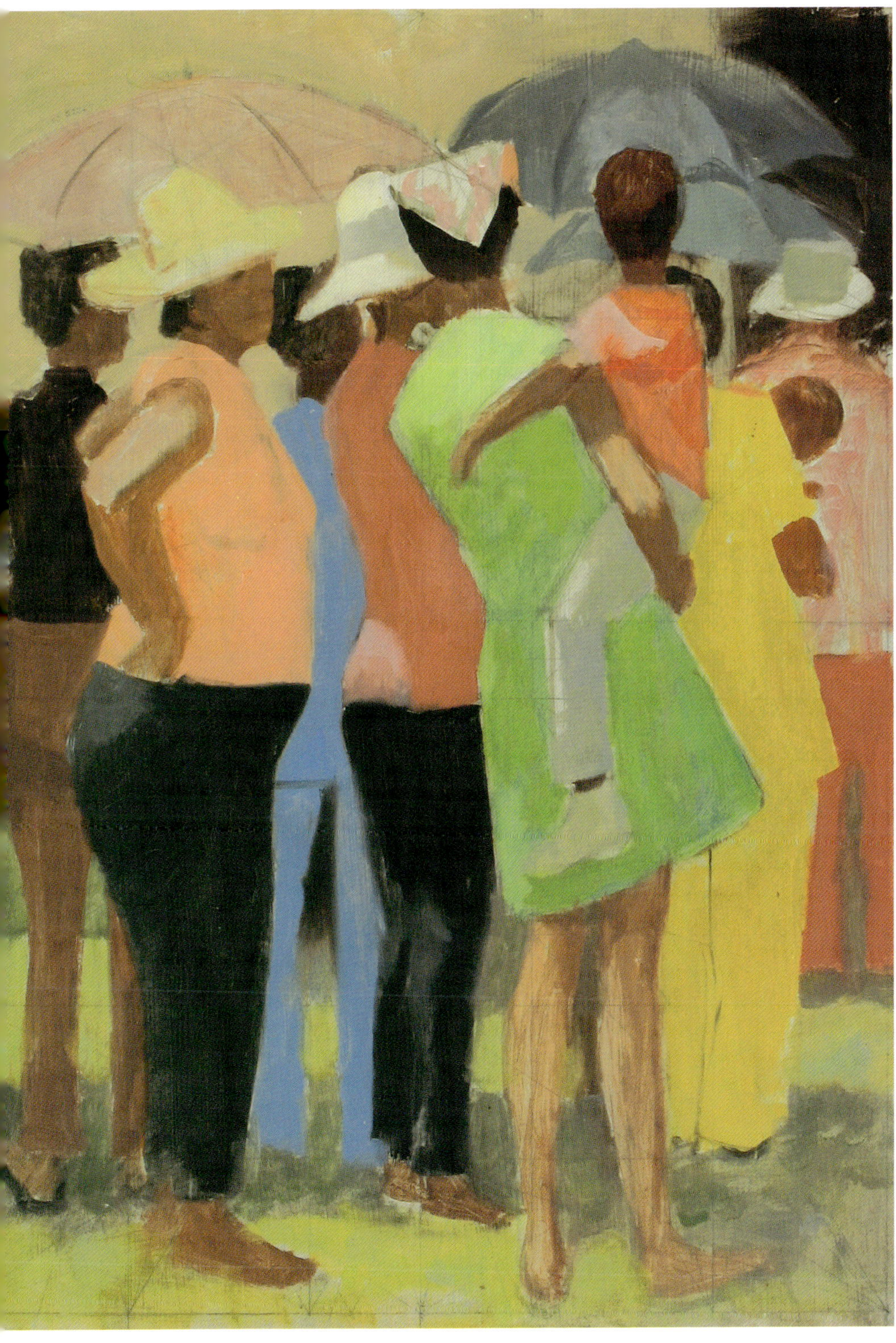

"Group of Women and Children," oil on canvas board, 18" x 14", 1980s.

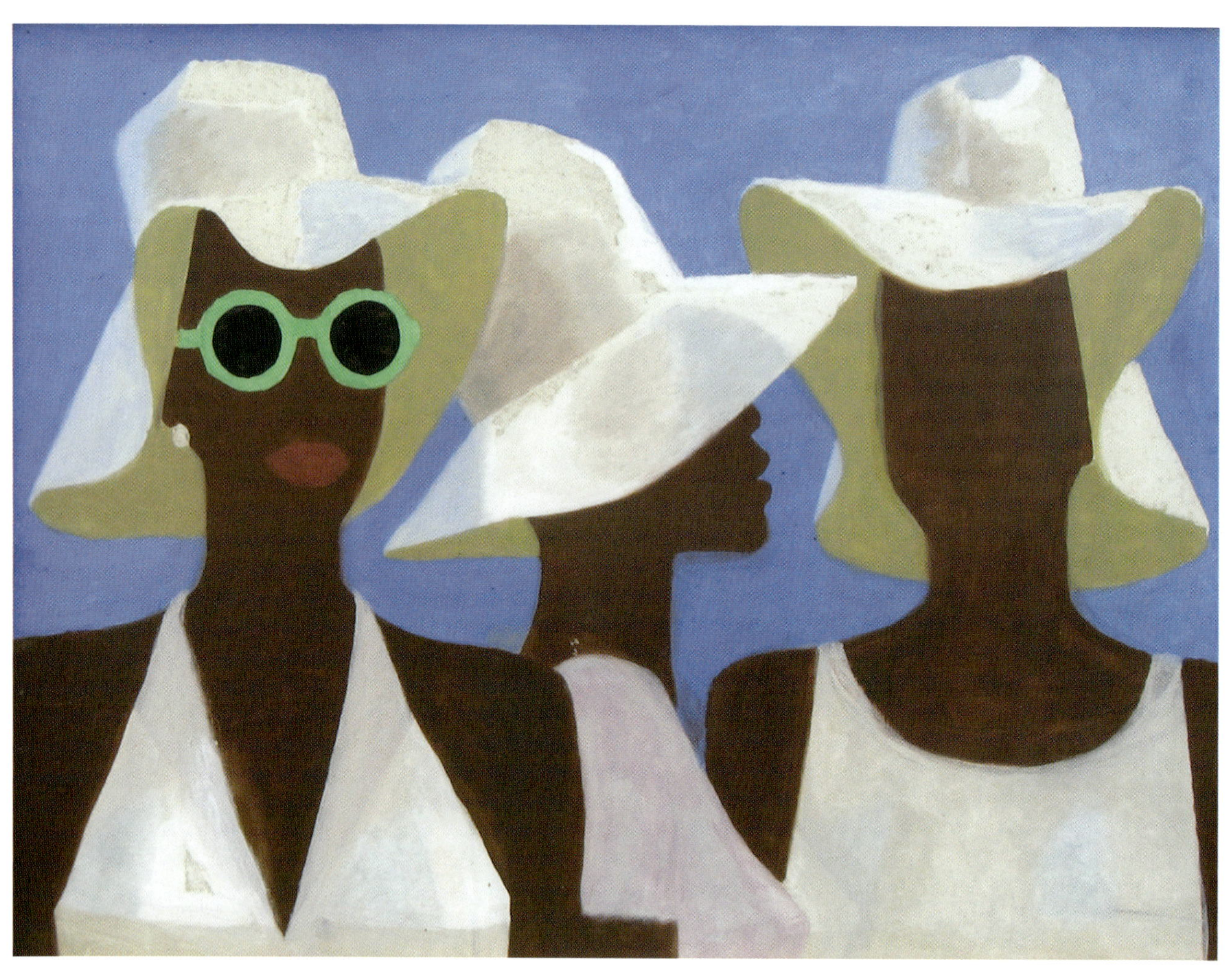

"Women in White with White Hats," oil on canvas board, 24" x 30", 1980s.

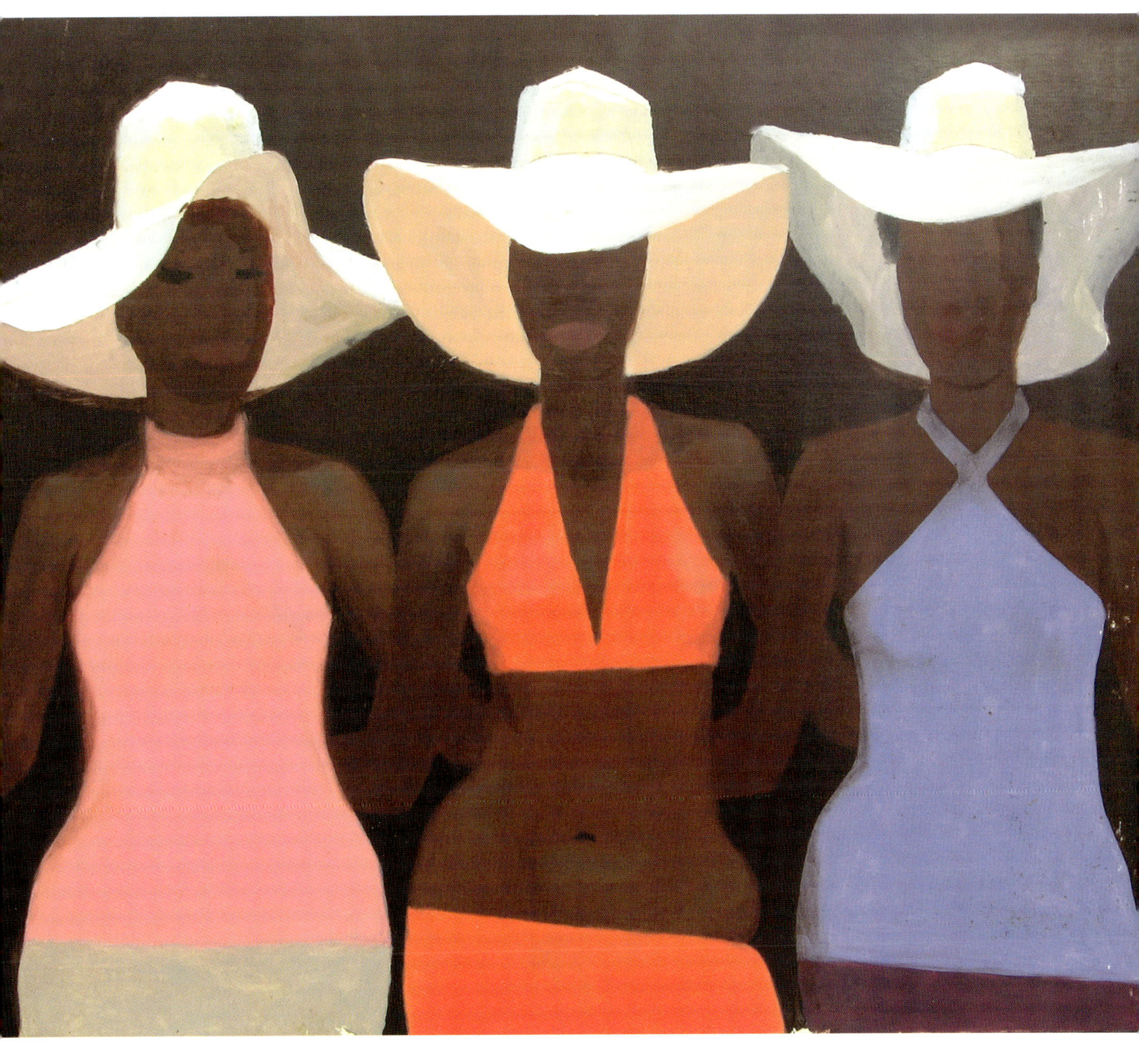

"Women in Pastels with White Hats," oil on Masonite, 24" x 30", 1980s.

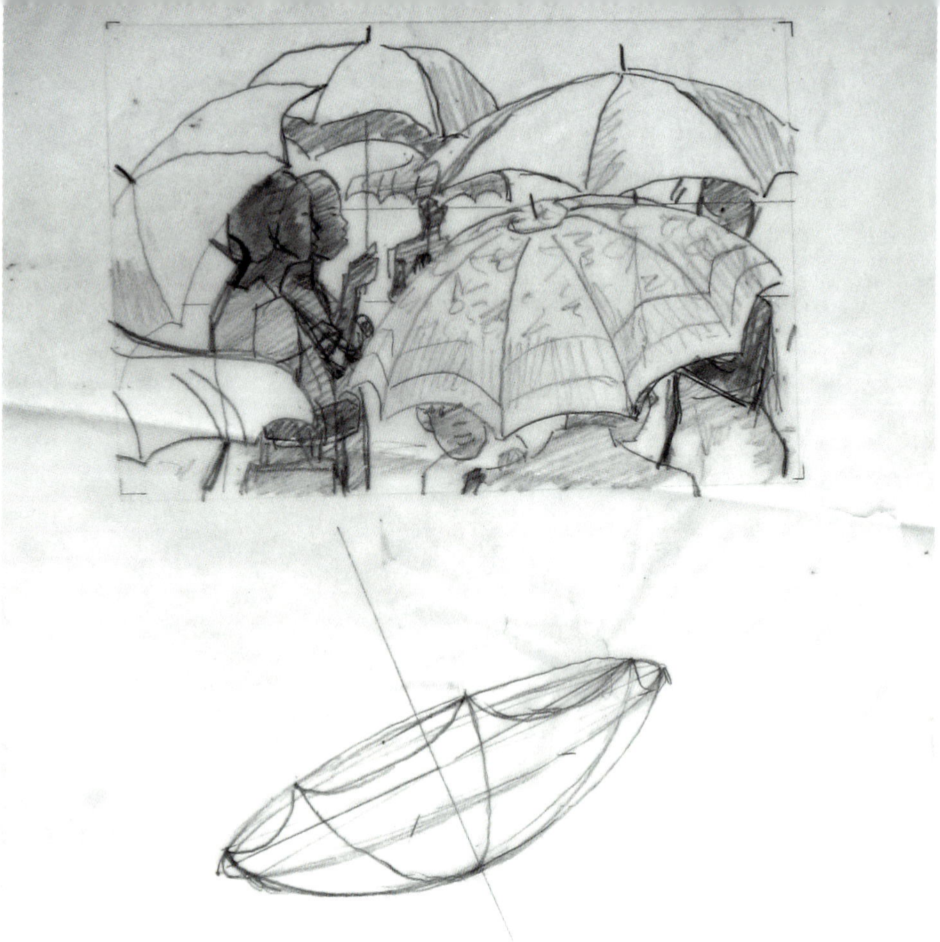

"Sketch of Women with Umbrellas," pencil on paper, 1980s.

"Sketch of Umbrella," pencil on paper, 1980s.

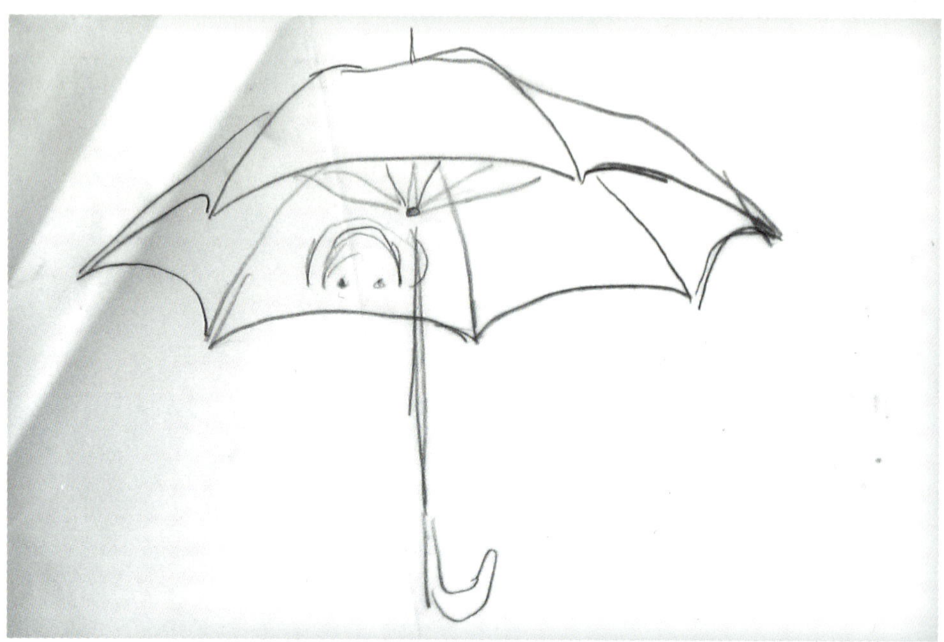

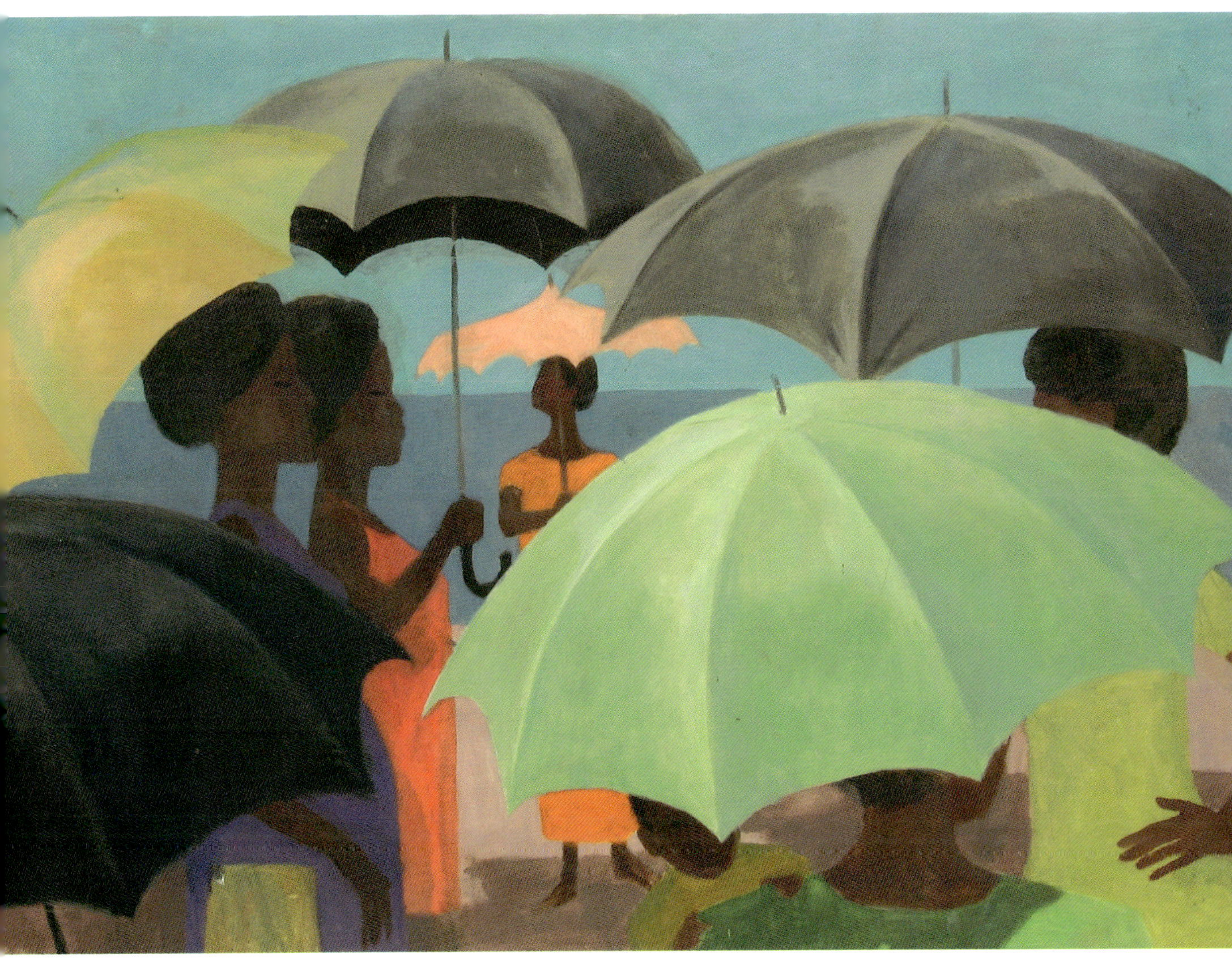

I love this painting.

"Women with Umbrellas," oil on Masonite, 20" x 30", 1980s.

"Boys with Snorkels," oil on masonite, 12" x 20", 1980s.

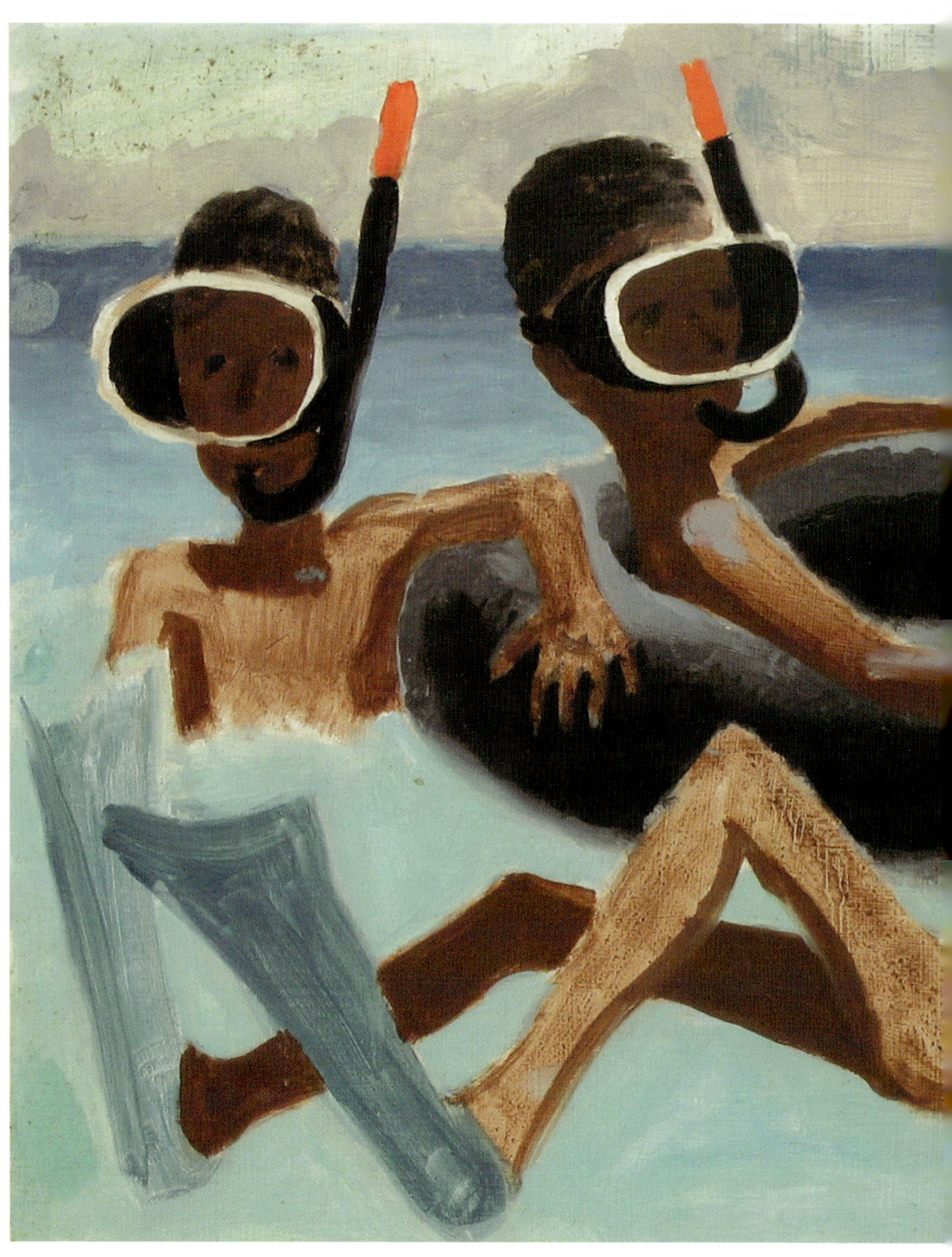

This is one of Sal's favorite paintings.

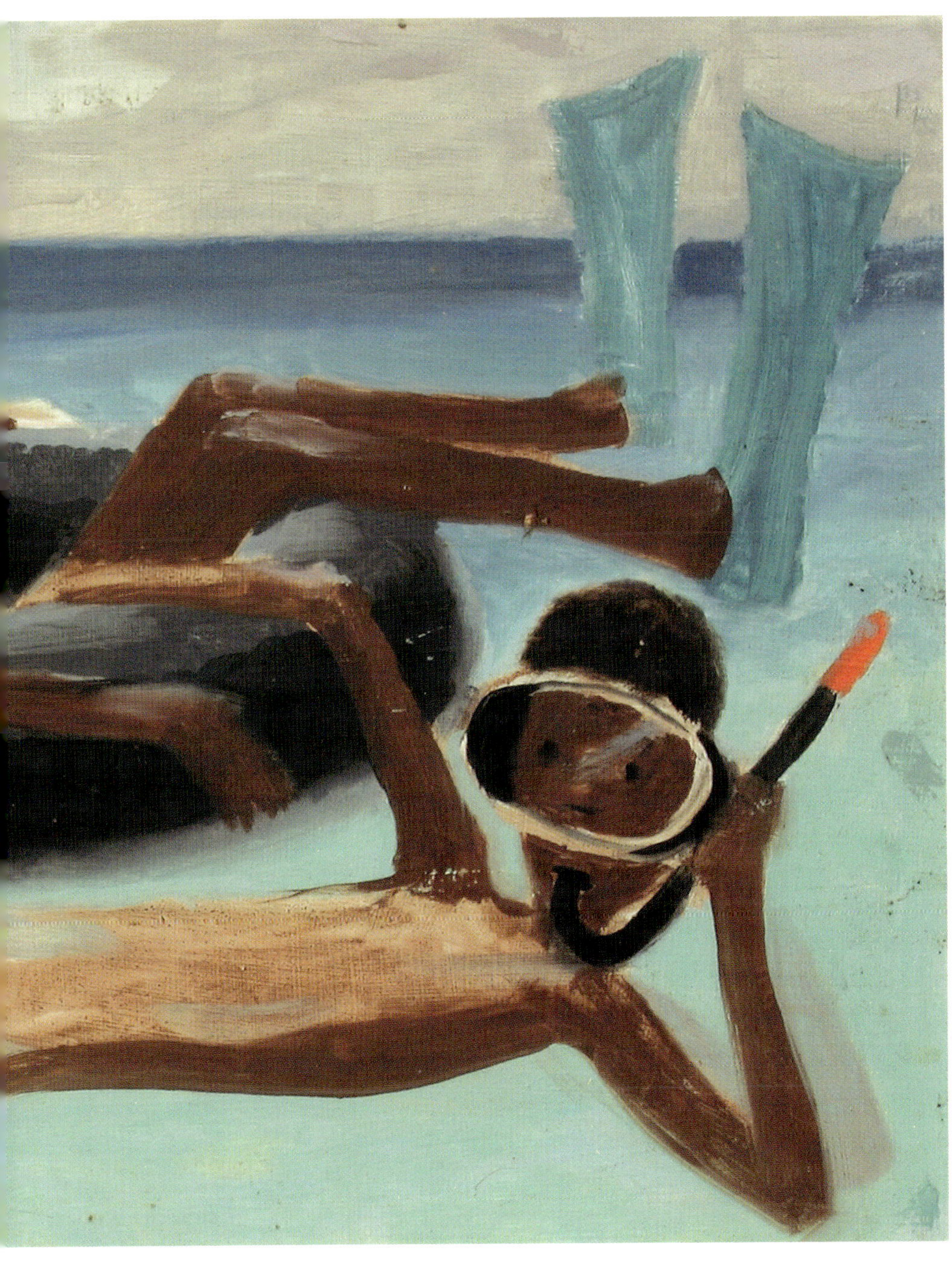

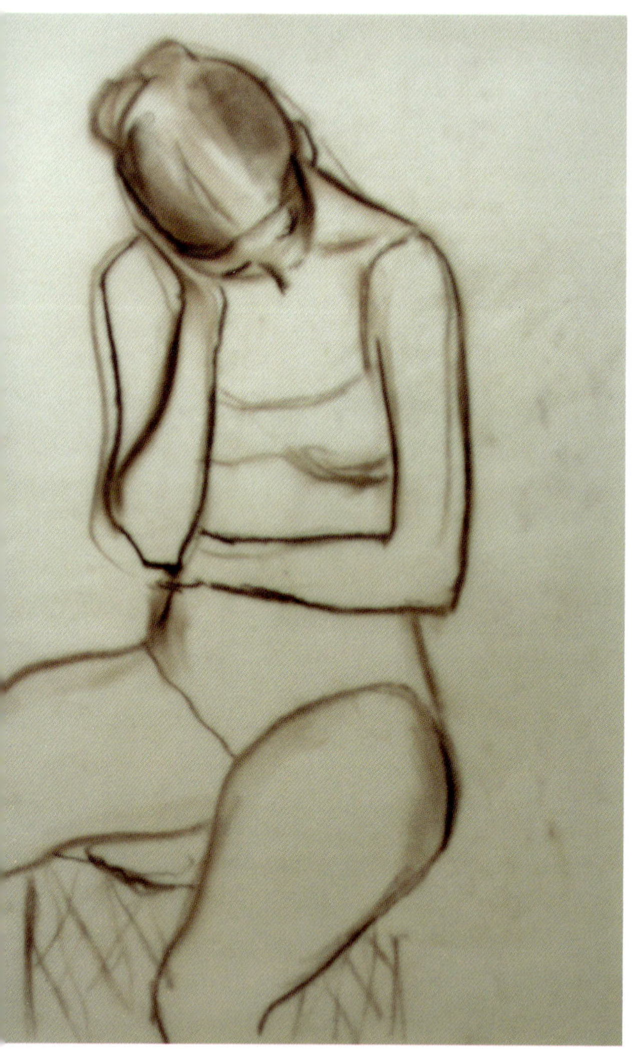

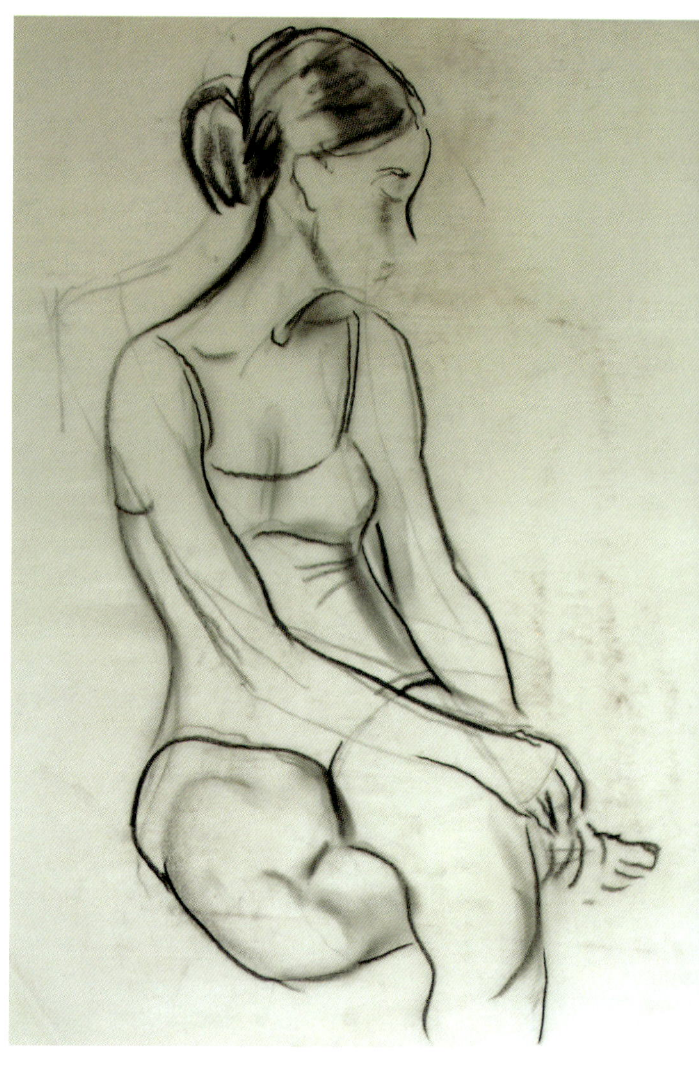

"Sketch of Young Woman Sitting," pencil on paper, 1980s.

"Sketch of Young Woman with Leg Tucked Up," pencil on paper, 1980s.

Here is a young woman who posed for Bob.

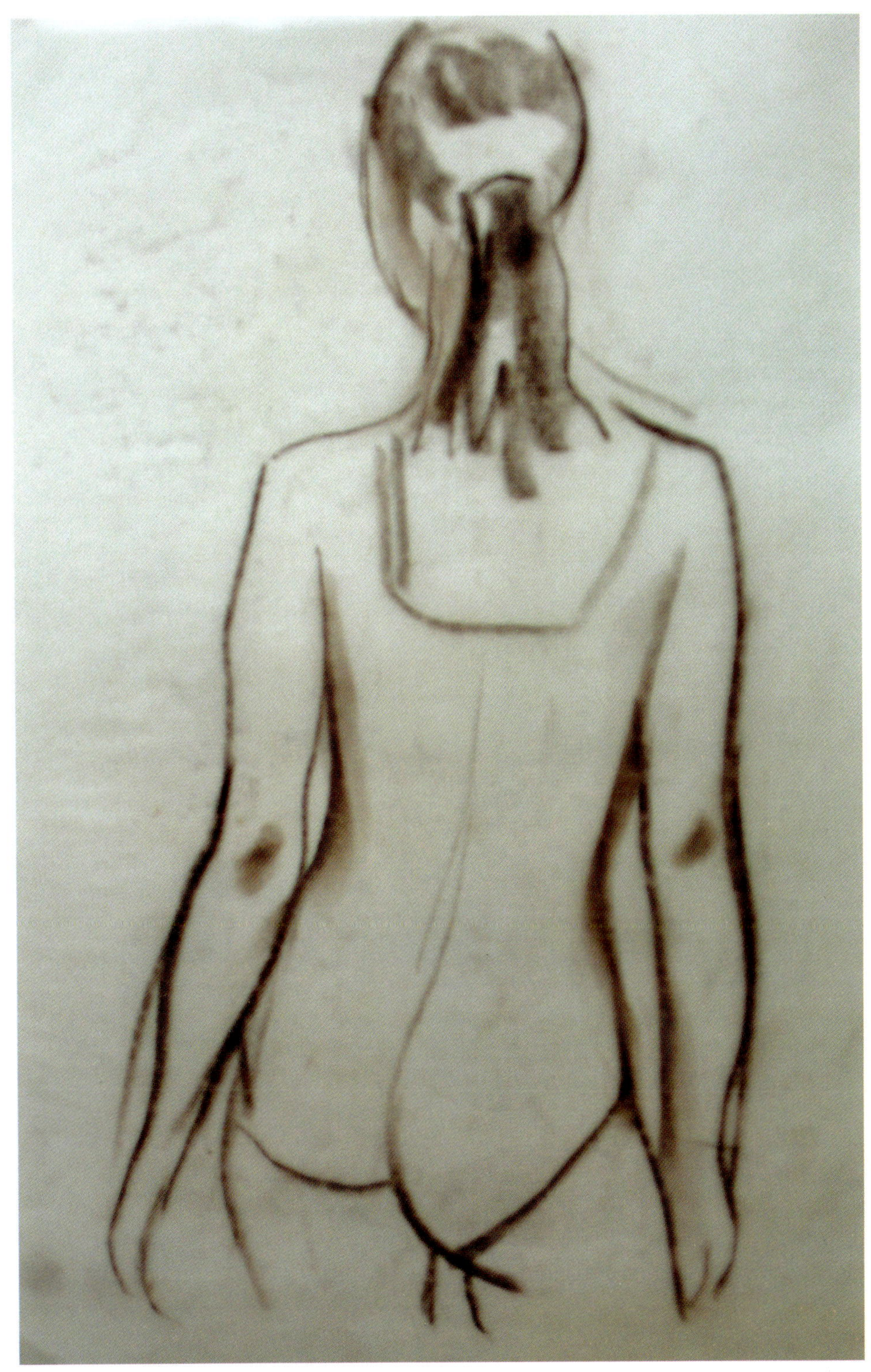

"Sketch of Young Woman Standing," pencil on paper, 1980s.

"Sketch of Woman with Box (upper body)," pencil on paper, 1980s.

My father drew women carrying baskets on their heads when we were in Mexico. The following sketches are from St. Thomas.

"Sketch of Three Women with Boxes (facing)," pencil on paper, 1980s.

"Sketch of Women with Boxes Walking (in profile)," pencil on paper, 1980s.

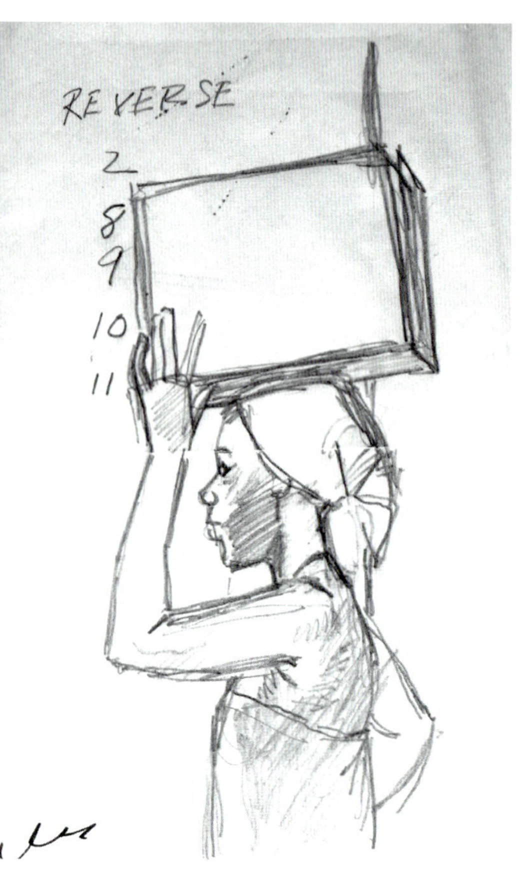

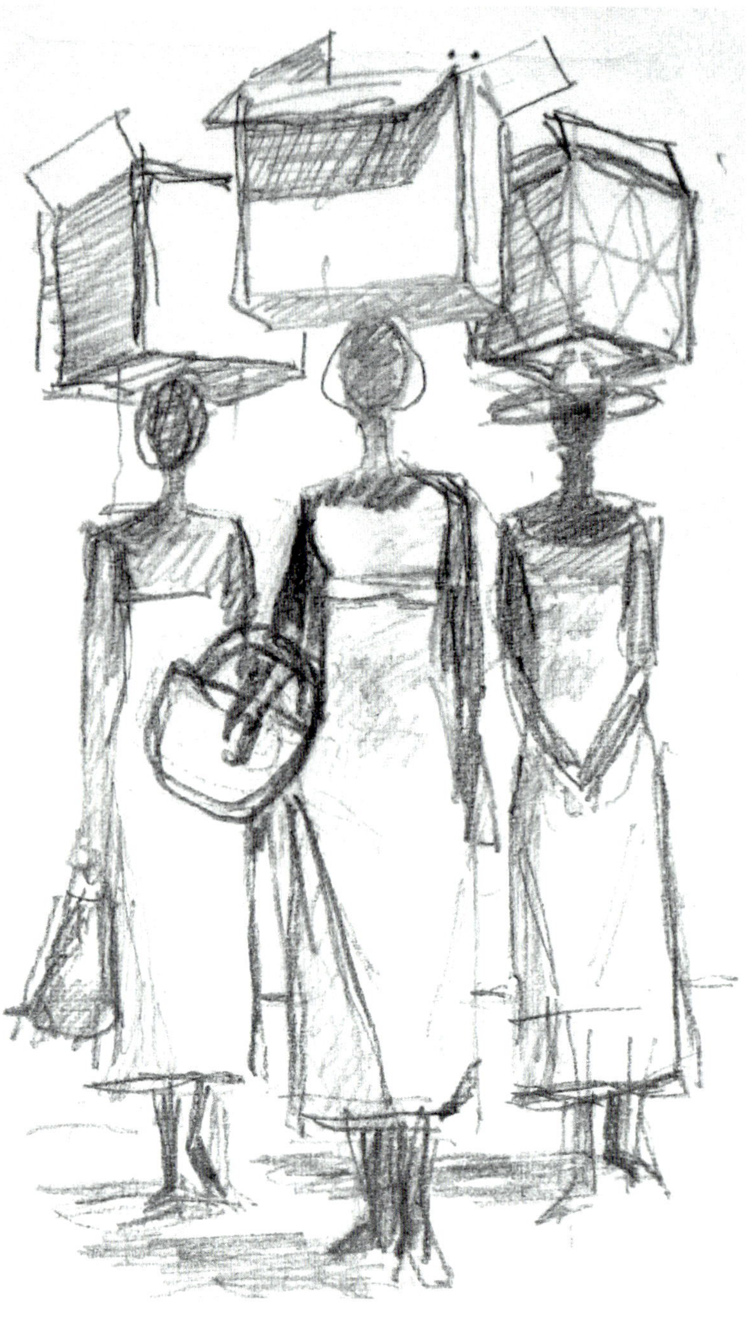

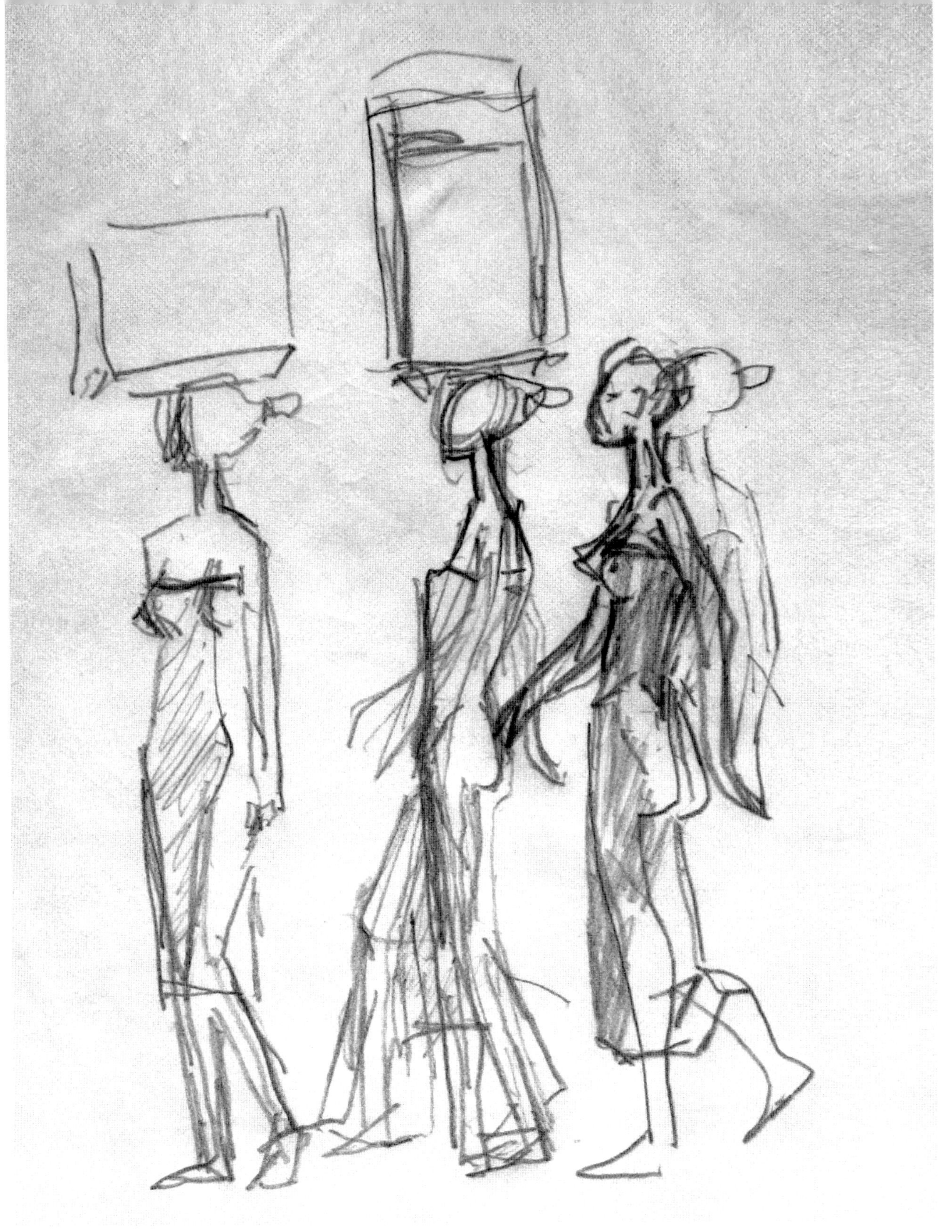

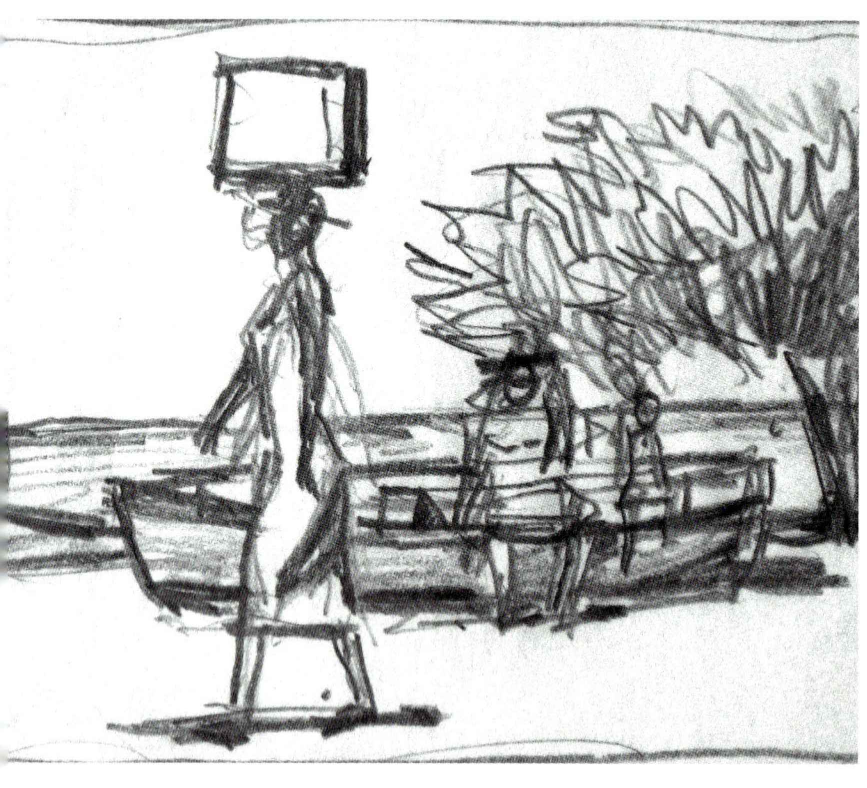

You can see that when this woman walks by a woman sitting on a boat, she is going efficiently about her business; but when she walks by a man sitting on a boat, she sways her hips and her body to get his attention.

"Women with Boxes" (facing page) is one of my favorite paintings.

"Sketch of Woman Passing Woman Sitting on a Boat," pencil on paper, 1980s.

"Sketch of Woman Passing Man Sitting on a Boat," pencil on paper, 1980s.

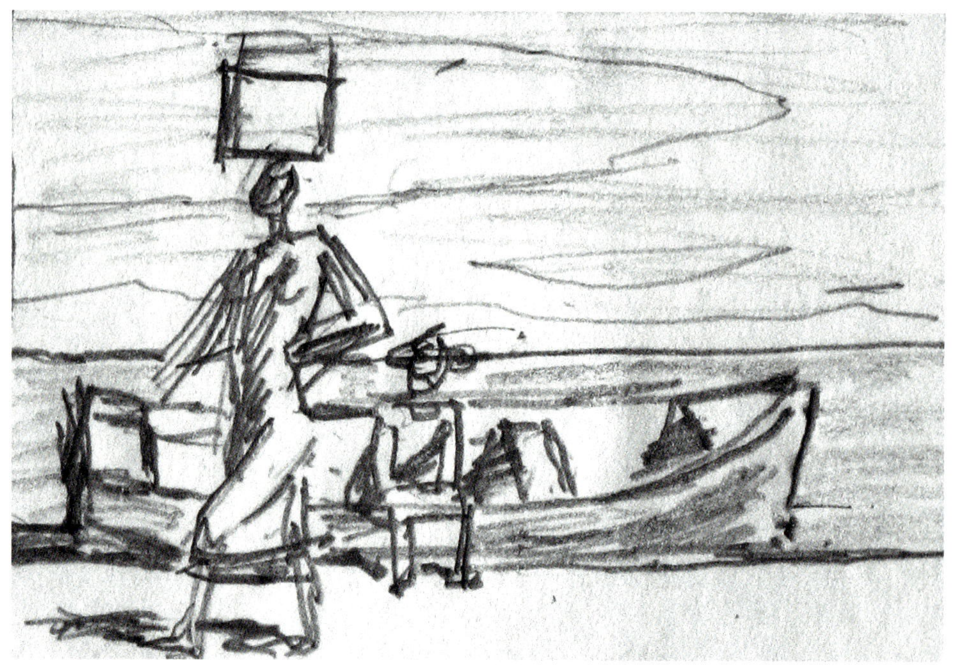

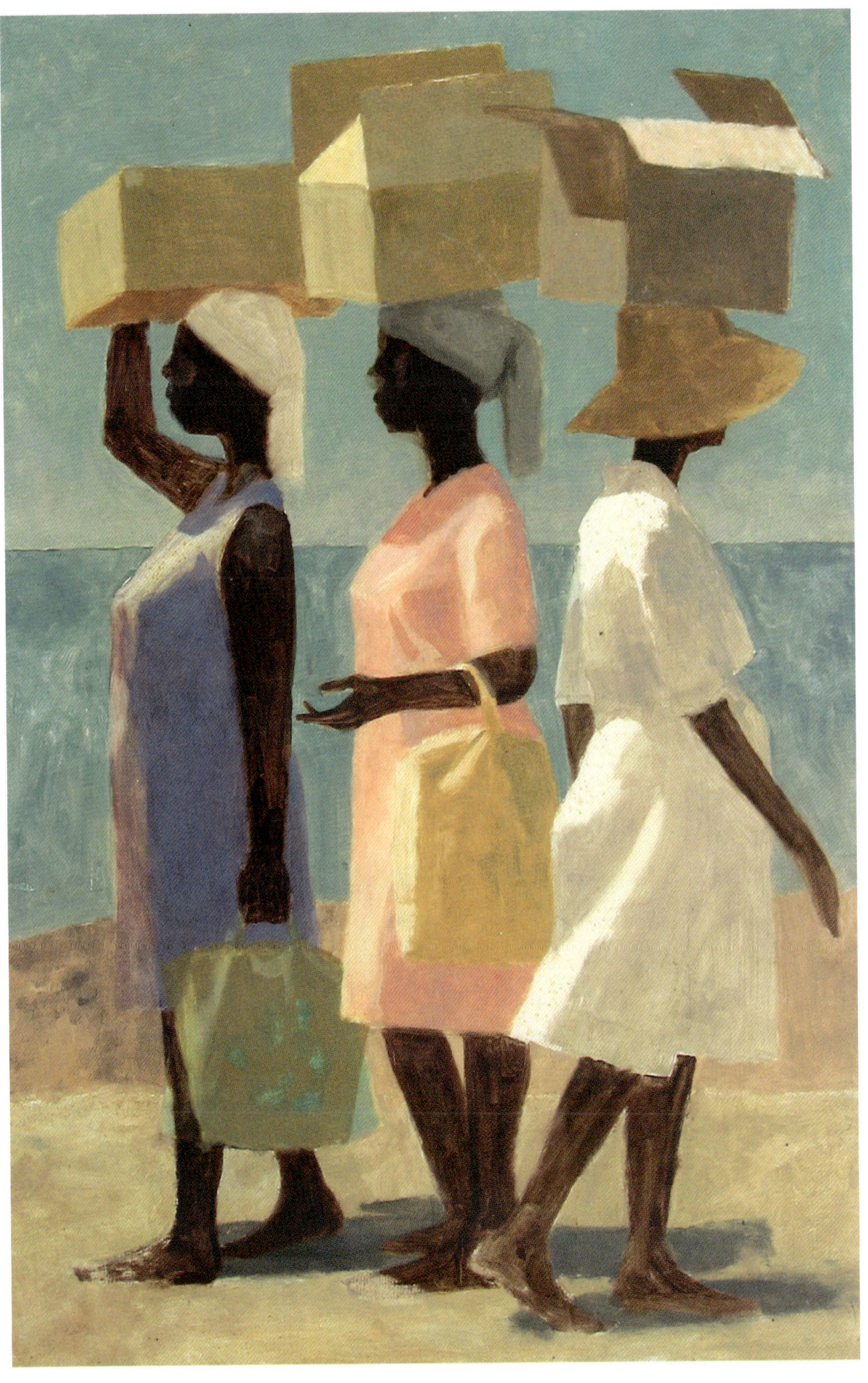

"Women with Boxes,"
oil on Masonite,
30" x 20", 1980s.

Bob's Thoughts About Art 8

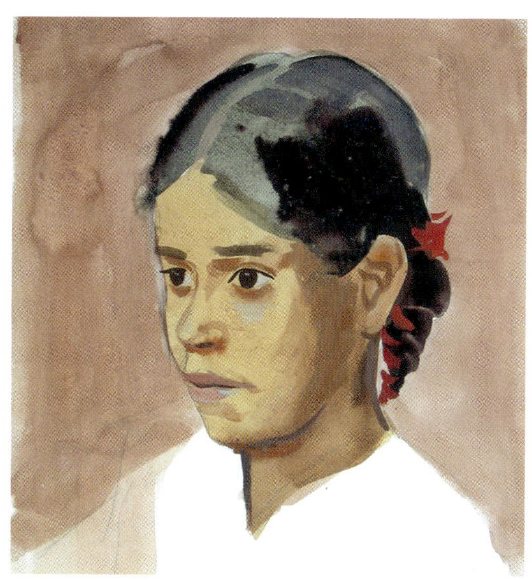

"Mexican Girl," acrylic on paper, 12" x 9", 1959.

Many people have wanted to know more about what my father was thinking when he did his art. The truth is, he rarely spoke about his artistic process. As I have said before, whenever people told him their idea for a book, he answered, "Don't talk about it, do it." As he got older, he became even more reserved, almost as if he thought that his artistic power was nourished by his silence.

Bob said that he learned to "See" in art school. He said that most people do not really see—that their idea of the world prevents them from seeing the world as it really is. When they draw, they draw their idea of what they see rather than what the object really looks like. For example, when I was eight and was drawing a girl, I drew her eyes about one third of the way down from the top of the oval that was her head, because I thought of eyes as being in the upper part of the head. Looking at my drawing, my father said that in fact, eyes are almost exactly half way down the head oval.

My father signed his pictures when he was young, but by the 1940s, he had stopped signing his work. I believe this was partly because he believed that people should look at a picture for itself, and not see it in terms of the name or reputation of the artist. Choosing artistic anonymity was an aspect of the value he put on Seeing: Seeing what is truly in front of you, and learning to ignore your idea of what is in front you. Of course, my father had begun to be published as a children's book author, so he no longer had to worry about selling his paintings. His painting became something he did in his spare time to please himself. And, while his name did not appear on his paintings, it was on the cover of all his books.

One summer, when I was about eight, my father encouraged me to draw in his sketchbooks. I know now that he was using me as a model for how kids draw. He used my drawings as inspiration for the way the Scribiller drew in the book Bob was planning. It was to be about a boy who found a magical blue pencil that would make whatever he drew into reality. The Scribiller drew like a kid, except better.

"Sketch of Drawing by the Scribiller," colored pencil on paper, 1950s.

"Sketch of Drawing by the Scribiller (black) and Bob (brown)," pencil and colored pencil on paper, 1950s.

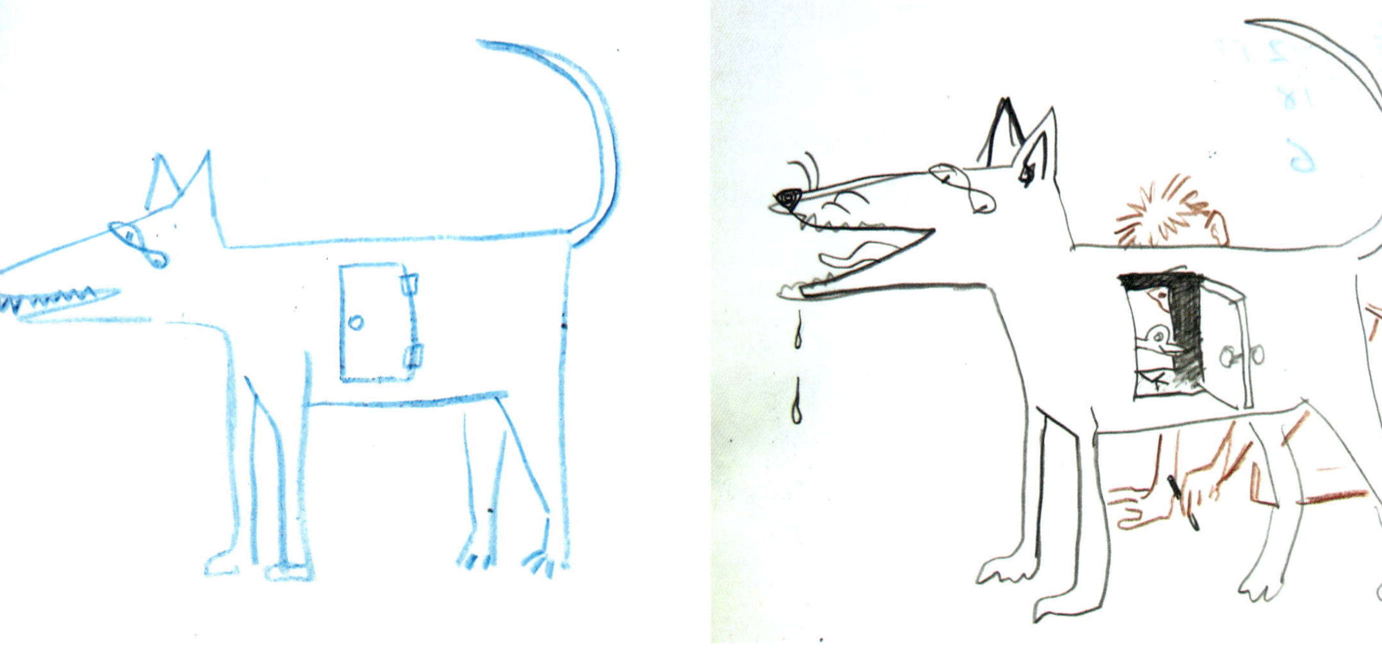

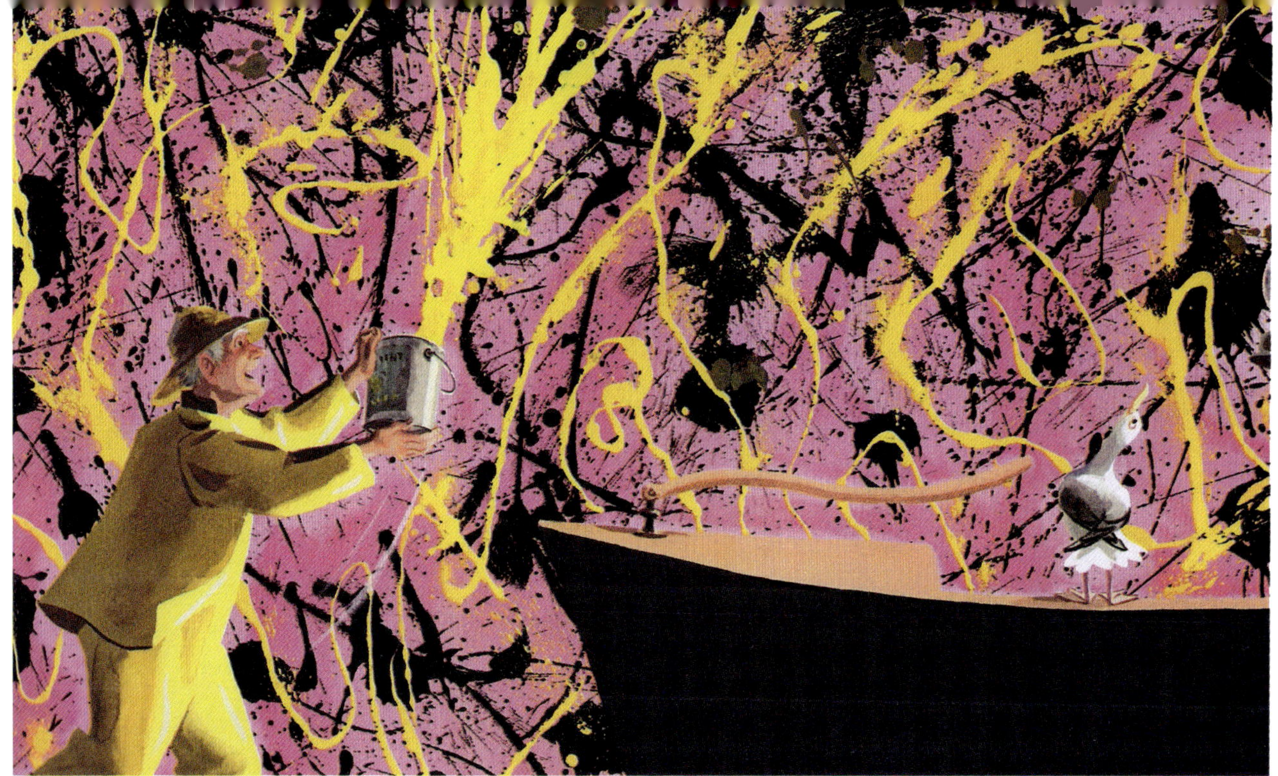

Burt Dow, Deep Water Man, "Burt Painting the Tummy of the Whale," Viking Press, 1963.

Here is an example of Bob's artistic process: he got a kid to draw for him, so he could learn to draw like a kid.

Bob abandoned the Scribiller before he got too far. My friend Anita Haviland suggests that he found out *Harold and the Purple Crayon* by Crocket Johnson (1955) had already been published. Harold's purple crayon made real whatever Harold drew. The Scribiller's blue pencil was too close for comfort to Harold's purple crayon, and Bob didn't want to copy the idea.

There was a period when Bob said that he was more of an illustrator than an artist. He liked to draw pictures to go with stories. Especially, he liked to make pictures that said things visually which could not be said verbally. I think that his identity as an illustrator, as opposed to an artist, peaked in the 1960s, when abstract art and pictures as pure image divorced from reality, feeling, and ideas were the fashion. The work of Paul Klee, Piet Mondrian, and Jackson Pollack exemplified this "modern" art. In Bob's *Burt Dow, Deep Water Man,* Burt Dow joined the modern art movement when he flung paint around a whale's belly to make it sick so it would vomit him back out. Burt discovered that he enjoyed expressing himself artistically.

Unlike Burt, Bob usually didn't want to make pure designs. He wanted pictures that had meaning and action and told stories. Later, as abstract, "modern" art became less fashionable, he went back to calling himself an artist. Well, also, he hadn't illustrated a book since the 1960s. He was painting pictures and making puppets, which made him an artist more than an illustrator.

Sal has pointed out that Bob tended to exaggerate the irregularities of the people he drew. She says that he worked for a syndicated cartoonist drawing comic strips for a couple of years after he graduated from art school. Then he worked for Francis Scott "Brad" Bradford on a mural that is now at MIT. Both of these experiences probably encouraged his cartoon tendencies: bold, simplified outlines at the expense of subtle lighting, texture, and detail. But Bob had a humorous streak anyway, so on top of his cartoon and mural experience, I think his cartooning came naturally. Here Bob drew a Greek fisherman who looks like a cartoon of a Greek fisherman.

"Sketch of Greek Fishermen," pencil on paper, 1960.

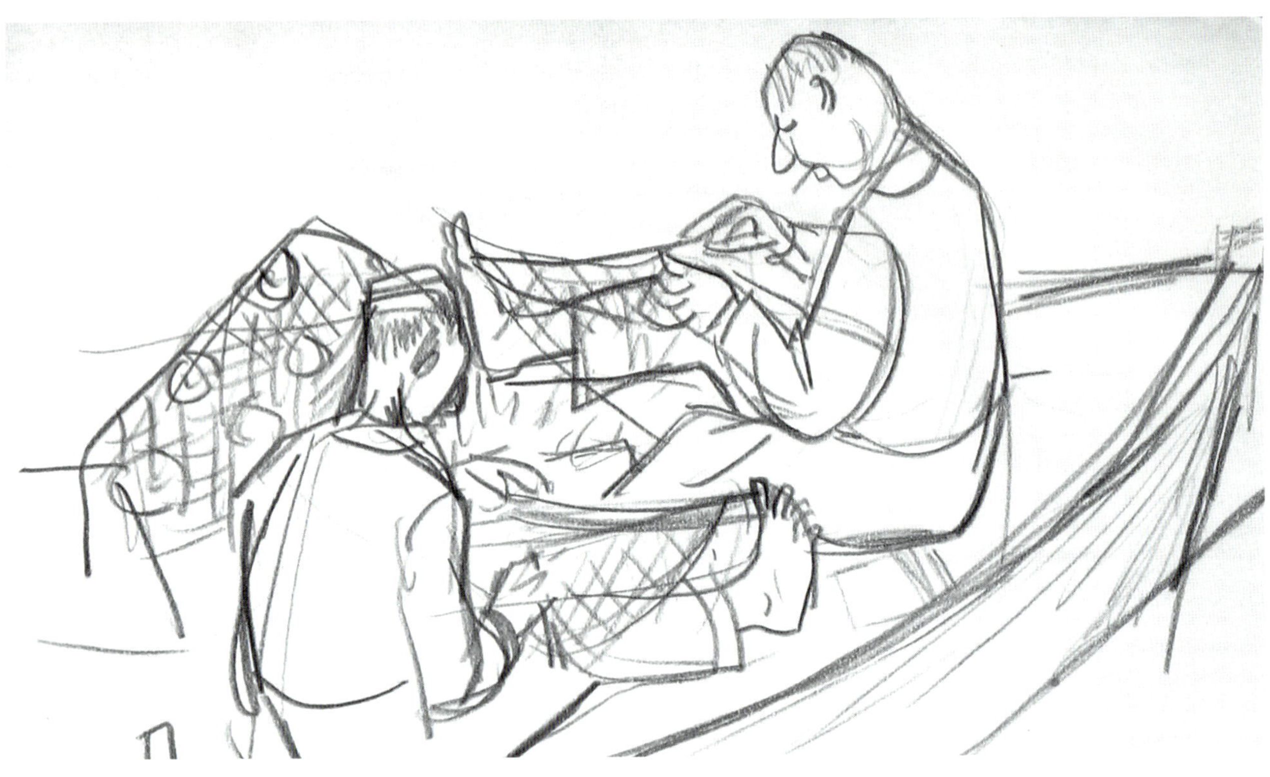

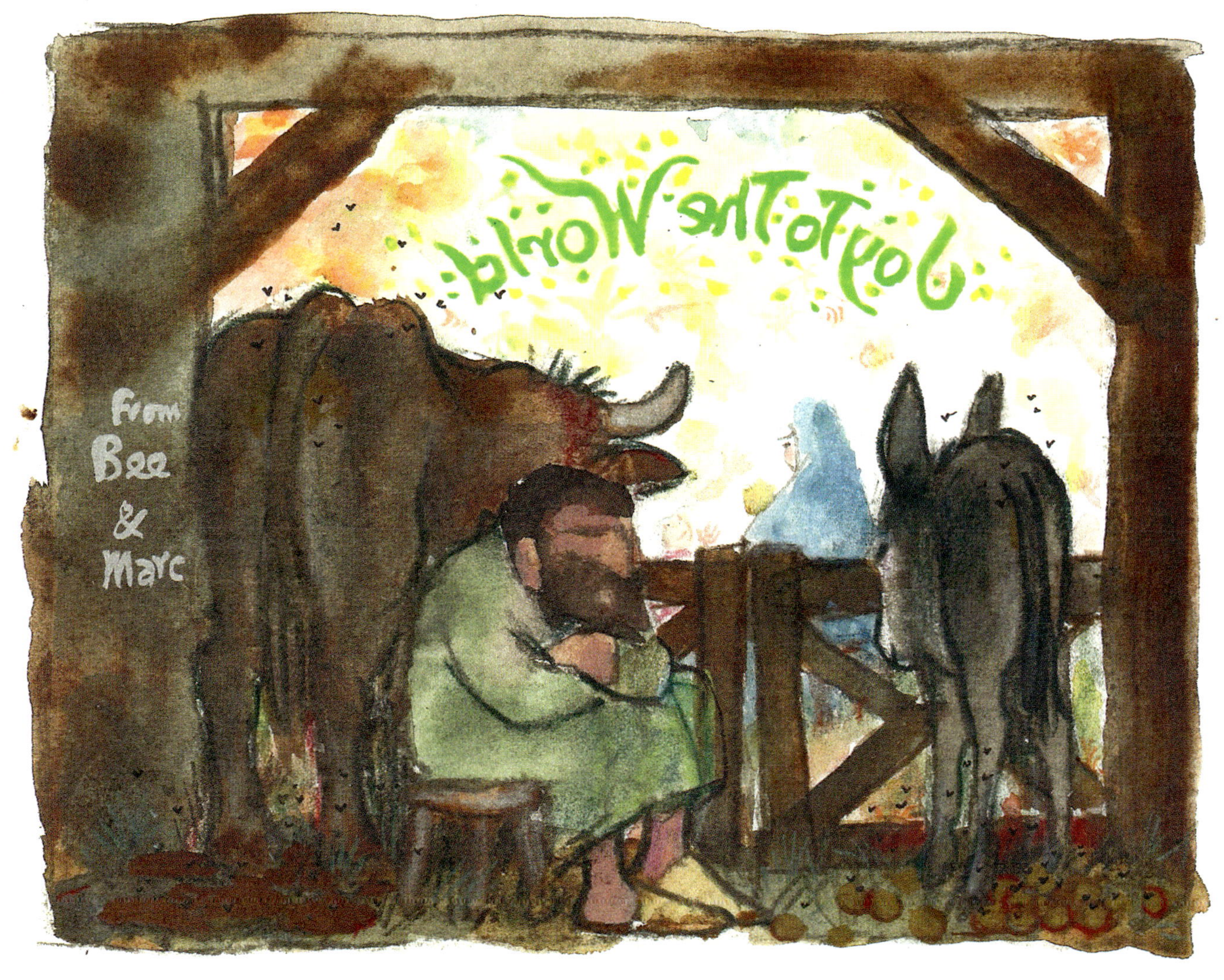

Christmas Card, by Marc Simont, 2010.

Bob and Marc Simont met in art school and became roommates and lifelong friends. Marc and Bob both worked with Brad Bradford on the MIT murals, so they must have worked to harmonize their styles with Brad's and each other's. Cartooning also came naturally to Marc. Here is a Christmas card Bee and Marc sent me a couple of years ago.

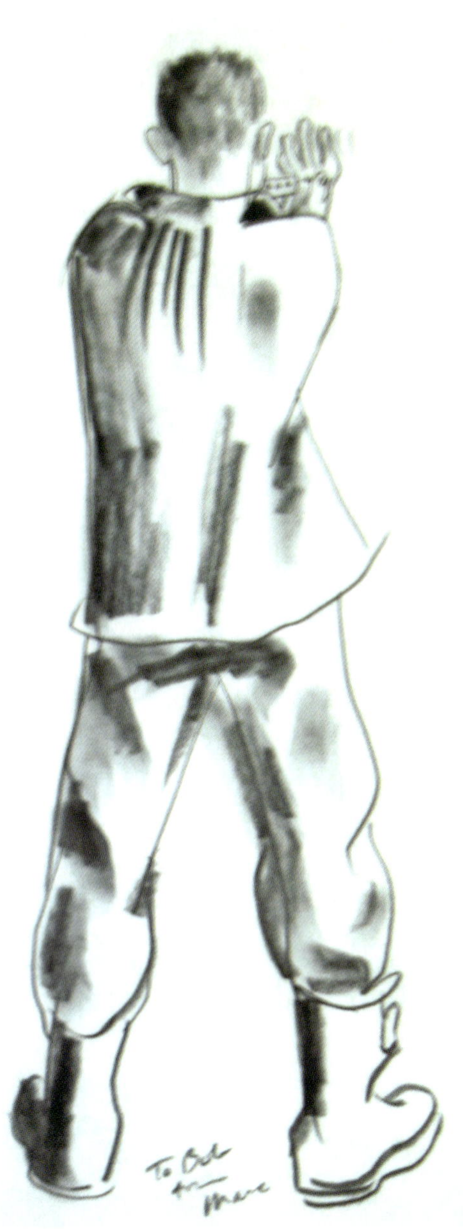

"Bob Playing his Harmonica," drawing by Marc Simont, pencil on paper, 16" x 7", 1930s.

Sally has a picture Marc drew of Bob playing the harmonica. It could have been Bob who drew it.

Both Bob and Marc drew with heavy, strong lines, though Marc's are usually heavier. They were both excellent at anatomy and perspective. They tended to exaggerate characteristics of their subjects in a cartoony fashion. I told Marc that I thought he was one of the major influences on Bob's art, and Marc answered, "It worked both ways." Marc died on July 13, 2013.

In studying my father's art, I have become increasingly aware of my father's ability to vary his style. He drew exquisitely realistic sketches of Reuben, my parent's dog before Sal was born.

"Sketch of Reuben," pencil on paper, 1940s.

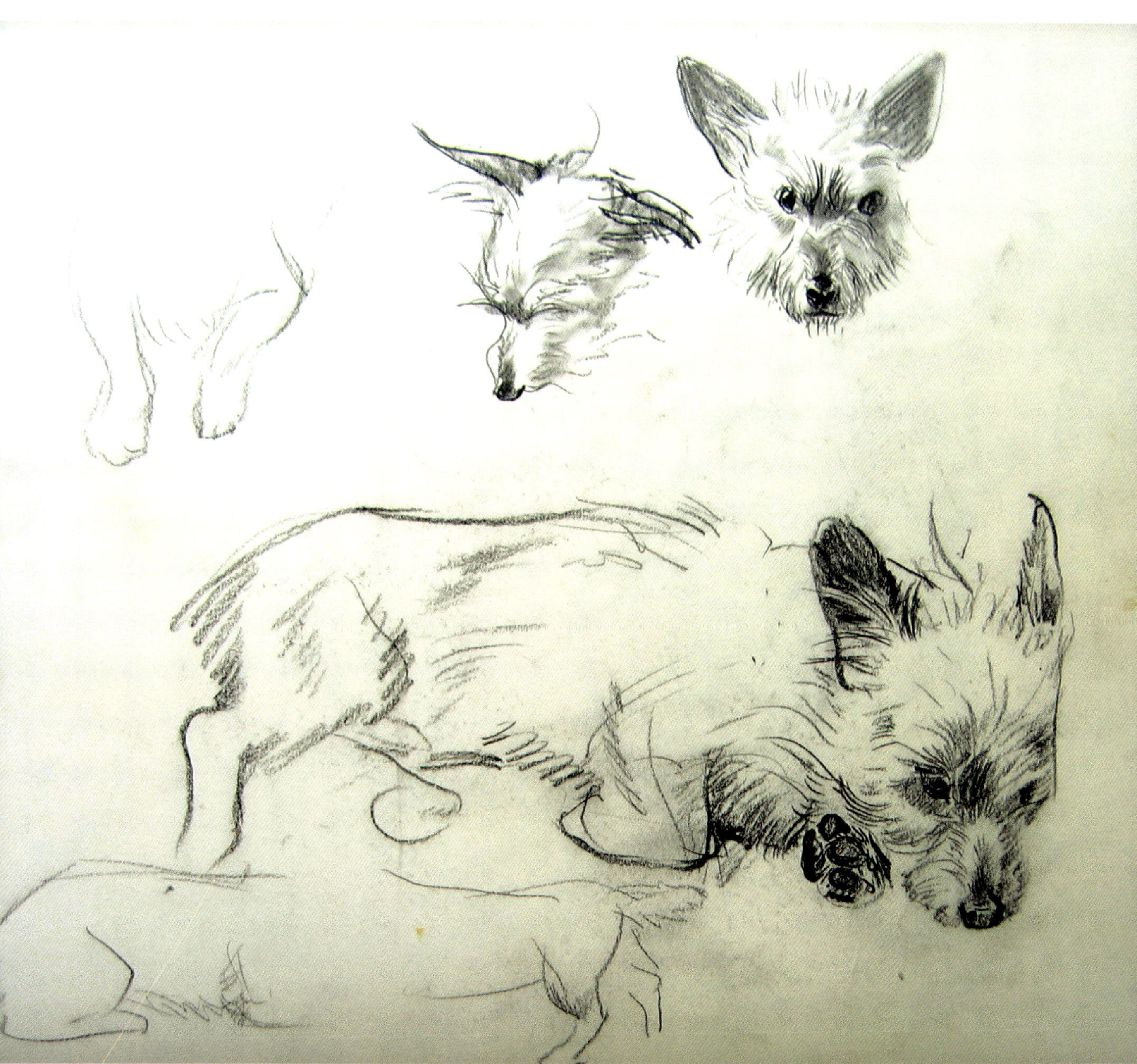

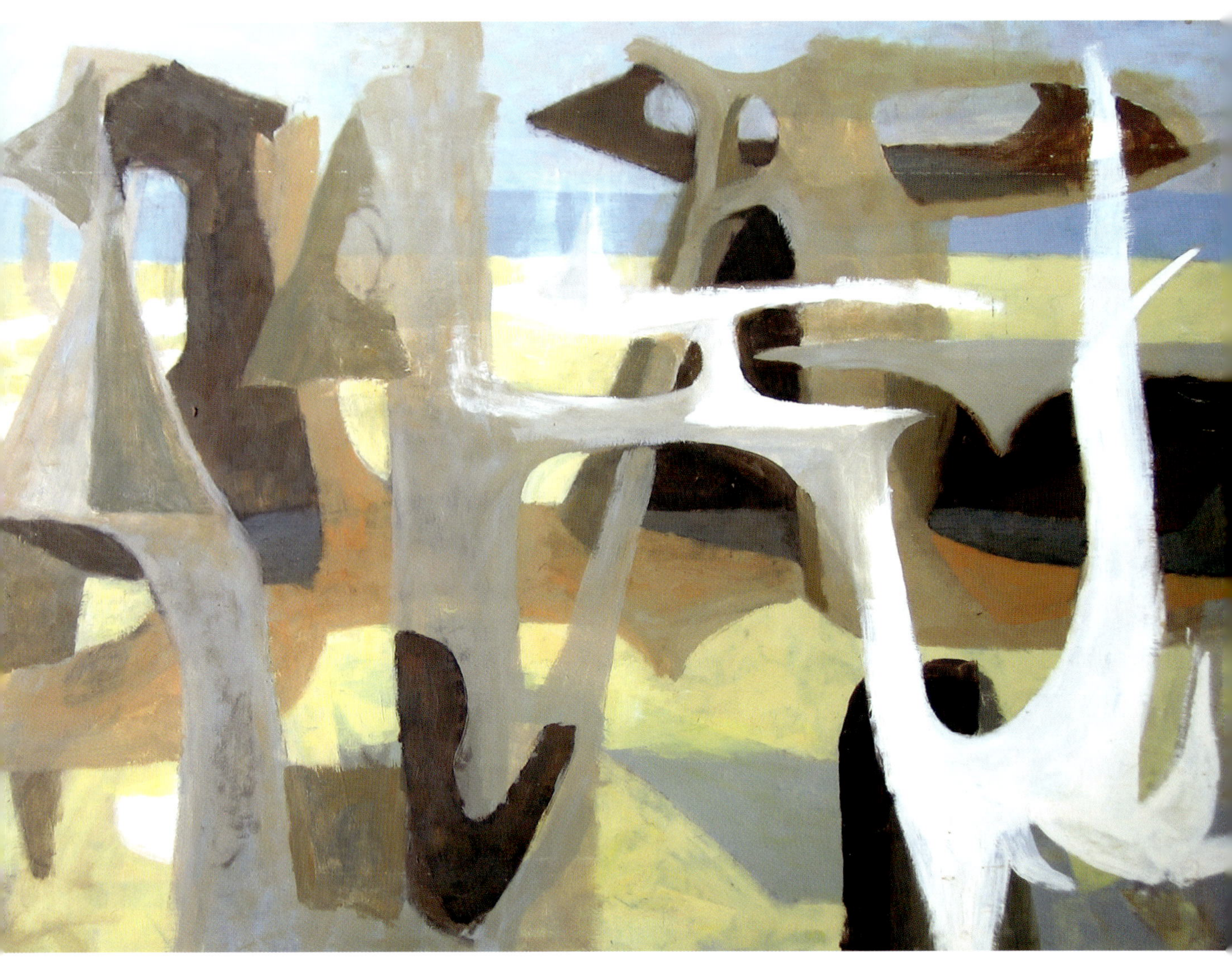

"Driftwood Fantasy," oil on canvas board, 24" x 32", 1970s.

He painted semi abstract and a few totally abstract pictures.

I think Bob was channeling both Picasso and Orozco in this etching.

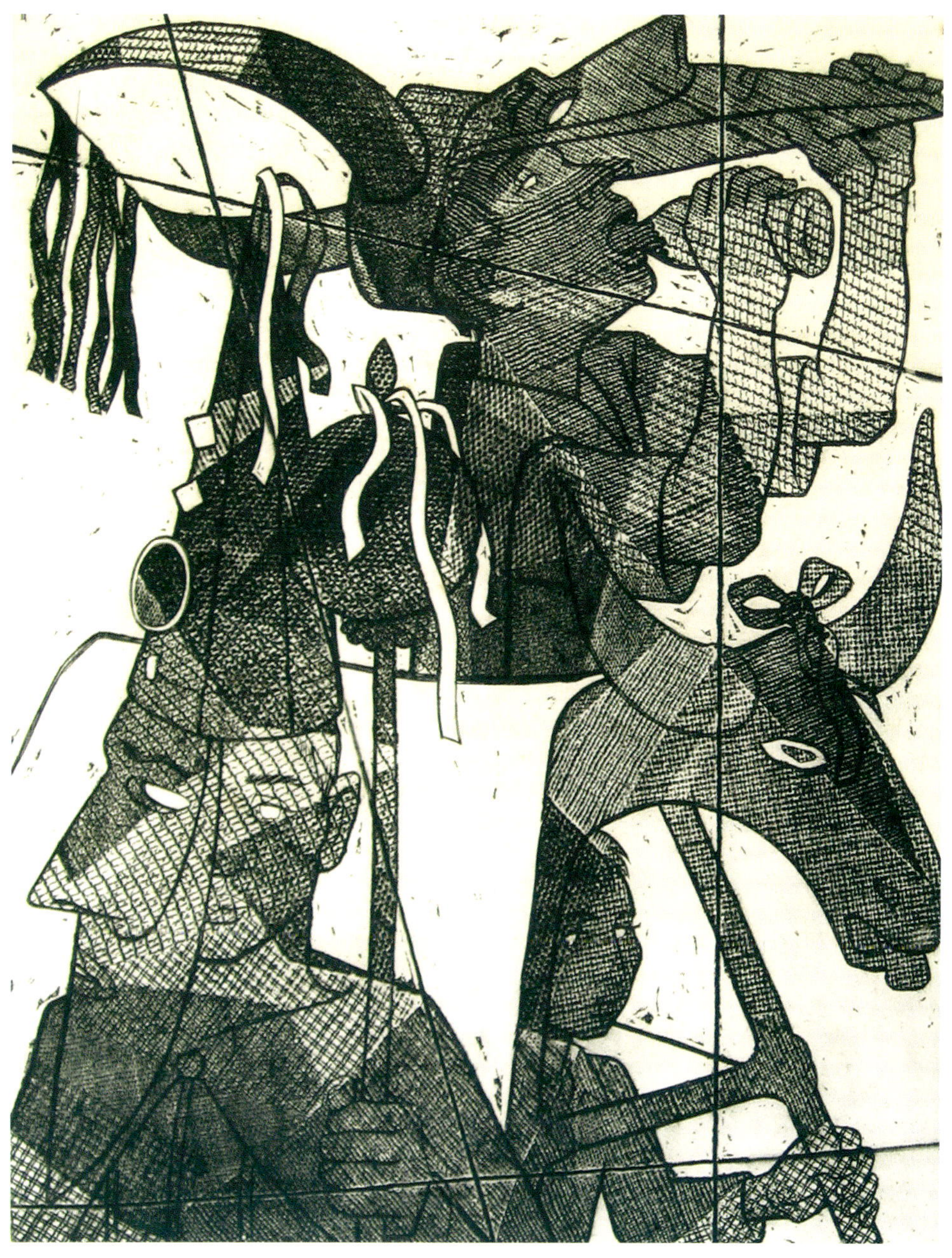

"Carnaval," etching
17" x 13", 1958.

Burt Dow, Deep Water Man, "Burt and Sea Gull in the Tummy of the Whale," Viking Press, 1963.

He used very bright, vibrant colors in some pictures, and very somber tones in others. He used soft, beautiful colors in *Time of Wonder,* and outrageous colors in *Burt Dow.*

He said that he liked pink. Sometimes, if it was a loud pink, he called it "pimpk." The whale's stomach in *Burt Dow* was pimpk.

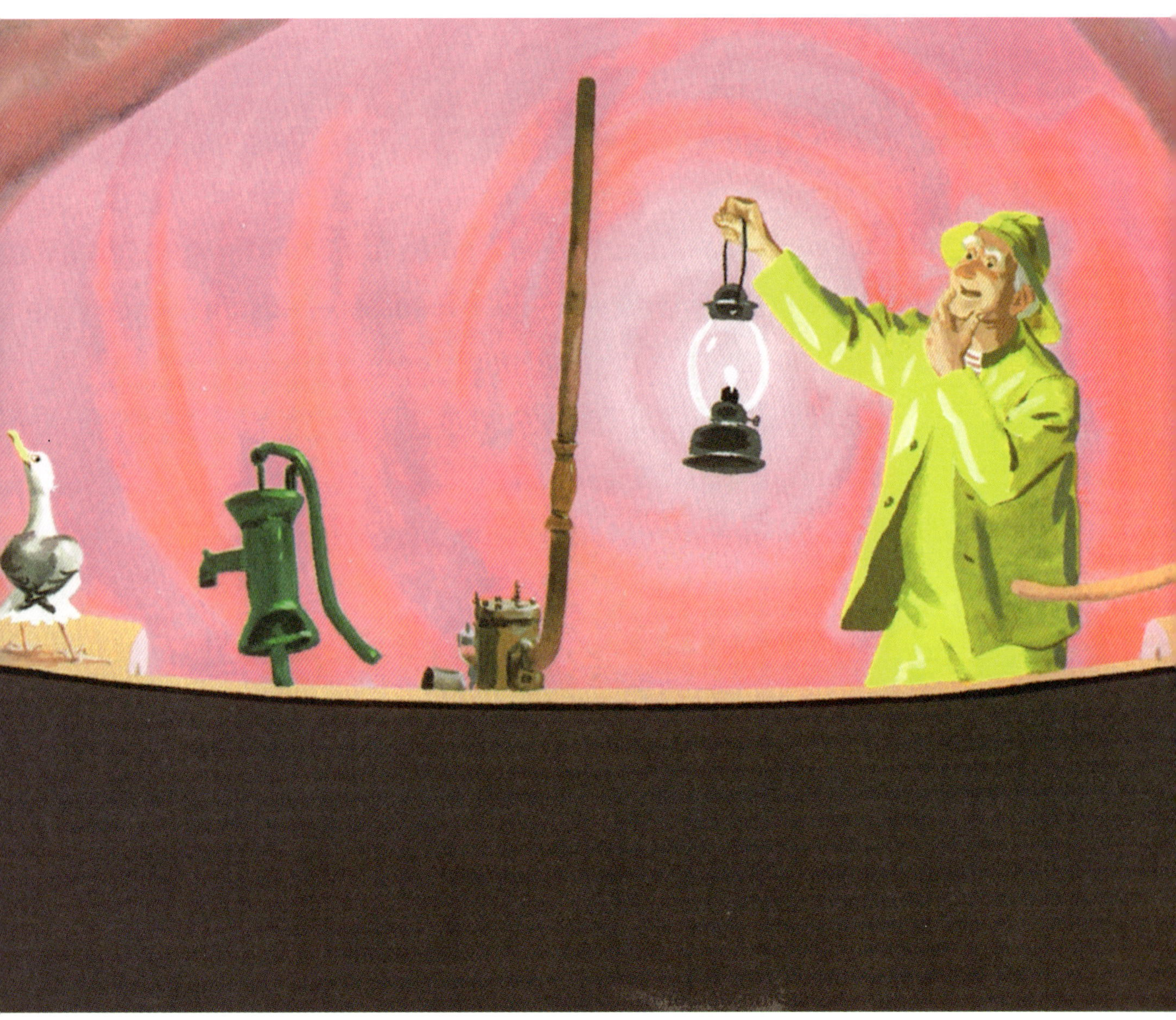

Bob worked in a wide range of mediums. At one time or another, he worked in pencil, charcoal, chalk, watercolor, casein, oil, and acrylic. He did wood and linoleum cuts, silk screen, murals, etchings, lithographic drawings on zinc, engravings, stone sculpture, clay modeling for both bronze and latex casting. He cast the latex for his puppets himself and used a metal lathe to make tiny toothed brass wheels for his puppets.

During World War II, Bob was stationed in Alabama, and was, among other things, in charge of decorations for officers' parties. He made a bronze sow for the officers' club, which I saw many years later. She was hollow, with a stoppered opening between her shoulders where you could pour in punch. You turned her tail to release the punch through her teats. That's how I know he cast in bronze, though he probably just made the clay model and sent it off to a foundry to be cast.

He was a meticulous craftsman. I remember when I was in sixth grade, he was in a fallow period. He used his time that winter to make a sample collection of every color on the color wheel, with fine gradations of the pure colors. He painted them in acrylic. Then he made fine gradations of every one of those colors from white to black. It took almost a year. Now, of course, you can call up this color wheel and color globe on Photoshop. Still, I saw my father use his samples over the years when he was mixing paint on his palette for an oil painting, or choosing an off white paint for the living room.

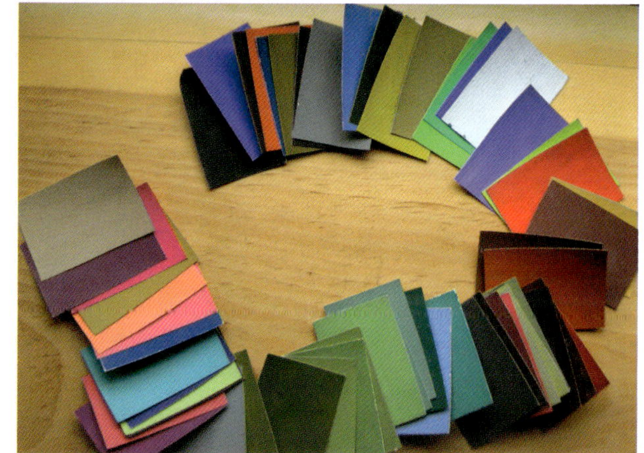

Color Chips, ca 1960.

I last saw the color samples in the 1980s, but researching this book, I found them again in the attic. Before, the samples were in order, hundreds of gradations of a single color: just like in the paint store and not too interesting unless you are looking for a particular hue. But when I took them out I saw that he had broken up the order, and put them into combinations he liked. I like them better this way, too.

My father taught me the basics of perspective. Some excellent artists don't concern themselves with perspective, but my father's work is usually impeccable in that regard. Bob's careful use of perspective was an expression of his admiration for renaissance art.

His anatomy was very accurate, unless he was drawing a fantasy figure, or doing an abstract, in which case, he took liberties. He said that his knowledge of anatomy when he drew Lentil was not as good as it later became. Looking at his sketch books, I believe that drawing Sal and me playing in hundreds of positions on the floor over a period of years is what perfected his knowledge of anatomy. He had a copy of Grey's Anatomy in his studio, which he used to look at from time to time. So did Sal and I.

Bob admired classical art, and took some woodcuts with classical themes to May Massee. She told him to ditch the classics and go home to Ohio and draw what he knew. He did, but he remained a closet classicist. In *Homer Price* and *Centerburg Tales*, Uncle Ulysses, Grandpa Hercules, and of course Homer himself, are named after Greeks or Romans. At least once a winter, my father took the family to the Metropolitan Museum in New York City to look at the Greek statues.

Bob disliked repeating himself. He might do many variations on an idea for a picture until he felt he had explored it entirely, but then he moved on.

He disliked sequels, because he said they were often just a rehash of the original material, and were rarely as good. He said that he thought *Centerburg Tales*, which was the sequel to *Homer Price* was the least artistically successful of his books. He did illustrate four Henry Reed books, but began muttering on the third, and quit after the fourth. Still, I like Henry Reed and I am glad Bob stayed with Henry as long as he did. Because of Bob's doubt about sequels, I thought carefully before I committed myself to writing this book—I didn't want it to be a rehash of my memoir about growing up with my father.

When Bob liked something, he rarely said why. He just said, "She does some very nice work."

He said that one of the reasons for the popularity of abstract art in the twentieth century was the emergence of photography. Photographs replaced art as the medium to show people what something looks like. In order to protect their turf, artists needed to find things that artists could do better than photographers. Many felt that a painting that was less realistic might express feelings or ideas or visions better than a photograph. Some artists went all the way to abstract, some to semi abstract, some just to a stylistic rendition of reality.

My father was usually at the realistic end of the spectrum, but one way he embodied the claim of his generation of artists that painting could do things that photography could not, was to draw or paint a made up scene that included elements from several different places. People wonder where Sal and Mom went blueberry picking in *Blueberries for Sal*. I always thought the blueberry field in the book was inspired by the Howland's blueberry field on Little Deer Isle. Some think they went to the blueberry fields at the head of Cape Rosier, others that it was the hill above Bucks Harbor, or maybe it was Caterpillar Hill, or even Blue Hill. It was really a classic Maine blueberry hill made up from Bob's imagination. Now, with Photoshop, photographers can make up their own blueberry hills, too.

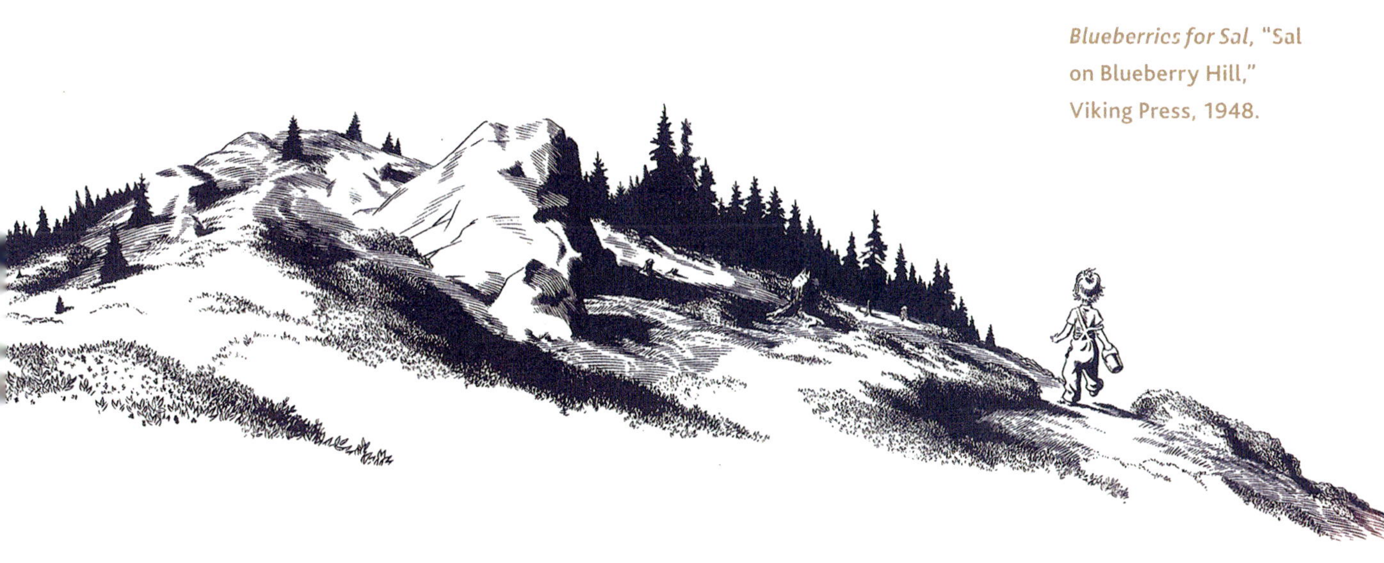

Blueberries for Sal, "Sal on Blueberry Hill," Viking Press, 1948.

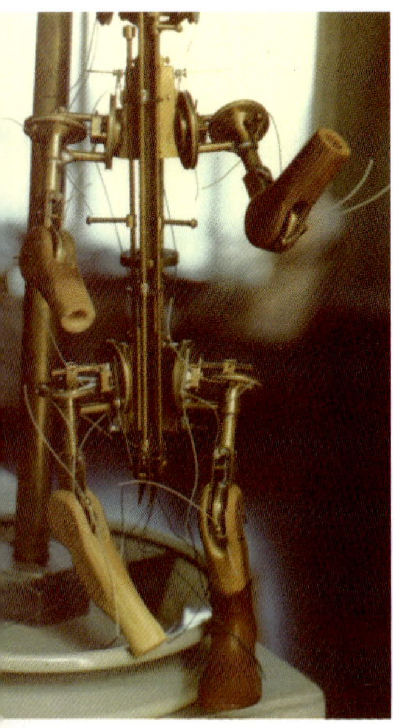

Twenty Twenty's innards, 1980s, photo courtesy of Westson Woods Studios.

In Mexico, when he was 44, my father had a nervous breakdown. I have considered many possible causes, according to the various psychological theories of the past fifty years; but the truth is, I don't know why he had his breakdown.

Maybe he felt he had reached the pinnacle of his creative life. He had set the bar so high by winning two Caldecott Medals and three Caldecott Honors, that there was almost no where he could go in the children's book world but down. How could he top his previous success? Also, his previous books had been based on his own childhood and Sal's and my childhoods. We were now entering adolescence, and maybe he felt he had explored our family life as far as he could in children's books. He had spent two winters in Mexico doing many sketches for a possible children's book about a Mexican girl, but maybe he realized that he was not going to be able to do it as he thought it should be done.

Maybe my father did not know where to go from there. Like Dante at midlife, maybe he found himself lost in a wood. Maybe, like Dante, he went underground. After a two-year interlude with Burt Dow in a whale's tummy, and some time with Henry Reed, he began a new career—making puppets.

The thing about these puppets is that they were doubles. On stage, "above ground" was the puppet that people saw. Under the stage, "underground," a skeleton puppet was attached to the stage puppet by gears and strings. Whatever the puppeteer made the underground puppet do, the above ground puppet did, too. These were extremely intricate and finely crafted puppets. My father spent thirty years working on them. He returned to the mechanical tinkering of his childhood.

There were three puppets who were friends: a mole, a mouse and a pigeon. The mole's name was Twenty Twenty. The mouse had no name for many years, but eventually became Mechanical Albert. The pigeon's name was Mr. Pinkerton.

Bob spent almost all his time on the mole. He said once he got Twenty Twenty perfected, he could adapt the parts to the mouse without much trouble. And, twenty years later, he did. The pigeon presented a problem, because the question was how far to modify the pigeon's wings so that they could function as hands. He never did actually make Mr. Pinkerton.

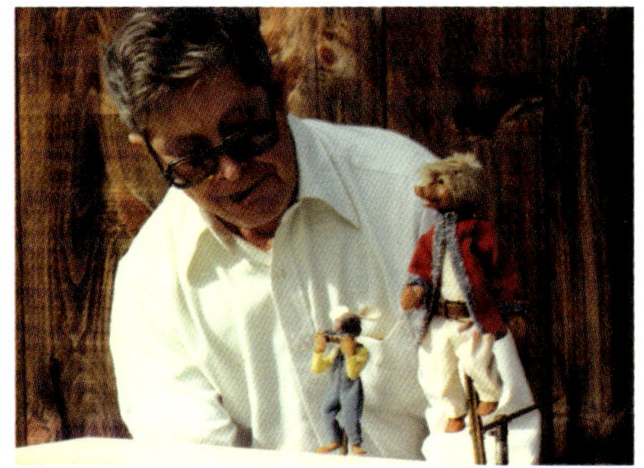

Bob with Twenty Twenty and Mechanical Albert, 1990s, photo courtesy of Weston Woods Studios.

The clothes for Twenty Twenty and the other puppets were made by Noni Cely, a fine doll maker and artist in Atlanta.

After his breakdown, my father seemed to have a different idea about "Seeing." He named a mole, which is nearly blind, Twenty Twenty. Maybe his youthful vision of the world no longer gave meaning to his life, and he felt blinded. But underground, a blind mole can see better than people with normal vision.

And, maybe the mole was also a spy. Perhaps an unseen spy of the underworld could see the world as it really was. Maybe my father wanted to learn to see the unseen, hidden underworld.

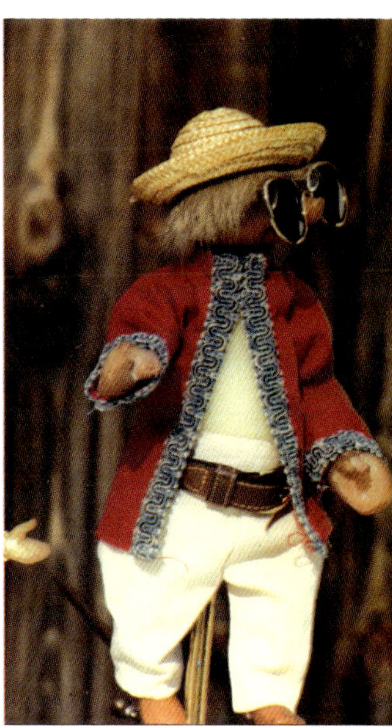

Twenty Twenty, made of wood, latex, brass, nylon fishing line, synthetic fur, clothing, 1990s, photo courtesy of Weston Woods Studios.

The mouse had no name for many years. Maybe he was, like the dormouse in *Alice in Wonderland*, a sleeper, another kind of spy, unnamed and unknown. Eventually, my father named him Mechanical Albert. Mechanical Albert could crawl inside a car piston and fix it from the inside out. So, "Seeing" was no longer looking at things from the outside, but rather going inside, and seeing and working from within.

In these pictures, my father and Twenty Twenty take turns wearing the shades of celebrities and spies. Mechanical Albert is holding a harmonica.

The Pigeon was named Mr. Pinkerton, with probably a pinkish greenish sheen to his feathers, and he worked as a detective at the Natural History Museum in New York. As Bob told me, Pinkerton men were detectives. Many Pinkerton men worked for the U.S. Government as private contractors. The Pinkertons also worked for businesses, spying on unions and attacking strikers. The logo of the Pinkerton Agency was an open eye with the slogan, "We Never Sleep." Because the Pinkerton Agency was a private agency, its detectives were called "Private Eyes."

Fame was a trial to my father. I think he felt singed by the glare of the public eye. For my father, retreating underground was a way of protecting himself from too much exposure. He found a new freedom and identity as a private eye, declaring independence from the public eye and the demands of fame. He was hidden under the stage as Twenty Twenty's underground self, and within the mechanical guts of his puppets, as Mechanical Albert was hidden within the mechanical parts of a car. My father also became a Pinkerton private Eeye. He liked "Pimpk," he was inside the flesh of the body, as Burt Dow was in the pink belly of the whale.

But things change. After my first book had gone to press, Bob's friend, Morton Schindel, sent me a DVD of a video of my father and his puppets at Weston Woods in the 1990s, thirty years after my father began work on the puppets in the 1960s.

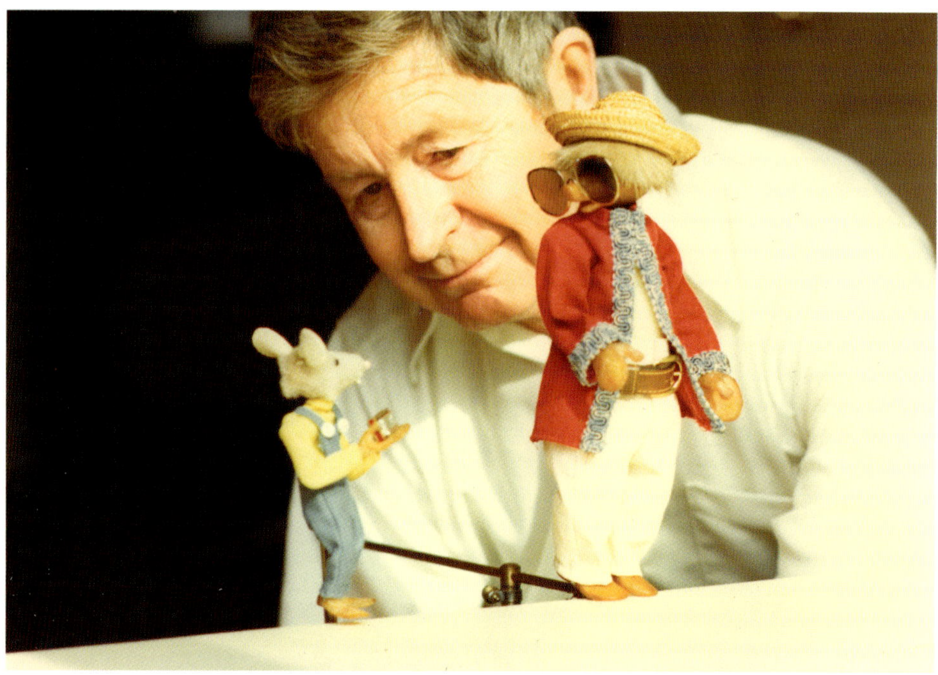

Bob, Twenty Twenty, and Mechanical Albert, 1990s, photo courtesy of Weston Woods Studios.

The puppets' characters and lives had changed. Originally, the puppets all lived in the back of a school bus, but in the video, the mouse, Mechanical Albert, hung out in an old beer can behind a garage, where he helped the mechanic fix cars. Albert's wife loved classical music and lived in the grand piano in the house next door. Albert sometimes stayed with her, and also helped her move out twice a year while the piano was being tuned. Albert and his wife had relatives "all over the place!"

Albert and Twenty Twenty had a new friend, a woodchuck called the Varmit. Twenty Twenty and the Varmit lived under an old tree in the woods near Mechanical Albert's garage. The Varmit was very wise, like Einstein, and spent most of his time laying around in bed, thinking. Twenty Twenty cooked and did the housekeeping. So Twenty Twenty had gone from being an edgy, mole-about-town spy to a staid, domesticated bachelor roommate, probably into hummus and kale.

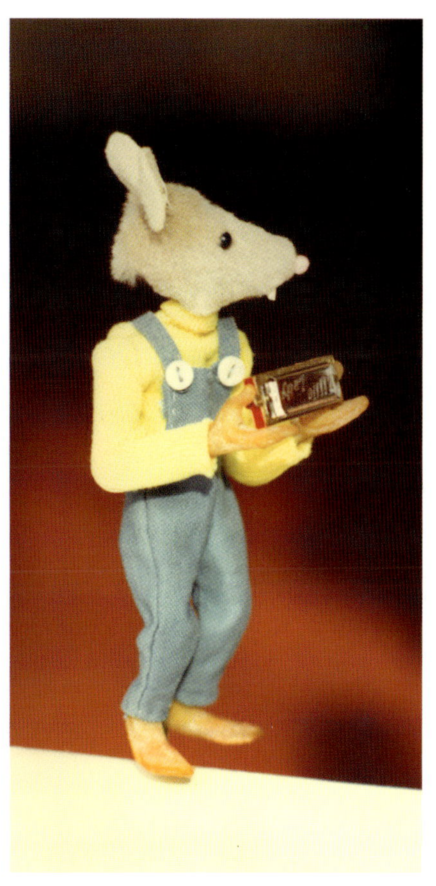

Mechanical Albert with his Harmonica, 1990s, photo courtesy of Weston Wood Studios.

Mr. Pinkerton, the pigeon, a detective for the Museum of Natural History, forty miles away in New York City, discovered that some ancient Egyptian wheat seeds were missing from the museum, and traced the seeds to Mechanical Albert. When he asked Albert if he had taken the seeds from the museum, Albert said, yeah, he didn't know they were anything special. He said they tasted terrible, all musty and moldy and he had to spit them out. He pointed to a nice stand of wheat growing behind the garage where the nasty seeds had germinated. So Mechanical Albert was instrumental in introducing ancient, heirloom Egyptian wheat to a suburb of New York.

These stories show that the puppets had evolved. All of them, except Mr. Pinkerton, were still what Bob called earth creatures, and lived on or under the ground, but they had settled into middle aged domesticity. They no longer seemed like creepy underworld spies. The Varmit looked pretty disreputable, but more like Einstein who preferred to dress in a sweatshirt and slippers

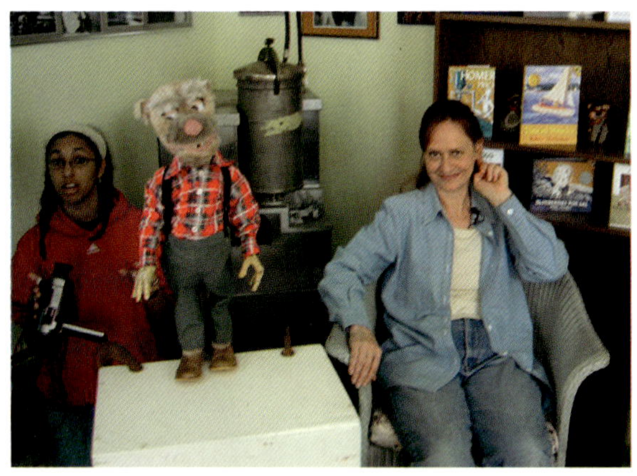

The Varmit and Friends at Weston Woods, 1990s, photo courtesy of Weston Woods Studios.

than like a criminal or spy. Maybe the spy aspect of their characters was largely a product of the 1960s, when spy stories became popular. In the 1960s, James Bond leapt to fame. There were many spy movies: *Our Man in Havana, North by Northwest, The Spy Who Came in from the Cold, The Manchurian Candidate. Mad* magazine ran a regular cartoon strip called "Spy vs. Spy." Of course, now reality has imitated art, and the NSA is peering over all our shoulders.

In my last book, exploring the spying aspects of Bob's personality, I wrote a chapter on the surprising number of spies who intersected our family life. After I wrote the book, my second cousin Anna Durand, from my mother's side of the family, contacted me. She said that her grandfather, Dana Durand, who was my mother's uncle and my great uncle, was also a spy, and a pretty important one. He was in the OSS during World War II, and the head of the CIA in Berlin right after World War II. Anna's mother Pat wrote in an e-mail to me that her father sent for the family to join him in Berlin. She wrote, "My mother and I knew perhaps a bit too much about my father's work, so it was an exciting time for us, tho' in retrospect maybe we should have been more anxious. As it was, we thoroughly savored it all, so for the little Quaker family this life of 007 dependants was an outstanding feature of our lives!"

Anna, commenting on her mother's e-mail, wrote,

"Cool, but she leaves out the really juicy parts! My memories of his legends are that he had a cyanide tooth, to crunch and vamoose if he was caught and tortured, that he and his minions were the first ones into Hitler's bunker after his death, and my mom had some creepy Nazi dishware that they 'liberated.' His later life as a CIA officer was spent getting us into some of the quagmire we're still in. He was supposedly involved in the CIA's overthrow of the democratically elected Mohammed Mossadegh and installing the Shah in Iran.

[He] was also involved in some weird scheme whereby he and a few others tried to repent of their sins via a new technology that allowed third world countries to sell and not burn the natural gas that was emitted when oil companies drilled wells. This, perhaps, was the situation that caused him to 'attempt suicide,' (it might actually have been attempted murder by the CIA to silence him,) but he got out of it and was allowed to resign."

Well! Maybe father knew about this family lore and it contributed to his interest in spies and the underworld. Anna's mother said that my parents spent their army leave with her parents in Florida during World War II, so maybe Dana or his wife talked about his spying duties. On the other hand, "loose lips sank ships," and maybe Uncle Dana and his wife kept mum. Or maybe my father suspected without being told. He was very intuitive.

Anyway, to return to the 1980s: what about the Varmit, who lay around in bed all day, thinking? I used to do that when I had mercury poisoning, so maybe the Varmit was me with a sex change. And in the video there was also a black female. She was totally unknown. The existing black female puppet is just an animal shaped head wrapped in black cloth, maybe an earth creature Black Madonna, or a woodchuck Great Kali. She is a mystery, and maybe the motive and goal of the spying after all.

In fact, spying may be a spiritual endeavor. As the Sufi poet Hafiz said, "Hafiz has become one of the greatest spies upon God this world has ever seen."

In my previous book, I wrote that Jim Henson, who created the Muppets came to Weston Woods Studios and looked at Bob's puppets after Bob died. I have learned that I was wrong—Mr. Henson died before my father did. Someone from the Ballard Institute and Museum of Puppetry at the University of Connecticut came and looked at the puppets. I have talked to several people there, but no one knows who it was. Anyway, that person said that the puppets were ingenious, but could never have been used in a real puppet show. It would take too many people with too many fingers to move the puppets under the stage. All those fingers and people wouldn't fit into the small space. Also, the nylon fish line that connected the parts would wear out rapidly and break.

I talked to John Bell at the school of puppetry at the University of Connecticut. With the help of John Bell, and Morton Schindel of Weston Woods, Bob's puppets have found a new home at the Ballard Institute and Museum at the University.

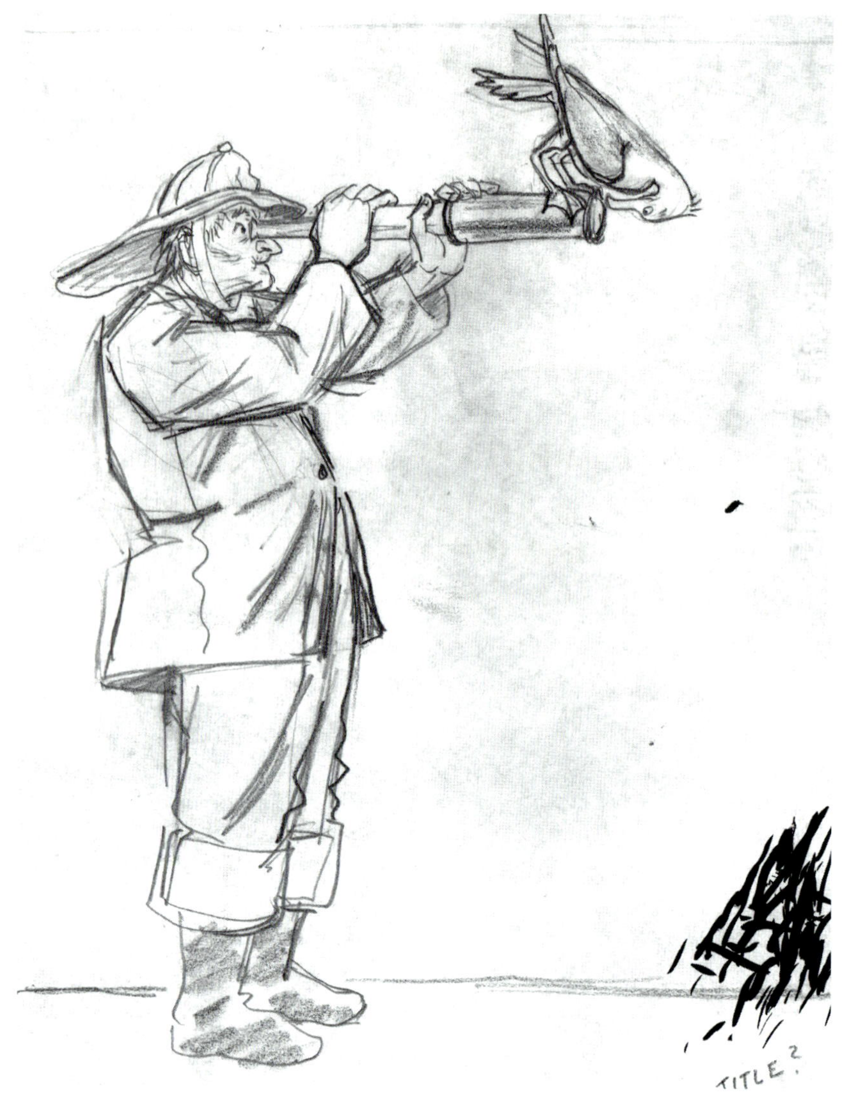

"Sketch of Burt Dow Spying on the Sea Gull Spying on Burt," pencil on paper, ca 1962, courtesy of May Massee Collection, Emporia State University.

Design and Dynamic Symmetry

10

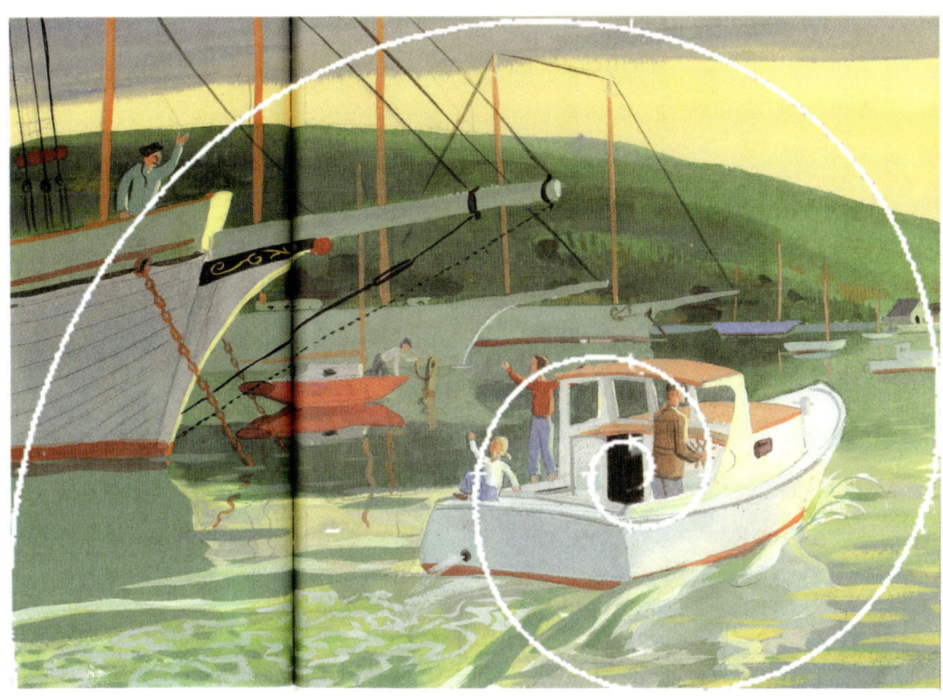

Time of Wonder, "Bucks Harbor," Viking Press, 1957.

If there was one word that my father used more often than any other when discussing art or design, it was "Proportion." When I was building my cabin, I was going to build it 24 x 16 feet, which has a proportion of 3:2, but Bob suggested that I build it 26 x 16, because it is a better proportion. 26 divided by 16 equals 1.625, so my cabin has a proportion of 1.625 to 1. We shall see that this proportion of 1.625 to 1 is very close to one of the most famous proportions in art.

My father gave formal voice to his interest in design in his acceptance speech to the American Library Association, when he won the Caldecott Medal for his book, *Time of Wonder.*

He mentioned five elements of design:

REPETITION is the first element of design: for example, many apples on a tree or a herd of horses. But the repetition is not exact, so good design has repetition with variation. These gulls sitting on a ledge in *Time of Wonder* illustrate my father's use of repetition.

Time of Wonder, "Gulls on Rock," Viking Press, 1957.

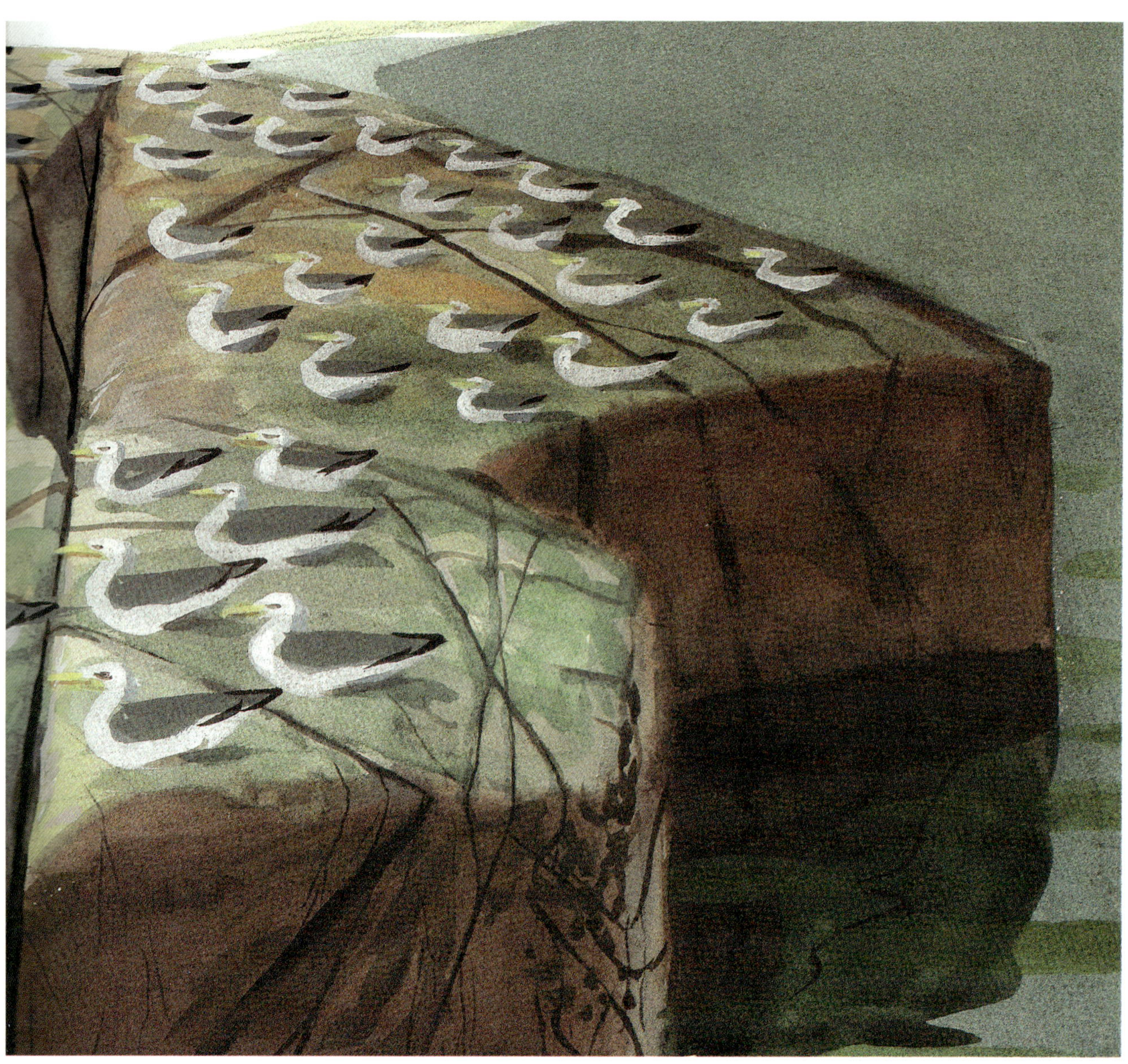

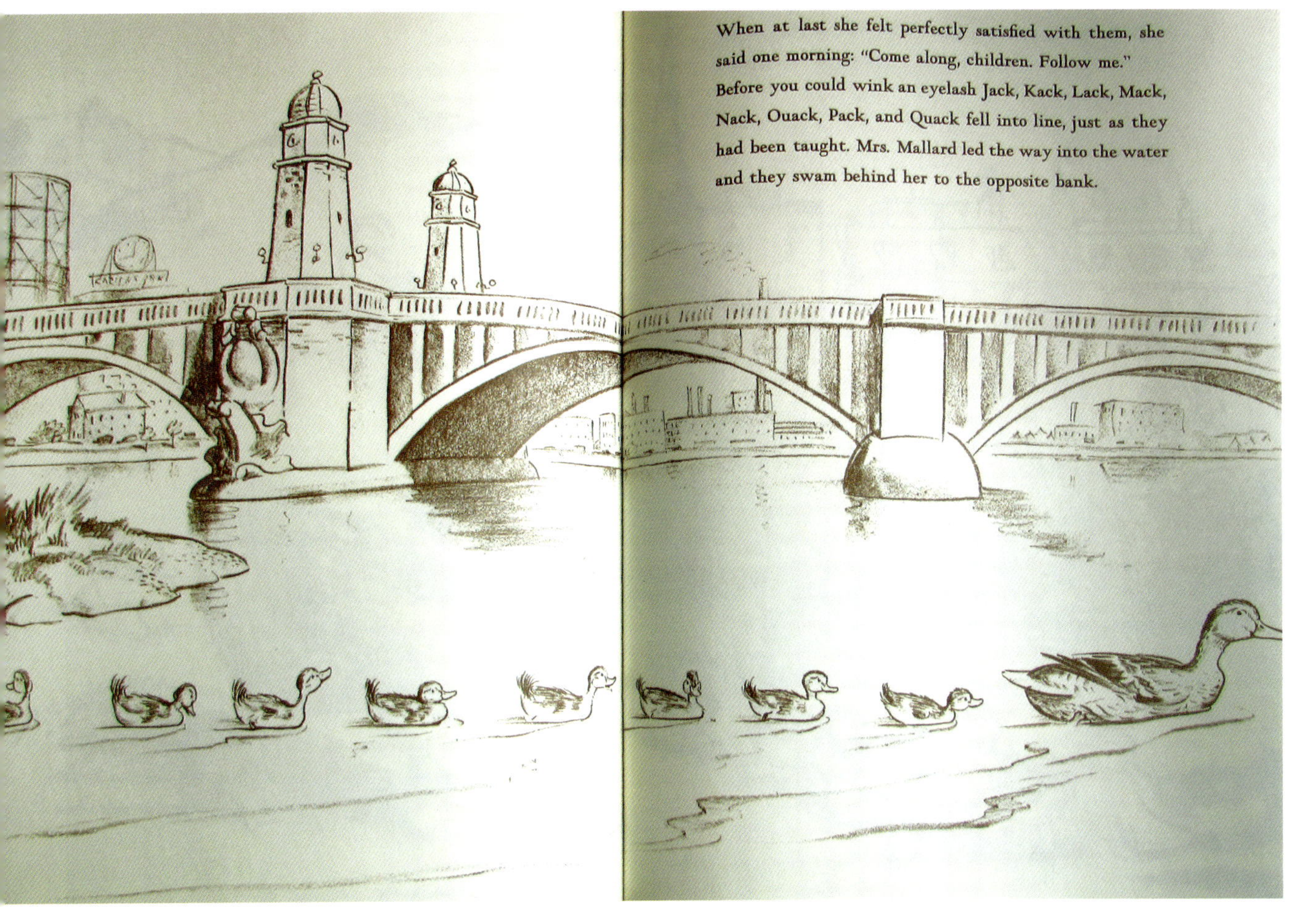

Make Way for Ducklings, "Crossing the Charles River," Viking Press, 1941.

These ducklings and the arches of the bridge show repetition as well.

RHYTHM is another element of design: of the seasons, of growing shells and plants, of waves on the water, and grass in the wind. If repetition occurs in space, rhythm happens in time and expresses itself through implied motion in the picture.

Blueberries for Sal is about Sal and her mother, and Little Bear and her mother, who are in the middle of the summer blueberry season. But they are already looking ahead to next winter, and getting ready for the cold time by stocking up on good blueberries. So *Blueberries for Sal* is about the rhythmic progression of the seasons. In this particular picture, Mother Bear is tramping through the blueberry field and munching on blueberries. Tramping and munching are both rhythmic motions in time and space. And Sal adopts Mother Bear's rhythm and tramps and munches right along behind her.

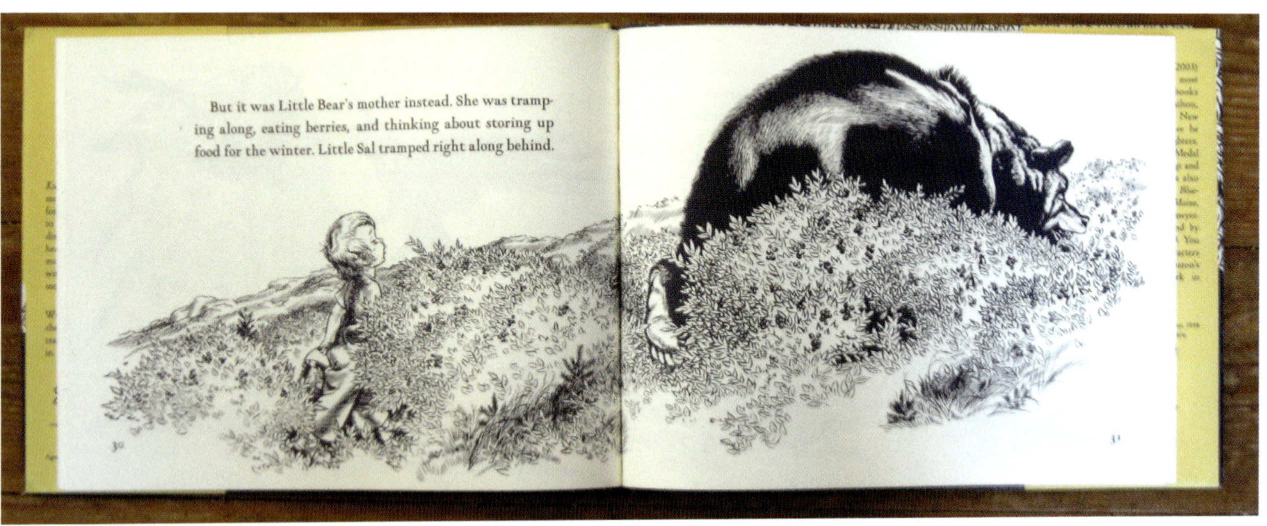

Blueberries for Sal, "Sal and Mother Bear," Viking Press, 1948.

COLOR is another element of design. As discussed in the last chapter, my father spent a winter making a complete set of colors, like the ones you see in paint stores. Nowadays, you could generate a set of colors with a few clicks of your mouse, but I think he found a deeper understanding of color by doing this work by hand.

TEXTURE is a fourth element of design: of wood, clay, sand, stone, and natural fibers. My father felt very close to the natural world after writing *Time of Wonder,* and all his examples were of natural textures.

Here, he shows the texture of rocks and sand.

"Scott Island, Rocks with Islands," watercolor, 15" x 22", 1940s.

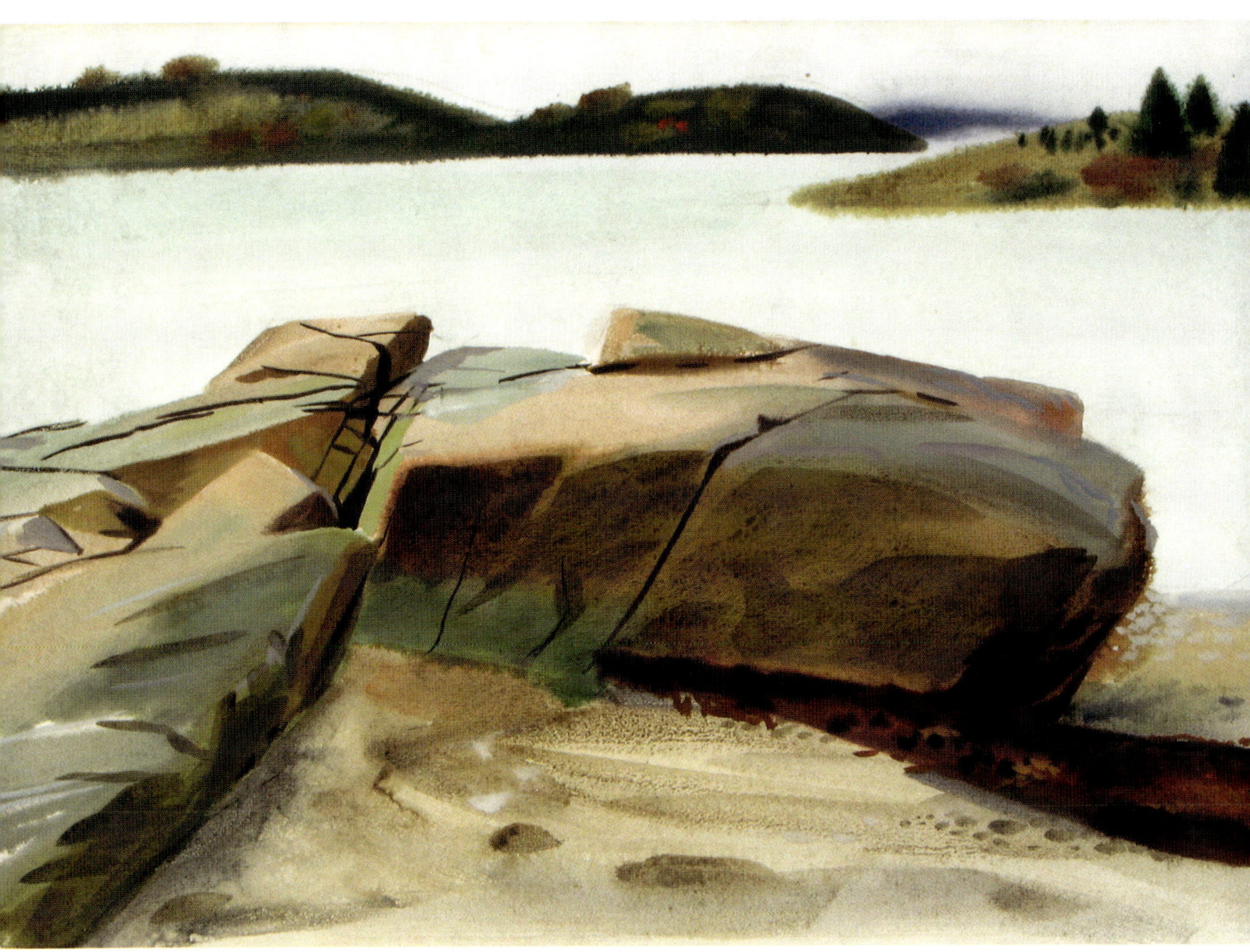

FORM is a fifth element of design: the forms of plants and animals, and forms made by wind and water. Here is a rowboat, a form made by a human being.

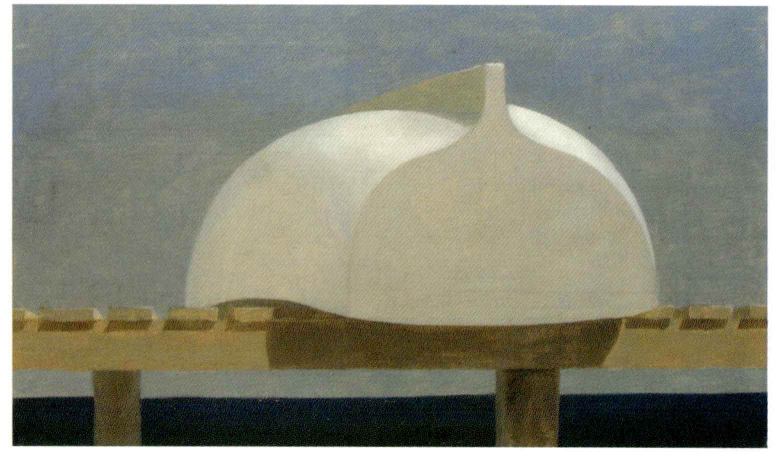

"Rowboat on Dock," oil on Masonite, 20"x 28", 1960s.

However, my father said that the most important element of design is Space Relationship: how all the various elements of a picture are placed in relation to each other. Space relationship is another way of saying proportion.

Symmetry is a kind of proportion in which two or more things are the same size and shape. Sand dollars and snowflakes are symmetrical on all sides of a center point. The sand dollar has five-pointed symmetry and the snowflake has six-pointed symmetry.

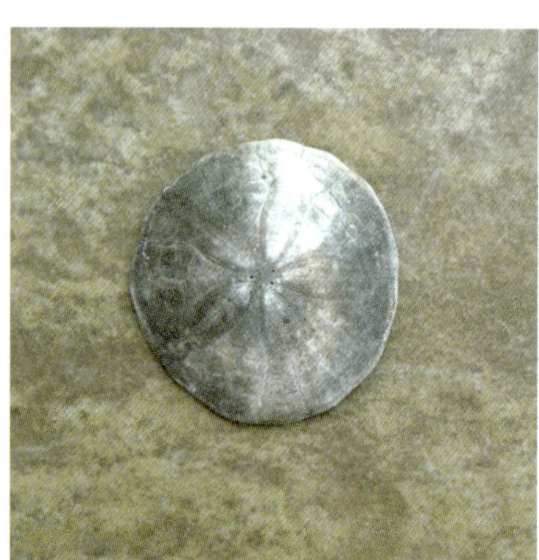

Sand Dollar, photo by Jane McCloskey.

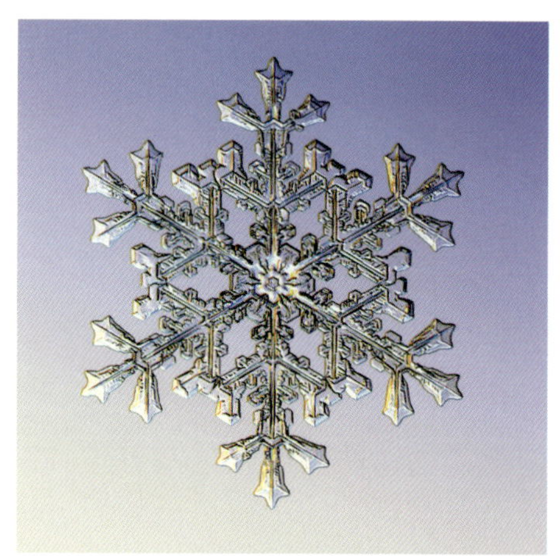

"Snowflake Libbrecht," courtesy of Kenneth G. kgl@caltech.edu.

Animals and people are often symmetrical around a center plane. Exact symmetry is rare: for example, lobsters have one claw larger than the other.

Art is often symmetrical around a center line. In art, as in nature, exact symmetry is rare. Leonardo's "Vitruvian Man" is symmetrical, except for his feet.

In Bob's picture of Sal knitting, she is almost symmetrical, but not quite. My father said that good design has repetition of shapes, but not exact repetition.

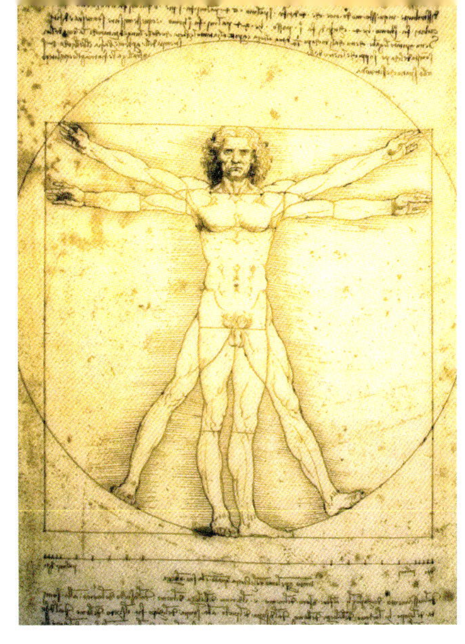

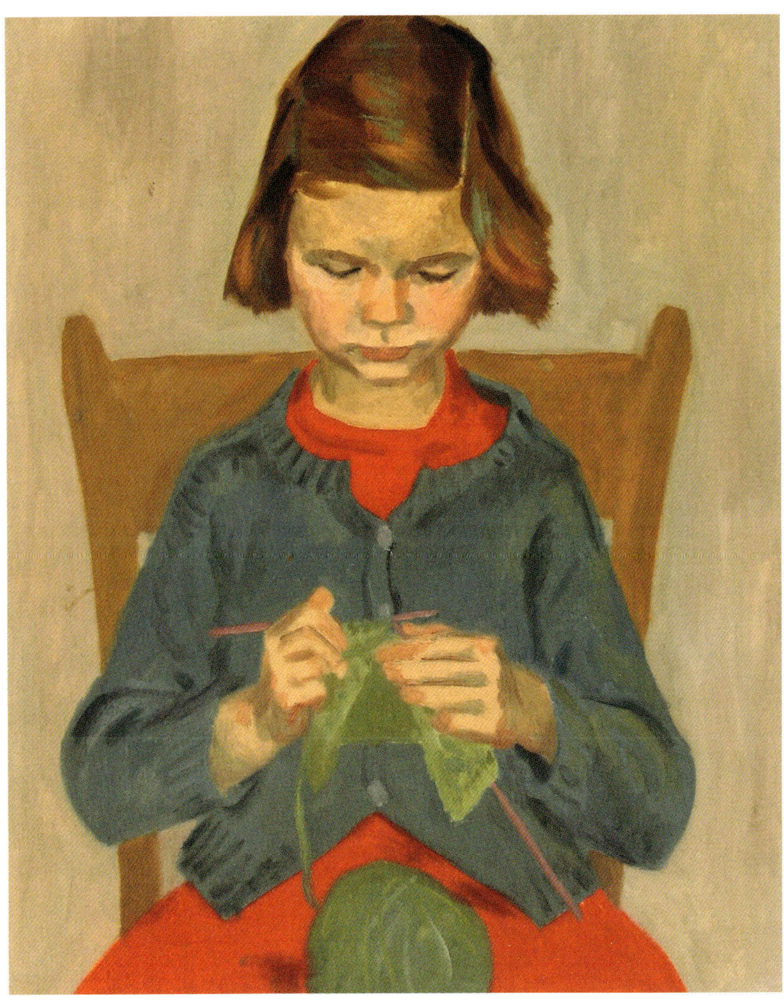

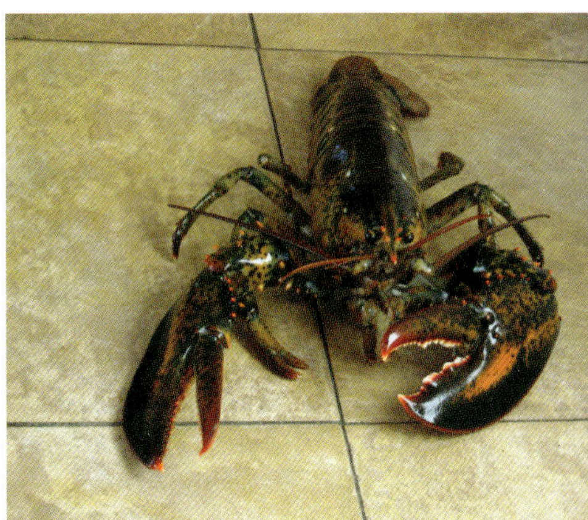

"Vitruvian Man," by Leonardo da Vinci, ink on paper, ca 1490.

Marsden: The Lobster, photo by Jane McCloskey.

"Sal Knitting," oil on Masonite, 20" x 16", ca 1954.

Writing in the early 1900s, artist and design theorist Jay Hambidge gave the term "static symmetry" to the kinds of symmetry we have discussed so far. In his book, *The Elements of Dynamic Symmetry,* Hambidge contrasted static symmetry with what he called "dynamic symmetry." In static symmetry, a shape is repeated around a center point, as in a snowflake, or repeated on either side of a center plane, as in a lobster; but in dynamic symmetry, a given shape is repeated, but its size and orientation change.

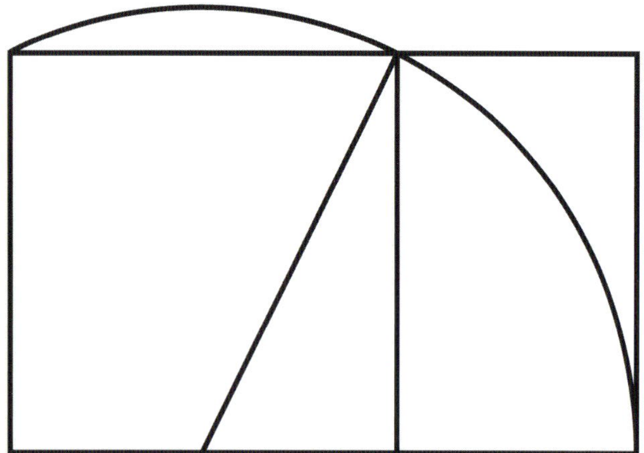

The Golden Rectangle.

The most famous example of dynamic symmetry is this rectangle. You construct this rectangle by finding the midpoint of the bottom of a square and putting your compass point there. You swing an arc as shown and that creates the proportion of this rectangle. This rectangle has the same proportion as the smaller rectangle to the right of the square. This rectangle does not show symmetry around a center point or line, but rather shows dynamic symmetry, in which two rectangles have different sizes and orientation, yet maintain the same proportion.

Luca Pacioli, who taught math and geometry to Leonardo da Vinci, called the proportion of this rectangle "The Divine Proportion." This proportion is an irrational number with decimals that go on forever : 1.6180539887. . . to 1.

This proportion is usually shortened to 1.618, with the 1 is implied, so the proportion is called 1.618 for short. The long side of the rectangle is 1.618, while the short side of the rectangle is 1.

1.618 is also called the "Golden Ratio." And the rectangle is called the "Golden Rectangle."

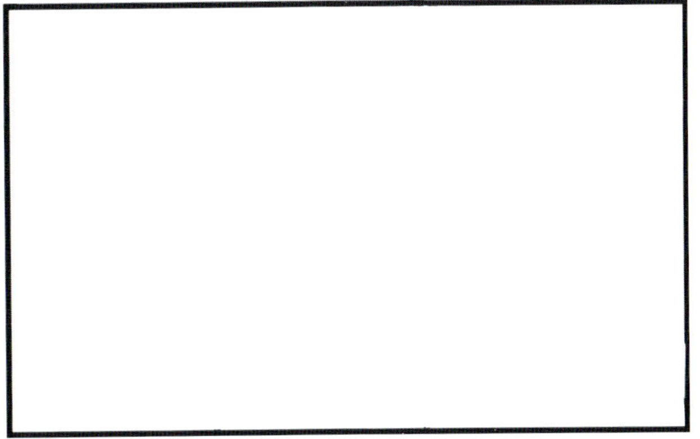

Golden Rectangle (empty).

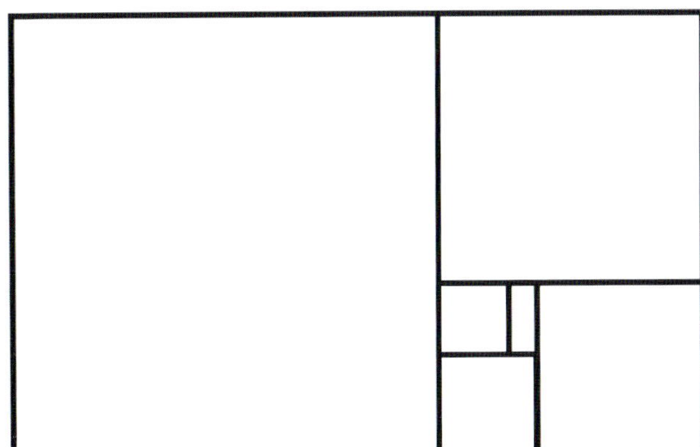

Golden Rectangle (also called the Rectangle of the Whirling Squares).

The proportion of my cabin, 26 x 16 feet, or 1.625, is only 7/1000s away from the perfect 1.618 proportion of the Golden Rectangle.

We saw earlier that you could divide a golden rectangle into a square and leftover rectangle, and that the smaller rectangle has the same proportions as the large rectangle. You can also divide the smaller rectangle into a square and leftover rectangle, and that rectangle into a square and leftover rectangle, and so on. Theoretically, the proportions remain constant forever, though in practice, some distortions set in as you draw smaller and smaller rectangles.

Golden Rectangle (with Golden Spiral).

So, you can see that these rectangles are dynamic, that is, always changing in size and orientation, and symmetrical in that they always have the same proportions, the square and the Golden Rectangle.

Using a compass, you can draw a "Golden Spiral" in this rectangle.

While this book is about my father's art, I want to show that other artists also used proportion in their work, so you can see my father as one of a long line of artists who worked consciously with proportion. Here is Winslow Homer's "Blackboard." You can see the precision of the various rectangles in this painting, and the precision of the blackboard itself. The rectangle on the lower right of the blackboard is a Golden Rectangle and will be the culmination of the school teacher's talk about geometric forms.

"Blackboard," by Winslow Homer, watercolor on paper, 9" x 12", 1877, courtesy of the National Gallery of Art.

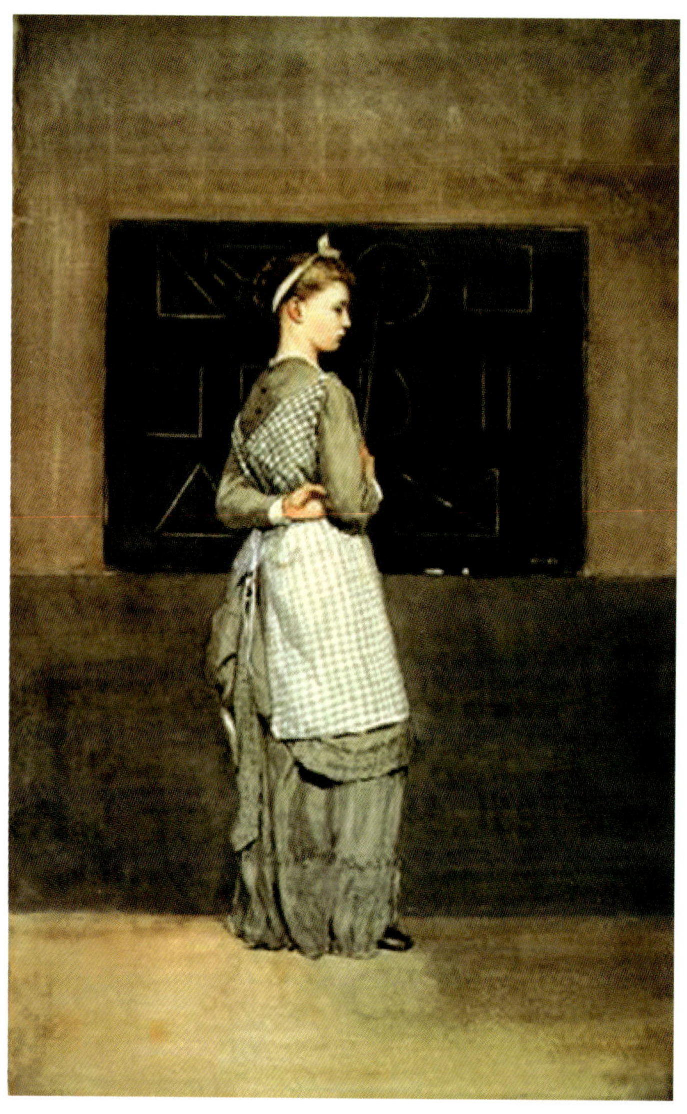

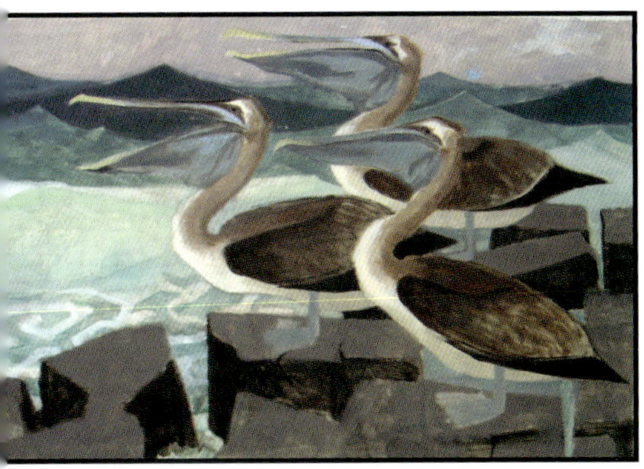

"Pelicans in St. Thomas," oil on canvas, 48" x 30", 1980s.

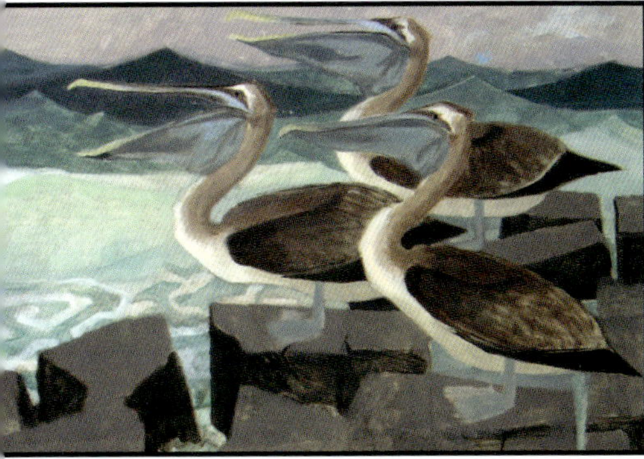

"Pelicans in St. Thomas" (detail: translucent paint with composition lines visible.)

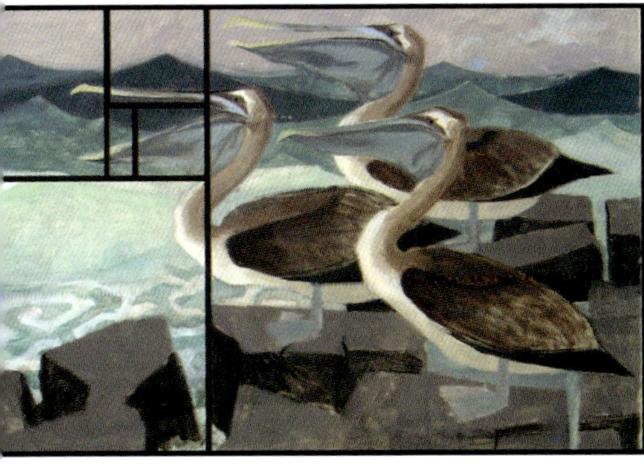

"Pelicans in St. Thomas" (cropped to nearly exact Golden Rectangle.)

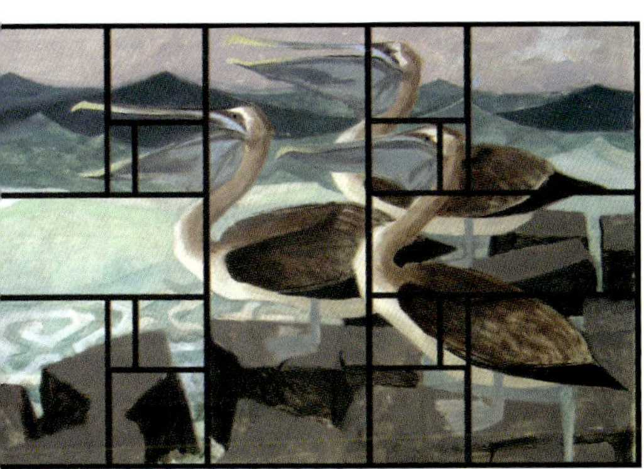

"Pelicans in St. Thomas" (with Golden Rectangle superimposed.)

"Pelicans in St. Thomas" (with four Golden Rectangles superimposed.)

Here is my father's picture of pelicans in St. Thomas. The canvas measures 48" by 30", which is a proportion of 1.6 to 1.

But you can see that there is a white border around the painting, and when you look closely, you can see lines under the paint that show he designed this painting to be exactly the size it is.

When I cropped the painting to remove the white border, the resulting image measured 1.616, or 2/1000s away from 1.618, the Golden Rectangle.

I superimposed the subdivided Golden Rectangle on the painting. You can see that in the lower left, the square corresponds to the light green water and rocks.

When we insert the golden rectangle in all directions in the painting, you can see that the lines of the divisions of the rectangles correspond to important horizontal lines in the painting.

Many of Bob's paintings have similar construction lines which are visible through the paint.

Root 2 Rectangle.

Let's look at some other rectangles. Here is a Root 2 Rectangle, which has a proportion of 1.414. . . to 1, or simply 1.414.

The blackboard in Winslow Homer's painting is a Root 2 Rectangle.

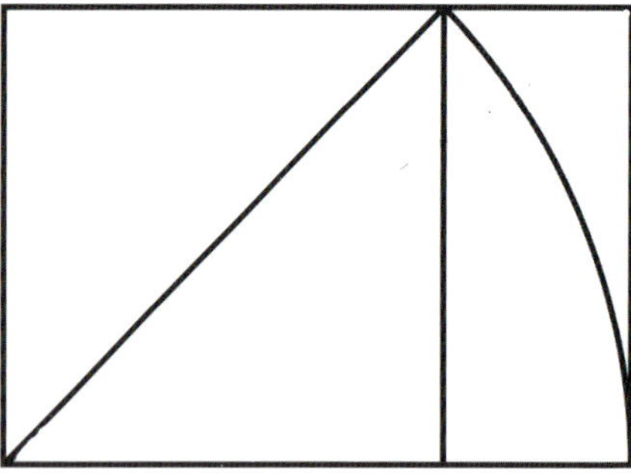

"Blackboard," by Winslow Homer, watercolor on paper, 9" x 12", 1877. courtesy of the National Gallery of Art, Gift of Jo Ann and Julian Ganz, Jr., in Honor of the 50th Anniversary of the National Gallery of Art. 1990.60.1

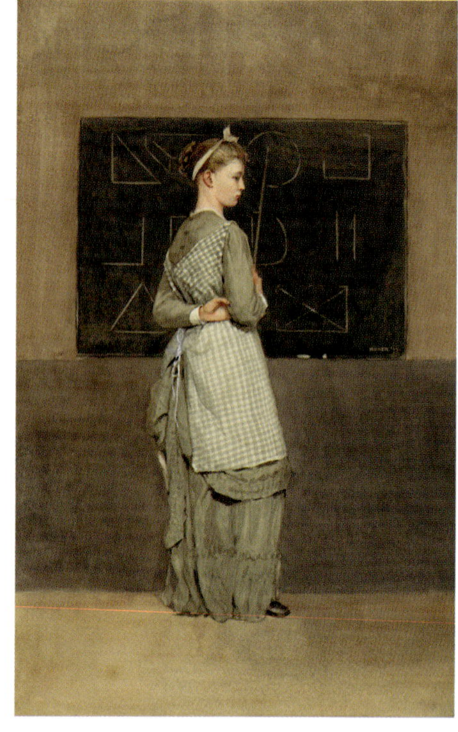

In Bob's book, *Time of Wonder,* most of the pictures are Root 2 Rectangles, with the square, the 1, on the right of the book's gutter, and the .414 on the left of the gutter.

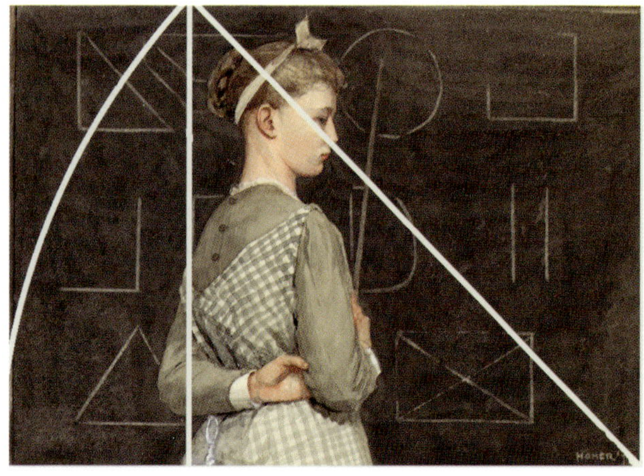

"Blackboard" (detail with Root 2 Rectangle superimposed.)

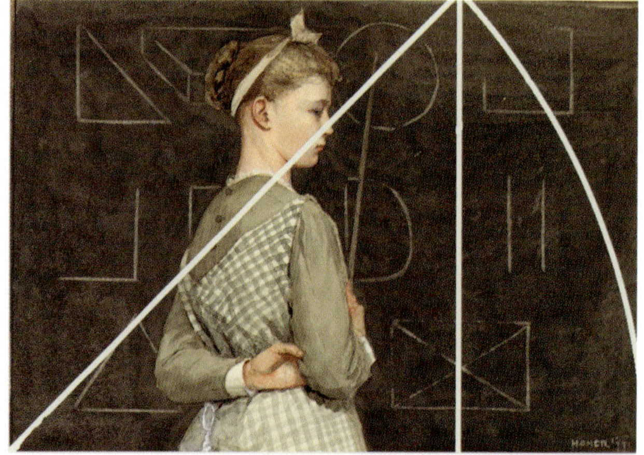

"Blackboard" (detail with Root 2 Rectangle superimposed.)

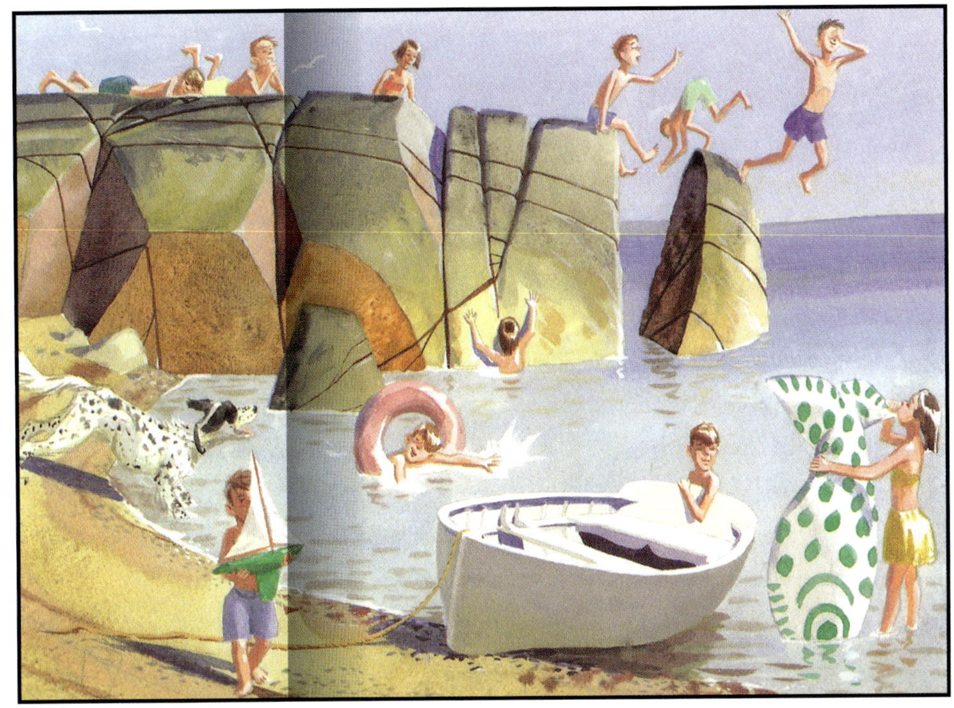

Time of Wonder, "Kids Playing on Beach," Viking Press, 1957.

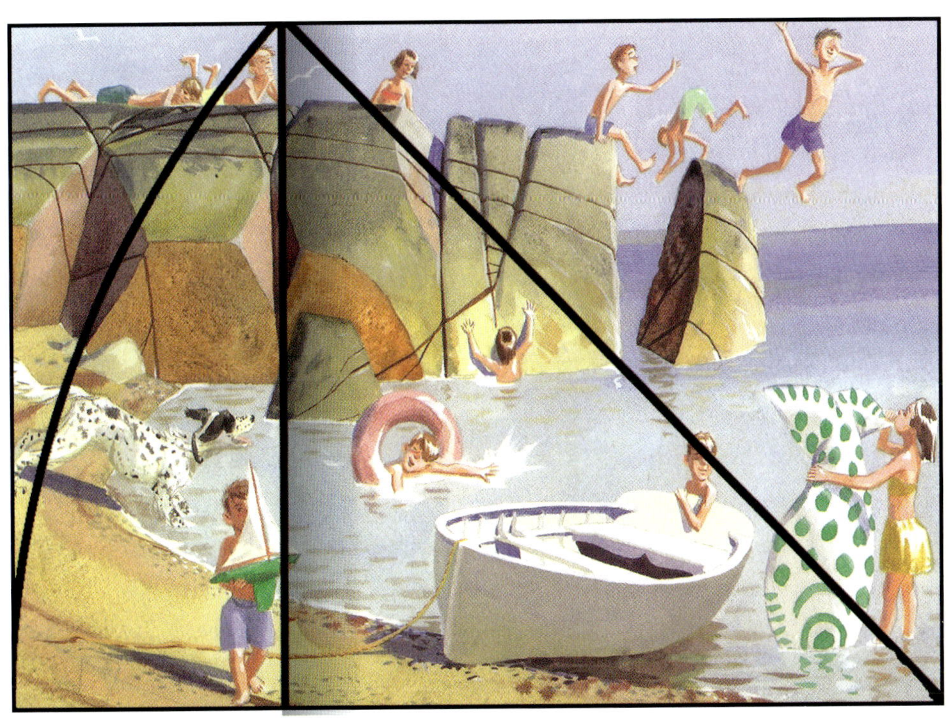

"*Time of Wonder,*" "Kids Playing on Beach" (with Root 2 Rectangle superimposed.)

Root 3 Rectangle.

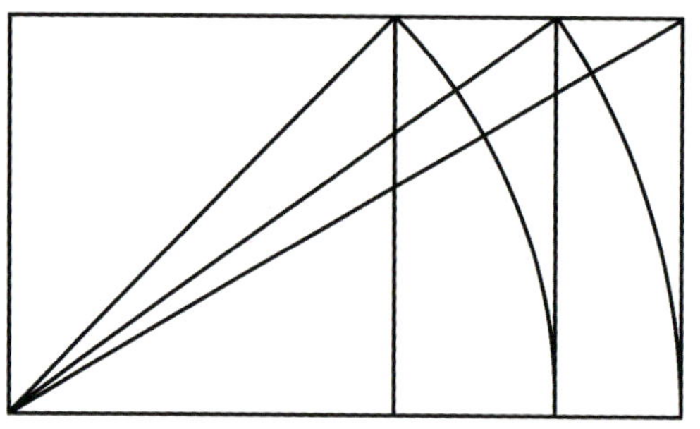

A Root 3 Rectangle has a proportion of 1.732 to 1.

Cimabue's "Maesta," in Florence, is based on a Root 3 Rectangle. The painting, 152" x 88", has a proportion of 1.727, which is 5/1000s away from 1.732 of the perfect Root 3 Rectangle.

You can see that the diagonal of the square follows the diagonal bottom of the Maesta's red skirt, and that the top of the square follows the level black cloak on her lap. The diagonal of the Root 2 Rectangle follows the main fold of the skirt in her black cloak. The top of the Root 2

Rectangle intersects the shoulders of the arch. A Root 4 Rectangle has a proportion of 2:1. You can see that it is made up of two squares side by side.

"Maesta," by Cimabue, tempera on panel, 152" x 88", ca 1280–1290, courtesy of the Uffizi Gallery, Florence.

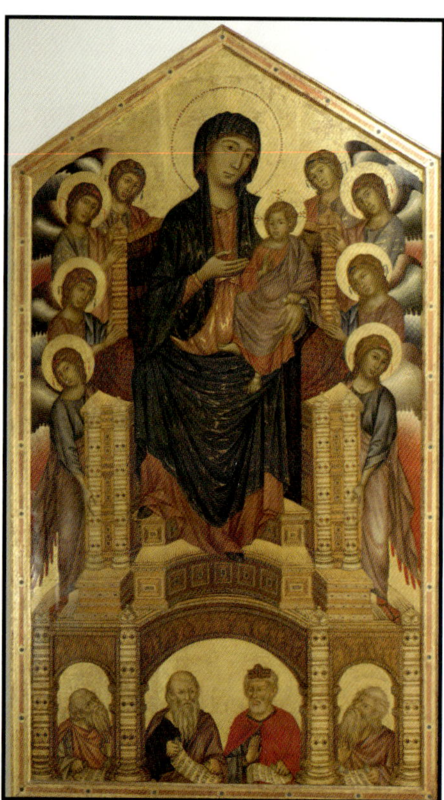

"Maesta" (with superimposed Route 3 Rectangle.)

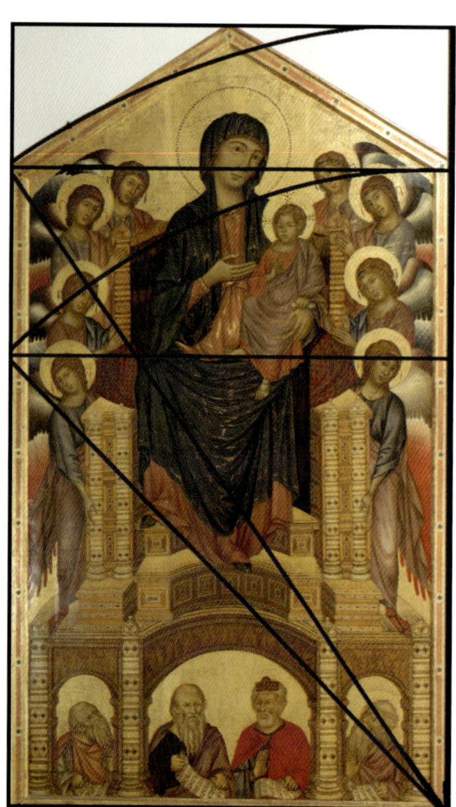

A few pictures in *Time of Wonder* are Root 4 Rectangles. The arcs and verticals intersect with the important parts of the boats and important parts of the right hand arch reflection.

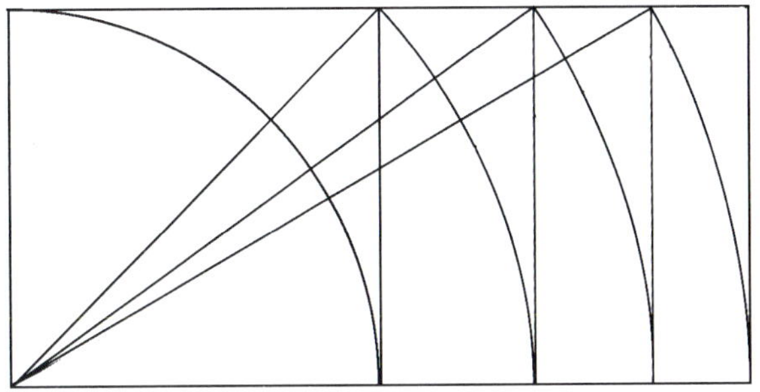

Root 4 Rectangle
A few pictures in Time of Wonder are Root 4 Rectangles.

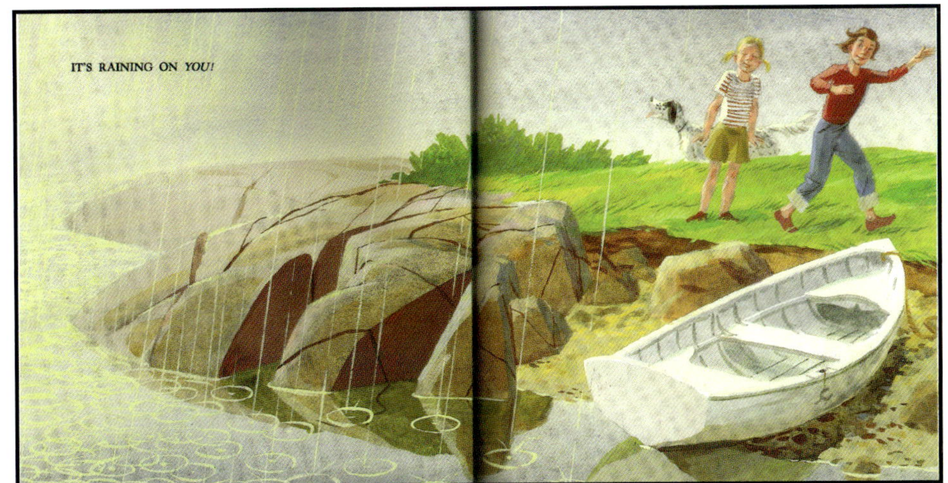

Time of Wonder, "It's Raining On You," Viking Press, 1957.

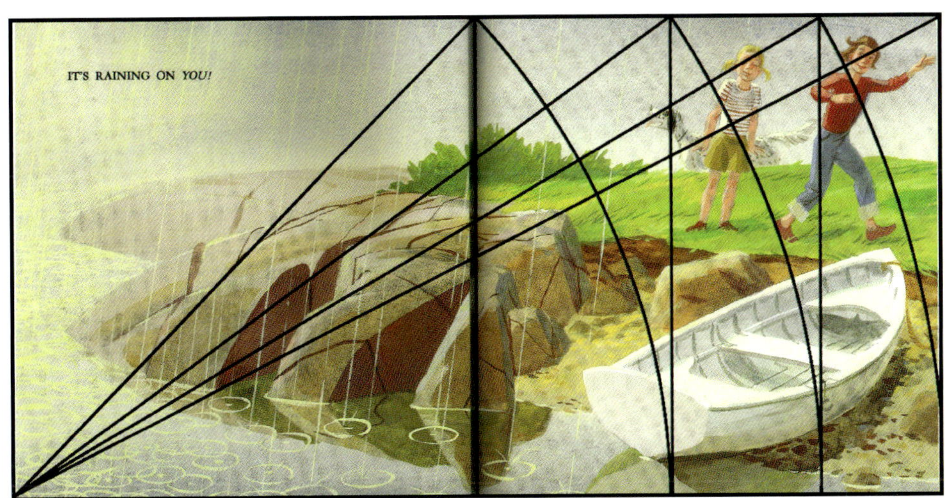

"It's Raining On You" (Root 4 rectangle superimposed.)

"Boats on Concrete Dock," oil on Masonite, 48" x 24", 1980s

Here is another painting with a Root 4 proportion. The arcs and verticals intersect with important parts of the boats and important parts of the arch reflections.

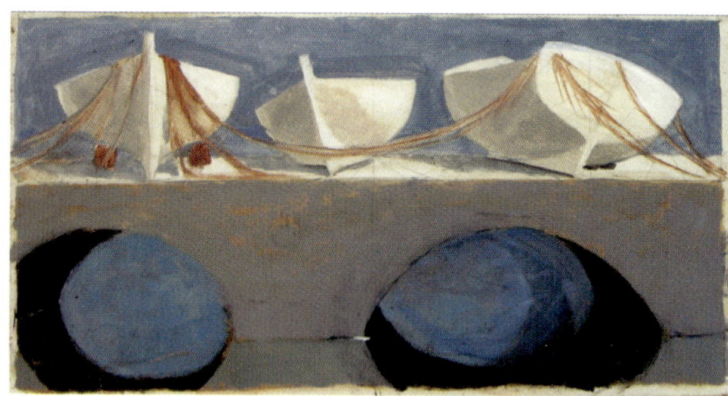

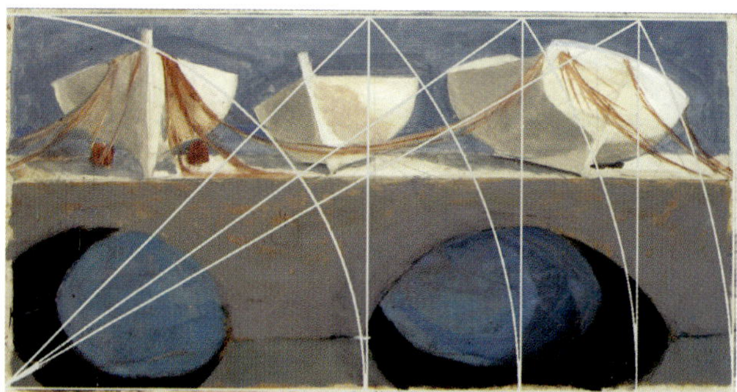

"Boats on Concrete Dock" (with Root 4 Rectangle superimposed.)

The Root 5 Rectangle has a proportion of 2.236:1. The front of the Parthenon, minus the roof and the steps, is a Root 5 Rectangle.

You can see that these Root 2, 3, 4, and 5 Rectangles are all related to the square and to each other, each building on the previous rectangle.

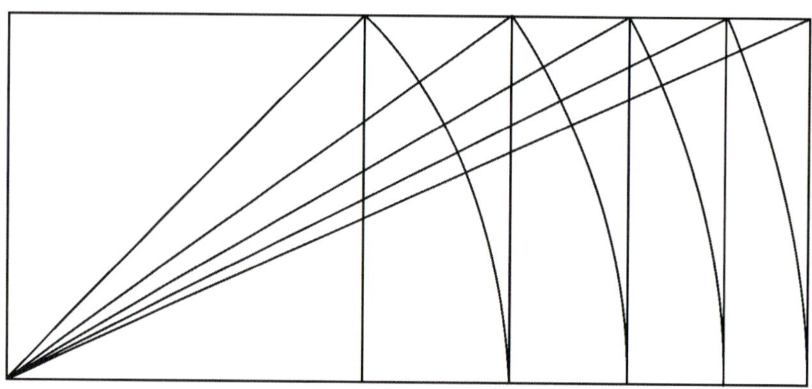

Root 5 Rectangle.

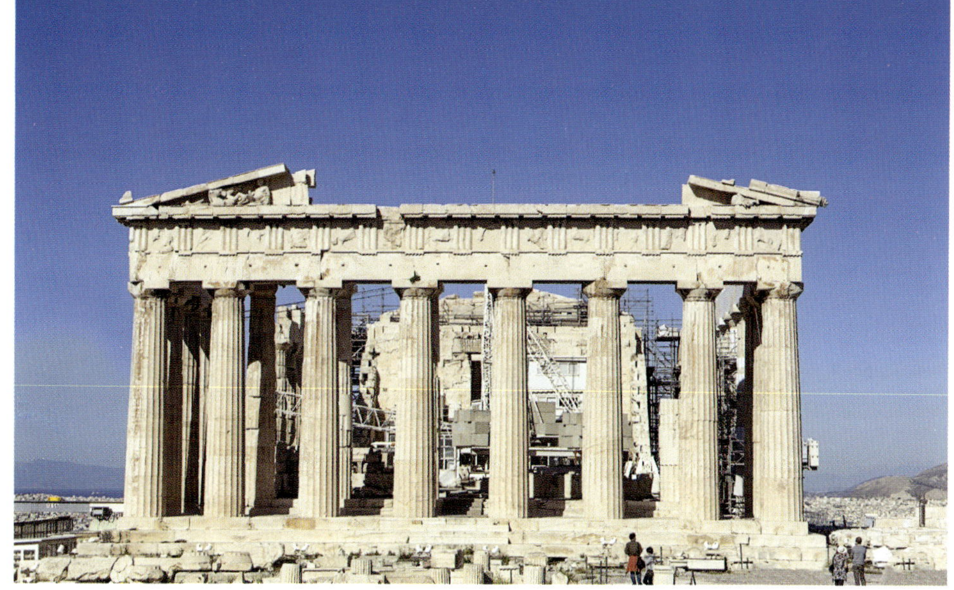

Parthenon. Courtesy of Shutterstock

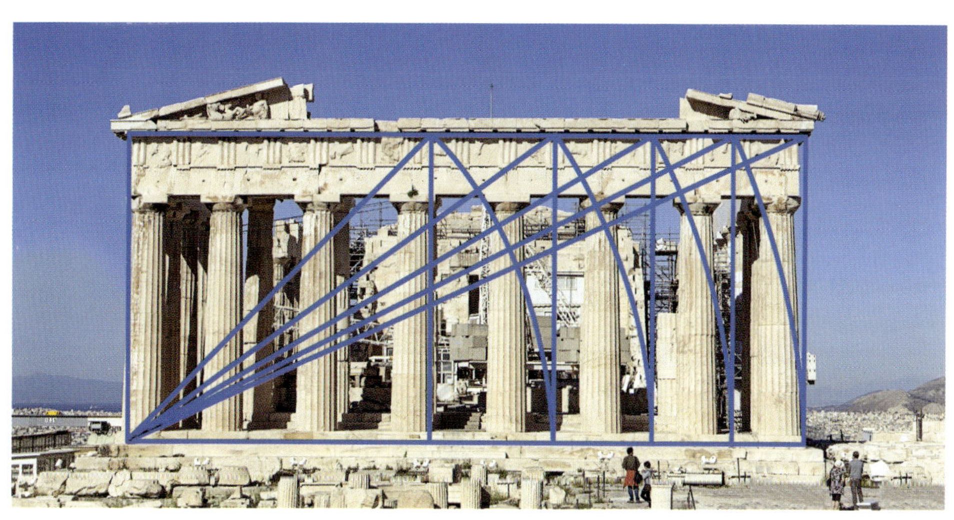

Parthenon (with Root 5 Rectangle superimposed.)

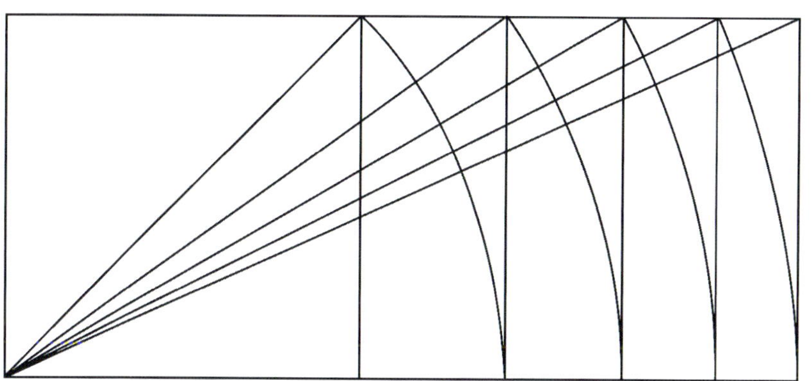

Root 5 Rectangle Construction.

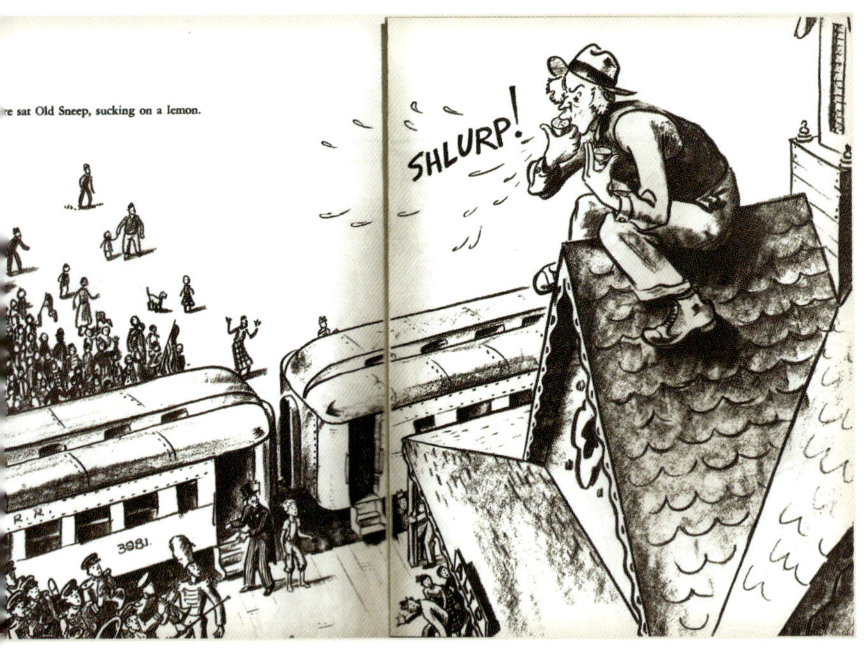

Let's take a break from these rectangles and look at a picture my father drew for the book *Lentil.* The story is about the town of Alto, which is welcoming home its famous native son. All the people have gathered to meet the train. The train has pulled into the station. The band is ready to play. But the town curmudgeon has commandeered the highest place around, and, in the sudden silence when the great man steps off the train, the old dude slurps on a lemon.

Lentil, "Old Sneep Sucking on a Lemon," Viking Press, 1940.

Here is a septagram, a seven pointed star, embedded in the illustration.

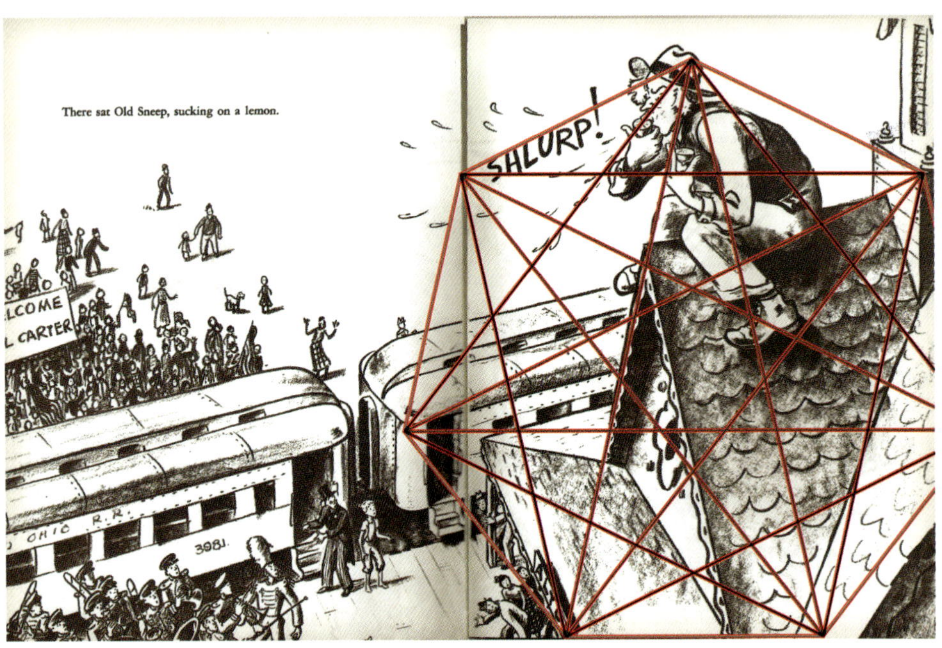

"Old Sneep Sucking on a Lemon" (with septagram superimposed.)

The position of Leonardo's "Vitruvian Man" is based on a septagram. There is a dot on his left big toe and another dot on his right instep where the two bottom septagram points land. His hands touch the upper septagram points and his arms follow the upper lines of the septagram. A horizontal line touches the top of his head, an intersection occurs at his heart, and a line passes through his sexual parts.

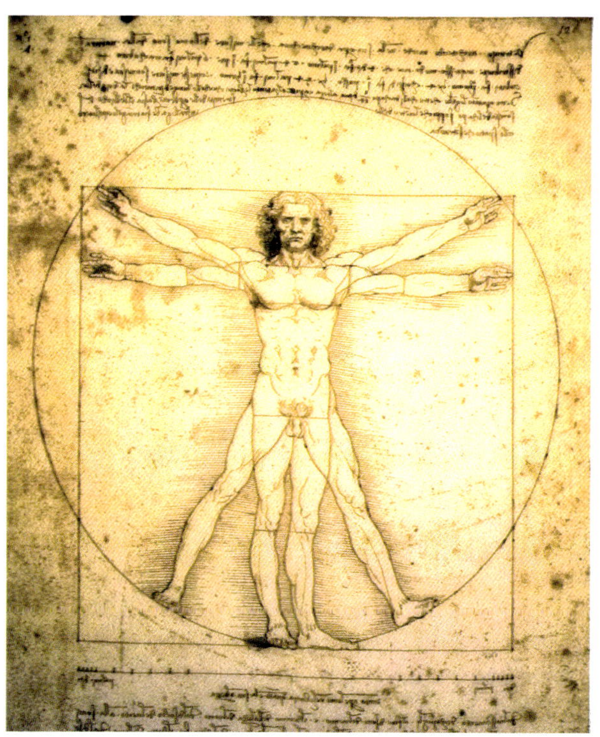

"Vitruvian Man," by Leonardo da Vinci, ink on paper, ca 1490.

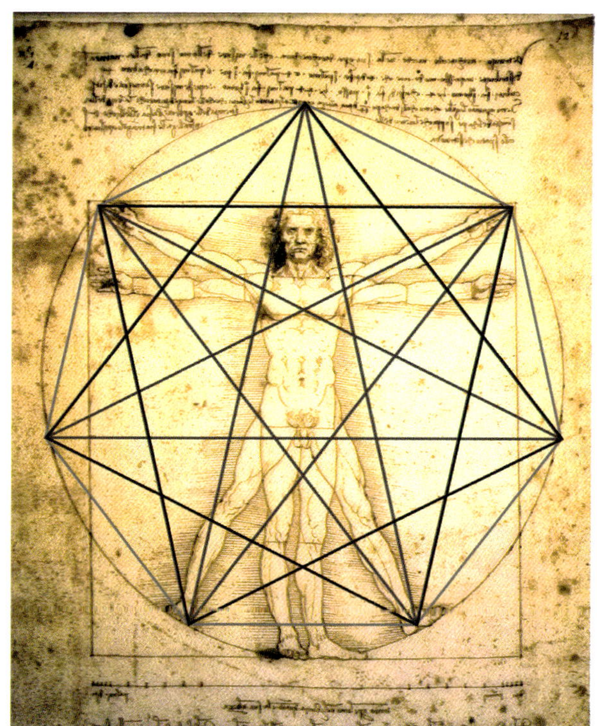

"Vitruvian Man" (with septagram superimposed.) Courtesy of Shutterstock.

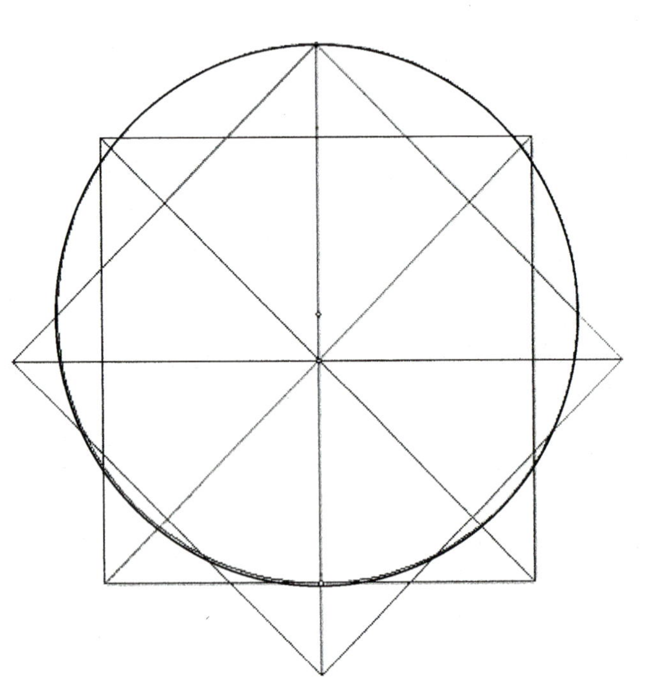

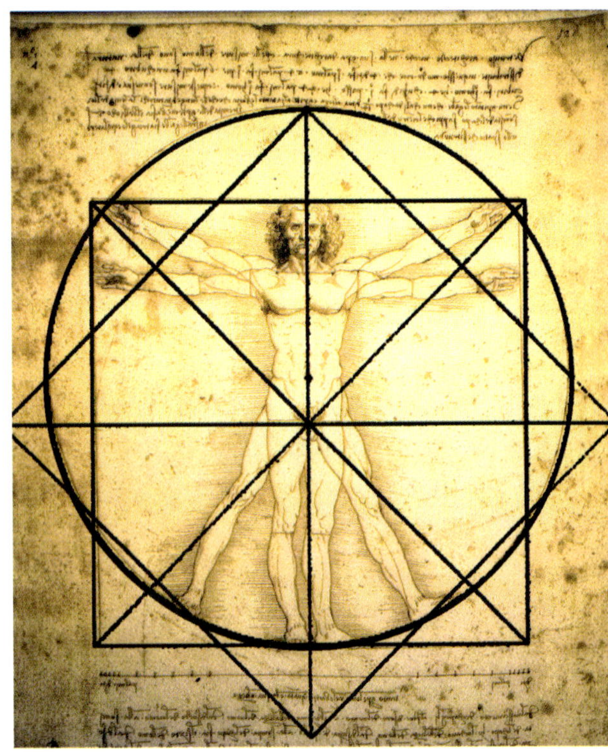

Construction of an Octagon.

"Vitruvian Man" (with Octagon superimposed.)

I always wondered how Leonardo decided on the size and position of the square and circle in "Vitruvian Man." The proportions of Leonardo's square and circle are based on the construction of an octagon. To construct an octagon, you rotate a square 45 degrees as shown. The midpoint between the bottom of the original square and the apex of the new square forms the center of the circle. If we superimpose this diagram on the Vitruvian Man, we see that Leonardo used the construction of the octagon as the basis for positioning his square and circle.

Winslow Homer used a hexagram as the basis for the composition of his painting, "Breezing Up."

The mast of the boat follows a line of the hexagram. When the hexagram is turned sideways, a line follows the deck of the boat. The lines of the waves in the lower corners of the painting follow the hexagram. The cloud in the upper right center follows another hexagram line.

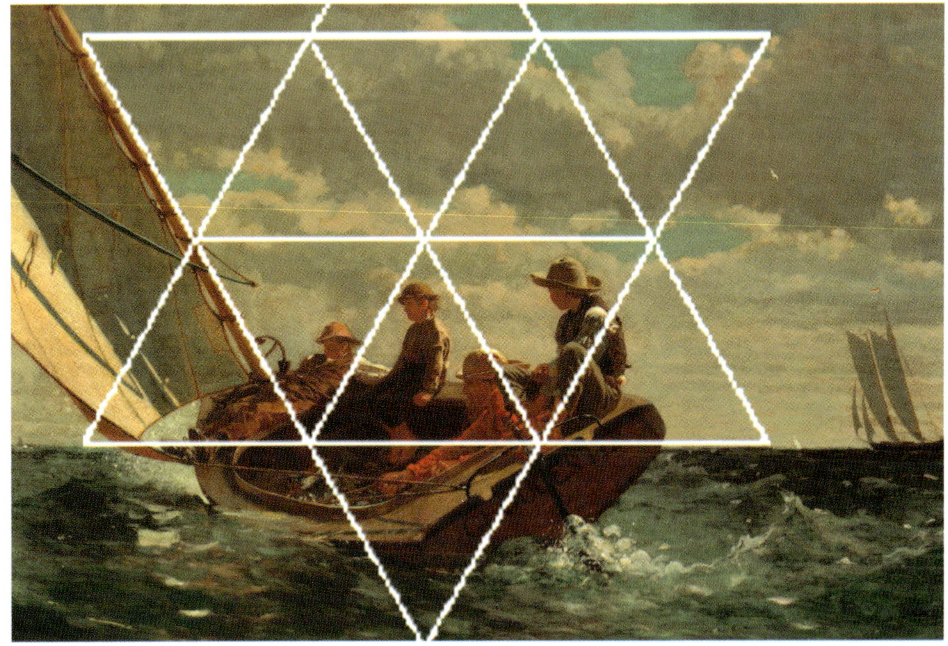

"Breezing Up," by Winslow Homer, oil on canvas, 1873-1876, 24.2" x 38.2", courtesy of the National Gallery of Art (with hexagram superimposed.)

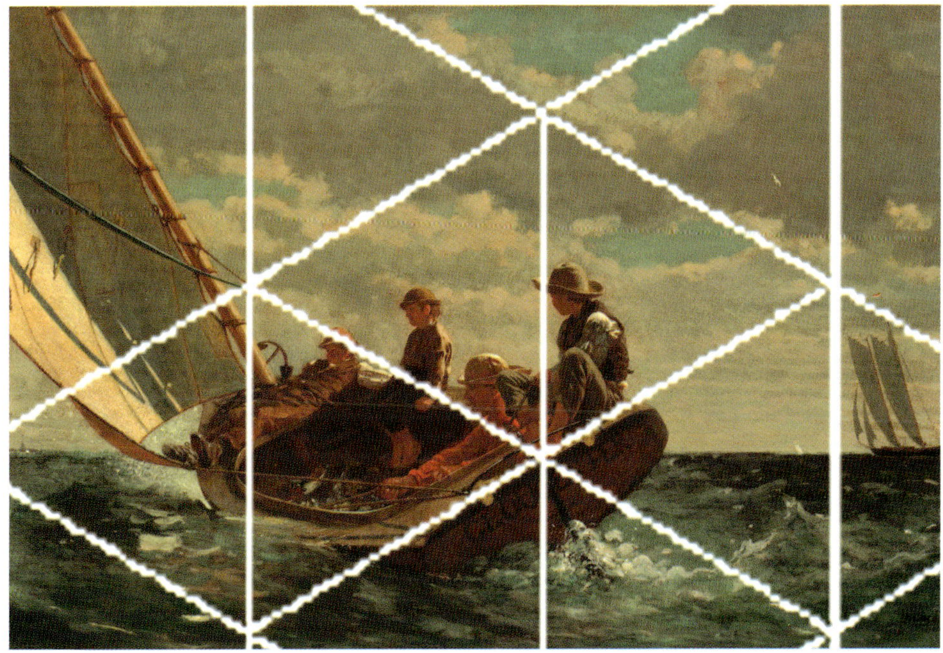

"Breezing Up" (with hexagram superimposed sideways.)

Let's return to my father.

Here is a picture from *Time of Wonder,* of my father, Sal and me on our boat in Bucks Harbor. We are coming into the harbor to buy groceries and emergency supplies for the approaching hurricane. Looking at that cabin door of the boat, it seemed very black, as if begging to be noticed. Suddenly it reminded me of the inner rectangle of a Golden Rectangle.

I tried out a rectangle in the picture, and look how it fits!

My father was a sly one. He painted this picture in the 1950s, when it was fashionable to see Freudian symbols everywhere. When you see the spiral connecting that dark cabin opening with the great, long, thrusting bowsprit, it becomes obvious that my father was symbolizing a nautical sexual couple—the secret life of boats!

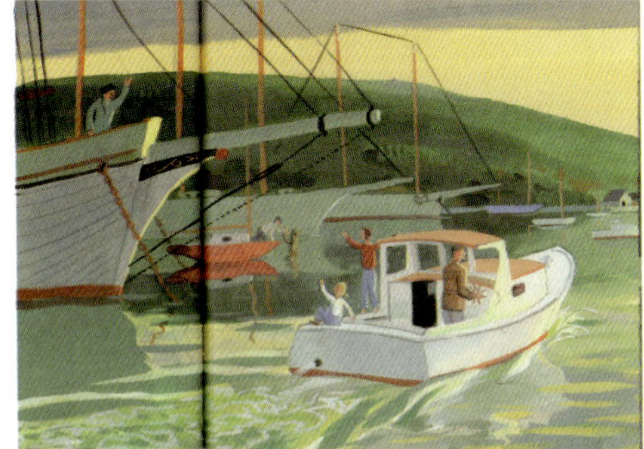

Time of Wonder, "Bucks Harbor," Viking Press, 1957.

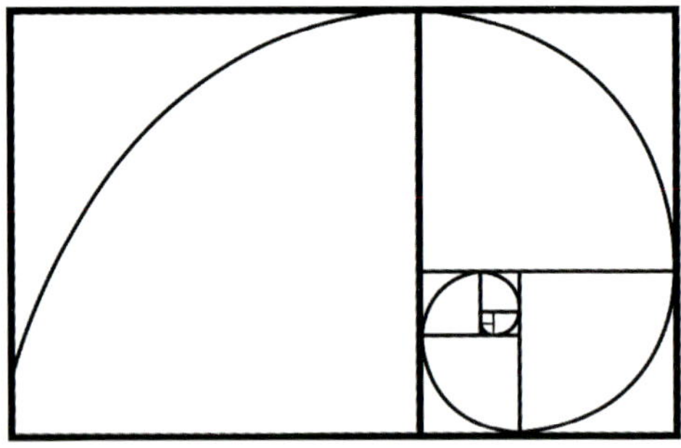

Golden Rectangle (with Golden Spiral.)

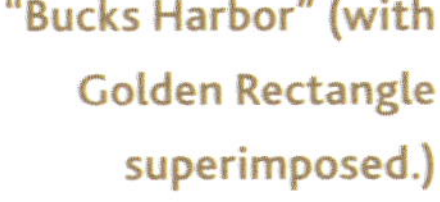

"Bucks Harbor" (with Golden Rectangle superimposed.)

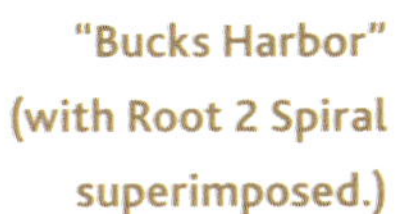

"Bucks Harbor" (with Root 2 Spiral superimposed.)

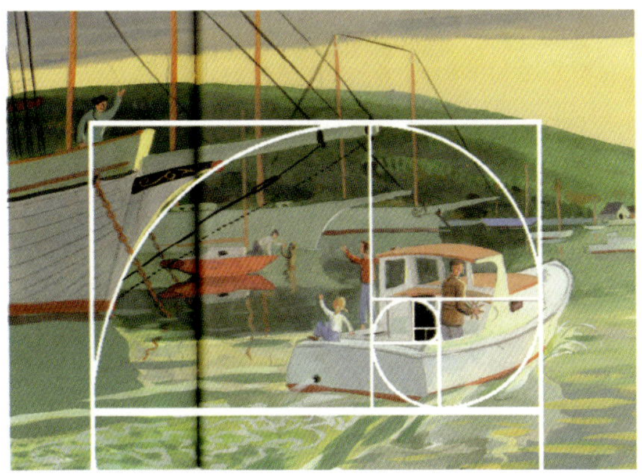

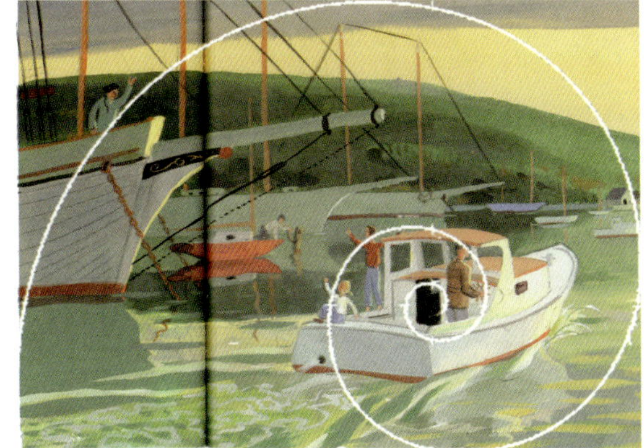

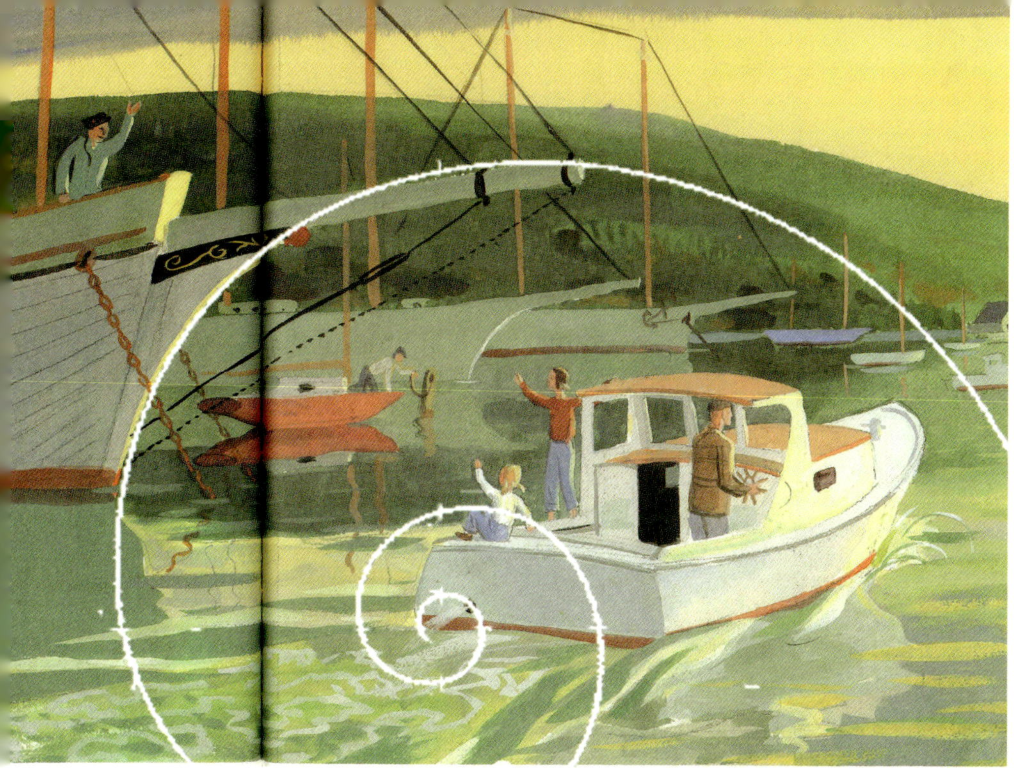

"Bucks Harbor" (with hexagram Spiral superimposed on the exhaust.

Trying a Root 2 Spiral in the picture, we see that the Root 2 Spiral has the same proportions as the Root 2 Rectangle of the picture. But the surprise is that the eye of the spiral, like the eye of the Golden Spiral, falls on the cabin door.

And, because that black exhaust pipe in the stern of the boat looks very black, like the cabin door, I put a Root 2 spiral on it, and this is what I found: the spiral follows the bow of the schooner.

There are human overtones to this spiral, too. In the yachting world, sailors sometimes call power boats stinkpots. So, the rear end of our boat is tooting its stink, which then spirals around and up the nose of that high and mighty schooner. My father and others often called the bow of a boat its nose.

Did my father intend some or any or all of these spirals? Or are the spirals a byproduct of his use of dynamic symmetry? Or, could I make these spirals "fit" any picture I tried them in? I don't know, but for me, the spirals add interest to the painting.

My father used grids to create the geometry in his work. This grid is 1/1000 away from a 1.618 rectangle. The second grid is two 1.618 rectangles side by side. The third grid is the one my father used to illustrate his books.

His grids have some curve balls, but the basic method of making a grid is to create what is called an armature. You draw the diagonals of the rectangles shown (facing) in red, then draw the horizontal and vertical axes, shown in black. Then you draw a line from one corner so that it intersects the red diagonal at right angles. There are four corners and four of these lines intersecting the red diagonals, they are shown in green.

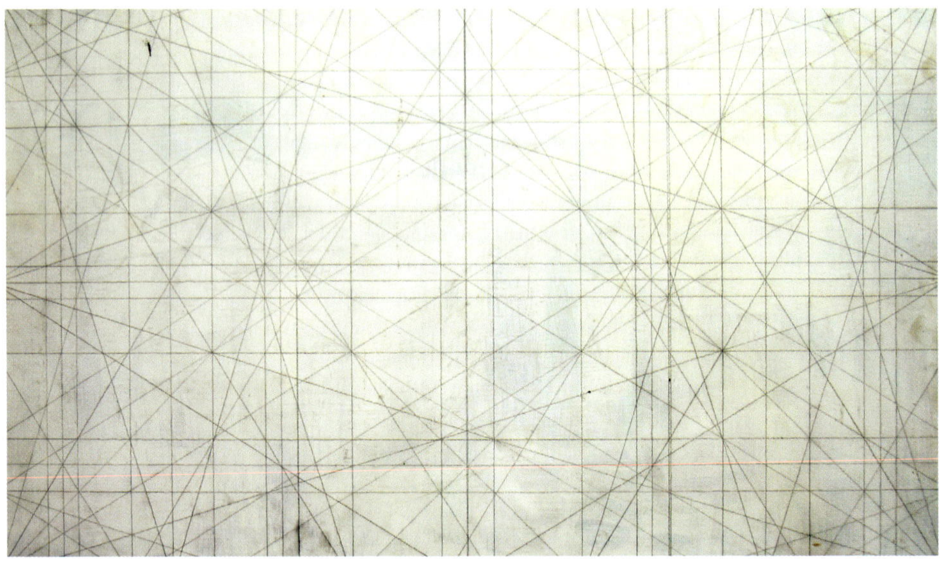

Bob's grid, Golden Rectangle pencil on canvas board, date unknown.

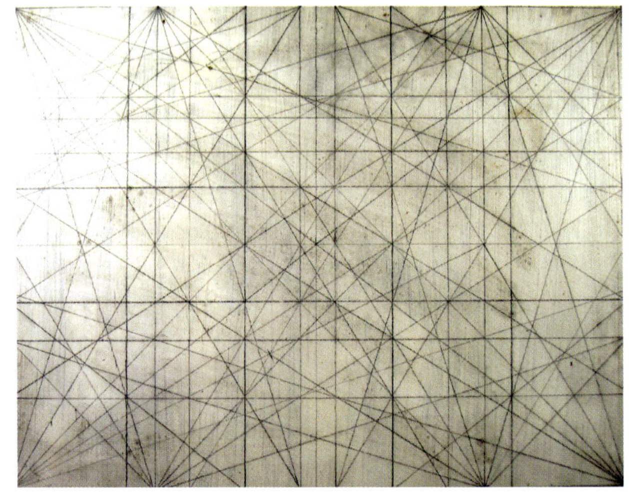

Bob's grid, proportion of 1.236, Two Golden Rectangles, pencil on canvas board, date unknown.

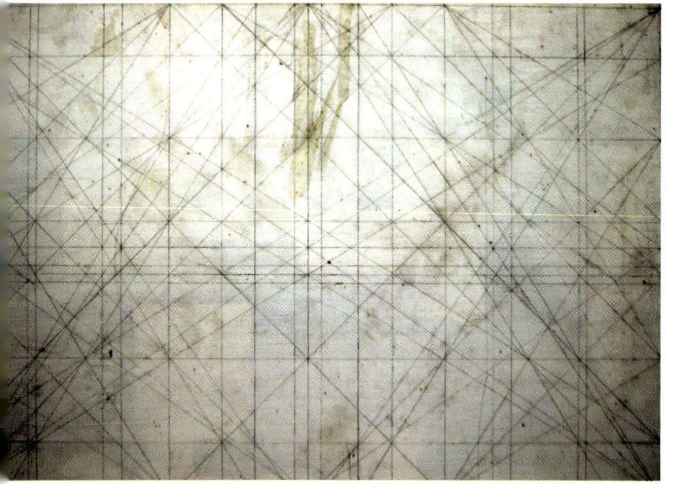

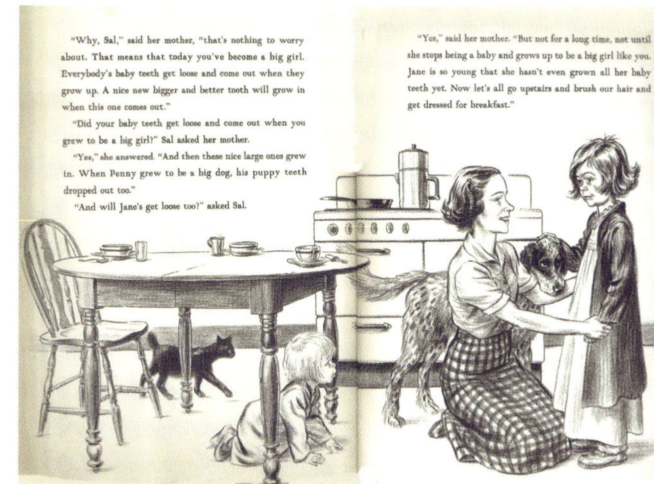

"Why, Sal," said her mother, "that's nothing to worry about. That means that today you've become a big girl. Everybody's baby teeth get loose and come out when they grow up. A nice new bigger and better tooth will grow in when this one comes out."

"Did your baby teeth get loose and come out when you grew to be a big girl?" Sal asked her mother.

"Yes," she answered. "And then these nice large ones grew in. When Penny grew to be a big dog, his puppy teeth dropped out too."

"And will Jane's get loose too?" asked Sal.

"Yes," said her mother. "But not for a long time, not until she stops being a baby and grows up to be a big girl like you. Jane is so young that she hasn't even grown all her baby teeth yet. Now let's all go upstairs and brush our hair and get dressed for breakfast."

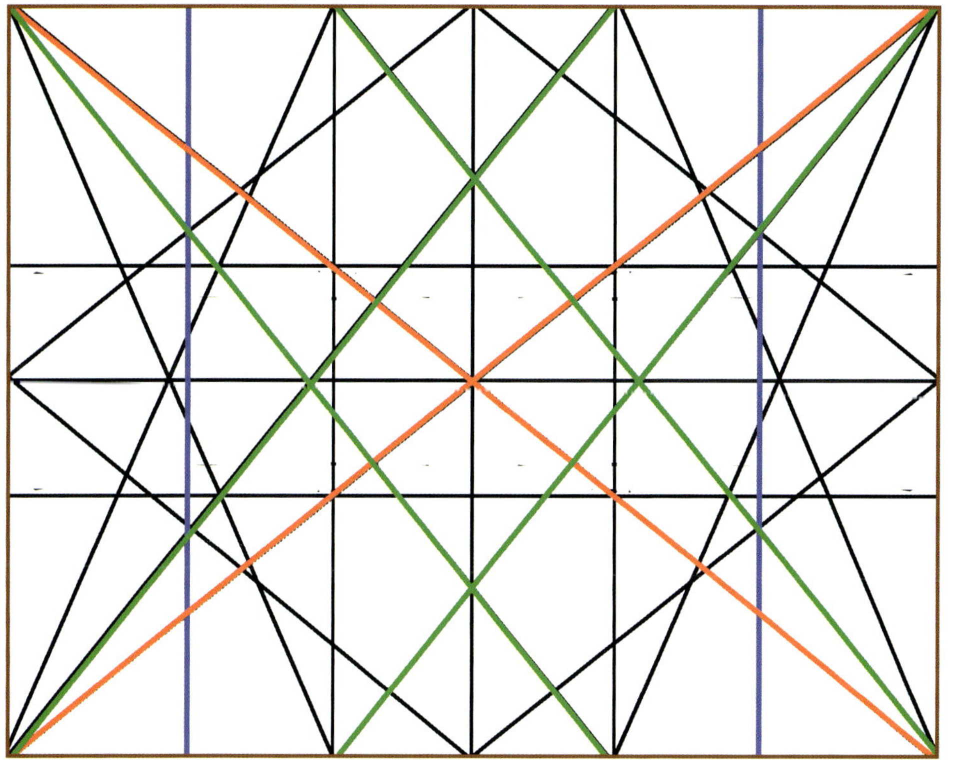

Bob's grid, Golden Bob's grid used to illustrate books, proportion of 1.457, pencil on canvas board, date unkown.

One Morning in Maine, "Mom Reassuring Sal About Her Loose Tooth," Viking Press, 1952.

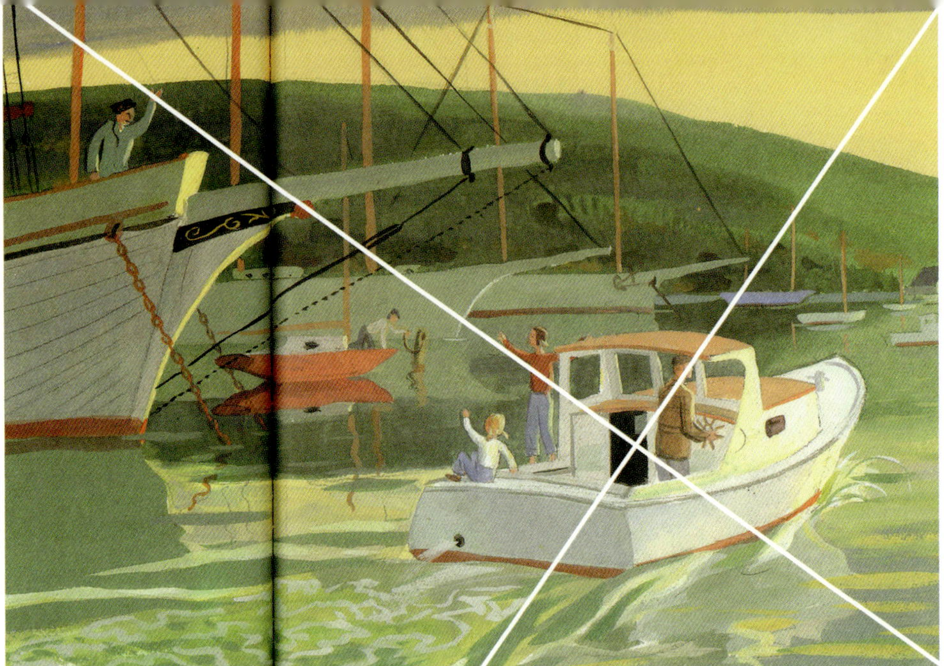

"Bucks Harbor," (with intersection of diagonal and diagonal of the reciprocal rectangle.)

The proportions of Bob's Bucks Harbor picture are different from the proportions of the armature, but the diagonal and the right-angle intersection of the diagonal still works. And you can see that, like the eyes of the spirals, the intersection lands on that cabin door.

Then, you drop perpendiculars, shown here in black, from where the green lines intersect the edge of the rectangle, which create smaller rectangles with the same proportions as the larger rectangle.

Here is a grid which I filled in more than the armature. You can see that you could go on indefinitely, generating horizontal and vertical lines wherever there is an intersection of two lines within the grid, or generating slanting lines between any points where lines intersect the edge of the grid. But, you need to stop before the grid becomes too crowded. I sense that my father only drew the basic lines and then filled in other lines as his picture called for them.

Jane's grid.

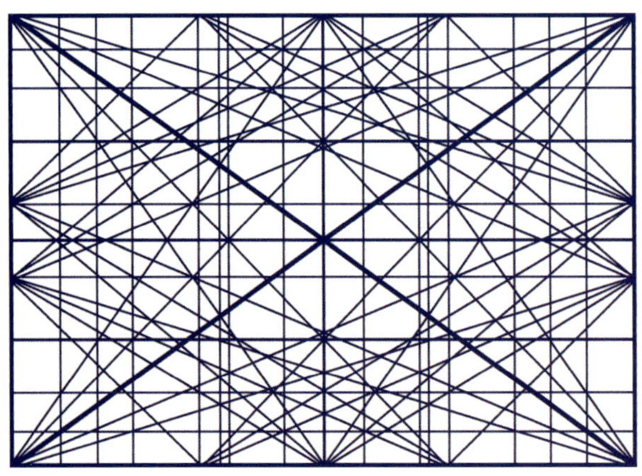

I became a fan of grids because I think that they give my doodley drawings an energy and interest that they do not have without the grid. I drew a goose using a grid, and pretty much slavishly followed the grid lines. Once or twice a line I wanted was missing and I put it in and then followed it. So, this isn't paint by the numbers, but paint by the grid. The reason the lines of this goose are pleasing, to me at least, is that all the lines of the grid are related to the whole rectangle and to each other, so the lines of the goose are also related to the whole rectangle and each other. They are proportional.

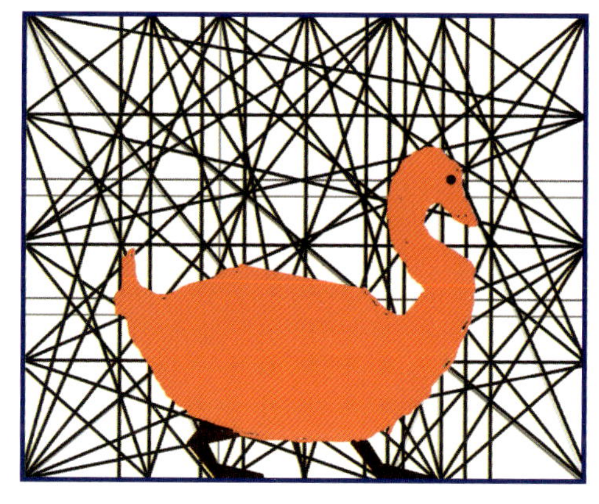

Jane's Goose on grid.

I don't think my father or other real artists who use grids are as dependent on the grid as I was, but I suspect the grid helps improve the proportions of their compositions and make them look more natural.

A final note on armatures. You can divide the side of a rectangle into two as I did, but you can also divide it into thirds or fifths to create an armature with different proportions and properties than the armature I showed here.

I am not sure how the artists created the various polygons in their paintings. I suspect that you can create a rectangle of a certain proportion whose armature will generate a particular polygon, but I haven't tried that experiment yet. Or, you can take a polygon and build a rectangle around it, using its base and peak and one side as three sides of the rectangle.

In other words, when artists put polygons in their paintings, the polygons are probably built into the grid, which guides the painting, and are not just plunked down randomly into the picture.

We have seen that artists use the Golden Rectangle and the Root Rectangles for the dimensions of their paintings. They also use variations on these basic rectangles if they want to make a painting of different dimensions.

The Golden Ratio is found in nature as well as in art. The Smith College Phyllotaxis website has a large number of pictures showing the mathematical basis for the arrangement of flowers, leaves, and pine cones.

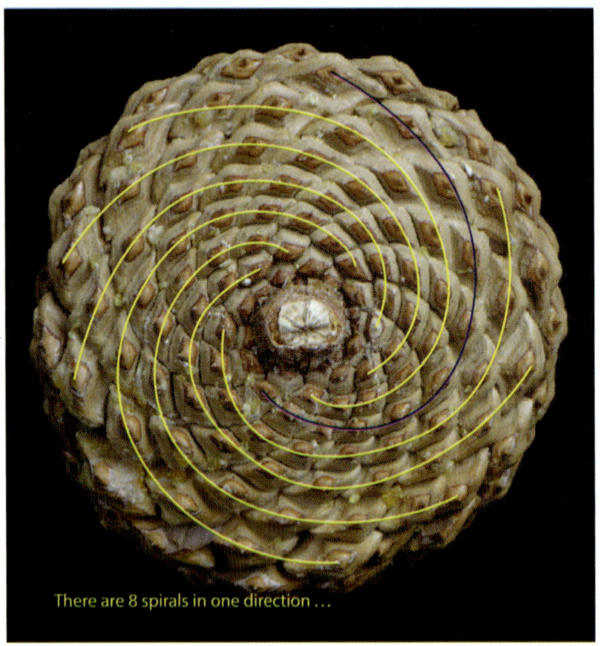

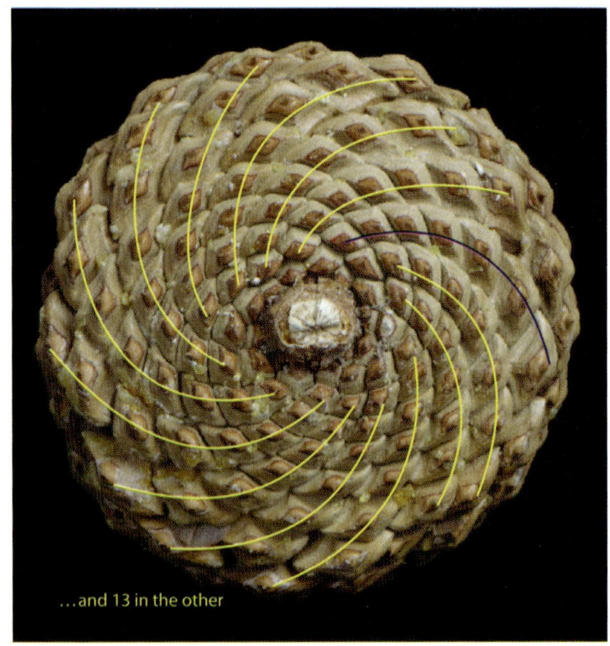

Pinecone with eight spirals.

Pinecone with thirteen spirals.

Apple (with Golden Spirals superimposed.)

In this pine cone, the arrangement of the "petals" forms eight spirals in one direction, and thirteen spirals in the other direction.

13/8 = 1.625, which is 7/1000 away from 1.618. Once I started looking for golden spirals, I saw them everywhere. What is interesting in these apple spirals is that the apple is not in exact profile, and yet we can find spirals in the apple anyway.

Did you ever wonder where the symbol of the heart came from? I think it must have come from the Golden Spiral.

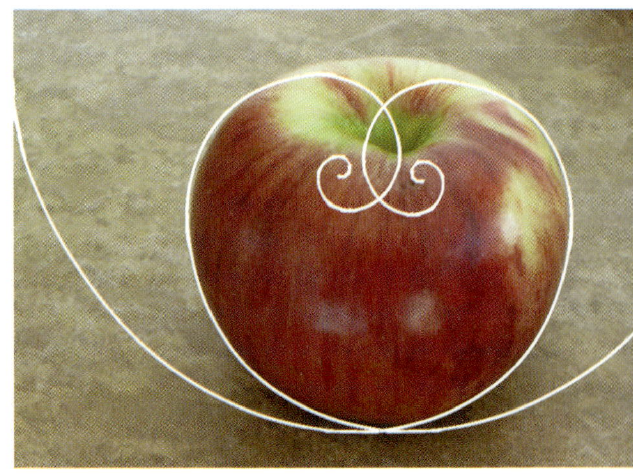

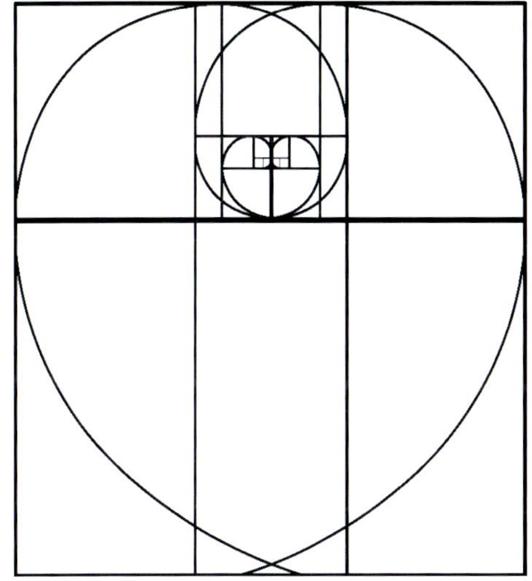

Heart made of Golden Spirals, by Jane McCloskey.

To return to my father, here is a picture from *One Morning in Maine,* in which Sal falls while showing her loose tooth to a curious seal.

I have embedded some Golden Spirals in this picture. Look at this spiral which starts on the curl of hair on her forehead. The spiral is maybe saying: this fall is making Sal's hair curl.

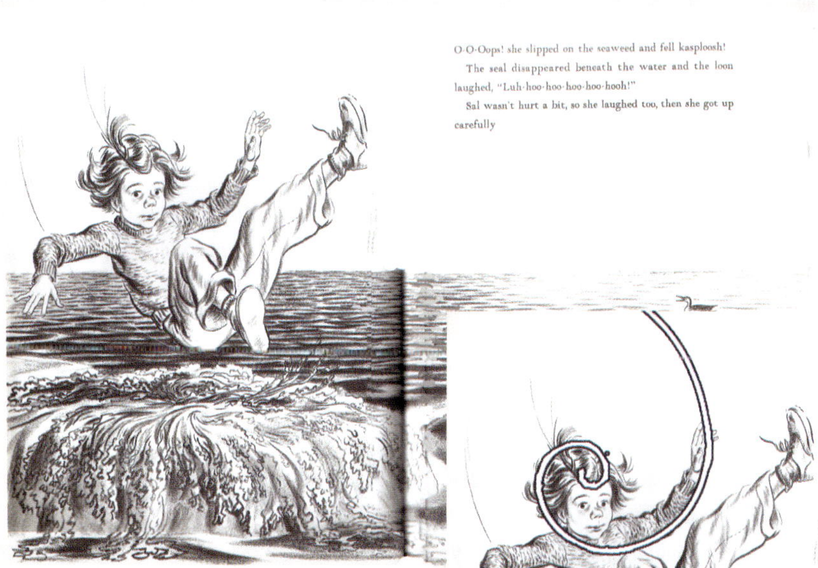

O-O-Oops! she slipped on the seaweed and fell kasplooosh!

The seal disappeared beneath the water and the loon laughed, "Luh-hoo-hoo-hoo-hoo-hooh!"

Sal wasn't hurt a bit, so she laughed too, then she got up carefully

One Morning in Maine, "Oops!," Viking Press, 1952.

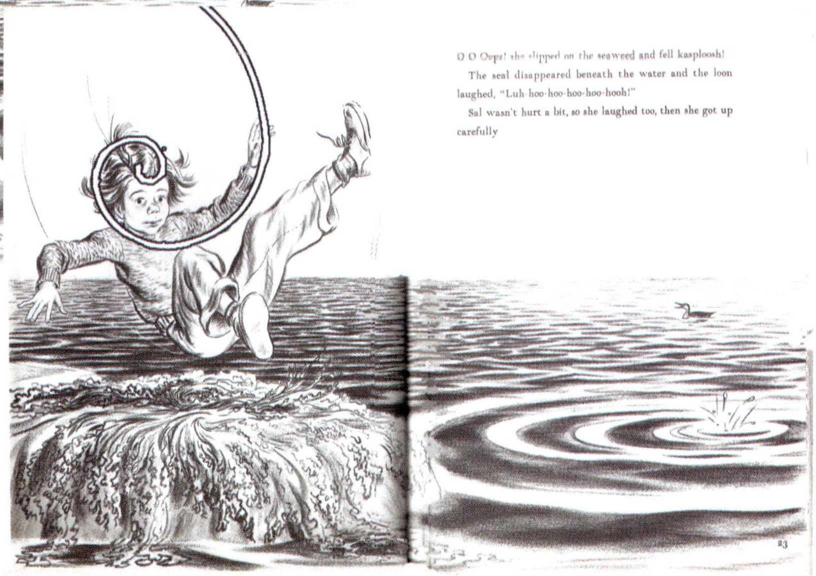

O-O-Oops! she slipped on the seaweed and fell kasplooosh!

The seal disappeared beneath the water and the loon laughed, "Luh-hoo-hoo-hoo-hoo-hooh!"

Sal wasn't hurt a bit, so she laughed too, then she got up carefully

23

One Morning in Maine, "Oops!" Head Spiral.

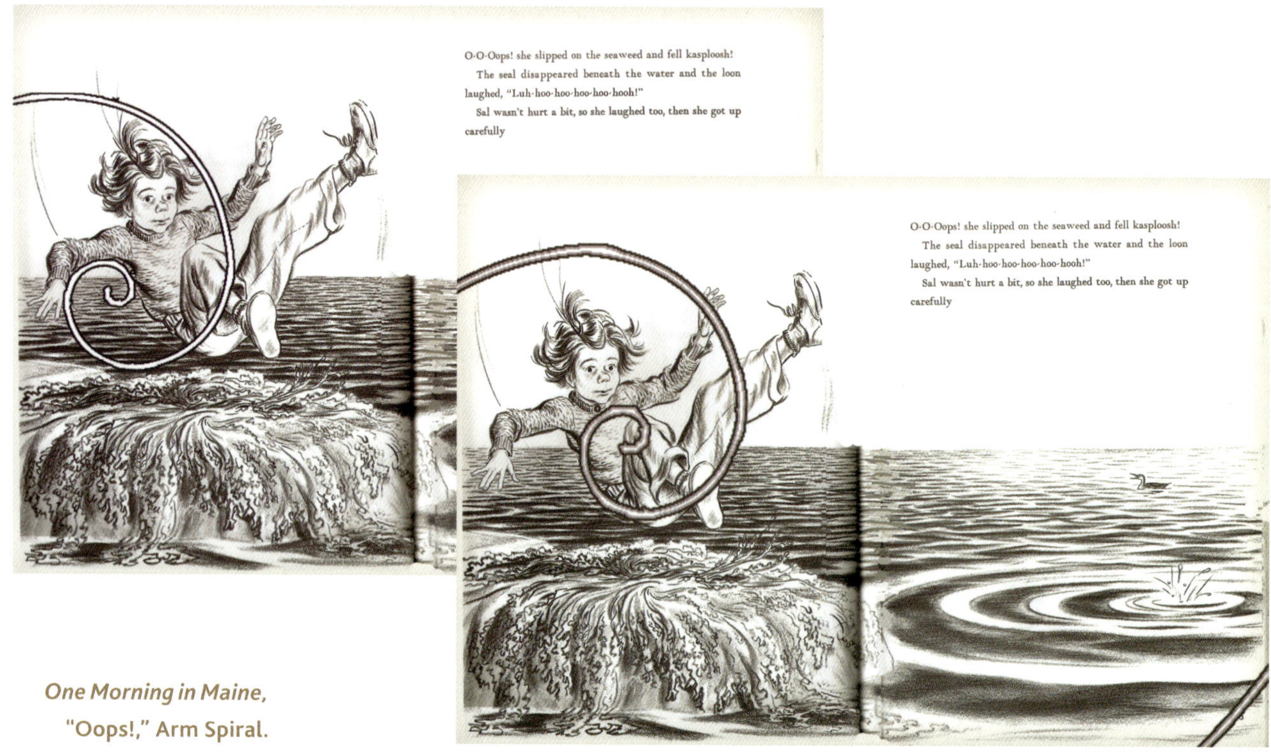

One Morning in Maine, "Oops!," Arm Spiral.

One Morning in Maine, "Oops!," Heart Spiral.

Another spiral begins under her arm, and looks like it intersects her bottom right where it will touch when she falls on the rock.

The spiral beginning on her chest may be saying that her heart is in a whirl. Or, as they say in Maine, maybe the spiral is saying she's going ass over teakettle.

This next spiral encapsulates the story of the whole picture. The eye of this spiral says that Sal was standing on the eye of the spiral in the seaweed when she slipped. Now, her bottom is in the air (but not for long) and her leg has flown skyward. The loon in the background is laughing, and the seal is gone.

It sometimes seems that the spiral, which shows spatial relationships among various elements of the painting, also works on an interpersonal level as well, showing the emotional, mental, and physical relationships among the entities of the painting. As we saw in my father's picture of Bucks Harbor, the spiral revealed sexual tension between two boats, and a social interaction between a stinkpot and a nose-in-the-air sailboat. In the illustration of Sal, the spiral shows the relationships among the seaweed covered rock, Sal's bottom, her upended leg, the loon, and the vanished seal.

One Morning in Maine, "Oops!," Master Spiral.

Here are the spirals for the seal and the rock. The seal spiral may indicate that the seal has ducked under water and resurfaced to the right, outside the picture, just in time to witness Sal land on the rock. Even the rock spiral may be saying something: the bit of air between the spiral and the rock top may be saying that the rock will try to cushion the force of Sal's fall.

One Morning in Maine, "Oops!," Seal and Rock Spirals.

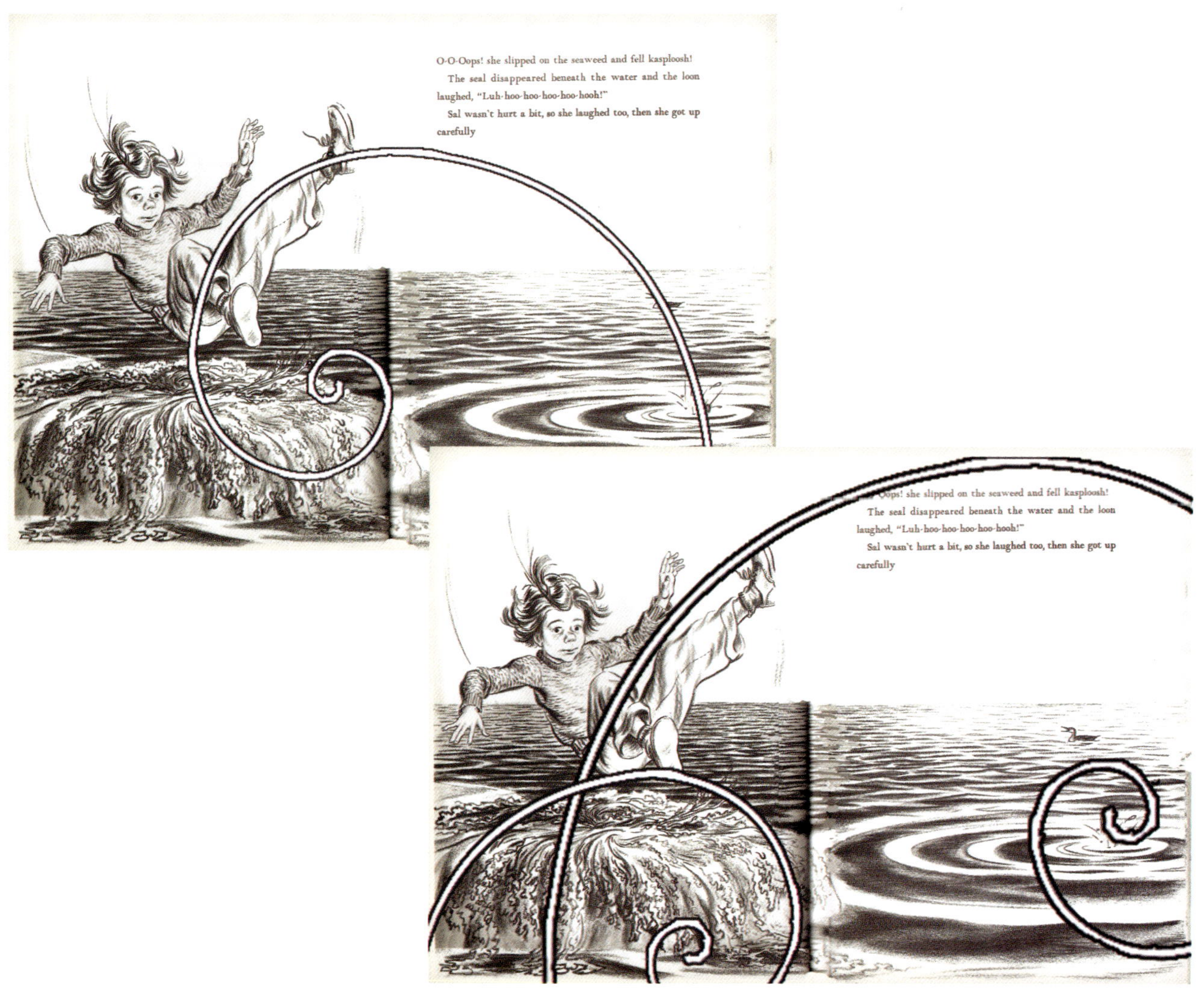

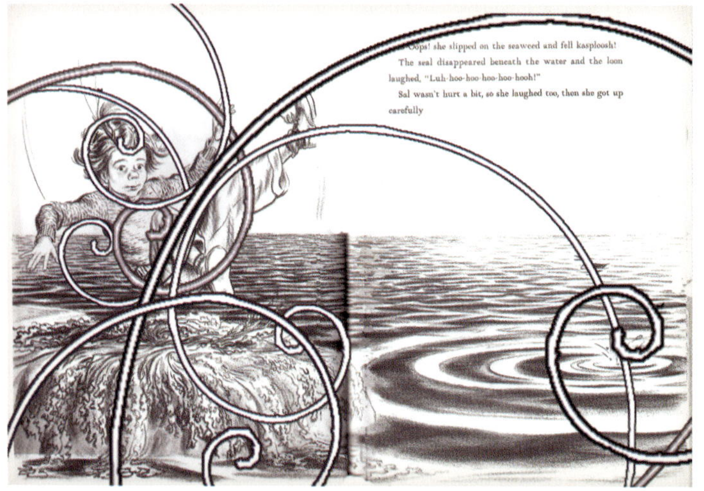

One Morning in Maine "Oops!," All Spirals.

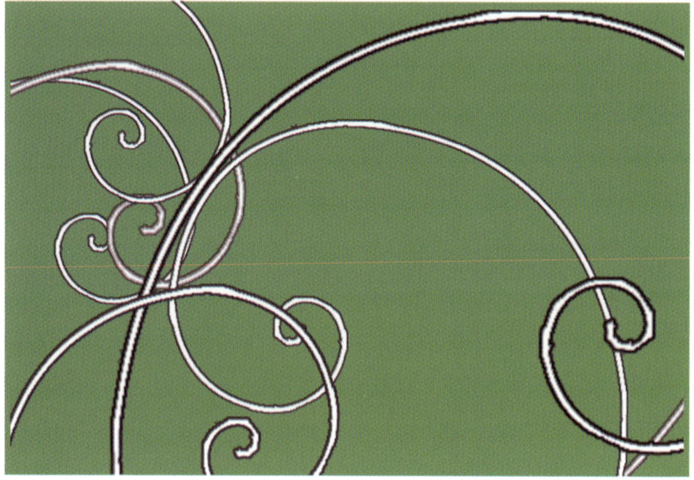

One Morning in Maine, "Oops!," Spirals on Green.

Here are all the spirals together.

And here are the spirals for this picture against a green background. If these spirals following the lines of the picture are harmonious by themselves, then they tend to confirm that there is harmony among the elements of the picture as well. The picture has good proportion.

I think these spirals are beautiful, but I don't know if Bob intended them. I am sure he intended at least some of the spirals in the Bucks Harbor picture. Maybe he intended the "Master Spiral" in this picture of Sal, relating all the elements of the image to each other. But maybe the other spirals are serendipitous, unintentional side effects of his use of a geometric grid. Maybe we can find spirals in any picture at all. In any case, my father cared deeply about good proportion, and he believed that dynamic symmetry and geometry helped him achieve it.

We will give the last word to my father. One day, when I said something about the Golden Rectangle and dynamic symmetry, he said, "You can do it with ANY rectangle." He meant that by using an armature and grid, you can set up a harmonious picture in any rectangle. He used geometry, but he didn't always use the Golden Rectangle, or the special rectangles of dynamic symmetry. He might use any rectangle.

ROBERT McCLOSKEY TIMELINE

By James E. Schwartz, Ph.D.

The Robert McCloskey Timeline was created in 2012 for the McCloskey Museum in Heritage Hall, Hamilton, Ohio.

1914

Born in Hamilton, Ohio on September 15 to Howard and Mable McCloskey.

1930–1931

Known by his nickname, "Clutch," McCloskey worked for two summers at YMCA Camp Campbell Gard north of Hamilton on the Great Miami River. He was dining hall steward, in charge of arts and crafts programs as well as musical activities. His most notable undertaking was carving a totem pole out of a cedar log. The design incorporated symbolism suggested by Native-American Isaac Greyearth.

1931

McCloskey illustrates his Hamilton High School Year Book.

1932

McCloskey begins three years study at the Vesper George School of Art in Boston.

1933

McCloskey receives commission for the sculptures at the new Municipal Building in Hamilton, Ohio. These sculptures may still be seen on the exterior and interior of the building.

1934

He meets May Massee and is told to go back home and learn how to draw and write about what he knows. He receives a commission for a new cover for *Trigger John's Son.*

1936

Begins study at the National Academy of Design in New York City. He is awarded the National Academy's President's Award.

1938

After returning from Ohio he shows a draft of *Lentil* to May Massee and the book is accepted. McCloskey accepts commission to work for Francis Scott Bradford on a mural in Cambridge, Massachusetts, now at the Sloan School of Management at MIT.

1939

He moves to Greenwich Village in New York City and begins work on *Make Way for Ducklings.* Wins Prix de Rome (now called the Rome Prize, which includes a year of study at the American Academy in Rome. He is also awarded the Tiffany Foundation Prize.

1940

Lentil, a book based on Hamilton is published, and on 23 November, Thanksgiving Day, he marries Margaret Durand.

1941

Make Way for Ducklings is published. He also illustrates *Yankee Doodle's Cousins,* by Anne Malcolmson.

1942

He receives his first Caldecott Award for *Make Way for Ducklings*. The Caldecott Medal is awarded annually to the artist of the most distinguished American picture book for children.

1943

Homer Price is published, his second book with a Midwestern setting.

1943

America is now at war and McCloskey enters the Army. For the next three years he is stationed at Fort McClellan in Alabama.

1945

Daughter Sarah (better known as Sally or Sal) is born in Ithaca, New York. The family moves to an island off the coast of Maine.

1948

Blueberries for Sal is published and daughter Jane is born. Now that World War II has ended and there is stability in Europe, McCloskey begins his year of study at the American Academy in Rome.

1949

He illustrates Tom Robinson's *Trigger John's Son* and is awarded a Caldecott Honor for *Blueberries for Sal*.

1950

Centerburg Tales published, the last of McCloskey's three Midwestern based books.

1952

One Morning in Maine published.

1953

He illustrates *Journey Cake, Ho!*, by his mother-in-law, Ruth Sawyer.
One Morning in Maine wins a Caldecott Honor.

1954

Journey Cake, Ho! wins a Caldecott Honor.

1955

McCloskey is illustrator for Anne White's *Junket, The Dog Who Liked Everything "Just So."*
Weston Woods films *Make Way for Ducklings.*

1956

Weston Woods films makes *Lentil.*

1957

Time of Wonder published.

1958

McCloskey receives his second Caldecott Award for *Time of Wonder,* becoming the first two-time recipient.

1958 (–1970)

He illustrates four books of Keith Robertson's Henry Reed series.

1960

Hi editor, May Massee, retires from Viking Press and becomes an advisory editor.

1961

Weston Woods films *Time of Wonder.*

1963

Burt Dow: Deep-Water Man is published, the last book written by McCloskey.

1964

Weston Woods films *The Doughnuts.*

On August 23 he receives an Honorary Doctor of Letters from Miami University in Oxford, Ohio.

1964

McCloskey begins making intricate puppets worked with clockwork gears and pulleys. He plans on making them into a TV show, but he becomes so engrossed in the mechanism of the puppets and he never does do a show. He works on them for nearly forty years. He also continues painting pictures, which are never shown during his lifetime.

1966

May Massee dies on Christmas Eve.

1967

Weston Woods films *Blueberries for Sal.*

An Honorary Doctor of Letters is awarded to McCloskey by Mount Holyoke College in South Hadley, Massachusetts.

The May Massee Memorial Committee is founded.

1971

McCloskey participates in Purdue University's Old Masters program, which brings distinguished persons to the campus to share their professional and personal experiences with Purdue students.

1972

The May Massee Collection is established at Emporia State University, Emporia, Kansas. McCloskey gives many of his sketches and book dummies to be archived there.

1973

The Regina Medal of the Catholic Library Association is awarded to McCloskey for continued distinguished contributions to children's literature.

1983

Weston Woods films *Burt Dow: Deep-Water Man.*

1987

Nancy Schön's bronze sculptures of the Mallard family are placed in the Boston Public Garden.

1990

Wife Margaret "Peggy" McCloskey dies in Ellsworth, Maine,on October 19, at the age of 74.

1991

Dedication of the *Make Way for Ducklings* statues on July 30 in Novodevichy Park in Moscow. McCloskey is present in Moscow for the dedication.

2000

He is named a Living Legend, one of 78 individuals so honored by the Library of Congress as part of its Bicentennial celebration. Those selected represent the breadth and range of America's cultural and civic heritage. The McCloskey Museum opens in Hamilton, Ohio.

2001

The Hamilton Community Foundation creates Lentil Park on its 50th anniversary in honor of McCloskey. Nancy Schön creates sculptures of Lentil and his dog, Harmony.

2003

Robert McCloskey dies in Deer Isle, Maine on June 30.

2010

Statue of the bear in *Blueberries for Sal* is dedicated at Coastal Maine Botanical Gardens in Boothbay, Maine. Nancy Schön created the statue.

Acknowledgments

I want to thank:

Robert McCloskey for being a good father to me, and for his art.

Spencer Smith of Seapoint Books for suggesting that I write a book about my father's art.

Michael Steere, editorial director of Down East Books for his guidance.

Michelle Franklin and Alexandra Lara at the May Massee Collection at Emporia State University in Kansas for their friendliness and help copying my father's book studies.

The Boston Public Library which sent sketches of the ducklings Bob made in preparation for *Make Way for Ducklings.*

Nancy Schön, friend of our family and sculptor of the ducks in the Boston Public Garden, who shared her duck sketches.

Dave and Marge Belew who have been the stars of Hamilton's support for my father. They and many good people from Hamilton have extended their support to Sal and me, with hospitality, kindness, and music.

James E. Schwartz, Ph.D. who gave me a tour of my father's childhood haunts in Hamilton. Jim also shared Hamilton historical lore, and sent me the Klippel paper written for a camp reunion. He allowed me to use his excellent timeline of my father's life, and, with his wife, Karen, has been fun, interesting and kind.

The Butler County Historical Association, The Robert McCloskey Museum, and the Lane Public Library for their support.

Anita Haviland, Lindsay Bowker, Samantha Hawkins, and Bruce Bulger who gave ideas, editing and encouragement.

Eric Rayman who gave encouragement and legal advice.

Sally McCloskey for her ideas and memories and support for this book.

And thanks, also, to the following for their generous permission and contribution of images:

Viking Children's Books of Penguin Random House for use of

Drawing of Bob by Marc Simont from *Make Way for McCloskey,* p. 8, Viking Penguin, 2004 in the introduction

Pictures of tiger from *The Man Who Lost His Head,* Claire Huchet Bishop, no page number, Viking Press, 1942 in New York chapter

Picture of journey cake and animals from *Journey Cake, Ho!,* Ruth Sawyer, pp. 34-35, Viking Press, 1953 in New York chapter

Picture of Henry and little girl from *Henry Reed's Baby Sitting Service,* p. 77, Viking Penguin, 1966 in New York chapter

Tom Leigh who took the photos of Bob's work for our archives

Janet Sohngen and Pat Brown Studios for their photos in the Ohio chapter.

James E. Noble, a neurologist in New York City, for sharing his picture of the Lord and Lady in the Boston chapter and his picture of Vacation Readers in the New York chapter.

Kenneth G. Libbrecht at Caltech for his picture of a snowflake in the dynamic symmetry chapter.

Smith College Phyllotaxis website for their pine cone pictures in the dynamic symmetry chapter

The National Gallery of Art for permission to use the Winslow Homer paintings, *Blackboard and Breezing Up* in the dynamic symmetry chapter

The Superintendence for the Historical, Artistic and Ethno-anthropological and for the Museum of the City of Florence for permission to use the Cimabue painting of the *Maesta* in the dynamic symmetry chapter

Clement Falbo for allowing me to use his diagram of the Root 2 Spiral, also called the silver spiral, in Bob's picture of us on our boat in Bucks Harbor in the dynamic symmetry chapter. He says the silver spiral has been in the public domain since the time of the ancient Greeks! Still, I wasn't able to find it anywhere else, and I didn't know how to construct it. So, thanks.

Morton Schindel, long time friend of my father and our family and founder of Weston Woods Studios, who sent the photos of Bob's puppets in the chapter on Bob's thoughts on his art

Shutterstock for the images of the *Vitruvian Man*, the Parthenon and the ear.

Sources and Comments

Charles Bouleau, *The Painter's Secret Geometry: A Study of Composition in Art*, 1963.

Since I began investigating my father's use of dynamic symmetry, I have discovered that the Golden Rectangle is somewhat controversial in the art world. Bouleau writes about the Golden Rectangle in geometry, but he does not limit himself to the Golden Rectangle.

p. 255. *The reserve shown by younger artists towards the golden proportion is a proof of the difficulties met with in applying it; and this reluctance has encouraged me to make my examination of composition throughout the different historical periods in complete freedom and without any preconception in favour of the golden number. Our analyses have, I think, shown how greatly the solutions adopted have varied according to individual temperaments, schools and periods. I have always tried to find the simplest scheme and to stick to it.*

In other words, Bouleau looks for the Golden Rectangle, but he also looks for other geometries in artists' work. He tries not to approach his analyses with preconceptions or bias.

Unfortunately, I did not often find Bouleau's analyses convincing. I believe this is a danger of geometric analysis: I have looked at some of my own armatures and polygons and spirals at a later time and found them almost irrelevant to the picture they are supposed to be following. What was I thinking? As I say, this is a danger of geometric analysis, but I have found that spirals are less prone to later repudiation than armatures and straight lines.

But even if it is prone to error, the process of geometric analysis, for me, is my most natural and pleasurable way of looking at paintings, and the world as well. I see the world and art in terms of form and line and space more than in terms of color or texture. Geometric analysis makes me slow down and look at a painting carefully, and evokes ideas and emotions about the subjects in a painting I did not know I felt.

Bouleau claimed that medieval artists used geometry, including the Golden Rectangle, more than the artists in and after the Renaissance. In this claim, he is in disagreement with Jay Hambidge who claimed that geometric painting died out with the Greeks and that Hambidge was the one to revive it. I tend to agree with Bouleau. I have seen medieval art that looks to me like it is based on geometry. And of course, Leonardo's "Vitruvian Man" is totally geometric.

p. 255. *I should add that, as a partisan of geometrical construction, I am delighted when I see it become, sometimes, the actual form which the picture presents to the view, but this does not make me think that geometry is everything in painting. The work of art draws its enrichment from the tension between its various components.*

He also shows sympathy for those who dislike using geometry or looking for geometry in art.

p. 255. *Today mathematics, through mechanics, have permeated and moulded our life to such a degree that many people have set up, in opposition to them, an art of negation and revolt, an extended expression of the self, a new romanticism or, perhaps, a simple explosive reaction of the individual against the tightening vice of conformism.*

Clement Falbo, "The Golden Ratio — A Contrary View Point," *College Mathematics Journal,* v36 n2,
p. 123-134, March 2005.

Falbo says that the evidence that the Golden Rectangle is used in art does not stand up, because of lack of standards for accuracy and other issues. He also proves wrong the often repeated claim that the chambered nautilus manifests a Golden Spiral. He found when he measured a number of them, that their ratios varied from 1.24 to 1.43, nowhere near the 1.618 of the Golden Ratio. I have to boast that I figured that out for myself from a nautilus picture I had from the web. My nautilus was about 1.25.

By extension, Falbo reminds us that there are many more spirals than just the Golden Spiral, and he discusses the Root 2 Spiral, aka the Silver Spiral. His mention of the Root 2 Spiral led me to look for the Root 2 Spiral in my father's Bucks Harbor picture from *Time of Wonder.*

Jay Hambidge, *The Elements of Dynamic Symmetry,* Dover Publications, 1967, first published by Brentanos in 1926.

Hambidge developed the rectangles we have seen in this book and guided my father's use of geometry. I believe that Hambidge gave a great gift to my father and other artists.

However, Hambidge made the unfortunate claim that art is inferior if it is not based on dynamic symmetry. This claim set up a needlessly adversarial relationship between those who use geometry and dynamic symmetry in art and those who don't. I prefer Bouleau's balanced remark about his enjoyment of geometry in art with the happy acknowledgement that geometry in art is not everything. It is a matter of personal preference.

Charles Klippel, Early Memories of Camp Campbell Gard and Robert McCloskey, 21 pages, 1994.

This paper was written for a camp reunion. Thanks to James E. Schwartz, Ph.D. for sending it to me.

Mario Livio, *The Golden Ratio, The Story of the World's Most Astonishing Number,* Broadway Books, New York, 2002.

This book is a wonderful tour for the non-mathematician of the Golden Ratio in history, math, science, and art.

Livio is skeptical that classical artists used the Golden Rectangle in their art. He says that Golden Ratio enthusiasts plunk down Golden Rectangles any which way in a painting, and are cavalier about precise measurement. In most cases, I agree with his skepticism, but I disagree with him about the Parthenon, which I believe was designed to contain Root 5, Root 4 and Golden Rectangles. This is precisely the kind of dynamic symmetry which Hammidge says emerges from using these rectangles.

The errors of the less knowledgeable Golden Rectangle enthusiasts should not make us deny all use of geometry by classical artists.

George Markowsky, "Misconceptions about the Golden Ratio," *The College Mathematics Journal,* Vol. 23, No. 1 (Jan., 1992), pp. 2-19.

Markowsky has some good ground rules for accuracy in finding Golden Rectangles in art, saying that the proportions of the ideal 1.618 ought to be within 2 percent accuracy of the proportions of the real piece of art. The geometric examples I have used have been accurate to within 1 percent of the proportions of the real piece of art.

He is skeptical that the Golden Rectangle is the most beautiful rectangle, as some Golden Rectangle enthusiasts have claimed. He made a chart of about forty rectangles, including the Golden Rectangle, and then asked people to choose which rectangle they thought the most pleasing. The Golden Rectangle did not win.

It is my belief that classical artists did not praise the Golden Rectangle for its beautiful shape, but because of its ability to generate related rectangles and subrectangles, which worked together in harmonious, beautiful interaction: because it generated art of good proportion.

However, even if the Golden Rectangle were the most beautiful rectangle just to look at, it would be difficult to decide from the way Markowsky presented the rectangles in his experiment. Since setting, size, and relationship are so important in aesthetics, I think that reducing a bunch of rectangles to about an inch in size and putting them in regimented rows makes it unlikely that anyone would be able to assess the true beauty of any of them.

http://www.world-mysteries.com/sci_17_vm.htm.

This is the website that shows that the octagon is the basis of the circle-square construction in Leonardo's *Vitruvian Man.*

Mike Spinak, "The Golden Section Hypothesis: A Critical Look." Web log: http://naturography.com/the-golden-section-hypothesis-a-critical-look/.

Spinak writes about the unfortunate effect that the popularity of the Golden Rectangle has had in the photographic world. He says that Golden Rectangle theory is so dominant now in photography that he has met professors who fail students who don't use it and judges who reject photographs which do not use it. Spinak is right. This ideological purism is nuts.

Spinak also says that artistic composition requires more than applying a formula such as adherence to the Golden Rectangle to a picture. He says that even if the Golden Rectangle does create pleasing proportions, then those proportions are still not sufficient for good composition, which is first about communicating. Sometimes a photographer may want to communicate anger or fear, where a "pleasing proportion" might be inappropriate because it soothes the mind and emotions of the viewer when the photographer wants them riled up.

I can agree with Spinak's dislike of prettiness in theory, but I have to say that I have been surprised by the way that Golden Spirals seem to work in the pictures I have analyzed, to awaken in me an understanding of the thoughts and emotions of the subjects in the painting. In Bob's pictures, the spirals are often playful. In other pictures, spirals have shown me a little girl's sorrow at being less valued than her brothers, a servant girl rebelling at her lot, a couple considering art and sex and death, a New England miss who might be channeling a Flamenco dancer, a saint criticizing the corruption of the Catholic Church, two saints discussing the need to remember death. These spirals evoke an understanding above and beyond what I see in the paintings themselves.

https://pavlopoulos.wordpress.com/2011/07/ "The Peacock's Tail, Essays on Mathematics and Culture." Website.

A passage from "The Peacock's Tail" elucidates my claim that these rectangles are praised, not for their beautiful shape, but because they have properties that help artists achieve good proportion in their pictures.

"According to Romanian polymath Prince Matila Ghyka (1881–1965)...root rectangles such as the sixton produce 'the most varied and satisfactory harmonic subdivisions and combinations:' drawing a perpendicular from a vertex to the diagonal 'produces automatically surfaces correlated by the characteristic proportion of the initial rectangle and also avoids (automatically again) the mixing of antagonistic themes.' A sixton [Root 3 Rectangle,] for example, produces smaller sixtons in an ad infinitum resonance of rectangles related to the square root of three and involving no other irrational ratio."

http://www.timelessbydesign.org/About.htm.

Timeless by Design promotes orthogons, but warns," Use of any design system does not guarantee quality."

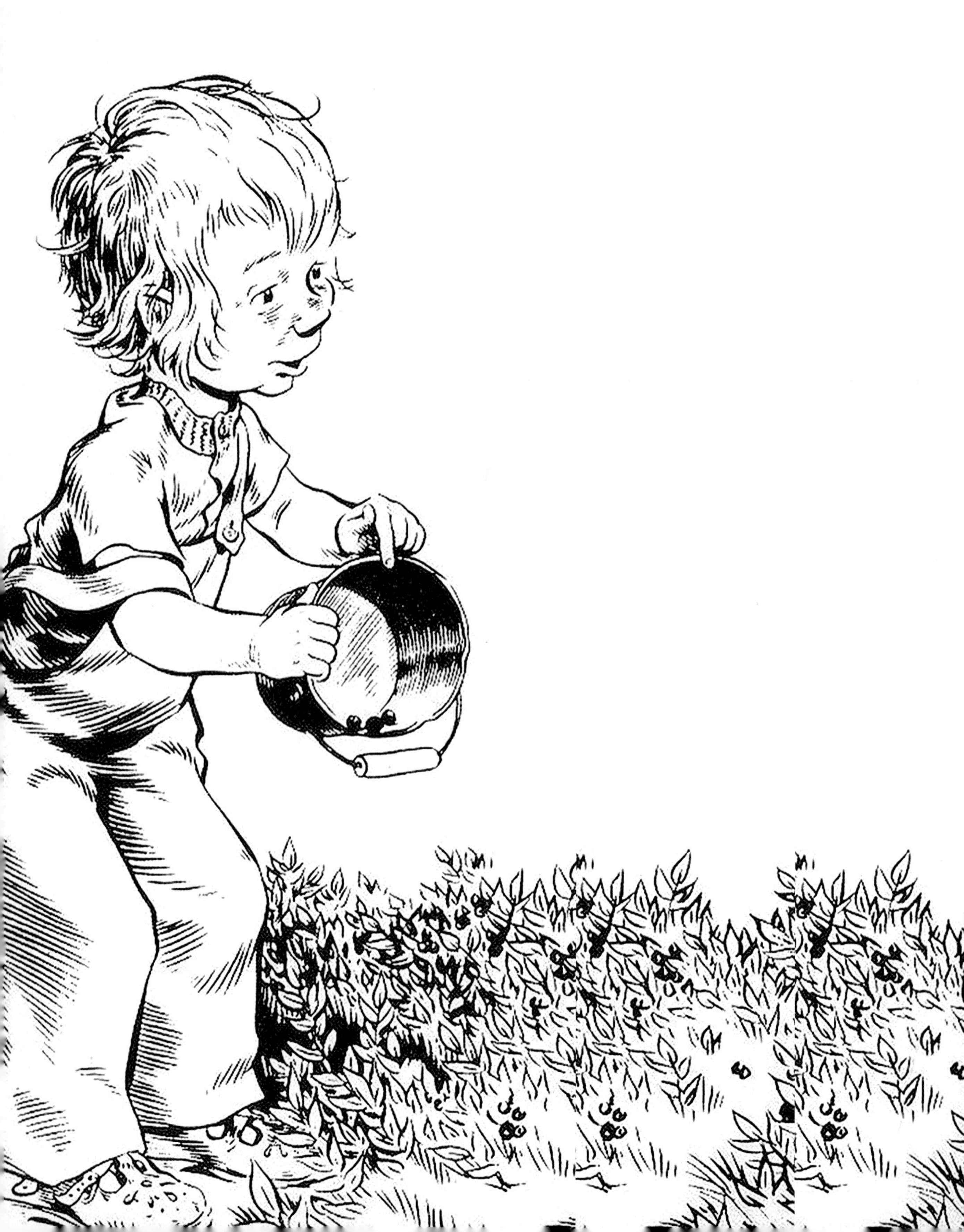

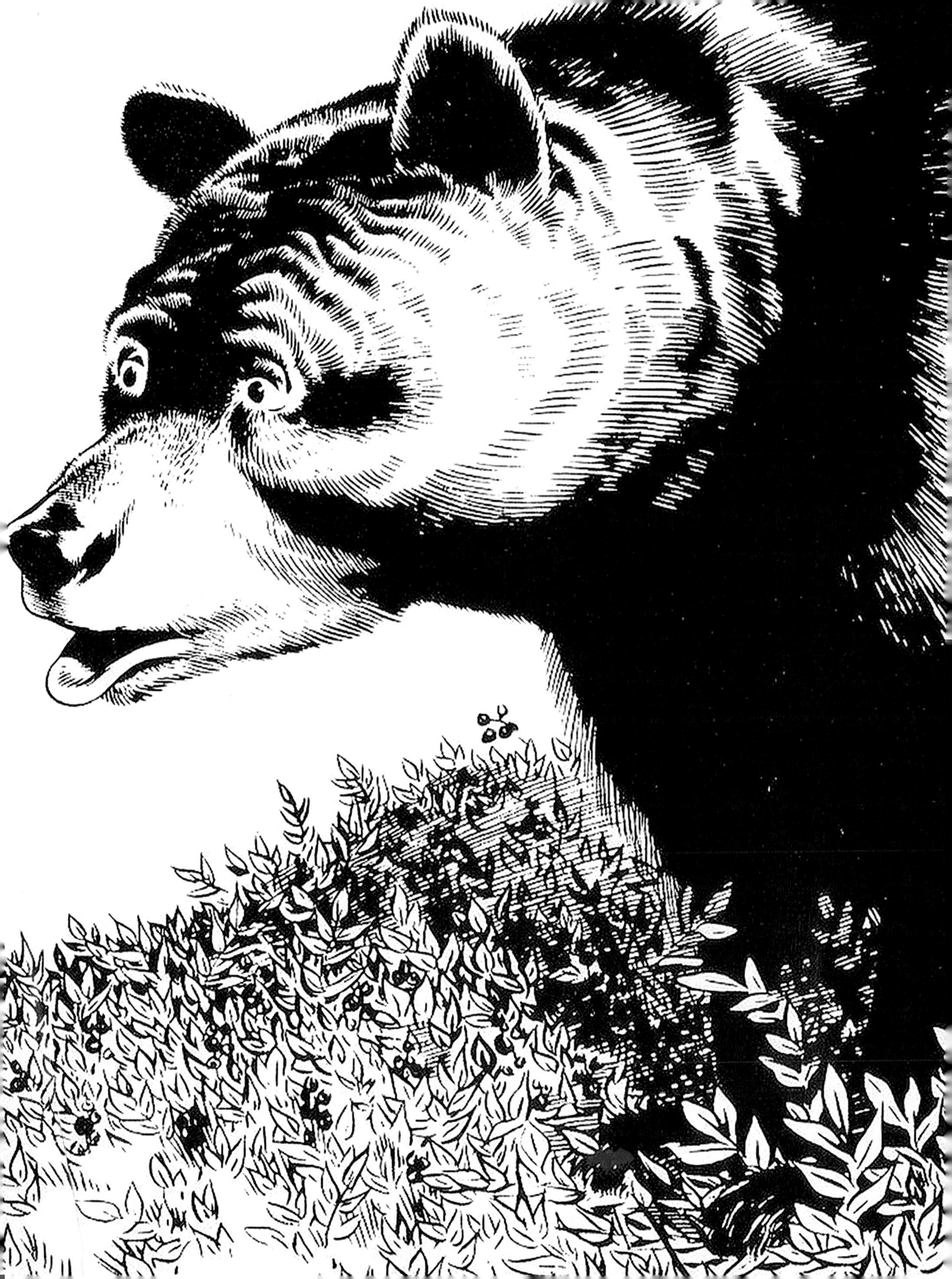